Nuns and Nunneries in Renaissance Florence

Nuns and Nunneries in Renaissance Florence

Sharon T. Strocchia

Johns Hopkins University Press
Baltimore

This book was brought to publication with the generous assistance of the Lila Acheson Wallace–Reader's Digest Publications Subsidy at Villa I Tatti.

Johns Hopkins Paperback edition, 2013
9 8 7 6 5 4 3 2 1

Johns Hopkins University Press
2715 North Charles Street
Baltimore, Maryland 21218-4363
www.press.jhu.edu

The Library of Congress has cataloged the hardcover edition of this book as follows:
Strocchia, Sharon T.
Nuns and nunneries in Renaissance Florence / Sharon T. Strocchia.
p. cm.
Includes bibliographical references (p.   ) and index.
ISBN-13: 978-0-8018-9292-9 (harcover : alk. paper)
ISBN-10: 0-8018-9292-9 (hardcover : alk. paper)
1. Monastic and religious life of women — Italy — Florence — History —
Middle Ages, 600–1500. 2. Monastic and religious life of women —
Italy — Florence — History — 16th century. 3. Florence (Italy) — Church
history. I. Title.
BX4220.I8S76 2009
271'.90045511090923 — dc22   2008054188

A catalog record for this book is available from the British Library.

ISBN-13: 978-1-4214-1184-2
ISBN-10: 1-4214-1184-9

Special discounts are available for bulk purchases of this book. For more information, please contact Special Sales at 410-516-6936 or specialsales@press.jhu.edu.

Contents

Conclusion

Tables, Graphs, and Figures

Preface

The study of religious women in late medieval and early modern Europe has recently emerged as a vibrant field in its own right. Drawing on an abundance of riches, scholars have explored various forms of female spirituality and cultural production ranging from food practices to female-authored texts and music. Whether motivated by intensely felt spiritual convictions or profound distaste for the cloistered life thrust on them, medieval and early modern nuns wrote chronicles, plays, and treatises of real merit; painted and illuminated devotional works in both normative and idiosyncratic styles; made celestial-sounding music in a distinctive female voice; and patronized art and architecture on a previously unimagined scale. The recovery of this cultural legacy demonstrates conclusively that religious life offered one of the most significant vehicles for the formation and expression of female subjectivity in the premodern period.

Less well established is the constitutive role that nuns and nunneries played in the grand narrative of early modern Europe, especially in its political and economic development. In general, the historiography of early modern state-building has not been in sustained conversation with studies treating gender, religion, and society. To date, the most heavily trafficked intersection maps political relationships between nuns and the post-Tridentine church around issues of compulsory enclosure. Recent studies by Ulrike Strasser on gender and religion in early modern Munich and Jutta Sperling on convents in late Renaissance Venice have broken new ground by showing the centrality of convents to the consolidation of political authority by both church and state in the late sixteenth and early seventeenth centuries. Similarly, the role of religious women in facilitating a capital-based economy as producers and consumers has received scant attention. Elizabeth Lehfeldt has shown that nuns in seventeenth-century Valladolid exercised economic clout as creditors to the Spanish crown, but there is still much to be learned about the situation elsewhere, especially in view of the considerable resources convents mobilized as institutions.[1]

Focusing on the role religious women played in effecting broad historical change, this study shows how nuns and nunneries helped constitute the social and political world of late medieval and Renaissance Florence from the Black Death (1348) to the fall of the Florentine republic (1530). During this period of stunning human achievement, female religious communities became central to virtually every aspect of the urban social order. Many of the features that defined Renaissance Florence — its marital strategies, property regimes, political aspirations, church-state relations, cult of remembrance, mechanisms for social welfare — were built on the backbone of female monasticism. Deeply bound up with secular affairs, convents experienced radical changes in terms of size, composition, and resources over this period. Richard Trexler's foundational study demonstrated that there was a steep rise in female religious professions after 1480, but it was not simply the explosion of convent populations that marked fifteenth-century Florence.[2] The very nature of female monasticism itself changed during the Renaissance. Over the course of the fifteenth century, Florentine convents were transformed from small, semiautonomous communities into large civic institutions serving family, state, and society. Far from being "dead to the world," nuns advanced the city's economic fortunes in their role as textile workers vital to the burgeoning silk industry. From a social standpoint, convents offered urban elites new patronage opportunities that translated into greater political influence and that amplified their control over local ecclesiastical resources. Religious women acquired a heightened role in civic ideology as intercessors for the city writ large; as a result, they quickly became ensnared in new regulatory schemes. The goal of this book is to explain how and why this transformation happened and to explore its impact on the thousands of women living in religious houses.

In emphasizing the socioeconomic and political dimensions of Florentine convent life, my intention is not to discount female religiosity but to place it in a new light. Spiritual intercession lay at the root of nuns' power, yet it was the sheer complexity of interactions binding convents to the city that made them such powerful institutions. Although few holy women and still fewer saints appear in the following pages, Florentine nuns nevertheless remained keenly alive to the religious currents of their day. Viewing these communities through social and political lenses — patronage networks, economic activity, neighborhood affiliations — throws into sharper relief how contemporaries themselves constructed the sacred. The permeability of Renaissance cloisters speaks to a religious sensibility in which the sacred was deeply embedded in the everyday. As consecrated virgins, Florentine nuns not only stewarded religiously charged spaces and objects but embodied aspects of the holy in their very persons. At the same time, however, groups of religious women acted as lightning rods for many of the contradictions riddling Italian lay piety. Because nuns helped bind the social and the sacred, conflicts over their behavior highlight crucial tensions in the contemporary religious landscape.

Studying Florentine convents from a predominantly social perspective also delineates the ways in which gender confounded religious ideals or made them more problematic. While values like voluntary poverty fired the late medieval religious imagination, these same ideals sometimes clashed head-on with contemporary gender norms, making it impossible for Italian nuns to beg for their living and remain cloistered at the same time. Questions concerning the appropriate level of nuns' reclusion, their ascetic practices, means of livelihood, models of community all fueled civic and ecclesiastical controversies throughout the Renaissance. In addition, Florentine nuns grappled with difficult issues of organization and self-governance distinctive to women's communities, especially as the resurgent fifteenth-century papacy brought greater regularity to a heady religious pluralism. Renaissance nuns paradoxically developed a strong political presence by playing on gendered rhetorical tropes that emphasized their fragility and dependence. Similarly, nuns' relations with male clerics, on whom they depended for cult life, were frequently marked by inversions of customary class expectations and power dynamics. Only by probing these gender-based tensions can we arrive at a full understanding of Renaissance religion as lived experience.

Besides illuminating crucial aspects of Italian religiosity, this study casts new light on the institutional history of the Florentine church, which remains poorly understood compared to other historical domains. Scholars like Roberto Bizzocchi, George Dameron, and David Peterson have done much to further our understanding of the complex relationships binding the Florentine bishopric, male clergy, and urban society together from 1100 to 1500.[3] Yet female monasticism has remained largely invisible in examinations of local church-state relations, despite the riches of suppressed convent archives. Even Trexler's precocious study did not take up the politics of the Florentine church in relation to convent life. This marginalization has important consequences, since the process by which the Florentine church became more aristocratic only becomes fully intelligible if one places convents at the center of inquiry. Moreover, since Italian history is largely local history, the distinctiveness of the Florentine church compared to its neighbors remains murky unless we take into account the relations between local bishops and the convents in their care. In addition, broader religious initiatives such as the Observant movement and Savonarolan reform acquire new dimensions when viewed through the prism of local convent experience. The present study makes no pretense of exhausting these questions but instead takes a step toward developing a wider research agenda.

One of the central arguments advanced in this book is that the fifteenth century was a decisive moment both for convents and for their relations with urban society. Despite deep continuities in monastic life, virtually every aspect of convent experience — economic foundations, social composition, labor patterns, enclosure provisions, naming practices, civic oversight — was transformed in the Quattrocento. As a result, religious women in 1500 contended with very different dynamics from that of their predecessors a century earlier. Rather than viewing the fifteenth century merely as a run-up to the Council of Trent (1545–63), however, it might be more apt instead to see Tridentine battles over enclosure, forced professions, and convent property regimes as the culmination of earlier trends that were given new force by changed historical circumstances.

The first chapter charts the explosive but uneven growth of Florentine convents between 1348 and 1530, systematically mapping for the first time monastic recruitment patterns in Renaissance Italy. Before the Black Death, the city boasted approximately five hundred nuns; by 1500, that number had increased fourfold to over two thousand before climbing to twenty-five hundred by 1515. Convent populations doubled yet again over the next forty years.[4] Expressed in terms of the urban population, nuns represented roughly 1 out of every 200–250 Florentine inhabitants in the late 1330s; by 1552, about 1 in every 20 residents was a nun, most of them involuntary. As Florentine girls flooded convents in nearby provincial towns in the later fifteenth century, they helped form a territorial monastic system that marks an unwritten chapter in the history of Italian state-building. Florence was among the earliest Italian cities to invest heavily in female monasticism, the growth of which was driven by local political dynamics as well as marital strategies. Throughout the Renaissance, Florentine political culture penetrated the very heart of convent life; in turn, nuns facilitated the workings of an exceptionally sophisticated political environment through their petitions, litigation, and chapter decisions. Religious vocation was not entirely absent from the constellation of factors driving monastic expansion, but its impact was not widely felt except in the 1450s and 1490s.

Chapter 2 extends this discussion by showing how Florentine convents became integral to the construction of ecclesiastical power bases by Renaissance urban elites. This process was intimately bound up with the redefinition of urban social geography and its characteristic bonds of neighborhood. Over the course of the Quattrocento, convents were transformed from local enclaves drawing their membership predominantly from surrounding neighborhoods into elements in a citywide network of urban institutions controlled or managed by the Florentine patriciate. In the late Trecento, neighborhood functioned as the major unifying element in convent life; a century later, common class origins filled that role. Casting daughters, sisters, aunts, nieces and cousins as agents of family ambition, Florentines used kinship instrumentally to achieve dominance over religious houses in more distant urban sectors. Changing patterns of convent property holdings in the fifteenth century, documented here for the first time, reinforced patrician control of top-tier religious houses. The chapter closes with two case studies illuminating the ways that interconvent rivalries further reshaped traditional neighborhood dynamics. These different angles of vision demonstrate that Florentine convents assumed a central place on the civic stage not only through strength of numbers but also by redefining neighborhood relations.

Chapter 3 examines the structures of corporate and personal wealth on which Florentine nuns relied and links the Renaissance convent economy to broader changes in the public fisc as the Medici gained ascendance. Florentine convents depended on a mixed economy combining revenues from rents, yields, monastic dowries, gifts, alms, interest payments, earnings, and individual living allowances. Convent tax reports show that underendowment was an endemic problem among female religious institutions; roughly three out of four Florentine nuns lived at or below the official cost of living set by civic tax officials, although gifts and other unreported income helped offset these shortfalls. Still, the majority of fifteenth-century Florentine nuns experienced the realities of monastic poverty, whether willingly or not. I also take up the vexed issue of "private" wealth within a communal setting. Nuns' living allowances introduced numerous paradoxes into monastic life, but perhaps the most significant was that convents could not balance their budgets without them. Despite deep continuities in convent finance, however, this economic framework was altered by the political consolidation of the Florentine state after 1450, which irrevocably tied convent budgets to state-run instruments of public finance. I argue that the explicit exchange of prayers for financial favors was one of the key mechanisms by which convents were transformed into full-fledged civic institutions in the second half of the fifteenth century.

The next chapter establishes that Florentine convents operated as important sites of commodity production that helped advance the city's commercial fortunes—a subject virtually untouched by historians. Renaissance nuns were working women as well as creative women. They provided a cheap, unheralded labor force for the burgeoning silk industry, primarily as producers of metallic thread essential to the "look" of high-end Renaissance clothing and decorative arts. Florentine nuns also speeded the growth of the industry in the Quattrocento by organizing preliminary production processes for silk firms; they further improved productivity by permitting their cloisters to be used as way stations for the consignment of goods. Three case studies presented here show that some convents developed specialized niches in the luxury market as producers of exquisite embroidery, an activity that simultaneously afforded avenues for creative expression and established partnerships with painters, goldsmiths, and other artisans. After 1500, some Florentine convents nimbly switched to lace making to meet changing market demand until compulsory enclosure later in the century restricted work opportunities. Other Renaissance nuns earned money as teachers and caregivers responsible for diffusing literacy, catechism, and proper deportment to young girls as a coherent educational package.

The final chapter probes the relationship between open reclusion and monastic discipline. I take issue with literary depictions of Renaissance convents that represent them as morally lax institutions simply because they did not practice strict enclosure. The often vaunted sexual transgressions of religious women have been considered not only fact but explanatory fact, with little critical attention paid to the quality of evidence or to the underlying assumptions and objectives of particular attacks. This chapter places questions of monastic discipline on a more complex footing by elucidating both the practice of open reclusion and the politicized nature of enclosure. Contemporary controversies over enclosure were only partially concerned with nuns' physical separation from the world. Ideologically speaking, these conflicts voiced larger social anxieties regarding both female agency and male sexuality. In practical terms, enclosure controversies articulated assorted claims to nuns and nunneries on the part of families, friends, clients, business associates, monastic supervisors, and civic officials. The stakes were high, since at the heart of Renaissance enclosure wars lay a battle for control over local religious resources. Given the growing importance of Florentine convents to the urban economy as well as to civic ideology, it is not surprising that these institutions came under increased civic scrutiny. In 1421 the Florentine commune took the unprecedented step of creating a civic magistracy charged with safeguarding nuns' sexual purity — the first of its kind anywhere in Europe. Previously untapped records left by this office paint an extraordinary picture of the culture of suspicion enveloping nuns' behavior; they also depict civic magistrates caught in a double bind between wanting to permit easy access to cloisters and yet needing to police transgressions. By 1500, contests over enclosure were heightened by new revenue-seeking practices of the Renaissance papacy, by the disastrous wave of foreign invasions that ushered in religious reforms and political regime changes, and by nuns' stalwart defense of open reclusion based on tradition and legally established privilege.

Running throughout my analysis is a consideration of female agency, both personal and institutional — an area fraught with contradictions. Scholars have noted that the convent offered unusual opportunities for the pursuit of learning as well as rare occasions for the formal exercise of power. Yet at the same time Renaissance nuns rarely chose their own destiny; instead, it was almost uniformly thrust on them by their families, often at an early age. Similarly, religious women created multiple models of governance to support diverse spiritual goals yet frequently relied on male benefactors to protect their distinctive way of life. Although Florentine nuns made autonomous corporate decisions — who to admit into chapter, how to allocate and embellish their living quarters, what type of market work to do — they rarely escaped familial suasion or the fact of their own poverty. As patrons and brokers in their own right, nuns' sphere of influence remained limited. I gauge the relative significance of these contradictions in order to evaluate how monasticism both constrained and empowered Italian religious women before the Catholic Reformation.

I also am concerned with illuminating the changing nature of communal life, albeit to a lesser extent. Florentine convent chapters were not only subject to the ordinary strains common among small groups but also managed overt tensions between women with strong religious convictions and those who had little vocation. These strains became more pronounced as forced professions multiplied circa 1500, giving rise to hothouse politics that sometimes ended in factionalism — the bane of sixteenth-century religious communities. Although they lack comparable drama, even the small politics of everyday life mark the cadences of nuns' lived experience as they moved through long years spent behind convent walls. Religious women wrestled repeatedly with implicit tensions between community and hierarchy as they endeavored to find the sacred in the everyday. Where possible, I have tried to elucidate the achievements of ordinary nuns whose historical legacy as scribes, stewards, artisans, caregivers, and convent leaders remained circumscribed by their small worlds.

The breadth of issues engaged here is made possible by the extraordinary range of archival sources that has given Renaissance Florence its well-deserved reputation as a historical laboratory. This study capitalizes on copious materials running the gamut from nuns' own writings — letters, chronicles, account books, tax petitions — to family diaries, ecclesiastical visitation records, civic tax reports, anonymous denunciations, and religious encomia. Given the existence of what is probably the most abundant set of documents for the study of European women before 1500, the attempt to situate Florentine convents in a web of goods and favors, influence brokerage, competing familial and ecclesiastical claims, class dynamics, artistic commerce, and civic aspirations may not seem foolhardy. To exploit this remarkable source base, I utilize a mix of interpretive tools developed by historians, cultural anthropologists, and literary scholars who have explored the symbolic and the sociological in imaginative ways. Enriching these multidisciplinary approaches are feminist perspectives that illuminate women's historical relationships to religion and power. Nevertheless, my fundamental goal remains a historical one: to show how the "nuns' story" intersected with and helped constitute the history of church, state, and society in Renaissance Florence.

A Note on Dates: In the Florentine calendar, the new year began on the feast of the Annunciation (March 25). Dates given in the text have been modernized to correspond to the calendar year beginning January 1. When citing archival documents in the notes, however, I give both dating styles when necessary to avoid confusion.

Nuns and Nunneries in Renaissance Florence

CHAPTER ONE

The Growth of Florentine Convents

Around 1338, the Florentine chronicler Giovanni Villani estimated that his native city supported 500 nuns out of an urban population of roughly 100,000 to 120,000, or 1 religious woman for every 220 inhabitants.[1] Villani's figures may be suspect, but they nevertheless capture an essential truth: nuns and nunneries were not a prominent feature in the urban landscape of late medieval Florence. That situation was utterly transformed over the course of the fifteenth century. By 1515, the number of nuns in the city and immediate environs had increased to over twenty-five hundred in an urban population of sixty thousand to seventy thousand, yielding a ratio of one nun for roughly every twenty-six inhabitants. Over the next forty years, the female monastic population living within the city and a four-mile radius rose by almost 40 percent, while the urban population remained relatively static. Hence the total of just over thirty-four hundred nuns reported in 1552 represented a ratio of one religious woman for every nineteen residents.[2] The dispersion of Florentine girls to convents in neighboring towns like Prato and Pistoia pushed this ratio even higher, despite local attempts to contain the influx of outsiders. As the pace of forced professions quickened,

Florentine nuns who were scattered throughout the dominion formed far-flung monastic networks that extended the reach of the Florentine state.[3]

This stunning institutional growth was deeply intertwined with the growing aristocratization of church, state, and society in Renaissance Italy. By the seventeenth century, almost half of Florentine patrician daughters became nuns; Jutta Sperling estimates that close to 54 percent of Venetian patrician women lived in convents in the late sixteenth century. As local variants of this pattern took root in Milan, Bologna, Naples, and other Italian cities between 1550 and 1650, female monasticism became one of the defining features of early modern Italy.[4] These high rates of profession are even more striking when placed in a wider European context. Although convents across Renaissance Europe gained ground in tandem with population recovery and favorable economic conditions, no comparable expansion occurred in England, France, or Germany.[5] Even early modern Spain did not boast an equal number of female religious communities or such high numbers of nuns.[6]

Such spectacular growth in convent populations represented more than an impressive numerical increase: it constituted a fundamental redefinition of female monasticism and its relationship to the urban social order whereby small communities that had been modeled on the apostolic family were transformed into a civic network of large custodial institutions serving family, state, and society. The peak in female monastic professions in late sixteenth- and early seventeenth-century Italy is well documented, but the trajectory leading up to this surge has not been studied as extensively. This chapter marshals various fragmentary data to chart systematically for the first time the growth of Florentine convents from the Black Death (1348–49) to the disastrous siege of Florence (1529–30). In documenting patterns of growth over this period, I look closely at the social processes that shaped them in order to understand why Florentines made significant investments in female monasticism at varying points in time. Operating within the limitations of the sources, I also differentiate the rate of growth at individual houses, establish the social identity of girls who became "brides of Christ," and probe the ways in which expansion impacted the dynamics of convent life.

The uneven trajectory of monastic growth over these two centuries is best conceptualized as three linked phases, each driven by different concerns. The first phase, running from 1350 to 1430, was marked by a protracted demographic crisis in which female religious communities struggled to maintain the threshold necessary for communal life. Since late medieval convents tended to be small-scale institutions in any case, recurrent epidemics pushed many communities to the brink of extinction. These decades were fraught with tensions pitting the spiritual value of monasticism against the social imperatives of reproduction; when deciding their daughters' destiny, Florentine fathers often had to choose between rendering divine service and keeping their lineage and city alive. Young widows sometimes made similar choices between remarriage and monastic withdrawal, guided by property considerations as well as piety.

The demographic rebound marking the second phase from 1430 to 1480 must be seen in relation to the decline of the late fourteenth and early fifteenth centuries. The mid-fifteenth century was a formative period in Florentine monastic life that welded the formation of a Medicean ruling class with the consolidation of elite control over the local church. Driving monastic expansion in these pivotal decades were political concerns, on one hand, and avid spiritual convictions, on the other. Women touched by the midcentury Observant movement joined religious communities in impressive numbers and even founded several of them; at the same time, young girls who became involuntary nuns helped bring patrimonial plans to fruition by deepening family footholds within specific religious institutions. Regardless of their spiritual zeal, Florentine nuns contended with new power relations—civic oversight, papal authority, the emergence of patronage as the dominant force in political culture—when rebuilding their ranks in the mid-fifteenth century.

The final phase witnessed a breathtaking explosion of convent populations. After 1480, female monasticism became integral to more systematized family strategies that advanced the collective fortunes of household and patriline at the expense of particular family members. Rising dowries and a complex marriage market meant that making a good match for one daughter increasingly hinged on another daughter remaining celibate. The extraordinary pace of growth in these years, however, must also be seen as a response to political turmoil and heightened religiosity. Paradoxically, these competing concerns only widened the gap between religious expectations vested in "brides of Christ" and the diverse social uses to which convents were put, transforming convents into fierce battlegrounds well before Trent.

The account of Florentine convent expansion presented here clarifies current understandings of Italian female monasticism in several ways. First, it demonstrates that Florence was at the forefront of the movement toward forced professions that eventually characterized the entire peninsula. Even compared to their neighbors in locales like Bologna and Milan, members of the Florentine middling and upper classes were among the earliest Italians to invest in female monasticism as a form of social and political power.[7] Second, it documents that growth was driven by a complex rationale extending beyond the purely financial considerations first proposed by Richard Trexler.[8] Propelling convent populations upward was a rich mix of local political dynamics, evolving marital strategies, the Observant movement, and the use of convents as urban welfare institutions. Finally, this account shows how monastic expansion altered nuns' lived experience. By 1500, higher populations posed structural and experiential problems that were the inverse of those confronting religious women a century earlier. Refracting nuns' lives through the prism of time and place reminds us that, although their stories have much in common, they still must be told in the plural.[9]

Convents in Crisis

Despite the extraordinary richness of Florentine sources, attempts to take an exact census of the city's convents at various checkpoints are riddled with challenges. Throughout the fourteenth and fifteenth centuries, the number of convents shifted constantly as new foundations came into being and older institutions were suppressed or put to new uses. The mid-Quattrocento saw exceptional volatility as Eugenius IV (1431–47) and his local representative Archbishop Antoninus attempted to reinvigorate the Florentine diocese. The ten-month siege of Florence by imperial troops in 1529 marked another watershed, when about a dozen convents on the periphery were destroyed for tactical reasons and their inhabitants permanently relocated. Complicating any census of religious women were informal clusters of female penitents who lived together without a rule or obligatory vows. These "semireligious" women — variously called *ammantellate*, *bizzocche*, or *pinzochere* — reflected both the sustained attraction of penitential ideals and the reluctance of a number of women throughout the Quattrocento to affiliate with formal monasticism, considered by some women to be an impediment to their spiritual development. Like the beguines of northern Europe, their goals ranged from retreating into a life of unfettered contemplation to running an active apostolate centered on charitable works.[10] As we will see, many informal communities became institutionalized over the fifteenth century; other groups simply died out or disbanded when finances collapsed.

The highly composite nature of female religious communities presents other challenges. Different classes of nuns living in the same house were not always counted in the same way in ecclesiastical visitation records, civic tax reports, and internal administrative records. The core group of professed choir nuns who formed an official chapter was supplemented by novices and "unprofessed nuns" awaiting final vows. Their reclusion was made possible by servant nuns (*converse*), mainly immigrants from the countryside, who were responsible for doing the community's heavy work and sometimes for transacting business outside the cloister. Other institutional residents included lay dependents and ancillary personnel — clerks, chaplains, unprofessed servants, annuitants, gardeners, other staff — who figured among the official "mouths" eligible for civic tax exemptions. In addition, before the advent of specialized custodial institutions circa 1550, convents provided the single most important extrafamilial residential option for women and girls of all ages. Stakeholders ranged from older annuitants (*commesse*), most often widows who donated goods or property in exchange for lifetime accommodation, to pupils, wards, and boarders at various stages of life. Given these considerations, census numbers are better understood as reasonable approximations than as definitive statements.

Although much has been written about the revitalization of religiosity in thirteenth-century Europe, the early fourteenth century proved more vibrant for Florentine female monasticism. George Dameron estimates that there were at least sixty-six female religious communities in the city circa 1330, far more than the twenty-four convents Villani reported. Many of these communities, however, were informal groups of female penitents, not incorporated religious houses. Still, the 1330s and 1340s — the great age of political factionalism — saw a spate of new convent foundations. In these years, when the ambitious, third circuit of city walls was completed, fourteen new convents sprang up in the city and environs.[11] This growth contrasted with the experience of neighboring Bologna, where Gabriella Zarri has shown that convent populations reached their numerical peak around 1300–15 before declining precipitously even prior to the Black Death, hitting a low ebb in the mid-fifteenth century.[12] A few of these new Florentine religious houses were founded by one or several women seeking spiritual perfection defined in a pluralistic rather than uniform sense. One of the most striking features of this upsurge was that only one new convent was a mendicant affiliate, in sharp contrast to numerous penitential groups inspired by mendicant ideals; the other new foundations followed the Benedictine or Augustinian rule, which accommodated a wider range of organizational practices and spiritual objectives. Some propertied families shied away from committing their daughters to mendicant convents partly because of their asceticism and partly because their central governance made it harder to exercise family influence over them. Far from being uniform, late medieval religiosity was a bundle of gendered preferences amply reflected in the landscape of female monasticism.

While Villani's estimate of five hundred nuns is probably too low, there is no question that the Black Death devastated an already small census. Because most Florentine nuns practiced open reclusion, their cloisters did not confer immunity against the pandemic. Only three of the one hundred nuns inhabiting S. Jacopo di Ripoli, the city's largest medieval convent, survived the first round of plague, while nine of the twelve nuns comprising the more typical community of S. Niccolò Maggiore succumbed to disease. Subsequent epidemics held even slight demographic rebounds in check. S. Niccolò was cut in half once again by the second wave of plague that hit in 1363 before losing almost its entire chapter in the virulent outbreak of 1400.[13] Convents in nearby towns like San Sepolcro experienced similar plague-related contractions, although the evidence is less complete.[14]

Our first comprehensive piece of evidence regarding Florentine convent populations dates from 1368, when the bishop distributed a huge pious bequest "among the paupers of Jesus Christ." Adhering to what Samuel Cohn has called a mendicant pattern of giving, the bishop parceled out bits of this legacy to the residents of eighteen convents and eleven male houses.[15] In contrast to the 205 male religious concentrated in several large mendicant foundations, the 202 nun-beneficiaries lived in small communities averaging just over 11 women. The largest convent was the house for repentant prostitutes (the Convertite), with twenty-five inhabitants. Despite their small census, female communities nevertheless showed a striking upper-class composition. Even though affluent convents did not figure among the recipients of this bequest, over 40 percent of nun-beneficiaries had surnames — still a relative rarity in the Trecento — indicating their prominent status. Old magnate lineages like the Adimari, Agli, Aliotti, Bardi, Cavalcanti, Spini, and Tosinghi made a strong showing in the census, but the majority of nuns bearing family names came from the newer mercantile elite — the Albizzi, Benci, Rucellai, Acciaiuoli, Bonsi, Medici — who rose to prominence in the fourteenth century.[16] The clustering of sisters and other kin at this early date is equally striking: at least 17 percent of nun-beneficiaries were blood relatives. This demographic profile suggests that, in this era of frail civic institutions and fierce political rivalry, aspiring *popolani* families were already appropriating the kinship-based strategy that magnates had used to gain control over ecclesiastical institutions in the late thirteenth century.[17] Unprecedented mortality caused by two successive plagues created opportunities for newcomers to achieve footholds in ecclesiastical institutions — one of the most valuable local resources that powerful families fought over.

Many of these same social and demographic features are apparent in the 1384 census, the first systematic survey of Florentine convents, taken by Bishop Angelo Acciaiuoli. Conducted on the heels of a yet another plague episode, this visitation of twenty-five convents turned up exactly three hundred nuns, novices, and professed servants; convents averaged just over twelve women.[18] A few houses — such as the wealthy suburban convent of S. Gaggio — were relatively robust, but the majority of communities struggled to sustain their numbers. S. Giovanni Battista di S. Frediano had lost half of its meager population to the recent onslaught; the episcopal vicar instructed them to admit new recruits in light of their sufficient endowment.[19] Although mendicant convents were not included in this census, given the bishop's limited jurisdiction over them, they too were minuscule communities. S. Jacopo — the largest pre-plague convent — housed seventeen nuns in the 1390s and remained at that level until the 1420s. The Poor Clares of Montedomini, one of the oldest convents outside the Florentine city walls, housed between ten and fifteen nuns in the early Quattrocento. Many Franciscan houses in the urban core — S. Francesco de' Macci, for example — were comparable in size or even smaller.[20] Even a generous estimate of mendicant convent populations in the city and environs would add only 100–150 nuns to the 1384 episcopal census, bringing the total number to 400–450 nuns out of an estimated population of sixty thousand persons. Importantly, however, although the actual number of nuns had declined since Villani's day, their percentage relative to the overall population had grown by a tiny fraction.[21]

The bishop's visitation also revealed that the majority of convents remained solvent and well governed, although the fragmentation of communal life was visible among some. While nuns often put their best foot forward to official visitors, they also took advantage of pastoral visitations to voice grievances that otherwise might go unheard, since visitation protocols gave each nun the chance to air individual complaints. Old Benedictine houses with stable endowments fared best in an uncertain post-plague environment. Abbess Angela Pecori of S. Niccolò Maggiore testified that her twelve nuns were "obedient" and performed all required liturgical offices; convent goods were stewarded effectively by a treasurer and a cellarer. She admitted, however, that while the nuns "observed silence," they did not keep it "very well." The highborn abbesses of S. Pier Maggiore and S. Felicita reportedly maintained good discipline: their nuns celebrated divine offices, slept together in the dormitory, and shared common board in the refectory. As heads of urban parishes, these two convents commanded deep-seated loyalties and a wealth of resources that enabled them to embellish their complexes with new altarpieces, chapter room frescoes, and beautiful liturgical books, even as they faced crushing tax burdens and substantial loss of life.[22] Other convents were less fortunate. Abbess Margherita Bindi of S. Giovanni Battista suffered from a prolonged illness, so there had been no "rule" for some time. With the nuns' consent, the vicar deputized a nun-lieutenant to act in her stead and instructed the nuns to obey her as if she were the "true abbess." Several convents showed minor lapses in discipline. Yet, although these communities were not vibrant centers of spirituality, it would be mistaken to consider them morally lax. Convent goods at S. Onofrio were well conserved, but the ten nuns did not sleep in the common dormitory. The nine nuns of S. Anna shared only a common table; those of S. Orsola "did not observe silence." The most serious disarray occurred at S. Ambrogio, where the weak-willed abbess Francesca Guadagni played favorites and dissipated convent goods.[23]

These communities were simply too small to be wracked by widespread factionalism, one of the principal scourges of sixteenth-century convent life. Instead, threats to communal harmony came from personal animosities that were toxic in a small-group setting. In addition, chapters confronted the repeated loss of experienced leadership. Rotating through different offices enabled abbesses and senior nuns to accrue deep organizational knowledge that made them conversant with customary privileges and practices. The sudden loss of experienced cohorts in plague episodes diminished the collective memory of house traditions governing daily life and external relations. Moreover, the deaths of mature women wise in convent ways shrank the leadership pool from which chapters elected top officers and further contracted the social networks on which houses could rely. Unfortunately, grooming new novices in corporate responsibilities often failed to pay dividends, since younger nuns remained susceptible to plague as well.

These problems take on a human face when one looks more closely at the city's premier convent, S. Pier Maggiore. Reduced to eight members by the Black Death, the chapter had regained its optimal number of twelve nuns plus two novices by 1370. Virtually all of these women hailed from what Anthony Molho has termed "high-status" lineages representing the 110 wealthiest families dominating political affairs throughout the Quattrocento.[24] One chapter member admitted after the Black Death, Suor Bartolomea Dini, had acquired sufficient experience to be appointed treasurer—a customary launching point for a career as abbess—but her death in the 1374 plague robbed the house of a seasoned leader. A slightly younger colleague, Suor Lisabetta Acciaiuoli, served several turns as treasurer in the early 1380s—the same years her brother Angelo won appointment as bishop of Florence. An obvious candidate for future abbess, she too was struck down by disease in the early 1390s.[25] Many of the new entrants intended to replenish convent ranks in these decades and sustain continuities in leadership—Flora Portinari, Taddea Dini, Spera Cambi, Piera Barucci, Maddalena Bencivenni, Bartolomea Ricasoli—died well before reaching maturity.[26] The convent was fortunate, however, in the longevity of its abbess, Benedetta Macci, who ascended to this position in 1350. Surviving several plague episodes, this hardy soul steered S. Pier Maggiore toward a state of strong spiritual and financial health. She showed real skill in managing the heavy civic taxes that subsidized military campaigns as well as in navigating prickly political circumstances. Abbess Benedetta occasionally capitalized on tense church-state relations by inserting herself into a complex dialogue of power that pitted old and new elites, the populace, commune, bishops, popes, and local clerics against each other in rapidly shifting alignments.[27] The Florentine see experienced a particularly rapid turnover during her forty-five year tenure, and she fictively "married" at least four incoming bishops as part of their installation proceedings before her death in 1395. Unfortunately, however, her successor Antonia Bardi succumbed to plague only five years after being elected "by sudden divine inspiration," depriving the community of a half century of organizational wisdom.[28]

Late Trecento convents also confronted shifts in pious giving that affected their finances. Cohn has argued that, after the second outbreak of plague in 1363, male testators in Florence and other central Italian cities transferred support from religious women and other "poor of Christ" to large civic charities like hospitals and dowry funds for poor girls. Female testators, however, continued to vigorously patronize convents, a practice that Cohn sees as conservative compared to men's more innovative stance.[29] This claim warrants closer analysis; for now it is important to note that shrinking postmortem bequests must be balanced against the lively stream of inter vivos contributions made by both women and men, especially to support nuns' caretaking role in the cult of the dead. Crucial to both convent demographics and finance was the fact that as Florentine lineages consolidated their sense of identity in the late Trecento, they enrolled their daughters as nuns to oversee tomb sites and steward commemorative programs. In the late fourteenth century, nuns already existed for the sake of others, whether as guardians of property, custodians of the dead, or propitiatory offerings to a seemingly vengeful God. The social value of female monasticism to lineage-conscious patrons is substantiated by the foundation of eight new Florentine convents between 1376 and 1400—a pattern that was not replicated in either Bologna or Venice, although other Tuscan and Umbrian towns saw informal women's groups proliferate.[30]

The emergence of new religious communities amid such precipitous decline, however, only intensified the competition between convents for new recruits, especially since the majority of nuns were placed in these institutions by their families. To combat declining numbers, virtually every Florentine convent decreased the amount of the dowry required to enter as an incentive to rebuild ranks after the virulent epidemic of 1400. Like convents all over Europe, Florentine religious houses relied heavily on dowries to build the property endowment on which nuns drew for a lifetime.[31] Although intended to create long-term financial security, these monies in practice were often used instead to pay off debts and taxes, maintain convent buildings, or launch ambitious decorative or architectural campaigns. Regardless of the uses to which they were put, dowries formed the lifeblood of any institution. Hence any decision to lower entrance payments systematically was a serious matter. To sustain its numbers, S. Pier Maggiore dropped dowry sums after 1400 by 35–70 percent from late Trecento levels, decreasing its "alms"—the euphemism for monastic dowries—from a range of 150–315 florins to a standard fee of 100 florins (although a few benefactors occasionally offered more).[32] This gambit quickly yielded several new novices. Across the river, S. Felicita reduced dowries from late Trecento norms of 120–130 florins to 90–110 florins. These nuns also played a spiritual card by ardently promoting the cult of archangel Raphael following his miraculous apparition to one of the nuns in 1424.[33] The Benedictine convent of S. Niccolò Maggiore opted for a radical solution to rebuild its chapter, which was possible only because of its ample endowment. In 1438 Abbess Taddea Ridolfi reported that "we are nine nuns, not including the abbess, among who are five girls. We accepted them without dowries and agreed that the convent would provide all their needs from great to small."[34]

Nor was this response merely a desperate attempt by traditional convents to compete with newer, more attractive foundations. Even the most rigorous Florentine communities discounted dowries to accelerate growth and build endowments. In the 1410s, S. Verdiana slashed entry payments by 20–40 percent, to 60 or 70 florins. Other new convents like the Paradiso targeted artisan and professional households by setting dowries at 40–80 florins, which enabled them to grow both their membership and endowment quickly.[35] Since dowries functioned only as a rudimentary social filter in these decades, nuns often made difficult pragmatic decisions when navigating between demographic demands and social selectivity. As chapter 2 shows, convents adopted different recruitment strategies in these troubled times. Some enlarged their customary recruitment area beyond the immediate neighborhood; others dug deeper into the social spectrum for local recruits or tried to assess strength of vocation. Yet virtually all convents aimed at the same goal: attracting new generations of nuns who simultaneously extended life-giving networks.

This economic strategy was key to the demographic rebound of Florentine convents in the early Quattrocento, especially since female monasticism faced stiff challenges in the form of widespread natalist concerns. Molho has shown that in the 1410s and 20s, preachers, moralists, and political theorists espoused a natalist mentality "favoring married life over the monastic condition," which culminated in the creation of the civic dowry fund (1425).[36] Enrolling thirty thousand girls over its 150-year history, the dowry fund gave Florentines a set of sophisticated financial instruments by which to integrate social and marital strategies. The fund's early provisions, however, discouraged monastic placements, since the initial objective was to stimulate reproduction through marriage. Only in 1437 did civic administrators allow convents to recoup the original investment if a girl professed instead of marrying.

As the urban population dropped to thirty-seven thousand in 1427 — less than half its size a century earlier — the commune and its citizens faced a dilemma. On one hand, monastic celibacy worked against the city's long-term viability; on the other, both civic honor and the desire to appease a wrathful God called for maintaining robust religious houses. While lower convent dowries provided a partial solution to this problem, equally critical was the transformation of female monasticism into a civic project tied to the financial mechanisms of the public debt. By extending aid to most Florentine convents via indirect tax offsets in 1415, city fathers took the first steps toward integrating female communities into civic policy.[37] Six years later, they made the unprecedented move of establishing a civic magistracy charged with supervising convents — the first of its kind anywhere in Europe — thereby acknowledging the centrality of convents to the social order.

In these decades of emerging civism and early state formation, the economic relationship between marriage and monasticism became firmly entwined in contemporary discourse. Blaming the rampant sins of sodomy, usury, and witchcraft for the divine wrath visited on the population, the Franciscan preacher Bernardino of Siena claimed that rising marriage portions were responsible for the city's inability to rebound demographically. In his famed Lenten cycle of 1424–25, he argued that "many parents, since they can't afford to expend such immense dowries on their daughters, keep them sterile . . . at home." This future saint also directly linked marital strategies to forced vocations. "What is even more cruel," Bernardino continued, is that households with several daughters and insufficient resources "lead one or two of the prettier ones to the altar with the largest dowries possible; and the others, especially if they are crippled, lame, blind, or in some other way deformed, they close in a convent like the world's spit and vomit."[38]

Bernardino's analysis mixed astute insight with misperception. As scholars have shown, the preacher was wrong about rising dowries, which did not grow perceptibly in the early fifteenth century. Nor were convent populations growing in absolute terms; in fact, the census of Florentine nuns reached a low ebb in the first three decades of the Quattrocento, much like the urban population itself. Decimated convent populations were obvious throughout the 1422 visitation conducted by Archbishop Amerigo Corsini, only the second such diocesan excursion on record.[39] In the forty-year interval between visitations, the surveyed population dropped from 300 to 229 nuns overall, while average convent size declined from 12.5 to 8.8 nuns; the largest urban house topped out at 19 women. Although the match with the previous episcopal census is imperfect, population in the nineteen houses visited by both bishops had fallen between the first and second visit by 20 percent (221 to 178 nuns). A few communities—S. Apollonia, S. Felicita, S. Giusto, the Portico—had made minor gains, and the inklings of monastic renewal can be detected in the inclusion of the little hermitage called Le Murate, where ten recluses had walled themselves up in a tiny bridge house perched over the Arno. When this group incorporated as a formal Benedictine nunnery in 1424, it became one of only two convents that were established in the first half of the Quattrocento.[40] Most convents struggled to maintain critical mass, despite dowry incentives. The six houses whose constitutions fixed an optimal number all fell short of their threshold. The majority modeled themselves on the apostolic community, setting perfection at twelve nuns led by an abbess, but even these low numbers proved difficult to meet.[41]

Table 1.1. Estimated Population of Florentine Convents inside the Walls, 1338–1552*

Year	Est. No. of Nuns	Urban Population	Approximate Ratio	As % of Urban Population
1338	500	100,000–120,000	1:220	0.45
1384	400–450	60,000	1:141	0.7
1427	500–520	37,000	1:72	1.3
1480	1,200–1,300	41,000	1:33	3.0
1515	2,500**	60,000–70,000	1:26	3.8
1552	3,419	60,000–70,000	1:19	5.2

Sources: AAF, VP, 1.1; ASF, Catasto, vols. 184, 185; Batarra, *Popolazione di Firenze;* Brucker, "Monasteries"; Goldthwaite, *Building of Renaissance Florence;* Herlihy and Klapisch-Zuber, *Les toscans;* Trexler, "Celibacy"; Villani, *Croniche.*

*In all cases where a range is given for either the number of nuns or the urban population, I have calculated approximate ratios and percentages from the midpoint of each range.

**Includes nuns in urban convents and within a four-mile radius of the city.

Yet Bernardino's insight that convent populations were growing relative to the overall urban population proved correct. To substantiate this point, we can turn to the snapshot of ecclesiastical institutions captured in the 1427 *catasto,* the first systematic tax survey of the entire Florentine dominion.[42] In their massive study of this report, David Herlihy and Christiane Klapisch-Zuber estimated that there were 906 religious women living in forty-eight institutions: 553 nuns housed in twenty-seven urban convents, plus another 353 nuns residing in twenty-one communities outside the walls. That estimate is almost certainly too high. Refining the criteria for types of religious communities, which were often hybrid in nature, as well as categories of personnel puts the number of nuns in 1427 closer to 800, with 500–520 women living in urban houses.[43] Despite sharp demographic contraction after the Black Death, convents nevertheless housed a greater fraction of the urban population—about 1.3 percent in 1427—than they had forty years earlier. As table 1.1 illustrates, about 1 in every 141 Florentine residents in 1384 was a nun; by 1427, that ratio had grown to roughly 1 in 72. In the early Quattrocento, Florentine fathers were already choosing to place their daughters in convents instead of marrying them. Part of the rationale was surely financial, in that the much-vaunted dowry fund initially did not permit investors to recover their capital in the event of a girl's death or religious profession.[44] Other social and political considerations that I analyze in chapter 2—local influence, social integration, political power—factored into familial decisions. Before affluent Florentines developed consistent strategies for plague management, the imminent threat of death made it advantageous to protect the patrimony and tend to the afterlife simultaneously by placing girls in divine service. The early Quattrocento struggle between marriage and monasticism may have pitted core values against each other, but monasticism was already beginning to win out.

This victory can be traced partly to the reshuffling of Florentine society in the aftermath of plague, which left a deep imprint on the social composition of convents. Defining nuns' social rank is challenging, given that Florentines used a complex calculus to determine status, ranging from wealth and officeholding to antiquity of lineage, fiscal probity, and individual moral character. Yet the *catasto* firmly establishes that convents were more socially diverse in 1427 than a half century before or after. Trexler noted that the economic position of nuns' families in 1427 leaned toward the middle, with few nuns coming from the city's richest families — a fundamentally accurate observation that nonetheless must be contextualized in several ways.[45] First, we can securely identify only one in every four or five nuns from tax reports; the remaining nuns either were not listed by name, were identified by first name only, or had a generic patronymic. Still, this very fact indicates that convents had not yet been saturated by elites in the early Quattrocento. Combining convent tax rosters with membership lists gathered from other sources, we can safely say that only 25–30 percent of Florentine choir nuns in 1427 sported a surname — the most basic status marker — compared to upward of 40 percent in 1368.[46] It was not only urban elites who invested in convents in the wake of the plague but a wide range of artisans and professionals such as notaries, physicians, goldsmiths, and even members of the building and food trades. There also were striking status differentials among nuns bearing surnames. Molho's identification of the 417 lineages comprising the fifteenth-century Florentine ruling class offers a useful tool here.[47] Two-thirds of the nuns bearing family names in tax rosters belonged to these lineages; among them, 41 percent (52 of 125) came from "high-status" families clustered in a few convents like S. Jacopo and S. Domenico nel Maglio. Yet not all nuns bearing family name came from the apex of society. A significant number of the remaining one-third belonged to moderately wealthy, politically active notarial households that proved unable to sustain their fortunes as political opportunities contracted. This element of diversity within a broad-gauged elite both enhanced the civic nature of convents as communal institutions and emphasizes the rapid aristocratization of Florentine convents later in the century.

Another legacy of plague was the steep age gradient among nuns, captured in the faces painted by Francesco Botticini later in the century (fig. 1.1). Although only six convents reported their members' ages in the *catasto*, these differences

Fig. 1.1. Francesco Botticini, *St. Monica Creates the Order of Augustinian Nuns.* S. Spirito, Florence, c. 1478 (detail). Scala / Art Resource, New York.

were equally pronounced at all houses.[48] The youngest nun at S. Maria di Candeli was eight years old, the oldest seventy-six. Between these extremes, the remaining twelve choir nuns clustered in distinct brackets: five were fifty or older; three were age twenty to forty, and six nuns were under twenty. Such sharp age demarcations must have spawned generational tensions, especially since many older nuns were described in tax records as ill, infirm, or "useless" (*disutile*). In the early Quattrocento, religious women by and large did not share experiences as members of the same cohort except if they were among the very young. Almost half of the nuns at the Portico were under twenty years of age; the four novices representing the future of S. Giusto were all six to eight years old.[49] These were indeed young, organizationally inexperienced nunneries, filled with undisciplined vitality. Still, the age pendulum might swing to the other extreme. In 1435, not a single nun or novice at Montedomini was under age thirty; the average age of chapter members approached forty-five. The challenge confronting this Franciscan community was not inexperience but recruiting new blood to ensure its future. The five women comprising S. Maria in Verzaia in 1438 formed a similarly mature lot.[50] Rapid turnover in convent populations due to plague meant that nuns showed great differentiation in age and class, as well as in forms of religious expression, throughout the early fifteenth century.

These age profiles also provide insight into familial decisions surrounding monastic profession in the early Quattrocento. Determining the exact age at which young girls were destined for either marriage or the cloister is complicated by the fact that households often deliberately falsified or omitted girls' ages in tax reports in order to widen their window of marriageability. We also must distinguish between the age at which girls entered a convent and the age at which they professed, since becoming a nun was a protracted, disjointed affair, much like marriage in Renaissance Italy.[51] Normally the process was divided into three stages, each marked by a public ceremony: entering the community, which disengaged girls from society; taking the monastic habit (*vestizione*), which gave them a liminal status as unprofessed nuns; and professing solemn vows, which rendered them legally "dead to the world." Nuns themselves figured their ages from different starting points in house chronicles and necrologies, recording both age at entrance and the number of years spent in religious life; however, seniority in chapter was determined by date of profession following strict rules of hierarchy.[52] Most nuns adopted a religious name heralding their new status either at entry or vestition, but some retained their secular names depending on house custom, especially in the first half of the Quattrocento. In this pluralistic environment, each order set its own age threshold for profession, although social norms rather than religious prescriptions carried the day.[53]

Catasto reports confirm that Florentine girls normally entered religious communities before age ten, which marked a crucial transition to nubile status in sumptuary legislation and other social arenas. Judith Brown has shown that many girls entering S. Jacopo in the early Quattrocento were less than ten years old, with entry age rising to twelve or more after 1500.[54] These early beginnings socialized girls into monastic life, protected their honor, and limited worldly exposure. Fathers who kept daughters at home too long were considered lax in their duty, since their failure to either marry or monachize them jeopardized family honor. Writing to his father in 1435, Pazzino di Messer Palla Strozzi expressed dismay that his unmarried sister still remained at home: "I believed that you had put Caterina in a convent some time ago. Now I see that you haven't done so, which amazes me. You will hold onto her so long she will be ready for a husband."[55] The experiences of Piera and Margherita Portinari, whose father, Folco, ran the Medici bank in Milan, were more normative. Armed with a 75-florin dowry each, they entered S. Apollonia at ages seven and eight and were

immediately renamed Filippa and Benedetta (1434). Their entry ceremony undoubtedly resembled the initiation of young Agnola Quaratesi into S. Niccolò
dei Frieri a decade later. The morning of her acceptance, "her uncle Lotto
brought the said girl to our convent in the company of her relatives." After mass,
the convent supervisor asked "if she wanted to be a nun and the bride of Lord
Jesus. She said: yes, I do. Two lit candles . . . were placed in her hands," then she
was led to the convent door. "All of the nuns were gathered in the passageway
holding lit candles. After we put the girl inside, the door closed and we returned
to the church."[56] Postulants usually spent a year or two in the convent before
taking the habit, although some houses "dressed" girls sooner. Young nuns-in-
the-making were easily identified in the interval by their hair worn loose to the
shoulders. Lay girls boarding at convents to "learn the virtues" — reading, sewing, catechism, moral deportment — pursued their education at a similar time of
life.[57] These practices suggest that, in the early fifteenth century, fathers decided
their daughters' destinies around puberty as defined in a social sense rather than
in infancy.

Only rarely did convent chapters accept girls under age five, since their vocation was doubtful, their care time consuming, and their presence disruptive.[58]
The large, socially inclusive convent of Le Murate was exceptional in its willingness to accept the very young. Drawing on now lost documents, Suor Giustina
Niccolini penned a house chronicle in the 1590s filled with stories about abandoned youngsters who later joined the chapter. Because the nuns enjoyed a
reputation for charity, toddlers age two or three were sometimes left in the
convent turnstile instead of being consigned to the civic foundling hospital.
Other girls arrived at Le Murate between ages three and six, although most
probably entered at the customary stage of life. Conversely, a sizeable group of
widows joined the house in their thirties and forties, as did Abbess Scholastica
Rondinelli, who transitioned from wife to widow to nun in the course of a single
year. Other women from propertied families like the Benci and the Gianfigliazzi
renounced worldly things and became nuns when they were "already old" (in
their sixties, seventies, and eighties), sometimes shortly before death.[59]

Age at profession was less normative, since it hinged on circumstances ranging
from dowry fulfillment to the festive calendar. As we will see, different methods
of paying dowries drove monastic biographies down different paths starting in
the 1430s. Generally, most girls in the early Quattrocento took vows around
age fifteen after gaining some experience with monastic routines. Dowry fund
records, which tilt toward the latter part of the century, show that before 1480

Fig. 1.2. Anonymous, *Veiling Ceremony of a Florentine Nun*. Gabinetto dei disegni degli Uffizi, Florence, c. 1500. Inv. 1890, no. 3334. Soprintendenza Speciale per il Patrimonio Storico, Artistico ed Ethnoanthropologico e per il Polo Museale della città di Firenze.

median age at profession for girls holding investments was 17.6 years old, compared to 19.9 years old for marriage.[60] Typical monastic experiences include those of the sisters Antonia and Camilla Bardi, who lived together in S. Apollonia for "several years" before professing together in 1435 at age sixteen and fifteen respectively. Although these profession ceremonies had not yet been fully transformed by the Renaissance culture of display, they were still festive occasions marked by feasting, decorations, music, and the inclusion of family, as suggested in one such visual representation (fig. 1.2).[61] The two Bardi sisters swore before Archbishop Corsini, Abbess Cecilia Donati, the assembled chapter, various priests and friars, and assorted kin that they would observe the Benedictine rule and house customs until death.[62] Taking solemn vows was a crucial rite of passage that forced girls to relinquish individual property claims and fully immersed them in the collectivity. Young nuns vested in the dowry fund could collect their dowries only by furnishing proof of profession.[63]

By 1430, Florentine convents were slowly emerging from a profound crisis period. As plague decimated urban populations throughout Italy, local convents furnished important venues in which to live out penitential ideals and perform other acts of propitiation. Florentine devotional culture was never far removed from financial and political considerations, however, and it was these drivers that ultimately assured convent survival. Families placed their daughters in religious service to protect family interests, tend the cult of remembrance, assert influence over valuable institutional resources, advance the social integration of their households, and promote civic honor. Although natalist concerns loomed large in this era of high mortality, the complex social functions of female religious communities anchored their continued growth.

The Midcentury Resurgence

Florentine convent populations began an impressive turnaround between the ecclesiastical tax surveys of 1427 and 1478, increasing by 40–50 percent to approximately twelve hundred to thirteen hundred nuns in the city and environs. Since the urban population rose more slowly to about forty-one thousand residents in 1480, nuns figured as roughly 3.0 percent of the population by that date, which translates to one nun for every thirty-three inhabitants.[64] By contrast, convents in Bologna, Milan, and smaller provincial towns did not make a similar demographic recovery during the same time period. In those places, both the number of female religious houses and their populations continued to decline at midcentury. Only Venice showed a fairly analogous development.[65] Signs of recovery were visible in the convent-building boom marking Quattrocento Florence; at least eleven urban convents undertook expansion projects during the fifteenth century, most after 1450.[66] Driving this distinctive pattern was a unique conjuncture of religion and politics. Fifteenth-century Italian oligarchies aligned their interests more closely with the Roman Curia, since control of civic life and control of ecclesiastical institutions formed two sides of the same coin.[67] Before the 1430s, however, Florence differed from other north Italian city-states in that its diocesan organization was weak and contested, its bishop was often absent, and its civic apparatus was strong enough to counter ecclesiastical claims.[68] Once the Medici returned from exile in 1434, growing collaboration between the papacy and the Medicean oligarchy smoothed over many of these problems and helped seal a fateful bargain between family, church, and state.

Still, this phase of monastic expansion was marked by uneven growth and pronounced stratification between Florentine convents. Selective urban houses — S. Pier Maggiore, S. Felicita, S. Ambrogio — maintained a policy of social exclusivity, holding growth firmly in check in order to retain a high standard of living. S. Pier Maggiore, which housed seventeen nuns in 1427, remained at roughly that level until the 1490s, while its counterpart across the river, S. Felicita, stabilized at twenty-four nuns between 1427 and 1478. The population of S. Ambrogio was somewhat more elastic, growing from nineteen to thirty choir and servant nuns in the same interval.[69] Like their Venetian counterparts, S. Zaccaria, S. Lorenzo, and Le Vergini, these traditional houses tightly controlled their populations in order to sustain the honor and privileges of the urban patriciate.[70] Old-line Benedictine and Augustinian convents remained attractive to prosperous families, whatever their pious leanings, because they could accommodate greater interaction with society and were more susceptible to local political pressure, being subject to episcopal rather than mendicant jurisdiction. As detailed in chapter 2, these top-tier convents formed the primary targets for elite Florentine families looking to establish additional power bases outside their immediate neighborhood around 1450.

New foundations grew much faster, both because their high ideals gripped the contemporary religious imagination and because their admission policies were socially inclusive. Le Murate (est. 1424) and S. Chiara (est. 1452) opened their doors to girls of diverse social status, provided that they displayed strong religious convictions and supplied a modest dowry. The nun-chronicler of Le Murate, Suor Giustina Niccolini, was proud of the fact that women came from all over Italy, Spain, and other parts of the world to join her community.[71] Subsidizing this growth was a raft of wealthy benefactors, who grasped the patronage opportunities new convents represented. Because of this inclusivity, Le Murate showed exceptional diversity in its social makeup and rapidly eclipsed all other Florentine convents in population, growing from 36 nuns in 1439 to 124 in 1458 and to over 200 in 1515.[72] By 1470 the nuns taxed their creativity simply to find suitable religious names for new entrants; the sheer press of bodies led Abbess Scholastica Rondinelli, who oversaw this surge from 1439 to 1475, to order a weekly change of tunics "on account of the stench" in the cramped choir.[73] Choir nuns admitted under her tutelage ran the gamut from high-status Strozzi girls to shoemakers' daughters. Several Italian noblewomen brought massive dowries up to 1,500 florins, which underwrote architectural expansion and enabled poorer girls to join.[74] Still, the dream of dissolving status distinctions in a shared spiritual enterprise proved ephemeral. Later in the century, Le Murate and similar houses reinscribed social differences, often becoming internally stratified in the process.[75]

Most convents steered a middle path between these two extremes. Only a dozen convents filed returns in the 1478 *catasto*, but the upward tick in populations is apparent throughout. Collectively, convent growth told a complex tale in which religiosity joined hands with secular ambition. The Dominicans of S. Jacopo expanded from twenty-nine to forty-nine nuns between 1427 and 1478, primarily because of the Observant movement. Reformed convents in Bologna saw a similar rise in professions in the 1450s, 1460s and 1470s.[76] By contrast, Medici preferment allowed S. Verdiana, headed by the avid newshound Abbess Piera de' Medici, to double its population from fourteen to twenty-eight choir nuns in the same period. In the 1460s the convent embarked on an extensive building program under the auspices of Giovanni di Cosimo de' Medici and his wife, Ginevra Alessandri, who undertook this project "for the love of God and the benefit of their souls, because they recognized that the convent of S. Verdiana was in extreme straits and great need." Outside the walls, the Poor Clares of S. Matteo in Arcetri grew from twenty-three to thirty-two "mouths" owing to the quest for patronage that immutably altered Florentine political culture after 1434.[77] The mid-fifteenth century was a pivotal moment in the conquest of female religious institutions by the urban elite, which simultaneously transformed convents into civic goods and instruments of familial power. In turn, convent chapters welcomed this growth, as the wider network of friends, clients, and sponsors they could draw on as a result of expansion enabled them to compete more effectively for favors and influence.

Setting the stage for recovery was the papal suppression of sparsely populated, underfunded houses by Eugenius and his successor Nicholas V.[78] Eugenius in particular used the Florentine diocese to showcase a resurgent papacy following the papal schism; his prolonged presence in the city throughout the 1430s was decisive in implementing reforms. After Archbishop Corsini's death in 1435,

Eugenius governed the diocese directly through a papal commissioner, leading him to lock horns with the Florentine *signoria* over numerous jurisdictional matters. There were clear winners and losers in this papal reform project. Both Eugenius and Nicholas capitalized on the legacy of plague to advance the Observant movement—one of the key forces of spiritual rejuvenation in fifteenth-century Europe stressing foundational ideals—which reached its peak of fervor in Tuscany at midcentury.[79] These popes seized the opportunity to remake female monasticism as a statement of religious renewal, transferring goods and personnel from small, struggling foundations to Observant convents to reward their rigor.[80] Observance did not simply renew discipline, however, but articulated a new vision of female monasticism predicated on ample populations, large portfolios, and greater uniformity of lifestyle across geographical regions—the hallmarks of what later became Tridentine monasticism. A century or more before Trent, a rejuvenated papacy tried to realize its centralizing ambitions in part by standardizing monastic pluralism. Papal privileges and exemptions, whether for taxation or diet, were made contingent on nuns' continued compliance with Observant practice as judged by pope or vicar. The influx of new resources into favored houses—S. Apollonia, S. Brigida del Paradiso, Le Murate—allowed them simultaneously to perform liturgical offices, manage external affairs, develop internal governance, produce commodities for the market, and still conduct a penitential life. Renaissance monasticism did not merely "change sex," as Trexler astutely noted; it was predicated on a different institutional model rooted in papal policy.[81]

The Observant movement in Florence stimulated new recruits and foundations, as it did throughout Europe. Florentine merchant diaries and convent records alike suggest a spike in genuine vocations in the 1440s and 1450s. Girls who actively embraced monastic life remained a small minority, but their fathers highlighted the divine favor visited on their households for the familial audience reading these accounts.[82] Convent records also noted with real pride the entry of girls like Alessandra Barbadori, "inspired by God to enter the convent of S. Ambrogio in order to serve God here," since their presence enhanced the community's spiritual reputation.[83] A number of female initiatives played out around this devotional upsurge. In the mid-1450s, two wealthy women—Maria Albizzi and Annalena Malatesta—"inflamed by the love of God" established the Franciscan convent of S. Chiara and the Dominican tertiary house of S. Vincenzo, sited near each other in the Oltrarno. Both women realized their objectives through the intervention of Archbishop Antoninus, who served as their spiritual director. Concerned that Conventual oversight of S. Chiara would not advance the nuns' spirituality, Antoninus "often went to visit Abbess Maria Albizzi" to nurture her commitment. This future saint counseled other abbesses, performed scores of vestitions at the Observant houses of S. Apollonia and Le Murate, and corresponded tirelessly with pious laywomen.[84]

Popes and prelates also transferred mendicant convents from Conventual to Observant oversight in these transformative decades. Eugenius himself supervised the reform of the Poor Clares of S. Maria a Monticelli who, "due to the negligence and poor governance of their superiors," reportedly had fallen into "grave errors, there being neither charity, nor obedience, nor enclosure among them." He forcibly removed nuns "who had deviated from the true path," dispersing them to other provincial convents "against their will, and with no little effort and expense," according to convent documents. At the same time, he transformed internal monastic life by importing four exemplary nuns from Bologna to serve as role models. S. Jacopo was reformed in similar fashion when the Dominican general transferred six Observant nuns from S. Pier Martire in 1458 to instill greater discipline and devotion.[85] This convergence — hands-on papal intervention, zealous pastoral attention, heightened religiosity — was unique to Florence and stimulated an exceptional turnaround in local convent populations.

While Florentine devotional culture partly fueled recovery, the worldly forces of finance and patronage drove convent growth more actively in these decades. A key enabler of recovery was monastic dowry practices. Historians have noted the disparities between secular and spiritual dowries without examining the trajectory of convent dowries themselves. In the 1420s and 1430s, when the city was gripped by a fiscal crisis, convent chapters deliberately kept monastic dowries low and accommodated diverse payment schedules. Entrance fees stabilized at 100 florins or less, thereby preserving the strategic drop-off from Trecento levels initially meant to repopulate religious houses. Chapters probably feared the loss of prospective recruits as well as the growing set of patronage channels they represented. No doubt nuns' kin also exerted pressure to keep spiritual dowries affordable — a definite advantage in view of new proscriptions following the return of the Medici. Throughout the 1430s, 1440s, and 1450s, convents provided receptive environments for the daughters and sisters of anti-Medicean exiles whose misfortunes barred suitable marriage matches.[86]

In consequence of these developments, monastic dowries stayed within a normative range across the city. "These are the things that girls entering the convent of S. Apollonia to become nuns bring with them," stated one convent record; "first, 100 florins, given as alms." Other high-status convents set the baseline for spiritual dowries at 100 florins. Entry payments at the middling house of S. Luca held steady at 40 to 100 florins from 1433 to 1502, with the vast majority pegged at the latter figure.[87] If spent in other ways, the sum of 100 florins could purchase the scarlet, fur-lined robe (*cioppa*) worn by Florentine priors or pay for a small transept chapel in the newly remodeled church of S. Spirito.[88] Lower-tier dowries of 40–60 florins were within reach of notaries, lawyers, physicians, goldsmiths, and silk weavers, nor were they necessarily beyond the range of artisans in the building, food, or textile trades. Among the choir nuns of the Chiarito and the Paradiso in the 1460s were the offspring of butchers, shoemakers, apothecaries, and linen makers. With their burning idealism, new convents like S. Monaca (est. 1442) and S. Chiara initially embraced a diverse social mix, including women from Bologna, Lucca, Pistoia, and other Tuscan towns. Tertiary communities offered still other options for cash-strapped households seeking to perform a devotional act, advance family fortunes, and provide a protective residential environment for their daughters. Most members of third-order houses like S. Onofrio lacked surnames, a rough indication of their modest status.[89] In other words, Florentine spiritual dowries represented only a rudimentary social filter that enabled and even encouraged professions. Supplementing dowries were monastic trousseaux comprised of everyday items: beds and bedding, linens, books, candles, devotional images, holy dolls. Although monastic trousseaux grew larger after 1460 as consumption levels rose throughout Italian society, the bulk of goods still consisted of daily wares like coarse linen curtains for privacy in crowded dormitories rather than luxury goods like the fancy maiolica tableware embellishing late sixteenth-century Venetian refectories.[90]

Further facilitating monastic growth in the mid-Quattrocento was the willingness of convent chapters to accommodate various payment schedules for spiritual dowries. Prompted by the deepening financial problems of patrons, benefactors, and "friends" in the 1430s, most Florentine convents pragmatically shifted to installment plans, abandoning the former practice of requiring single advance payments. In the late fourteenth and early fifteenth centuries, convent dowries were customarily paid in cash, often in the form of gold coins placed in a sealed purse on the main altar of the convent church. Cash payments were also the norm in pre-Reformation Strasbourg.[91] This practice symbolically extended the metaphor that nuns were gifts given freely to God, transforming the dowry into a voluntary ritual offering, much like the girl herself. Vestiges of this custom remained in later years; nuns joining S. Domenico nel Maglio in the late fifteenth and early sixteenth centuries placed a single gold florin on the sacristy altar to mark their entry into the community.[92] However, advance payments incurred steep financial risks for families, who stood to lose a considerable sum without reaping expected dividends if a girl died soon after admittance. In the plague-ridden fourteenth century, the kin of Selvaggia Alberti and Spera Cambi forfeited dowries upward of 300 florins when the girls died only a few months after entering S. Pier Maggiore.[93]

After 1430, convent chapters regularly permitted households to spread out dowry payments over several years, with uniformly positive results for families. Installments alleviated cash flow problems and limited financial loss in case of premature death. The pact struck between Bernardo de' Medici and the nuns of S. Gaggio is typical of what became a commonplace arrangement. In 1431 Bernardo pledged a generous 150-florin dowry for his daughter Lena, giving 30 florins in cash on admittance. The balance was to be paid over five years by rents assigned from two shops in Mercato Vecchio run by a barber and ironmonger.[94] Well into the 1470s, well-off businessmen from prominent families — the Alessandri, Altoviti, Barbadori, Bonvanni, Machiavelli, Strozzi, Tanagli, della Tosa — made small down payments at entrance and then assigned annual rental income from houses, workshops, stores, farms, and vineyards to underwrite the balance. Other fathers or kinsmen paid dowry installments by designating the interest from credits in the public debt, whose payment schedule was notoriously slow and sporadic.[95] Still other fathers retired dowry payments through circular schemes that directed debts from third parties to convents instead — an inherently risky business.

Concessions to patron families yielded more recruits, but the social and financial consequences for nuns and nunneries were mixed. These accommodations enmeshed convents in a vast civic bookkeeping operation as well as in private credit networks that made clients, tenants, and business partners responsible for monastic professions. On the plus side, nuns acquired a larger circle of contacts that included artisans and tradesmen across the city. New dowry practices inextricably wove convents into urban commercial life, giving them a capillary reach well beyond their immediate network of dependants and friends. By the 1450s, these practices elevated convents' civic profile as institutions belonging to the city writ large. Shopkeepers, tradesmen, peasants, and the complex apparatus of the public debt all directly supported "consecrated virgins" who, as the chronicler Benedetto Dei exclaimed, "spend day and night in prayer asking favors for the most esteemed Florentine *signoria*."[96]

Yet dowry installments also put nuns at the mercy of the current business climate and often proved difficult to collect. Consequently, chapters often found themselves having to balance financial promises against a girl's formal integration into the chapter. Since most houses required full payment before allowing final vows, delays in payment delayed profession. Elena Bonvanni, "called" to be a nun at S. Ambrogio in 1459, had to wait fourteen years before taking final vows because her father repeatedly fell delinquent in paying her dowry.[97] Dozens of other girls in the mid-Quattrocento postponed this solemn step due to unpaid dowries; their monastic life course diverged radically from nuns vested in the dowry fund, who by necessity professed quickly. Suor Lisabetta Strozzi poignantly expressed the anguish of this extended novitiate. "It's already been seven years since I entered here in God's service," she wrote to her kinsman Matteo from S. Jacopo, "and I grow more content from day to day, although I exhaust myself by constant striving and learning the virtues required by my sisters. But since I wish to conform to the chapter in all things, it is necessary that I be consecrated to my spouse Jesus and take the black veil like my peers."[98] At S. Gaggio, Piera Altoviti's monastic progress stalled after her father, Sandro, pledged a 100-florin dowry in 1431, to be paid within five years from assigned bakery rents. Although Sandro obligated his heirs to fulfill these terms, two decades later 40 florins still remained outstanding, forcing the nuns to file suit in 1453 in the archbishop's court. Antoninus brokered a compromise whereby Piera's brother pledged 8 florins annually until the balance was retired; in the interim, the convent held title to one of his farms as surety.[99] Taken collectively, these new financial practices heightened convent dependence on their patrons rather than advancing traditional goals of monastic self-sufficiency.

Importantly, the dowry fund—unique in all of Italy—played little role in the recovery of convent populations. In the half century from 1437, when the commune first allowed investors to apply their investments to monastic dowries, to 1489, a mere 1.8% of girls invested in the fund became nuns. The ease of transferring dowry credits from one sister to another after 1460 accelerated professions, but the fund itself did little to spur innovative monastic dowry practices.[100]

Despite inherent financial disadvantages, convent chapters were willing to trade immediate revenues for longer-term patronage rewards. By the 1450s, convents were becoming enmeshed in the vast web of goods and favors—gifts, loans, tax concessions, liturgical furnishings—that constituted the stuff of patronage.

Medici patronage enjoyed the greatest visibility, but it was unique mainly in the range of favors on offer, a range attributable to the family's political influence. Although Cosimo's patronage of male religious houses and charitable confraternities is well recognized, he also satisfied requests from Italian nuns as far away as the Friuli. Especially numerous were his clients in Pisan convents. Closer to home, the nuns of S. Francesco offered Cosimo exclusive patronage rights to their convent in exchange for money to enlarge their dormitory and build a new church.[101] Moreover, the transgenerational nature of Medici patronage enabled wives to extend the family's capillary reach. Natalie Tomas has shown how numerous Medici women — Contessina de' Bardi, Ginevra Alessandri, Lucrezia Tornabuoni, Clarice Orsini, and the much-reviled Alfonsina Orsini — exercised considerable power both as intermediaries and as patrons in their own right.[102] Among their many clients were nuns scattered across the Florentine dominion. Ginevra Alessandri, married to Cosimo's son Giovanni, maintained an active profile at her natal family stronghold of S. Pier Maggiore, to which she and other kinswomen made substantial loans, sometimes through the Medici bank. Giovanni procured a precious relic for S. Verdiana in 1452, and then commissioned an elegant silver reliquary that was subsequently donated to the convent in a triumphal procession staged as civic festival. He also furnished a partial dowry for a client's daughter at the same convent, which was returned to his mother, Contessina, in 1451 when the girl refused to become a nun.[103]

As patronage took firm root as a governing process, nuns established themselves as both patrons and clients to advance their communities and individual reputations. Since the story of every nun formally began with her dowry, nuns concentrated much of their leverage in this area. In the 1450s and 1460s, the highborn nuns of S. Felicita, S. Ambrogio, and S. Apollonia admitted several dozen patrician daughters with dowries of 50–70 florins — half to two-thirds of the standard amount — on the assumption that their families would reciprocate in other ways.[104] Religious women also procured spiritual dowries as intermediaries in longer patronage chains that included the Medici. Writing to the young Lorenzo in 1472, Abbess Scholastica Rondinelli thanked him for enabling Piero Vespucci's daughter to profess at Le Murate, presumably by arranging her dowry. The same year, Suor Filippa Portinari of S. Apollonia requested charity from him on behalf of a poor woman who had "a flock of grown girls" but no means to dower them. Hoping to place one of her daughters in the house, the woman enlisted the savvy nun Filippa as a go-between, who successfully engineered the girl's admission after obtaining dowry funds from Lorenzo.[105]

Yet convent patronage networks cut still deeper into the social spectrum as part of a rich female devotional culture whose features are just coming to light. Nicholas Eckstein has argued that charity-minded laywomen were key contributors to the vibrant religiosity around S. Maria del Carmine.[106] In particular, convents anchored important coordinates on the charitable map by providing safe residential options for poor girls or those at risk, often by securing them positions as servant nuns via women's networks. To take one example: in 1445, an ironmonger's wife named Nanna and her daughter-in-law Agnoletta visited S. Niccolò dei Frieri with Nanna's young niece, the offspring of a deceased dyer. "As they had done on other occasions," the women implored the nuns to accept the girl as a *conversa* "to avoid evil befalling her, since she is poor and has nothing." Fearing a quick descent into prostitution, they targeted this house because Agnoletta's aunt was a nun there; with her recommendation, the chapter agreed to take the girl without dowry "for the love of God." A few days later, the girl's brother brought her belongings to the convent: a "broken and rotten" bedstead, "a torn, vermin-filled mattress," and a ragged overdress "of little value." After five years in convent service, however, she notified the nuns that "she didn't want to remain here, so we surrendered her to her aunt Nanna."[107] These caretaking functions highlight the range of female agency, demonstrating the support that could be mobilized via women's networks as well as the civic value of convents as custodial institutions.

In the mid-Quattrocento, Florentine convents experienced a demographic resurgence unusual among its neighbors. While Bolognese convents plunged to their nadir in the mid-fifteenth century, Florentine houses were already on the upswing. This reversal of fortune stemmed from a complex conjuncture of civic, oligarchic, and Medici interests with those of the papacy. The collaboration of convent chapters in promoting these interests proved decisive in mapping a distinctive Florentine trajectory. Although David Peterson reminds us that not all Italian religious activity should be read through a civic lens, any account of the exceptional expansion of Florentine convents in these decades must be framed by local political explanations.[108]

The Rush to the Convent

Building on their midcentury recovery, Florentine convent populations began an inexorable rise after 1480, with the greatest crush of professions coming after 1500. The rapidity of growth was breathtaking. The number of nuns shot up from roughly twelve hundred in 1478 to two thousand in 1500 before climbing to twenty-five hundred in 1515. That year, the average size of fifteen major convents approached one hundred women; Le Murate topped the list at two hundred nuns.[109] To accommodate demand, four new convents were founded in Florence between 1500 and 1520 alone, and three additional houses were established in nearby Prato in the same period. All convents saw their ranks swell, but the most pronounced growth occurred in Observant mendicant foundations and third-order houses. The Poor Clares of S. Chiara, whose core group had numbered 8 women a half-century earlier, counted 110 nuns in 1515; the Dominican tertiaries of the Annalena housed an identical number. The chapter of S. Apollonia stood at seventy-four nuns, while the Franciscan tertiaries of S. Orsola grew from nine women in 1427 to eighty-seven in 1515.[110] The closest organizational models for these burgeoning communities were large custodial institutions like the civic foundling home opened in 1445.[111] Not only were these communities more affordable and inclusive; their rigorous asceticism also helped offset the growing culture of consumption in an increasingly complex spiritual calculus. In addition, the willingness to invest valuable human resources in these institutions shows just how confident the middling and upper classes felt about their ability to influence the full range of Italian ecclesiastical affairs.

This surge in convent populations raises complex interpretive issues. Certainly the general demographic recovery of Italian cities enabled expansion at the most basic level. Richard Goldthwaite estimates that the Florentine urban population grew from 41,590 in 1480 to 70,000 in 1520 — an increase of nearly 68 percent.[112] By contrast, convent populations doubled in this same period, rising from approximately twelve hundred nuns in 1480 (3.0 percent of the urban population) to twenty-five hundred in 1515 (3.8 percent); expressed another way, roughly one in twenty-six inhabitants was a nun in 1515, up from one in thirty-three. To explain this disproportionate rise in religious professions, scholars have pointed first and foremost to changing marital strategies that made it financially advantageous to monachize some daughters so that their sisters could marry well. The 1480 *catasto* is filled with young patrician girls who became nuns because they possessed little or no dowry.[113] Molho has shown that average dowries among the Florentine elite rose by almost 45 percent over the fifteenth century, from 1,009 florins in 1425–49 to 1,430 florins after 1475. Marriage portions increased still further in the Cinquecento, reaching an average of 1,852 florins between 1500 and 1530. The destinies of girls enrolled in the dowry fund dramatically illustrate the results of this escalation. Only 3.6 percent of the nineteen thousand girls enrolled in the fund between 1425 and 1499 took vows. This figure jumped to 15.5 percent between 1500 and 1529 — over a fourfold increase — then nearly doubled again to 28.2 percent in the years after 1530. The greater number of religious vocations also stemmed from the practice of endogamy among propertied families, which made it increasingly difficult to secure acceptable matches. "The primary force behind the rush to the convent," Molho argues, was not purely economic but also followed from "the progressive complexity of the marriage market."[114]

Further propelling forced vocations was the growing disparity between monastic and secular dowries. Not only had secular dowries increased by 1475; monastic dowries declined, both in nominal and real value. In the last quarter of the Quattrocento, top-tier convents regularly satisfied the demands of principal patrons by accepting their daughters or those of their clients with inferior dowries of 40–70 florins, entrenching an earlier practice based on necessity. These modest sums were the monastic equivalent of a "mere artisan's dowry," to borrow Alessandra Macinghi Strozzi's stinging phrase. Additional savings were provided by the low value of monastic trousseaux compared to wedding finery.[115] Lacking the means or ability to make a good marriage match, elite households traded on their family name, political reputation, kin connections, and clientage ties to secure comfortable monastic posts for their daughters, assisted in this endeavor by family nuns. At the same time, the standard 100-florin entry fee was declining in real value. The florin dropped 42 percent in value over the Quattrocento, accelerated by a coinage reform in 1472; new coins were worth 20 percent less than "good" coins. The loss of purchasing power became acute by 1500, and convent scribes noted the depreciation, remarking that 100 *fiorini di suggello* was the equivalent of sixty-two to seventy *fiorini d'oro*.[116] With spiritual dowries representing only 25–45 percent of their value a century earlier, it was obviously cheaper to place girls in religious service in Laurentian Florence than in the calamitous fourteenth century.

Yet only after 1520 did monastic dowries function as a significant social filter in tandem with the growing aristocratization of Florentine society. The Medici restoration in 1512 both legitimized the culture of display and gave it added impetus. As the city became a major international player, many aspects of Florentine life, from clothing and ceremonies to domestic interiors, grew more ostentatious. In the 1520s, spiritual dowries doubled to 150–200 ducats, where they remained until the 1540s. Still, convent chapters were willing to make exceptions for "special" patrons; S. Pier Maggiore happily admitted Gostanza Alessandri in

1526 "as a favor with only 100 florins, even though the most recent entrants gave 170 florins."[117] Although increases in dowries helped recoup value lost over time, their primary purpose was to screen clientele. Many of the customs associated with early modern aristocratic convents — the transfer of private cells among nuns and lavish profession ceremonies — had their roots in these decades.[118] After 1520, the age difference between those girls invested in the dowry fund who married and those who professed also diverged more sharply. Age at profession dropped from 17.6 years before 1480 to 16.9 years after 1520, while over the same period girls' average age at marriage rose from 19.9 years to 21.2 years. As Molho argues, this evidence strongly suggests that in the sixteenth century, fathers made decisions about girls' destinies at an earlier point in their daughters' lives than they had in the fourteenth and fifteenth centuries.[119]

By the end of the Florentine republic, the economic motivations behind rising religious professions were widely acknowledged. The commune tried in vain to cap secular dowries in the 1510s and 1520s because they led to forced vocations. A 1519 decree acknowledged that fathers unable to afford large marriage portions "have been forced either to make [their daughters] nuns against their will, or to keep them at home, or to marry them" beneath their station. This assessment precisely captured the experience of the apothecary Luca Landucci, who made one daughter a nun at S. Onofrio and kept his other two girls at home. The twenty-seven-year-old daughter of the painter and Savonarolan adherent Francesco Rosselli was finally settled as a tertiary in 1499, but only after her grandmother scraped together the entry fee. Thirty years later, a nun of S. Agata remarked that the merchant Francesco Dazzi canceled payment of his daughter's 165-florin dowry "because he did not want [her] to become a nun in our convent. Instead, he made her a nun in the convent of Foligno in order to spend less."[120]

Despite its importance, the marriage market does not fully exhaust the reasons for rising religious professions, at least not before 1530. Other political and religious forces multiplied vocations, both genuine and forced: the cataclysmic foreign invasions that ushered in regime changes and the Savonarolan movement after 1494; the resulting politicization of convents, as Savonarolan and Medici sympathizers battled for control of the city's holy women; the aristocratization of Florentine society and the corresponding exploitation of the local resources convents represented; the search for safe residential options in a world seemingly gone mad. All of these factors worked synergistically to push up religious professions among different sectors of society.

These braided processes were most evident at fast-growing tertiary houses, which traditionally showed great social diversity. Throughout the fifteenth century, elderly pious widows from prosperous Florentine families brushed shoulders with younger women from the territorial periphery who shared their spiritual convictions and desire for continued freedom of movement. Among the tertiaries of S. Lucia in the late Quattrocento was the seventy-three-year-old widow Costanza Vettori, whose activities included a regular trek to nearby S. Marco, where she cured her ailments by donning Antoninus's garments. With their low dowries and permeable enclosure, tertiary communities like S. Orsola and S. Giorgio were the convents of choice for professional and artisan households squeezed out of other neighborhood options. Few tertiaries had surnames even in the late Quattrocento, despite the growing prevalence of these status markers in society.[121] Women from modest backgrounds continued to populate tertiary houses into the early sixteenth century, but after 1500 their top officers invariably came from well-connected lineages. Early sixteenth-century *ministre* at S. Orsola belonged to the Guardi, Mazzinghi, and Ridolfi families situated in the mid- to upper echelons of the Florentine ruling class.[122] Although convent officers used their influence to benefit their communities, they also openly facilitated the entry of upper-class recruits. As nuns of lower status died out over the first few decades of the Cinquecento, S. Orsola acquired a pronounced patrician cast. When the majority of the chapter attested to a 1539 financial transaction as signatories, all of the nuns showed the hallmark of high birth by signing the agreement in their own hands.[123] A similar process of aristocratization transformed the Crocetta, founded in the heady, contested religious climate of the early Cinquecento. At its foundation in 1511, its intake consisted largely of women belonging to the lower social orders; within five years, however, its recruits were coming from such eminent families as the Medici, Pitti, Gondi, Albizzi, and Ardinghelli.[124] The ability of members of the Medicean governing class to control these resources solidified the consensus politics and marriage alliances binding them together.

The political shock wave induced by the French invasion of 1494 spawned numerous prophecies, visions of religious renewal, and charismatic "living saints" across the Italian peninsula.[125] In Florence, foreign invasions led to the ouster of the Medici and the rapid rise of the Dominican preacher Girolamo Savonarola (1452–98), both of which contributed to the politicization of Florentine convents. The factionalism that gripped Le Murate during the siege of Florence —one camp pro-Medici, the other staunchly republican—is well known.[126] Lorenzo Polizzotto has shown how Savonarola and his followers assiduously cultivated convents in Florence and the surrounding district as part of an all-out battle

Fig. 1.3. Woodcut, *Nuns of Le Murate Receiving Savonarola*, 1497. Frontispiece to Girolamo Savonarola, *Operetta sopra i dieci commandamenti di Dio*. Florence, 1497. Palat. E. 6.2.70. Biblioteca Nazionale Centrale, Florence.

to win their allegiance. Savonarola and his disciples at S. Marco founded and reformed convents, preached rousing sermons to crowds of laywomen and tertiaries, and counseled nuns via letters and personal visits like the one paid to the Murate nuns portrayed in figure 1.3.[127] With his charismatic appeal and rhetorical flair, Savonarola found a receptive audience not only among the Murate nuns but also among the Medici clients of S. Verdiana. During his lifetime, the preacher sustained special relationships with four Dominican houses: S. Lucia and S. Caterina da Siena, both under the direct supervision of S. Marco; the Annalena, which successfully resisted the friars' repeated attempts to impose solemn vows on the community; and S. Jacopo di Ripoli, whose members achieved a major victory by moving into the official Savonarolan fold in 1507. Each of these houses commanded significant financial and social resources, with large populations ranging from 50 to 130 nuns. After his execution, Savonarola's apostolate spread to other convents in Florence, Tuscany, and parts of north-central Italy.[128]

One of the new Savonarolan foundations, the tertiary house of S. Caterina da Siena, which was established in 1496 by Camilla Bartolini Rucellai, built its ranks quickly by removing financial barriers to committed Piagnoni — or "weepers," as the preacher's followers were called — irrespective of social status. Inspired by Savonarola's sermons to abandon the world, Bartolini Rucellai had recruited over a hundred members to her community by the time she died in 1520. Two-thirds of the dowries paid to S. Caterina between 1498 and 1510 were 70 florins or less, with some dipping down to 30 florins.[129] These low entry fees allowed a wide spectrum of sympathizers to demonstrate their commitment to the movement by means of their daughters' lifeblood. Among the early recruits to S. Caterina were the offspring of apothecaries, stationers, notaries, barbers, shoemakers, linen weavers, doublet makers, and painters attracted to the Savonarolan message. As the movement spread across north-central Italy, adult women from surrounding towns, as well as from Milan, Urbino, and the Romagna, flocked to the house. These women, together with young women joining of their own volition or because they lacked marriage prospects, gave the house an unusually mature complexion in its early years. Twenty-seven of the ninety-six nuns entering S. Caterina between 1497 and 1520 (28 percent) were age twenty or older; only seven girls were fourteen years old or younger, with the youngest admitted at age twelve.[130] Florentine laywomen, who figured among the preacher's staunchest supporters, enthusiastically backed this new venture by donating a few florins to its endowment; others, anxious for the spiritual well-being of younger kin, cobbled together money for their entry payments.[131] Even after internal quarrels ruptured the Savonarolan movement in the early sixteenth century, sympathizers renewed the cause by placing girls in affiliated convents in Florence, Pescia, and Prato, where they advanced a Piagnoni religious vision by making innovations in the liturgy, copying forbidden texts, admitting new clients, and committing social resources to the cult.[132]

Still, disagreements between nuns and their S. Marco supervisors erupted frequently. Although Savonarola himself showed a deft touch in managing convent affairs, after his execution his followers were criticized for depriving women of an independent spiritual voice. At S. Lucia, resistance to Savonarolan control emerged in the form of "devil possession"—blaspheming, swearing, sexually explicit visions—which fractured the house in 1498. Mass exorcisms proved ineffective; order was restored only when nearly half the nuns were transferred to other convents or sent home.[133] A less dramatic duel emerged at S. Jacopo, where the primary flashpoint was the community's rapid expansion after 1507. Once the convent was securely within S. Marco's jurisdiction, the Piagnoni hierarchy packed the house with their clients, as they did other Savonarolan foundations. By 1522, the senior nuns voiced opposition to accepting so many new recruits, concerned "not to burden the convent with too many girls." The nuns preferred to meet financial needs through increased production of gold thread, but the friars squashed this proposal and set strict limits on commercial earnings. At issue were not only the perceived distraction of market work and the "frivolous" nature of the product but the autonomy nuns exercised through business networks that undercut Savonarolan control.[134]

The series of acute political crises from 1494 to 1537 amplified the civic value of convents as custodial institutions. Throughout the Quattrocento, Florentine convents provided an invaluable service to state and society as caretakers of vulnerable women and girls, offering refuge to older annuitants as well as young boarders placed in temporary guardianship.[135] The perilous years after 1494 in particular saw a sharp increase in custodial activities as households sought to preserve the honor and safety of their womenfolk from rampaging armies. Since boarders were often related to nuns in a particular house, their presence both reinforced ties of kinship and class and highlighted the value of having a nun in the family. The bitter siege of Florence lifted up convents' civic role, making their control by urban elites imperative. A thousand women reportedly jammed into Le Murate for an entire month in early 1530, sleeping on the ground and in the scriptorium. Even the haughty nuns of S. Pier Maggiore sheltered dozens of female parishioners and peasant women "on account of the war."[136] Italian noblewomen from north-central Italy capitalized on kin relations, patronage ties, or personal friendships with Florentine nuns to secure refuge in local convents.[137] All of these factors—political traumas, marital strategies, aristocratization, heightened religiosity—jointly reconfigured the monastic landscape of late fifteenth- and early sixteenth-century Florence.

By 1500, the burgeoning number of nuns had decisively altered communal dynamics. When Archbishop Cosimo Pazzi made pastoral rounds in 1509—the first local visitation since Antoninus surveyed the diocese a half century earlier—

the strain on physical spaces was apparent. The Paradiso nuns were unable to observe the proviso in their rule that "each nun have her own cell" for prayer and reflection, since their population exceeded the "perfect" number of sixty nuns set by St. Bridget. Seeing that S. Pier Maggiore housed more than twice its *numerus clausus*, Pazzi instructed the nuns "not to accept another novice for whatever reason" under pain of excommunication. The archbishop issued similar injunctions at numerous other convents—a dictate that countermanded nuns' need to accommodate family strategies.[138] While Pazzi may have tried to give chapters cover for refusing new postulants, he placed nuns in the impossible position of navigating these conflicts on their own.

The rush to the convent also created a pronounced cohort effect that jointly impacted nuns' lived experience and convent leadership. Cohorts of six or seven girls entering at the same time experienced their novitiate together, ate together in refectory, were admonished by same novice mistress, took vows together, and sat together in chapter and choir for the rest of their natural lives. While these shared experiences sometimes created strong interpersonal bonds, they also introduced rivalries for leadership positions. Large communities required many different kinds of officers: sacristans, cellarers, gatekeepers, wardrobe mistresses, official "listeners" stationed in the convent parlor, and so forth. Fulfilling a ladder of duties allowed nuns to demonstrate competence and versatility, but it also pitted members of close cohorts against each other for top positions at similar points in their monastic careers. Short-term rotations of two or three years as prioress alleviated animosity at mendicant foundations, yet these convents often permitted repeat terms that smacked of monopolies on office.[139] Problems were more egregious at Benedictine and Augustinian houses, where abbesses were elected for life. The admission of nuns at widely spaced intervals had made it easier to distinguish qualified senior candidates still in their prime. This demographic pattern did not preclude tensions or even outright conflicts over election, but it certainly led to stable leadership, whether for good or ill. S. Felicita was governed by only five abbesses from 1386 to 1520; S. Ambrogio was headed by only four women over the entire fifteenth century and S. Pier Maggiore by just five.[140] By contrast, in the first half of the Cinquecento these houses experienced rapid turnover in office, since abbesses were already in their sixties or seventies when elected, and sometimes they were unable to perform their duties because of illness. Six abbesses served at S. Felicita in the half century from 1520 to 1571, after which the Council of Trent mandated three-year rotations.[141] Similarly rapid turnovers occurred at S. Pier Maggiore, S. Ambrogio, S. Apollonia, and Le Murate, where nuns from prominent families vied for top posts. In addition, monastic expansion exacerbated factionalism, with nuns often forming voting blocs based on kinship. The 1517 Florentine synodal constitutions recognized this problem by futilely prohibiting convents from accepting more than two nuns "of the same blood and family . . . for experience shows that factions and divisions are often engendered by the multiplicity of family ties in the nunneries."[142]

Growing numbers made it difficult to sustain a sense of cohesion, while large clusters of novices waiting in the wings skewed interpersonal relations. At the time of Pazzi's visit, S. Maria di Candeli housed thirty-two professed nuns and twenty novices who had yet to be fully integrated into the chapter.[143] Even in relatively harmonious, well-governed convents, expansion highlighted corporate qualities at the expense of face-to-face relations apparent a century earlier. In the sixteenth century, Florentine nuns belonged to their family, class, and cohort, but it was a challenge to function as a unified community expressing the monastic ideal of "one heart, one will, one soul." To strengthen corporate bonds and sustain house traditions, Florentine nuns constructed fictive family ties by trans-mitting religious names, which by the late Quattrocento increasingly mimicked secular naming practices, "remaking" a deceased sister in religion by giving her name to an entering novice.[144] This profound act of remembrance cast new nuns as placeholders in a system of filiation particular to that group. Other means of constructing community in burgeoning sixteenth-century convents included the circulation of material goods, joint profession ceremonies that doubled as im-pressive statements of display, collective activities such as convent theatre, and the beginnings of a rich tradition of convent chronicle writing.[145] In searching for commonality, nuns developed innovative cultural practices that reinforced a self-conscious corporate identity.

To conclude, the spectacular but uneven growth of Florentine convents from the Black Death to the end of the republic was the product of several different historical forces, both secular and spiritual. In the late fourteenth and early fif-teenth centuries marked by epidemics, exile, and social mobility, "new men" used convents to establish and defend property interests, much as magnate lineages had done before them. For some fathers, giving a girl to God blended worldly ambitions and penitential ideals in a deep act of propitiation. Demographic cri-sis provided new opportunities for affluent artisans and professionals to inte-grate their households into ecclesiastical arenas traditionally dominated by their superiors—a process that convents facilitated through dowry incentives. Still, Florentine convents faced a serious contraction between 1350 and 1430, during which they nonetheless competed successfully against a pronatalist discourse.

The midcentury turnaround of convent fortunes distinguished the pace of Florentine monastic expansion from neighboring locales. The intensely felt religiosity of the Observant movement converged with Eugenius's local, hands-on reform program, which was extended by his successor Nicholas and their representative Antoninus. Suppressions, mergers, and a rush of new professions at socially inclusive convents marked the religious landscape in the mid-Quattrocento as Florence became the showcase for papal-led monastic reform. Convent chapters enabled this recovery by adopting flexible payment plans for dowries, especially for principal patrons. Undergirding this resurgence was civic recognition that the urban social order simply could not function without strong, well-governed convents. Medici patronage also spurred this demographic comeback, as the city's first family seized new opportunities for political control and sought to expand client networks.

The final phase of expansion considered here that ran from 1480 to 1530 was driven principally by the difficulties of the marriage market, which scholars have emphasized almost to the exclusion of other factors. Rising dowry prices and class endogamy certainly forced countless girls into an unwanted monastic life. Yet other historical events and processes—political instability, newfound religiosity—contributed to multiplying numbers of nuns. Religious women contended with spatial constraints, internal rivalries, and the loss of close face-to-face relationships as their numbers expanded almost beyond recognition. Their often innovative responses to these challenges showed signs of strain as well as cultural creativity as they tried to fashion meaningful lives in mostly unchosen environments.

CHAPTER TWO

Nuns, Neighbors, and Kinsmen

Nuns and nunneries were bound up with the physical, social, and spiritual geography of Renaissance Florence in complex ways. Richard Trexler was among the first to argue that the dense concentration of nuns living around vulnerable spatial zones like walls and gateways bolstered divine protection of the city.[1] A few convents — S. Pier Maggiore, S. Ambrogio, S. Anna — became destinations for public ritual enactments and thereby helped map a sacred topography of power.[2] More generally, convents and their churches functioned as sacral nodes housing holy images and miracle-working objects; they also served as repositories for the beloved dead and provided lively meeting places for local confraternities and self-styled festive "kingdoms" that organized a diverse citizenry.[3] As the number of consecrated virgins multiplied in the late Quattrocento, nuns' social and symbolic influence became more capillary and pervasive. By 1500, convents were the most prevalent type of institutional building inside city walls, enclosing large expanses of urban space.

From a social standpoint, however, Florentine convents made their deepest impact on lived experience at the local neighborhood level. Across urban Italy, neighborhoods were the primary place of communion with others, forming "one of the natural and necessary contexts of civilized life."[4] Neighborhood dynamics profoundly conditioned the tenor of female religious houses; conversely, local convents linked neighbors physically and psychologically by entangling them in skeins of relationships that stretched beyond kinship, friendship, and clientage. Florentine public spaces were hypermasculine, making the all-female worlds of convents crucial hubs of sociability for laywomen. The steady stream of female friends and family who came to exchange news and gossip, pay boarding fees, or seek spiritual solace transformed convents into the most visible node of female homosociality in the city.[5]

Beyond exerting a profound impact on the cityscape, Florentine convents played an unrecognized role in remaking Renaissance social geography. Scholars have shown that neighborhood ceased to function as the locus of political activity after 1450, largely owing to the creation of a Medici party that superimposed citywide clientage networks and Medicean allegiances on an older set of local loyalties. The political character of heterogeneous urban neighborhoods had been further diluted by 1600, by which point civic elites had pushed artisans and laborers out of the city center toward the urban periphery.[6] Changing patterns of monastic recruitment and convent property holdings played a significant role in these redefinitions of the city and its locales. These changes form subject of this chapter. I begin by showing how new recruitment patterns taking hold after 1450 transformed convents from neighborhood enclaves into citywide institutions dominated by the Florentine elite. The second section shifts the vantage point from personnel to property, documenting how alterations in the geographical distribution of convent property reinforced patrician ascendance. The third section investigates how two of the city's oldest convents, S. Pier Maggiore and S. Ambrogio, preserved neighborhood preeminence by constraining competition from local convent rivals. Viewing convents through these different lenses makes it clear that they achieved civic prominence not merely by virtue of expanding numbers but also by redefining relations between nuns and their neighbors.

From Neighborhood Enclaves to Citywide Institutions

Despite its centrality to Italian urban life, neighborhood was a fluid, ambiguous concept. Local definitions of neighborhood turned partly on the sixteen wards (*gonfaloni*) into which the city was divided in 1343, which formed the backbone of civic life as the basis for electoral scrutinies and tax levies. The city's fifty-two parishes formed yet another overlay on the urban grid, distinct from civic administration. Topographical neighborhoods — spatially amorphous entities mapped out by a tangle of streets, intersections, and landmarks — commanded strong feelings of association that supplemented or even transcended the identities imposed by ecclesiastical and civic organization. As Nicholas Eckstein has observed, this ambiguity about what constituted a neighborhood gives the concept a certain analytical weakness but also aligns it more closely with lived experience.[7]

Trecento convents were overwhelmingly local institutions with limited geographic reach, both in terms of recruitment and social influence. The vast majority of nuns living in any house hailed from the immediate district in which the convent was situated. These local recruitment areas can be defined in various ways that reflect the amorphous nature of Florentine neighborhoods at the time. Most nuns came from the convent's home ward or those immediately adjacent to it. Yet recruitment areas might be defined almost as accurately in an aural sense as embracing those households lying within earshot of convent church bells or in kinetic terms as constituting those residences situated within a five-minute walk. In other words, the zones from which Florentine convents drew the bulk of their membership in the later Trecento were the everyday products of propinquity and patterned use. In the following discussion, I use the term "immediate vicinity" to designate areas lying within short walking distance from a convent, whether or not these areas were located in the same civic ward, although I also note ward affiliations when known for greater precision. When I refer to "local recruitment" I mean recruitment from these areas.

This localism was a historical outgrowth of older medieval behaviors centered on the *vicinantia*, the fundamental association for mutual assistance and defense that gave rise to the Florentine commune in the thirteenth century. Neighbors were seen as part of an extended household group that shared common, reciprocal interests and formed the first line of extrafamilial support, even when sharp disagreements about politics or tax assessments arose. Many medieval convents were founded as clusters of kin and neighbors sharing similar spiritual convictions; S. Gaggio resembled a joint household writ large at its foundation in 1345, and similar patterns shaped other houses in this spiritually fertile period.[8]

The local nature of Trecento convent life can be brought into sharper focus by examining the recruitment areas for S. Felicita and S. Pier Maggiore, both founded before 1100. Sited just across the Arno from the main part of the city, S. Felicita was dominated by Oltrarno families. All of the thirteen nuns inhabiting the house in 1332 hailed from the S. Spirito quarter comprising that side of the city, and this same local base prevailed for the rest of the century.[9] Families that constructed chapels at S. Felicita during the late fourteenth-century building boom also placed their daughters in the convent to tend this legacy. Most of these patrons — the Guicciardini, Rossi, Ridolfi, Canigiani, Barbadori, Benizzi, Mozzi, Machiavelli, and Pitti — resided in the Nicchio and Scala wards that formed principal convent turf. The experience of Agnola Benizzi, the chapter's newest nun in 1396, was typical in its deep neighborhood associations. Her relatives, who made their living as bankers, lived just down the street on Via Guicciardini across from Piazza Pitti; their tombs studded the convent church that doubled as their parish headquarters.[10] Before 1400 there was little crosstown traffic in monastic professions; only a handful of girls crossed the river to join S. Felicita. A similar localism obtained at S. Pier Maggiore, located in the urban core in the quarter of S. Giovanni. Ten of the thirteen nuns inhabiting the house in 1370 came from the Chiavi ward in which the convent was situated. This pattern, whereby the convent attracted nuns predominantly from the immediate vicinity, continued over the next quarter century, with most recruits hailing from Chiavi and adjacent wards.[11]

These local patterns permeate the available evidence for other Trecento convents. At the 1384 episcopal visitation, twelve of the thirteen nuns inhabiting S. Ambrogio came from households located within a five-minute walk in the S. Giovanni and S. Croce quarters. S. Niccolò Maggiore, situated on present-day Via Ricasoli near the Medici palace, drew all but one of its members from immediately adjacent wards; it defined its own topographical neighborhood (its official radius spanned three quarters owing to its location in the old urban core). Convents lying outside the walls necessarily had a different geographic reach, but they too displayed telltale signs of propinquity in their social composition. In 1384, a third of the nuns at S. Gaggio outside the southern gate had family origins in the Oltrarno, while well over half the nuns at S. Matteo in Arcetri further south came from the far side of the river. Conversely, S. Baldassare in Coverciano north of the city recruited all of its members from the northernmost quarters of S. Giovanni and S. Maria Novella.[12] The 1427 *catasto* affirms the continued predominance of local recruitment, although the intake net had widened slightly. Of the ninety-six nuns listed on urban rosters who can be securely identified by surname, household, and ward, almost three-quarters came from the immediate vicinity; only twenty-six nuns (27 percent) lived in convents located across the river from their family residence.[13] Since Florentine lineages tended to cluster in the same locale for generations, the tendency of convents to recruit nuns locally enabled prominent neighborhood families to put a distinctive stamp on a house. Local recruitment was not merely a matter of convenience but an established strategy designed to create privatized bailiwicks serving God and lineage. Baronial families viewed ecclesiastical institutions as an extension of private interests; their ownership was reflected in the names attached to certain convents in everyday usage.[14] Magnate clans expressed their sense of proprietorship by attempting to dominate convent personnel, spaces, and even ordinary transactions — a practice that animated church-state conflicts throughout the medieval period.

What gave these proprietary behaviors tremendous historical dynamism was the way that newer lineages adapted them in the second half of the Trecento. The disruption caused by the Black Death, the resulting redistribution of wealth, and ongoing political turbulence brought a number of "new men" to social and political prominence after 1350. The most successful *popolano* lineages among them emulated magnate families in using local monastic institutions simultaneously as investments, fortresses, and safe havens. The key to creating local family strongholds was the concurrent transfer of real estate assets to convents and enrollment of kinswomen there to tend the patrimony. This property regime exchanged religious service for lifetime usufruct of houses, shops, and sometimes farms; after a nun's death, neighborhood property reverted to the convent, where it awaited stewardship by the next generation of family nuns. In other words, the new mercantile elite used convents as holding corporations, much as feudal families had done from the eleventh century onward. These time-tested strategies were extremely advantageous to aspiring lineages beset by crushing taxation and a high risk of exile in the turbulent decades of the late fourteenth century, which took an enormous financial and psychological toll.[15] Although families surrendered title to nearby properties to convents, they also shifted a portion of their tax burdens to the nuns in the process, all the while retaining control over local holdings — and by extension the neighborhood — through personal oversight by daughters and sisters in religious service. Local monastic recruitment thus conserved patrimonies while enabling newer elites to establish nodes of ecclesiastical and social power within the city. Transferring property to religious institutions also prevented outright confiscation by the commune in the event of exile, whether by the artisan-based Ciompi regime (1378), its proaristocratic successor (1382), or anti- and pro-Mediceans in the 1430s. Even the massive confiscation of church property following the disastrous "War of the Eight Saints" (1375–78) saw assets gradually restored over the next half century.[16]

Convent localism thus was interwoven not only with a strong sense of place but also with specific strategies that safeguarded property interests in a politically volatile age. Late Trecento nuns performed similar custodial roles as laywomen like the Alberti, who kept family fortunes alive following the massive exile of their kinsmen in 1400.[17] Fathers and brothers conceived of the daughters and sisters they gave to God as existing for the lineage and, to a lesser extent, the *vicinanza*. At the same time, however, local recruitment catalyzed the more transcendent aspects of monastic life. By performing continuous prayers, nuns sanctified urban locales and assuaged some of the social and political tensions characteristic of late Trecento neighborhoods. In an agonistic social world riven by competition, mistrust, and political differences, nuns symbolically enacted some of the peacemaking functions traditionally ascribed to women. Convents also helped organize neighborhood devotional life, as female friends, relatives, and neighbors flocked to their churches and parlors. Although the presence of local nuns could never completely dissolve social differences, their participation in neighborhood affairs nevertheless promoted a spirit of harmony that gave late medieval religiosity much of its social force.

A close examination of S. Pier Maggiore offers a detailed picture of these practices. This venerable old convent enjoyed a special relationship with the Albizzi and its offshoot, the Alessandri, which split off from the main family line in 1372. One of the most prominent *popolano* families in its quarter, the Albizzi were successful wool merchants, international bankers, and arch-Guelfs who rose to the heights of the officeholding class after 1350. By the early fifteenth century, the family was one of the few lineages that could rival the Medici before its political fortunes declined precipitously following Cosimo's return from exile in 1434.[18] The family palaces were located a stone's throw away on the street originally called Borgo S. Pier Maggiore and later renamed for the Albizzi. Family tombs lined the convent church, where both the Albizzi and Alessandri staged frequent festivities honoring name saints and revered family dead.[19] As the Albizzi lineage gained prominence in the later Trecento, it packed S. Pier Maggiore with nuns to oversee this growing family legacy—a process facilitated by the decimation of the chapter in 1348 and again in 1363. By 1370 five of the convent's thirteen nuns came from Albizzi households, with two more Alessandri nuns joining soon after; together they easily swayed corporate decisions.[20] Still, these Albizzi nuns varied widely in age, talent, and experience. Dominant among them was Suor Francesca di Manno Albizzi, who spent a half century in the convent before her death after 1413. Clearly an able manager, Suor Francesca

served several turns as treasurer, frequently negotiated deals with local parishioners on the convent's behalf, and made small gifts to underwrite convent repairs.[21] When handling these transactions, this nun represented a nexus of family,
convent, and neighborhood interests. Part of her financial clout stemmed from
ownership of several properties in the zone, including a large house on Via
Scarpentieri realized from a family legacy. After her father's death (1380), she
sold one of the smaller properties to the convent in return for a sizeable annuity.
Five years later, she loaned the abbess 100 florins to pay clerical taxes and assist
purchase of another rental property on Via Torcicoda. She continued to receive
other property-based annuities until her death, acting as a clearinghouse for the
circulation of both convent and family properties in the vicinity.[22] Virtually all of
her fellow nuns from prominent neighborhood families — Della Rena, Da Fili-
caia, Turradini, Buonafede — were supported by similar family legacies.[23]

The chapter of S. Pier Maggiore was thus in a sense an extension of existing
neighborhood alliances and animosities. Since nuns remained stakeholders in
outside affairs, taking turns as treasurer helped them adjudicate competing family
claims and hammer out corporate decisions in light of a common agenda; but
internal house politics and chapter meetings must have been fraught on many
occasions.[24] Smoothing over some of these differences was common charitable
work such as distributing bread to parish poor, which also served to bridge differences in wealth and political affiliation among neighbors. The densely packed
zone surrounding the convent was home to a large contingent of Ciompi sympathizers as well as their adversaries; tensions between them erupted in the street
brawl that marked the symbolic "marriage" of Abbess Benedetta Macci to Bishop
Angelo Acciaiuoli at his installation in 1384. As spokesperson for the parish and
the embodiment of the Florentine church, the abbess simultaneously affirmed the
particularist interests of local politics and the transcendent claims underpinning
late medieval religiosity.[25]

Not surprisingly, such entrenched localism invited lay involvement in convent
affairs — a situation churchmen decried as fostering undue meddling in chapter
decisions.[26] Kin and neighbors played a particularly prominent role in financial
oversight, with an eye to gauging the quality of investments as well as the honesty
of convent procurators. Faced with heavy tax burdens and cash shortfalls in the
late Trecento, the nuns of S. Pier Maggiore repeatedly dipped into the social pool
of kin and neighbors for financial expertise.[27] When the next generation of nuns
petitioned the archbishop for license to conduct a major audit (1433), they once

again turned to "good and wise parishioners and kinsmen"—Andrea Fortini, Bernardo Turradini, and the noted statesman Niccolò Alessandri—who were the uncles and brother of three nuns.[28]

Florentine families sustained their local institutional dominance by grouping several sisters or cousins in the same community. Although Trexler noted this practice in his foundational analysis, he did not link it to property transmission or to local political interests.[29] While sharing daily routines with close relatives must have given nuns a sense of psychological security, this strategy also made sense from a property standpoint. Since Florentines practiced partible inheritance, it was more convenient to transfer shares in a family-owned house or shop to sisters sharing the same residence than to disperse them among several institutions. This kinship pattern was already well established by the mid-Trecento, as seen in the 1368 census discussed in chapter 1. Bishop Acciaiuoli's 1384 visitation documented the continuation of this practice, although the timing of his visit on the heels of plague meant that both the number of nuns and the percentage of siblings was lower (35 sisters out of 275 nuns, or 12.7 percent) than in 1368. Most houses counted no sisters or only a single pair; S. Gaggio—the largest convent the bishop visited—had the highest density of kin, with twelve sisters in a group of thirty-seven nuns.[30]

Continued decline in convent populations between 1384 and 1422 allowed members of a broadly defined urban elite to extend the practice of clustering siblings in order to gain or solidify a hold over local ecclesiastical institutions. By the time of the 1427 *catasto*, convents of every order, even those observing rigorous religious routines, were being shaped by similar forces of kinship.[31] Tax rosters identified only one pair of sisters living in separate communities; about one-third of the nuns of S. Jacopo, where admitting siblings was a long house tradition, were related by blood.[32] Similarly, 30 of 162 nuns (18.5 percent) listed on eleven tax rosters in 1438 were either sisters or cousins sharing the same surname. The greatest concentrations of kin were found in small, poorly endowed houses, which welcomed sisters as a way to replenish their numbers, and in elite communities destined to become family enclaves. Slightly more than half of the nuns at S. Apollonia had an immediate relative in the convent, hailing from prominent families like the Portinari, Bardi, da Rabatta, and Donati. Sibling ties continued to color monastic experience at S. Ambrogio well into the 1460s. At the other end of the spectrum, three pairs of siblings figured among the impoverished nuns of the Portico, while three Spinelli sisters monopolized the tiny Franciscan convent of SS. Jacopo and Lorenzo on Via Ghibellina.[33]

After 1400, continued demographic decline further loosened the grip of localism as convents opened their doors to a wider membership simply to maintain critical mass. These problems were compounded by political misfortunes when new waves of exile in the first decades of the Quattrocento made some daughters more valuable as prospective wives. Hit hard by political adversity, the Albizzi did not place a new nun at S. Pier Maggiore between 1413 and 1507, although they continued to patronize the church and to meet their commemorative obligations.[34] One way many houses coped with the decimation of the convent population was, as we have seen, by offering financial incentives in the form of reduced dowries. The nuns of S. Pier Maggiore and S. Felicita recruited wellborn girls from more distant urban sectors or seized novel opportunities to infuse new life into the house.[35] The most common tactic for replenishing convent populations, however, was to admit local girls from a wider class spectrum. In the 1420s and 1430s, convents recruited from the households of notaries, physicians, goldsmiths, and other successful artisans. In this recruitment effort, local ties proved decisive in recovering numerical strength.

The experience of S. Ambrogio illuminates how class and locale intersected to combat or even reverse declining convent populations. Situated on the urban periphery where cheaper property values invited a steady influx of artisans and immigrants, S. Ambrogio developed a rich social mix in these decades. Between March and July 1400, the convent lost nine nuns to plague, including the abbess, reducing the population to well below its optimal number of fifteen nuns.[36] To prevent further collapse, the chapter reached out more broadly to local parishioners. In 1422, S. Ambrogio enrolled the nine-year-old daughter of a table maker living in the parish, whose monastic dowry was guaranteed jointly by her brother and his business partners. Two years later, the nuns accepted the daughter of a goldsmith, also a fellow parishioner. These girls rubbed shoulders with other novices like Caterina Buonaccorsi, daughter of a prominent lawyer and sister of Abbess Niccola Buonaccorsi. Over the course of the 1420s and 1430s, when the urban population remained low, S. Ambrogio enrolled a notary's daughter, the granddaughter of a physician, five girls lacking surnames, and four merchants' daughters from the parish and nearby wards.[37]

Girls from notarial families were among the biggest winners in this outreach. Deeply invested in written culture and socially well connected, notaries linked the world of high politics and learning with everyday affairs. The emphasis on written records and a pronounced respect for texts formed an intrinsic part of both monastic and notarial culture, making notaries' daughters among the most

avid consumers of convent learning in the late fifteenth and early sixteenth centuries.[38] Not only would these cultural affinities have made the idea of placing
their daughters in convents appealing; gaining a toehold in well-respected convents also must have seemed attractive to notaries eager to advance their social
ambitions just as their influence within the guild of judges and notaries was
waning.[39] Even the venerable house of S. Pier Maggiore admitted the daughters
of two notaries in the 1430s to restore its numbers. The father of one, Maria
Fortini, sported extraordinary credentials, having served a brief stint as Florentine chancellor after Coluccio Salutati.[40] An added bonus was the family's longtime residence in the Chiavi ward where the convent was located. Still, elite
convents kept a tight hold on admissions. Maria's younger sister Piera did not
gain entry into S. Pier Maggiore but was sent instead to the "very poor" nuns of
the Paradiso, then populated mainly by artisans.[41] Virtually all of these girls
secured their places with a standard dowry rather than buying entry through
larger sums. Moreover, there are no indications that they were marginalized
because of their status. Indeed, several of them went on to serve distinguished
careers as convent treasurers and sacristans.

By using locale as a social filter and tapping local knowledge to glean clues
about a girl's character and family background, convent chapters retained control
over their membership. Small monastic populations and similar neighborhood
origins ensured that nuns knew each other and each other's families well. Neighborhood girls gave institutions a local feel and, more importantly, extended those
institutions' capillary reach into local affairs. The flow of news, gossip, gifts, food,
cash and religious objects back and forth across convent walls integrated the
monastic community into neighborhood rhythms, while lay visitors from different walks of life enabled nuns to keep their finger on the pulse of neighborhood affairs. Nonetheless, there were limits to how deep this local diversity could
go. Girls from the ranks of wage laborers became servant nuns instead of chapter
members at prestigious neighborhood convents or joined houses outside the city,
along with illegitimate patrician daughters.[42]

There were also important gender differences in the local uses to which convents were put by kinsmen and neighbors prior to the mid-fifteenth century.
Wealthy Florentine men tending family legacies expected their nun-daughters to
protect those interests in exchange for an infusion of resources. By contrast, men
of middling status used these institutions more explicitly as a means of fostering
vertical social integration within their locale. Convent management brought
together a mixed group of neighbors outside the structures of guild, ward, or

parish. In consequence, well-placed artisans and professionals gained greater local visibility and influence through their daughters, with convents serving as the nexus for contact with social higher-ups. Neighbors separated by wealth or political faction considered substantive issues together, participated in convent rituals side by side, shared intrigues sparked by the election of a new abbess, and took joint action over fiscal mismanagement or convent disorder. In this sense, convents resembled other forms of religious association that mediated cross-class relations, especially before the full effects of Medicean patronage took hold.

Less wedded to concerns of lineage, Florentine women maintained different stakes in female religious communities centering on sociability, education, and economic support. Dennis Romano has argued that neighborhoods, parishes, and convents in Renaissance Venice were constructed as gendered spaces forming women's primary social terrain.[43] A variety of transactions helped constitute Florentine convents and their locales as similarly gendered products of a dynamic social process. As legitimate destinations for female excursions, convents gave laywomen sanctioned use of the streets — a significant feature given the hypermasculine nature of Florentine urban space — and figured prominently in the social learning of respectable girls, who ideally imbibed the pious words and controlled behaviors of the women sequestered there. Girls deepened their acquaintance with convent life while learning the rudiments of reading, catechism, and modest deportment firsthand as pupils and boarders. At the same time, their mothers and aunts who made regular treks to visit them or pay boarding fees earned social credit among neighborhood spectators and civic moralists alike for fostering their proper upbringing.

Convents further cemented female loyalties by providing an array of financial services, which were especially crucial for Florentine widows exposed to social and financial risks. As a result of the wide age gap between spouses at first marriage, widows comprised 25 percent of the Florentine urban population in 1427; nearly 14 percent of heads of households in the city were widows, very few of them rich.[44] In this patrilocal society, propertied widows might live in different areas from their husband's family or their own natal family, where they remained vulnerable to gossip. By utilizing convents as institutional resources, widows could avoid suspicion while brokering complex transactions, safeguarding precious funds, or simply prepaying burial expenses.[45] Less prosperous widows often leaned on convents as sources of charity or livelihood; semiliterate widows who could read but not write made use of graphic services nuns provided.[46] Moreover, convents extended affiliations built up over a lifetime by offering women the unique privilege of burial in a nun's habit, sometimes in a choice location, thus enabling them to join a select community of the dead.[47]

Considering this rich nexus of sociability, support, and remembrance, it is not surprising that Florentine women tenaciously favored convents in their wills long after men had shifted attention to "newer" forms of charity like dowering poor girls. Samuel Cohn has argued that "women supported nunneries and nuns more than any other pious cause" in testaments written between the second wave of plague in 1363 and 1425.[48] In endorsing these institutions, propertied women clearly recognized the value of convents in their own lives. Their reluctance to endow new — often pronatalist — causes they had little hand in shaping reflects less a religious conservatism, as Cohn suggests, than a deeply rooted investment in institutions that proved responsive to their needs. Moreover, convents opened a space for pious women in which they could articulate their own forms of community independent of official notions. As devotees walked to a nearby religious house, they mapped a female-defined vision of urban neighborhood based on voluntaristic association. Conceived as process rather than artifact, convent locales can be considered "practiced places" formed by everyday use and widespread agency.[49]

In the second half of the fifteenth century, these characteristic features — local recruitment, the transmission of property to convents by local families, neighborhood integration, kinship patterns — gave way to a complex transformation that permanently altered the Florentine religious landscape. Fueling convent growth after 1450 were girls recruited from the city at large, not just local neighborhoods, which diluted the distinctive local traits and integrative functions of religious houses. As upper-class girls from more distant urban sectors gradually displaced neighborhood recruits, convents were transformed from local enclaves into an urban network dominated by the patriciate. The twin processes of aristocratization and privatization that gripped these institutions in the sixteenth and seventeenth centuries had their roots in the new, citywide recruitment patterns established after 1450. Various historical factors drove this transformation. The rise of the Medici as the city's main power brokers after 1434 demoted neighborhood from the primary node of political activity to "an important but by no means exclusive nucleus" around which aristocratic patron-client relations turned.[50] Relative political stability, coupled with the ongoing crisis of the public debt, made it more advantageous for families to assign nuns *monte* credits than to transfer property assets to them — an economic regime whose impact on convent finance and nuns' discretionary income is taken up in the next chapter. New recruitment patterns indicate that the function convents performed as social institutions was changing rapidly in the second half of the Quattrocento. Rather than primarily safeguarding local interests, convents proved increasingly useful as platforms for establishing social networks and enhancing patronage opportunities in other parts of the city and as a means for reinforcing alliances outside the cloister.

Although the pace of change differed according to convent size, wealth, and rigor, the displacement of neighborhood as the chief unifying element in monastic life was apparent across the city by 1480. As noted earlier, Observant, poorly endowed houses like Le Murate welcomed girls irrespective of locale as long as they met the dowry threshold and showed some sense of vocation. Although the convent eventually developed important connections with Italian and European elites, its initial intake groups in the 1440s and 1450s included numerous girls lacking surnames or who were unable to read. Spiritual conviction similarly trumped status markers or neighborhood affiliation at newly founded S. Chiara, as devout women from Florence, Tuscany, and central Italy flocked there to live out their spiritual dreams. The sole requirement for new members beyond the dowry was a burning desire to lead an austere life of prayer. Within a generation, however, this diversity was already giving way to more uniform considerations of class.[51] Similarly, shared spiritual ideals played a more significant role than neighborhood origins in recruiting tertiaries to the Annalena and later Savonarolan foundations like S. Caterina da Siena.

But common class interests were already superseding local neighborhood origins at the city's most affluent houses in the mid-Quattrocento. By 1475, more than half of the nuns entering S. Pier Maggiore and S. Ambrogio came from beyond the immediate vicinity, reversing earlier recruitment patterns. New chapter members included girls from the Ardinghelli and Gianfigliazzi families, whose strongholds lay in the Unicorn ward in the western part of the city; they were joined by new nuns from the Boncianni, Buondelmonti, and Carducci families, prominent residents of the Viper ward near S. Maria Novella across the city. Especially impressive was the accelerated traffic over the river. In contrast to limited crosstown placements in earlier decades, distinguished Oltrarno families like the Alamanni, Gualterotti, Biliotti, Ridolfi, and Vettori regularly enrolled their daughters in S. Pier Maggiore and S. Ambrogio after midcentury. To accommodate them, these chapters filtered out local girls from respected professional and artisan families, who were thrust instead into less affluent suburban houses like the Paradiso and the Portico or removed to neighboring towns. The last girls from professional households entered S. Pier Maggiore in the 1450s, securing places through the powerful conjunction of kinship and locale.[52] The loss of middling local families, coupled with the influx of upper-class girls from distant urban sectors, weakened the dense local associations binding these houses to their districts. By the 1480s, similarly selective convents had lost much of their local integrative role.

These changes turned primarily on patronage concerns rather than on economic criteria. Selecting new entrants was a matter of internal governance, with the chapter deciding which prospective entrants to accept.[53] Some nuns may have recognized the inherent value in broadening their geographic reach, but chapters were mainly responding to persuasion, both internal and external, when they selected girls from outside their immediate locale. Such persuasion commonly took the form of sponsorship or intervention of power brokers like Lorenzo de' Medici, who secured the acceptance of Ippolita Baroncelli, the daughter of a Medici client, at S. Apollonia in 1490 with only a half dowry; her sister Francesca entered S. Felicita the same year with the standard entrance fee.[54] Neither convent lay in the Baroncelli home ward of Carro in the S. Croce quarter. More subtle and compelling were the pleas of in-laws, extended kin, and convent "friends" who recognized an untapped opportunity to extend their influence over expanding institutional resources or who otherwise sought a comfortable situation for unwilling nuns. The considered choices of fathers, brothers, and uncles to situate vulnerable female kin at a greater distance signals both the strength of the imagined civic community with which they associated and the level of confidence they had in their ability to control its affairs. Religious women themselves lobbied to admit relatives and family friends as a form of internal patronage and instrumental use of kinship.

Enlarged recruitment areas resulted from various contingencies as well. As competition mounted for limited spaces in top-tier convents, it became increasingly difficult even for elite families to place sisters together. Some convents like S. Jacopo and S. Donato in Polverosa staunchly maintained a house tradition of admitting siblings because it was linked to their idiosyncratic economic organization. Buttressed by nuns' longevity, siblings still exercised a significant convent presence across the city in the 1540s.[55] Nevertheless, the evidence that a gradual change was taking place, especially at the most selective convents, is compelling. In 1471, S. Gaggio — the wealthiest suburban convent in the early Quattrocento — housed no sisters, compared to six pairs a century earlier. By 1480 there were no sisters living in S. Felicita.[56] S. Pier Maggiore admitted its last pair of sisters, Maria and Scholastica Vettori from the Oltrarno, in 1471–73. Caterina Gian-figliazzi gained entry to that house in 1473, but five years later her sister Lisabetta was enrolled instead at S. Ambrogio.[57] Andrea and Laudomina Buondelmonti, impoverished daughters of a distinguished magnate lineage, traced an identical route, with the elder sister Andrea gaining a spot at S. Pier Maggiore through the beneficence of Abbess Antonia Acciaiuoli, who was her in-law, despite her half dowry.[58] In the 1480s and 1490s, the Boncianni sisters Nannina and Leonarda were split between these same two houses, while Cosa and Paola Carducci went to S. Apollonia and S. Pier Maggiore.[59]

The experience of Andrea Minerbetti's eight surviving daughters exemplifies the blend of strategy and contingency that divided sisters among institutions. Anthony Molho has shown how this long-lived scion of an important Florentine family carefully plotted his children's destinies while responding to unforeseen events such as illness and a profusion of daughters.[60] A close Medici ally living in the Red Lion ward of S. Maria Novella, Andrea made an advantageous marriage match for his first daughter, Gostanza (b. 1493). In 1506, he placed his second girl, eleven-year-old Francesca, in the affluent Benedictine house of S. Niccolò Maggiore only minutes away from the family stronghold. The third girl, Ip-polita, entered the Augustinian convent of S. Marta a Montici outside the walls at the tender age of three-and-a-half, "to save her soul if it pleased God," since a bout of measles had left her blind in one eye and thus unfit for marriage by contemporary standards. Since the nuns of S. Marta had served as Ippolita's godparents, her entry there in 1502 closed the spiritual circle. In 1506 — the same year he monachized Francesca — Andrea sent his fourth daughter, Maria, to S. Felicita. Although this five-and-a-half-year-old was described as "sickly," a status that sealed her destiny, Maria defied expectations by living a long life, eventually serving as abbess of that esteemed house from 1571–74. After his first wife died, Andrea married off the firstborn daughter from his new union. He put his next daughter, eleven-year-old Bartolomea, in the Medici stronghold of Le Murate (1517), where he had Bini in-laws hailing from the south side of town. In making this choice, Andrea capitalized on both his political and kin connec-tions; neighborhood ties played no role. Another daughter, Lucretia, apparently showed more religious vocation, resulting in her placement at age sixteen in the stringent Dominican house of S. Pier Martire in the Oltrarno (1518). Andrea married off his last daughter, the product of his third and final union. Twenty years later, Andrea's son Tommaso widened the monastic net still further by putting his two daughters in the suburban convent of Faenza, where their aunt Gostanza had boarded as a youth.

In little more than a quarter century, this Minerbetti household strategically created alliances with six different convents of varied orders, only one of which stood in proximity to the family residence. Equally striking was the weak affinity shown for Dominican convents in light of staunch Minerbetti patronage of S. Maria Novella, site of the family tombs. And Minerbetti was only one example among many of the diffused convent patronage that became commonplace among premier Florentine families irrespective of neighborhood. This scattering of daughters across a broad urban map contrasted sharply with the tightly focused patterns of artistic patronage reconstructed by Jill Burke for the fifteenth-century Oltrarno.[61] The divergence between dispersed convent placements, on one hand, and the more concentrated investment in works of art locally that advanced familial reputation, on the other, suggests that the Florentine elite relied on a multipronged, gendered strategy that differed by objective and domain when constructing a self-conscious, geographical definition of itself. Building family chapels or lavish tombs in the local neighborhood church fashioned one kind of familial statement; spreading daughters and sisters over a broader institutional web brought other kinds of rewards. This latter practice guaranteed families ongoing access to decision making within institutions that were growing in civic importance; it enabled households and lineages to accrue social capital outside their immediate neighborhood while giving them broader influence with confraternities and other convent affiliates, and it provided ready-made havens crucial to survival in times of crisis, like the ones that struck Florence repeatedly after 1494.[62] In the later Quattrocento, there was much to be lost in sustaining a narrow localism and much to be gained by widening the net.

This kind of diffused patronage gradually transformed the predominant form of convent kinship from sibling bonds to intergenerational ties between aunt and niece, which allowed patrician families to build permanent institutional niches. Gabriella Zarri first noted the common dyad of aunt and niece in northern Italian convents by 1500 but did not delineate its historical roots.[63] The practice of using aunts as the thin end of the wedge to persuade tightly controlled chapters to admit their nieces became a defining feature of Italian female monasticism at its peak. Various early features of this process shine through in the story of Giardesca Piccardi, a young ward who was the niece of two S. Ambrogio nuns, Lena and Giuliana del Caccia. In 1456, their widowed sister Nidda Piccardi pleaded with them to enroll her five-year-old daughter Giardesca, who report-edly expressed a religious vocation. According to this concerned mother, only divine inspiration could account for a child of such tender years having "the intelligence to recognize the means of her salvation" as well as the heartfelt desire "to be deprived of the world"—familiar tropes that must have resonated well with these religious women. No mention is made in convent records, however, of Nidda's straitened financial circumstances or her status as a still marriageable widow. Having become quite familiar with convent ways over the course of almost two decades through her sisters, Nidda not only was in a position to praise "the goodness, great virtues, holy habits, and exemplary life" of the S. Ambrogio nuns; she also knew how to get things done by leveraging kinship. After ap-proaching her sisters and the abbess to accept Giardesca despite her youth, she then asked her father to press the case again. To ensure smooth sailing, they pledged the full amount of the customary monastic dowry plus trousseau. The chapter succumbed to their joint suasion and accepted the girl "unanimously." Thirty years later, the mature Suor Giardesca, who eventually rose to the posi-tion of abbess (1527–34), sponsored her own niece Maria Piccardi as a postulant, while the two original del Caccia nuns secured entry for yet another niece in the mid-1480s.[64]

The instrumental use of intergenerational kinship ties was even more obvious at S. Pier Maggiore in the late Quattrocento, where established nuns acted as patrons and mentors to their young relatives. Suor Maddalena Salviati paired with her aunt Lisabetta in a variety of property transactions after her entry in 1498; together they formed the nexus for a whole coterie of female friends who subsidized convent decorative schemes.[65] As a prospective nun, Cecilia Pan-dolfini enjoyed the dual sponsorship of her aunt Alessandra Pandolfini, a chapter member for almost forty years, and that of her great-aunt Gostanza Alessandri, the current abbess—a fact that no doubt accounts for her admission with half dowry in 1493. This trio's collective status and seniority made it a formidable voting block within the chapter. As she matured, Suor Cecilia herself became a force to be reckoned with, serving frequent turns as treasurer and second in command from the 1520s until her death after 1548. These positions allowed her to tend the family interests of both the Pandolfini and Alessandri, whose influ-ence in the convent stretched back to the fourteenth century.[66] At S. Ambrogio, Suor Laudomina Buondelmonti groomed her niece Clementia to perpetuate the legacy she had staked out since entering thirty years earlier in 1482.[67] Corbinelli, Donati, and Portinari nuns ensured familial longevity at S. Apollonia by these same means. As these aggregations of relatives multiplied by the early sixteenth century, the Florentine archbishop barred more than two nuns "of the same blood and family" from joining the same house. The stated objective was to prevent the formation of factions, but a more intractable problem lay in the deepening privatization of women's religious houses.[68]

As convent populations swelled in the late Quattrocento, other forms of kinship were pressed into service. Aunts and nieces solidified dynastic footholds in particular convents at the same time that patrilines secured influence over several institutions simultaneously by the distribution of first cousins among different houses. Through the strategic use of kinship and increasing tendency to select specific convents beyond the immediate neighborhood, a minority of Florentine families "drew to their advantage communal institutions accessible to all."[69] Take the case of the three Gualterotti brothers, Jacopo, Piero, and Niccolò, who were residents of the Oltarno Scala ward and Medici in-laws famous for their hostility to the Medici.[70] Between 1473 and 1491 they placed four daughters at different convents. Piero landed a spot for sixteen-year-old Gostanza at the parish stronghold of S. Felicita despite her meager dowry, probably through the good graces of his neighbors (1486). A few years earlier, he had complained to tax officials that marrying off three daughters had "consumed [his] substance and being."[71] His brother Jacopo — the beleaguered father of twelve in 1480 — situated two of his undowered daughters — Lucretia ("Suor Agnesa") and Albiera ("Suor Benedetta") — at S. Apollonia about a decade apart (1473 and 1485 respectively).[72] The widow of the third brother, Niccolò, secured a place for their daughter Laudomina at S. Pier Maggiore, possibly through her Medici connections. Two of these Gualterotti nuns rose to the position of abbess — Agnesa at S. Apollonia and Gostanza at S. Felicita — and their overlapping tenures from 1521 to 1528 gave the patriline concurrent direction of two of the most prominent Florentine convents for the better part of a decade.

Three Alamanni brothers, also residents in the Scala ward but Medici partisans instead, traced a similarly successful path by placing their daughters in three different Benedictine houses between 1497 and 1507. Bartolomea exercised a strong hand in decision making at S. Pier Maggiore in her frequent capacity as treasurer; Margherita became abbess of S. Felicita in 1534; another Bartolomea took a prominent leadership role at S. Apollonia until her death in 1555.[73] Similarly, in the 1490s the Bini, also Medici clients from the Oltrarno, cultivated ecclesiastical nodes across the city via first cousins simultaneously inhabiting S. Niccolò dei Frieri, S. Ambrogio, S. Pier Maggiore, and Le Murate, which Elena Bini directed as abbess from 1498 to 1504. In other words, powerful Florentine families, now galvanized primarily via Medici networks, appropriated the female branch of the local church through kinship, much as they had monopolized appointments of male clergy earlier in the Quattrocento.[74] In contrast to the selection of cathedral canons or the acquisition of patronal rights, however, this dominance was anchored less by formal ecclesiastical privileges than by the bodies of nuns themselves.

From the standpoint of religious women, these extended kinship ties helped stimulate new forms of exchange between houses, from financial transactions to symbolic gift giving.[75] Everyday items — bits of cash, candles, foodstuffs, medicinals, devotional objects — circulated within an expanded web delicately stitched together by class and kinship. Institutional linkages were strengthened still further by the involvement of nuns' clerical kin, who supervised other female houses in the city and surrounding district. As the role of neighborhood in convent life diminished, nuns fashioned a new sense of cohesion among themselves as a fictive family by means of imaginative naming practices that "remade" beloved monastic ancestors.[76] The dispersal of nuns beyond the immediate locale also enabled respectable laywomen to stretch definitions of the neighborhoods to which they belonged. Although there was no Florentine corollary to the Venetian spectacle of taking noble brides by gondola to visit convents "where they have either sisters, kinswomen or relatives," wellborn Florentine women and their companions nevertheless publicized convent ties by visiting religious houses from one side of the city to another.[77] Their greater visibility outside parish or neighborhood may have contributed to growing calls for policing enclosure in the late Quattrocento, discussed in chapter 5.

In sum, changing monastic recruitment patterns provide insight into how the Florentine patriciate came to dominate ecclesiastical and social affairs as the medieval city evolved into one of the major centers of Renaissance Italy. As urban elites transcended local loyalties, they enlarged networks of clientage and translated control of ecclesiastical institutions into expanded political influence. This remaking of Florentine urban social geography points to historic realignments between the Italian church and civil society marked by the interpenetration of secular and ecclesiastical interests.[78] The evidence presented here indicates that a significant step toward the princely worlds of court and cloister had already been taken when elite families moved out of their local enclaves to conquer the city.

Property and the Topography of Power

Another way that convents remapped Florentine social geography was through redistributed property holdings. From the Trecento on, convents concentrated their real estate holdings around the physical node of the house itself, which enabled nuns to control their immediate environment and exercise capillary influence in the neighborhood as proprietors. The three convents heading parishes — S. Ambrogio, S. Felicita, and S. Pier Maggiore — showed the most localized density as the single largest proprietors dominating their neighborhoods. In 1478, S. Ambrogio's holdings fanned out in a tight circle around it: it owned nineteen houses in Via Pietrapiana, which ran right into the convent square; eighteen houses in Via Pentolini; three in Via de' Pilastri; one each in Borgo Allegri, Via Ghibellina, and Via dell'Agnolo; plus three houses and a shop in Chiasso della Mattonaia. Even several convent-owned farms were situated within the sprawling parish. Similarly, most of the sixteen houses and three shops owned by S. Felicita stood on the church square and nearby streets; only one urban property lay outside the parish.[79] The portfolio of S. Pier Maggiore showed an identical pattern. Its extensive holdings — thirty-six houses, eleven shops — encircled the convent, with only two properties lying outside the parish. "In order to better recognize the houses belonging to our convent," S. Pier Maggiore systematically marked its properties in the 1520s with sculpted stone slabs bearing the convent emblem of two crossed Petrine keys surmounting its three initials (fig. 2.1). These visual markers left no doubt about who owned the neighborhood.[80]

This localized pattern was not unique among convent portfolios. Residential properties belonging to S. Apollonia were nestled together near its site on Via S. Gallo; in 1438, only one urban property lay beyond the immediate district. Six of the ten houses owned by S. Niccolò Maggiore were situated on its home street, with the other four properties located on adjacent streets. By 1478, its real estate holdings had become slightly more dispersed but remained centered on the convent.[81] Suburban convents exhibited similar property-holding patterns. After moving into their permanent complex in 1353, the nuns of S. Gaggio aggressively acquired surrounding properties over the next three decades until "the hill of San Gaggio" became predominantly their land.[82] They concentrated urban holdings in the parish of S. Felicita, gateway to the southern countryside; by 1495, S. Gaggio owned six shops in that parish, including two on Piazza S. Felicita. A bit further south of the city, the convent of S. Matteo in Arcetri — best

Fig. 2.1. Convent emblem of S. Pier Maggiore, Borgo
degli Albizi, Florence. Author photo.

known for housing Galileo's daughters — owned eight shops just across Ponte
Vecchio, the main bridge giving north-south access. Major Florentine monasteries adhered to the same local outlines, except they owned a larger number of
rural holdings, which fed their many inhabitants.[83]

Convents across the Italian peninsula held remarkably similar portfolios, documenting the extent to which ecclesiastical institutions controlled the landscape
of late medieval Italian cities. The 1452 census depicted the venerable Venetian
convent of S. Lorenzo at the physical center of its urban patrimony, with numerous tentacles extending into other areas of the city.[84] Owing to the different
topographies of the two cities, however, Florentine convent portfolios were more
physically compact. Roman convent holdings were more comparable, although
the evidence is less comprehensive. For instance, S. Maria in Isola, located on the
tiny, historically rich island of Isola Tiburina, had consolidated virtually all of
its urban holdings within a one-mile radius by 1483. Convent property spilled
across Ponte Fabricio into the parish of S. Gregorio — later the gateway to the
Jewish ghetto — and into the streets across from Ponte Rotto. Even convent
vineyards were distributed across the southern meridian of Rome from east to
west. Nor was S. Maria's island location a decisive factor in its accumulating

property this way. The convent's mother house showed virtually the same localized distribution in its 1492 inventory.[85]

Although convents acquired many of these properties piecemeal through gifts
and bequests, nuns also pursued a deliberate economic policy targeting local real
estate. To take a typical example: in 1423 Suor Caterina Buonaccorsi bought a
partial, lifetime interest in a house located a stone's throw from S. Ambrogio.
Generating an annuity for three decades, her share passed to the convent upon
her death, after which the chapter raised money to purchase the remaining shares
under the energetic leadership of her sister, Abbess Niccolosa Buonaccorsi. This
house remained one of the core convent properties for centuries.[86] When nuns
acquired more distant holdings through donation or inheritance, they frequently
sold them in order to reinvest locally. Departures from the norm usually stemmed
from powerful personal connections with a property. Abbess Piera de' Medici of
S. Verdiana proudly obtained the house with attached tavern called the Ship, in
which dwelling her father, Bivigliano, had "lived the whole of his life." Having
purchased lifetime rights to this property in 1445, she set her sights on permanent
ownership after becoming abbess six years later. Combining cash legacies from
her aunt and father with profits from the tavern and a farm, she "bought this
house free and clear for our convent," despite its location outside the immediate
neighborhood.[87]

This local concentration gave nuns and their agents real familiarity with their
neighbors, who doubled as tenants, clients, and dependants. As Eckstein has
argued, neighborhoods were conceptually activated by people and by the sum
total of their personal relationships.[88] In his 1470s rent book, the procurator of
S. Pier Maggiore traced both the map of convent property and a social history of
its occupants.[89] This priest began his administrative itinerary with "the house
next to the priests' refectory, across from Giovanni Corbizzi," which was leased
by the barrel maker Stefano. Organizing his book by location, he proceeded
mentally down the street to "the house next to the one just above, where Giorgio
the tailor lives," currently rented to the linen weaver Piero di Michele. Vaggia di
Messer Rinaldo degli Albizzi lived in the house opposite the nuns' dormitory,
which had been "sold to her for her own lifetime." Other tenants included the
noted humanist Matteo Palmieri, who ran an apothecary's shop still extant today.

Property management exposed nuns to tenants from every walk of life —
mercers, bakers, shoemakers, secondhand dealers, goldsmiths, drapers, farriers,
carpenters, other tradesmen — which in turn fostered firsthand knowledge about
the current economic climate and gave nuns tremendous discretionary power as

landlords. The affable treasurer of S. Jacopo, Suor Beatrice Panciatichi, exercised typical latitude of office when negotiating tenancy agreements in the 1510s and 1520s. Arranging a repayment plan with a longtime tenant who had fallen seriously behind on rent, Suor Beatrice explained in her account book that "he lives by his own physical labor; if he doesn't have work, he says that it's not possible to give more than this sum. When he is able to give more, he will do so willingly. If he doesn't pay monthly as intended by this promise, then he will still be responsible for the full amount, obligating himself and his heirs and all his goods, present and future." A month later, she struck a very different note when dealing with a new tenant. Should he fall into arrears, she asserted that "we are free to rent the house to whoever is available or pleases us . . . and to have his household goods thrown into the street."[90]

However, the localism of several convent portfolios was radically altered by papal reform efforts in the mid-fifteenth century. As noted in chapter 1, both Eugenius and Nicholas transferred property from small or insolvent institutions to Observant houses, which they considered the vanguard of religious renewal.[91] Although Eugenius's heavy-handed actions provoked stiff opposition from lay patrons as well as from the civic government, they were greeted approvingly by such zealous supporters of Observance as Cosimo de' Medici, who capitalized on these developments.[92] This story must be read in part through a Medicean political lens, but papal mergers advanced the aristocratization of the Florentine church more generally by concentrating greater wealth in the hands of fewer convents controlled by leading families. Rewarding favored convents with other institutional patrimonies enabled them to establish social relationships far from their own neighborhoods. In addition, the acquisition of new farm holdings created the potential to exercise managerial influence in the countryside.[93] Occasionally the process moved in the other geographical direction, with a favored suburban convent gaining an urban presence.[94] Regardless, creating these megaportfolios reinforced the new intake patterns just discussed, setting the stage for the development of a regional monastic system controlled by a pro-Medicean patriciate in the late Quattrocento.

S. Apollonia provides one of the clearest illustrations of this process. Situated in the sprawling, northwest parish of S. Lorenzo, this house took instant advantage of its new property base acquired through papal favor between 1438 and 1446, when it absorbed three ecclesiastical institutions and their prodigious holdings.[95] In 1438 Eugenius ceded the hospital of S. Paolo a Pinti to the "most observant" nuns of S. Apollonia, noting their "lack of income" and steeply rising population. Virtually overnight, the hospital's centuries-old patrimony, concentrated in the parishes of S. Pier Maggiore and S. Ambrogio, fell into convent hands.[96] The nuns moved swiftly to establish their presence at the hospital, successfully petitioning the pope to build a chapel and altar there.[97] From this merger, the nuns obtained two revenue streams flowing from the eastern side of the city: one from new spiritual services, the other from rents. Eugenius continued to shower S. Apollonia with spiritual favors as well as material assets.[98] At the same time, this acquisition elevated the profile of certain families like the Donati, to which both the abbess and convent syndic belonged, since the Donati already held patronal rights to several transferred properties. When final details of the merger were negotiated in 1439, the terms were highly favorable to the convent and specifically to its Donati nuns.[99] Consequently, what began as a papal reform effort ended with property flowing from one local institution to another via the customary channel of kinship.

Over the next twenty years, this new patrimony introduced the nuns to new webs of clients, sometimes via litigation. In 1443 the nuns embarked on a fierce campaign to recover use of illegally occupied properties, a campaign that entailed appeals and counterappeals involving the pope, assorted abbots, bishops from Verona and Faenza, and wellborn Florentines from all quarters.[100] In the 1450s, rents from hospital properties underwrote new convent construction, which had stalled for lack of funds.[101] Ten years later, these same properties provided the nucleus of a complex transaction with Cosimo de' Medici, who had obtained papal permission to construct a Franciscan convent on the former hospital site in 1464. Since this building project required the destruction of sixteen convent-owned houses and gardens, Cosimo agreed to substitute other property generating 50 florins annually.[102] The convent never completely surrendered its hospital properties; it retained four houses from the original transfer as late as 1495.[103]

Shortly after annexing the hospital, S. Apollonia petitioned the pope for a still bigger prize, pleading financial need and growing numbers. Eugenius responded by awarding them the venerable Benedictine convent of S. Maria a Mantignano, located three miles beyond Porta S. Frediano, along with its goods and property.[104] Citing poor governance and the "dishonest way of life" prevailing there, Eugenius forced Abbess Bartolomea Biliotti to resign, then relocated the nuns to the more rigorous atmosphere of S. Apollonia. Financially, this second merger was no small gesture. Mantignano enjoyed roughly comparable assets (5,271 florins) to those of S. Apollonia (5,360 florins), but its annual revenues of 600 florins gave it a per capita income of 85 florins — ten times the amount at S. Apollonia.[105]

The convent's entire urban patrimony consisting of twenty-seven houses was concentrated in Borgo S. Frediano, a major street traversing the Oltrarno.[106] Mantignano had built this portfolio around the urban toehold of a house, oratory, and cemetery in the working-class district of S. Frediano, which the nuns had obtained by papal license in 1370 to use as a refuge in times of warfare.[107]

This annexation not only doubled S. Apollonia's treasury overnight but in one fell swoop gave it an impressive patrimony in a distant zone where the convent previously had exercised no influence. Instead of being concentrated in a single area, convent tenants now extended across the city, augmenting the nuns' social capital and amplifying their patronage prospects. The merger brought an even larger rural patrimony.[108] Painstakingly assembled over three centuries, this massive portfolio could be used, managed, or disassembled as its new owners saw fit. Former Mantignano tenants swore "to work the land well" on behalf of their new superiors, directing rents and yields to their portals.[109] Although S. Apollonia sold a few urban properties, in 1495 it still owned nine houses and a shop on Borgo S. Frediano from the original transfer that netted 50 florins annually.[110] By 1450, S. Apollonia was developing durable client relationships with its new tenants through leases lasting two or three decades, which aligned with the convent's general preference for lifetime leases of residential and commercial properties.[111] The Mantignano legacy made S. Apollonia the institutional guardian of strangers' remembrance and enmeshed the house in various property disputes over the next half century.[112]

This windfall positioned S. Apollonia to undertake ambitious building and decorative projects in the 1440s and 1450s that secured its urban prominence.[113] With newfound assets and guaranteed revenue streams in hand, Abbess Cecilia Donati was pursuing the expansion of the main cloister by March 1442—a project that had been planned since 1418 and partially begun in 1429 but then stalled for lack of funds (fig. 2.2). The refurbished refectory, with its elegant fresco of the Last Supper painted by Andrea del Castagno circa 1447, was merely the most prominent among other embellishments made in these years.[114] Eugenius enabled further growth by allowing the nuns to sell properties valued up to 1,000 florins, which underwrote construction costs for the main cloister.[115] In a landmark move, the pope assured their long-term fortunes by exempting them from all ecclesiastical taxes, including papal imposts, and by placing them under direct papal supervision on condition that they remain Observant.[116] Antoninus followed papal instructions to visit the convent every five years, declaring after his first visit in 1448 "that he had found nothing in need of reform, either in the

Fig. 2.2. Upper loggia of cloister, S. Apollonia, Florence. Photo: Kunsthistoriches Institut in Florenz — Max-Planck-Institut.

spiritual or temporal realm, or in head or members." Given this clean bill of health, the convent retained its papal privileges.[117]

Not surprisingly, this annexation also provoked tensions between members of the newly united communities. Abbess Bartolomea Biliotti of Mantigano had deep knowledge of property rights as well as a long family history of involvement in local ecclesiastical affairs. Although the pope called her administration "negligent," the suppression had turned on the fact that her brand of monasticism clashed with the papal vision of renewal. Supposedly the abbess resigned voluntarily because of advanced age and "other just causes."[118] Once stripped of office, however, she stubbornly refused to take up residence in S. Apollonia. By means of two papal accords worked out in 1441, in which her kinsman Sandro played a critical role, the former abbess retained her lifetime right to a "proper portion" of Mantignano's income. She was permitted to live in the former convent refuge in the Oltrarno — her ancestral stronghold — and to use goods and furnishings necessary to her comfort, supported by former convent servants and an annual pension of 100 florins.[119] The six other displaced nuns from political families reportedly refused to engage with their new sisters in the choir and refectory.[120] Other frictions surfaced over the years, especially over the restoration of monastic dowries. Although the Mantignano nuns eventually became full-fledged chapter members, irritating reminders of papal fiat remained.[121] Whenever the nuns ambled through the upper loggia of the cloister's north wing, they encountered Paolo Schiavo's fresco of the Crucifixion commissioned by Eugenius before his death in 1447, which featured his monumental coat-of-arms.[122]

These were pivotal decades not only for S. Apollonia but for the transformation of urban social geography. Enacted in the name of reform, papal favors set in motion an upward spiral of success that launched S. Apollonia as one of the premier Florentine convents for the remainder of the Renaissance. Throughout the 1450s, the nuns capitalized on their growing prestige among distinguished families like the Guasconi, Donati, Corbinelli, Tornabuoni, Gualterotti, Bardi, and Portinari, who eagerly placed their daughters as nuns and boarders in this rapidly rising community.[123] The chapter embraced both sides of the Medici political divide, leaving nuns to negotiate the delicate balance between them. From this point forward, the recruitment policy for S. Apollonia nuns shifted from one based on neighborhood to one based on class. Nuns from across the city brought with them kinship ties that simultaneously enabled the convent's continued success and opened new locales to familial influence. After 1450, S. Apollonia owned and managed properties in the Oltrarno, in northeastern parishes, in the countryside, as well as in its own immediate zone—all now accessible to families with daughters in the convent.

The mid-fifteenth century once again proved decisive in the ways it linked convent property to forms of social and political power. Convent portfolios were always supported by local scaffolding that permitted nuns to exert varying degrees of influence over their immediate surroundings. Well into the sixteenth century, convents retained core local holdings, many of which figured in the 1561 ducal property census.[124] Surrounding streets were lined with houses and shops whose owners were increasingly secluded behind ever higher walls. Yet the expansion of several convent portfolios into distant urban sectors after 1450 helped shake loose old loyalties, scramble social networks, and bind the city into a more coherent entity open to patrician influence. From an urbanistic standpoint, convents helped fashion the Renaissance city out of an older medieval template not only by enlarging their physical complexes but by consolidating a range of new social dynamics.

Defenders of the Parish

Rivalries between convents also reshaped Florentine neighborhoods by limiting the establishment or expansion of new foundations, resulting in their uneven insertion into the cityscape. Because so many resources flowed from the immediate vicinity, religious houses showed fierce sensitivity toward perceived territorial competitors. In one celebrated case, the friars of the Carmine took the extreme measure in 1448 of destroying the door frames of S. Monaca, a new Augustinian convent under construction, to eliminate challenges posed to their own protégé, S. Maria degli Angeli, located a few blocks away. Construction continued only after repeated complaints from S. Monaca prompted papal intervention. Still, the Carmine successfully protected Carmelite interests in the vicinity by restricting S. Monaca's growth.[125] In an important sense, Florentine neighborhoods were the product of institutional as well as personal contestation.

Much of what we know about nuns' behavior as institutional neighbors comes from litigation. Like early modern Spanish nuns, Florentine religious women often initiated legal action to protect personal legacies, recover dowries, and defend collective property interests. Three nunneries — S. Ambrogio, S. Felicita, S. Pier Maggiore — not only had to engage these commonplace activities but also had to navigate more complex jurisdictional waters as heads of urban parishes.[126] All three were Benedictine communities founded in the formative medieval period, when the Italian church hammered out the skein of urban parochial rights; all three constrained the growth of rival female religious houses by zealously defending those rights. S. Pier Maggiore was the most populous of the three parishes, claiming forty-two hundred inhabitants in 1509. The parish of S. Ambrogio figured among the physically largest and most socially heterogeneous in the city but was more sparsely settled by twelve hundred parishioners. Across the river, S. Felicita dominated its sector of the Oltrarno, where it ministered to twenty two hundred souls.[127]

Irrespective of these differences in size, parish and convent administration were deeply intertwined at all three houses. Revenues were fungible, resulting in complex paper transfers between accounts; convent chapters bore responsibility for feeding local poor and disposing of commemorative bequests. Moreover, these nuns enjoyed collective rights to select the chaplains who ministered to parishioners, making lay influence over these convents of particular import. Their abbesses negotiated agreements with parish confraternities regarding local celebrations, meeting places, and fees. Managing the parish also meant managing the cult of the dead—chapels, altars, tomb sites, and the commemorative programs attached to them. Consequently, strong administrative skills were required on the part of their officers, who often showed exceptional legal and financial literacy based on a firm grasp of convent archives and historic privileges. In order to track revenues owed when a parishioner elected burial elsewhere, Abbess Maria Barbadori of S. Ambrogio "ordered and had made" a new burial register in 1478, while her counterpart at S. Pier Maggiore, Andrea Buondelmonti, initiated a complete administrative review shortly after her election in 1507 to clarify property holdings, commemorative obligations, and outstanding debtors to parish and convent.[128] Having worked out their respective spheres of influence in the twelfth and thirteenth centuries, these two houses heading contiguous parishes subsequently honored each other's dominance throughout the Quattrocento. Although bishops traditionally protected convent rights to ensure that parochial responsibilities were met, the rising tide of religious professions in the late fifteenth century recontextualized customary defenses of parochial rights and invited papal intervention.

As the city's premier convent, S. Pier Maggiore enjoyed enormous success in defending its territory from female rivals. As early as 1325, S. Pier Maggiore established ground rules that seriously disadvantaged the Cistercian nuns of S. Maria Maddalena di Cestello, sited in the parish. At issue was the thorny problem of burial rights, which brought immediate revenues as well as ongoing patronage around remembrance. Defending both parish and convent, the nuns of S. Pier Maggiore denied burial at the Cestello to anyone except their own nuns, although laywomen living in the house might obtain special permission.[129] Similar battles raged throughout the fourteenth century as new foundations settled in the heart of the city. Because repeated warfare had left their dwellings outside the walls "half ruined," the nuns of S. Maria di Candeli transferred to a new, in-town location in 1365. S. Pier Maggiore owned that property—a street corner called Monteloro—and sold it to the newcomers "with various pacts and conditions" that ensured its parochial rights.[130] Especially galling were the annual tributes of wax, capons, veal, and incense payable on major feasts that signaled Candeli's subordinate status.[131] For the next half century, the Candeli nuns seethed over these terms, which in their eyes had become "onerous." Reopening the battle in 1419, they petitioned Martin V for release from these conditions. The rebuttal from S. Pier Maggiore was swift and sure. It countered that any change would bring "grave prejudice and little honor" to the house and would "diminish its estate and honor." After referring the case to the Florentine arch-bishop, Martin confirmed the initial agreement.[132] By invoking parochial rights, S. Pier Maggiore both contained the institutional prestige of other local convents and capped revenues flowing to them.

In the fifteenth century, the convent showed its customary zeal in stifling lo-cal competition. The congregation of the Santuccie, founded by the thirteenth-century holy woman Santuccia of Gubbio (d. 1305), had its first Florentine incarnation in the parish of S. Pier Maggiore sometime before the mid-Quattro-cento.[133] The distinguishing features of this congregation, which adhered to the Benedictine rule and observed individual poverty, were centralized governance under an abbess-general and modified enclosure, both of which brought it into frequent conflict with local bishops. No traces of the original Santuccie archive remain, forcing us to reconstruct the story from the vantage point of the victor. The history of this foundation is bound up with that of its successor, also called "the convent of the Santuccie," founded in 1475 by Alessandra degli Alfani, a young, charismatic Florentine noblewoman known for her austerity and "holy ways." Sixtus IV granted her permission to found a cloistered convent dedicated to S. Giovanni Battista on the former Santuccie site, "under perpetual enclosure and regular observance."[134] The new nuns enjoyed the same spiritual privileges as other houses belonging to the Jerusalemite order, alternately known as the Hospitallers, Knights of Malta, or the Order of St. John of Jerusalem.[135] This new foundation not only posed the usual challenges but also introduced a crusad-ing affiliate into the neighborhood. Declaring a new crusade in 1479, Sixtus dubbed the Hospitallers "athletes of Christ" who defended the faith against the "perfidies" of Turks and infidels. With its pan-European chivalric associations, the new "Santuccie" house offered a fresh vision of female monasticism aligned with current papal preoccupations. Perhaps the greatest danger lay in the papal license permitting Alessandra to found other similar houses in the Florentine diocese. Had she been able to act on that license, her foundation could have served as the nucleus of a competing monastic network whose headquarters would have been located right next door to the old Benedictine bulwark. Given the generally strained relations between Florence and Sixtus, who placed the city under interdict in June 1478, the need to curry papal favor was apparent. S. Pier Maggiore held its ground by making a major donation to the crusade, which reaped both spiritual and practical rewards.[136]

Contrary to Machiavelli's dictum, fortune favored the old in this case. Ales-sandra Alfani, who served as both financial mainstay and moral center of the new enterprise, died only four years after founding her convent. Its still meager endowment, comprised mainly of her dotal wealth, proved insufficient to support the community. Since her followers now found themselves "destitute," Sixtus suppressed the house in January 1480 to "avoid scandal." The crusading pope ceded convent buildings to the male Hospitallers and transferred the nuns to another approved order of their choice, replete with soothing words and threats of excommunication for noncompliance. This mandate reportedly caused great consternation among the displaced nuns, some of whom resisted this forced adoption of a different religious lifestyle.[137]

The so-called Santuccie nuns apparently reconstituted the house under the aegis of the Lateran canons in Rome, from whom they obtained a major indulgence in December 1481.[138] However, these clever moves did little to resolve their financial problems or improve relations with their institutional neighbors. By the early 1490s, the third incarnation of the Santuccie was crumbling financially, and S. Pier Maggiore stepped in eagerly to acquire divested holdings and eliminate the local competition. In 1493 the nuns of S. Pier Maggiore repaid the 40-florin dowry of a certain Suor Eugenia on the condition that she renounce any interest in the Santuccie convent or its property. Shortly afterward, the abbess of S. Pier Maggiore transferred the monastic dowry for "one of the girls" from the da Verrazzano family, "who was at the Santuccie to become a nun," to her new Altoviti husband.[139] This lengthy drama concluded in February 1495, when Alexander VI granted S. Pier Maggiore full possession of Santuccie "with all its goods and appurtenances." Soon after, the Lateran canons in Rome consented to this merger "so as not to reduce Santuccie to a secular place." Besides absorbing the remaining endowment, S. Pier Maggiore also acquired the considerable spiritual patrimony the Santuccie had accumulated.[140] Once again S. Pier Maggiore proved itself an aggressive adversary. It successfully cleared the parish of rival convents, especially those with timely political connections and distinctive religious appeal. In the process, it acquired substantial spiritual privileges and annexed a potentially valuable piece of real estate. When official bulls announcing the merger arrived in May 1496, the nuns celebrated by throwing a banquet for the priests "who came here to see the bulls about Santuccie." These battles later cleared the way for local neighborhood spectacles that ironically showcased the nuns' generosity. As devotional and festive life began to crystallize around the parish in the early sixteenth century, S. Pier Maggiore transformed the distribution of alms to parishioners into part of the growing culture of display.[141]

In the adjacent parish, the nuns of S. Ambrogio proved equally fierce defenders of local territory but met with less success. Like their counterparts at S. Pier Maggiore, they amassed episcopal privileges that prohibited the foundation of other religious houses in the parish without their express consent. In the 1340s Bishop Andrea Acciaiuoli confirmed S. Ambrogio's privilege to exercise veto power over new foundations, which reiterated older episcopal favors. In 1368 Bishop Piero Corsini renewed this right, on the grounds that "the income of the convent being sparse, the nuns need to avoid losing any alms."[142] However, the story took a new turn in the fifteenth century, when the recluses of Le Murate relocated from their bridge house to a site on Via Ghibellina within parish boundaries in 1424. The charismatic zeal of the dozen women who had immured themselves there challenged S. Ambrogio's more traditional form of monasticism. To curb their influence, S. Ambrogio made the newcomers almost completely dependent on their parish supervisors for cult life. According to the 1424 pact, the Murate nuns could provide tombs for their own use but had to employ the S. Ambrogio chaplains for any commemorative services performed there. The pact also required those chaplains to officiate at Le Murate's main feast and barred the nuns from setting up a basin to collect alms.[143] The Murate nuns chafed under these conditions for ten years, and their resentment toward their parish supervisors became embedded in convent lore. Suor Giustina Niccolini, the house chronicler, accused S. Ambrogio of constant harassment in these early years, although she prudently blamed parish priests instead of the nuns.[144]

Once again, Eugenius intervened to reward Observance, this time trumping parochial rights in the process. The pope instructed the respected Portuguese friar Gomez, abbot of the Florentine Badia, to put Le Murate on a more formal footing. In 1435 Gomez annulled the previous agreement and replaced it with one more favorable to Le Murate, marking what Suor Giustina called the convent's "liberation" from parochial clutches. The new pact retained only a few features that directly protected S. Ambrogio's income while granting full monastic status and privileges to the Murate nuns.[145] As Eugenius showered additional favors on the community in the 1440s, Le Murate grew into an imposing physical complex supported by wealthy patrons like Giovanni de' Benci, a trusted representative of the Medici bank and the second wealthiest man in Florence after Cosimo.[146] As noted in chapter 1, devout women and young girls from all quarters and classes streamed into the house. Although the Murate nuns and their parish superiors at S. Ambrogio grew more cooperative with each other over time, papal intervention irrevocably reversed the customary power dynamics between them.

This prismatic look at nuns' neighborhood origins, property portfolios, and institutional relations traces the complex process by which the city's leading families asserted control over a crucial branch of the Florentine church. Convent recruitment patterns sketch the transition from the deeply rooted localism of the medieval city to broader, citywide social networks oriented around the Medici. In the process, relations between nuns, neighbors, and kinsmen were fundamentally reoriented. The mid-fifteenth century was a watershed that witnessed not only the erosion of local neighborhood associations but also a sea change in the function of convents as social institutions. Moving from local holding corporations to spearheads for far-flung patronage relations, convents helped reconstitute the social geography of the city. Although financial considerations permeated virtually all family decisions, conserving dowries was only one of several precipitating factors accounting for explosive convent growth after 1450. Still greater rewards came from translating convent control into expanded political influence. The Florentine oligarchy was aided in this endeavor by papal reform efforts, even though the net results often supported secular ambitions more directly. Many nuns avidly embraced their expanded role as familial agents; others sought the spiritual egalitarianism and simplicity embedded in monastic ideals. Although the Italian church had been caught up in previous cycles of renewal, the Quattrocento proved a decisive turning point that permanently aligned the interests of family, church, and state.

CHAPTER THREE

The Renaissance Convent Economy

The Renaissance convent economy not only conditioned the nature of monastic experience but formed a pivot around which complex political and moral questions turned. Religious women in late medieval and Renaissance Europe defined their religiosity in part through their relation to money and property, which at times brought them into conflict with ecclesiastical authorities and contemporary gender norms. Public begging espoused by female penitents like Claire of Assisi posed clear dangers to female honor in the eyes of church officials; hence spiritual quests based on radical poverty and the renunciation of worldly goods were quickly transformed into more traditional forms of monasticism stressing property endowments.[1] Conversely, ample endowments that supported comfortable living standards sparked concern about nuns' lax observance and the corrosive effects of excessive wealth. Maintaining this elusive balance — between income and expenses, between shifting moral conceptions of wealth, between reclusion and survival — presented Italian religious women with one of their greatest challenges. Practical administration of convent finances proved equally vexed. Although bishops and monastic supervisors identified sound financial management as a top institutional priority, clerics often operated on the gendered assumption that nuns could not manage their own finances effectively. Nonetheless, they generally failed to provide adequate oversight to prevent procurators from mishandling funds, leaving that task to nuns' kinsmen instead. Finances were also an ongoing source of tension among nuns themselves. Signs of mismanagement or favoritism in allocating communal resources sparked internal convent quarrels far more often than frictions over diverging religious practices.

These pervasive problems were made more complex in Florence by the intersection of convent finance with the public fisc. A leading commercial and political center, Florence developed a number of innovative financial instruments that helped maintain the city's sovereignty. In addition, the commune faced an almost uninterrupted set of fiscal challenges from 1350 to 1430 resulting from ongoing military campaigns against Milan and Naples. Military expenditures to maintain security and extend territorial control translated into high taxation, and the years of peace were few.[2] David Peterson has shown that one conflict in particular — the War of the Eight Saints (1375–78), waged against Pope Gregory XI — had a lasting impact on monastic portfolios. Searching for new sources of funding, the commune enacted the greatest lay seizure of monastic property prior to the Reformation. Although these political developments hit property-rich monasteries the hardest, convents did not escape unscathed.[3] It took fifty years for the commune to make partial restitution to ecclesiastical institutions, either by returning properties to their original owners or by compensating them with credits in the public debt (*monte*).

These high political dramas and their aftermath forged indissoluble links between civic and monastic finances. During the first half of the fifteenth century, Florentine convents became more heavily invested as stakeholders in the public debt, subjecting religious institutions and their inhabitants to fluctuating civic policies. The municipal dowry fund made it possible to fund spiritual dowries through liquid capital investments — an innovative mechanism that often replaced customary lump-sum cash payments with a state-run installment plan.[4] Financial relationships tying convents to the city were consolidated in the 1480s, when the commune issued waves of tax concessions to female religious communities. Even nuns' personal living allowances were increasingly bound up with the public purse as the form of their annuities shifted from property rents to interest-bearing *monte* credits. Florentine nuns helped to redistribute capital held in government funds through their very persons, since these credits generally reverted to the convent after death. This wide range of financial instruments fully enmeshed nuns and nunneries in the ebb and flow of urban economic life.

This chapter examines the Renaissance convent economy in relation to broad changes in Florentine politics and the urban economy, especially those spurred by state formation and the development of new markets. The first section examines the structure of convent finance in the early Quattrocento, using civic tax records to compare the distribution of wealth among Florentine convents, between male and female religious institutions, and between religious communities in Florence and other parts of the Italian peninsula. The second section takes up the vexed issue of "private" wealth within a communal economy, focusing on the relationships between nuns' discretionary income and corporate social practices. The third section analyzes ordinary budgetary challenges and the types of expenses that conditioned material life to show how nuns balanced their budgets. The final section links changing convent economies to Medicean patronage and the political consolidation of the Florentine state after 1450. In the second half of the Quattrocento, Florentine civic officials irrevocably tied convent budgets to state-run instruments of public finance. By systematically trading financial favors for prayers, the Florentine state fully harnessed nuns' spiritual power to civic objectives—an exchange that only heightened tensions between nuns' salvific service and other social roles.

The Structure of Convent Finance

As Jo Ann McNamara has argued, nuns' reclusion was impossible without an assured income.[5] To enable withdrawal from the world, Florentine convents relied on a mixed economy that combined various revenue sources that were partly private in nature. Staples of communal income included rents from residential and commercial properties as well as yields from farm holdings. These regular sources of income were supplemented by monastic dowries, liquid capital investments, and earnings from different kinds of work, along with gifts, episodic civic subsidies, and tax exemptions. In addition, many nuns had personal living allowances (*vitalizi*); the relationship between these supplementary funds and the house treasury varied by institution. Convent wealth was further enhanced by the material goods each nun furnished upon entry. Reconstructing Renaissance convent economies using the available evidence tells us more about income and expenses, however, than about total institutional wealth. Unfortunately, there are no comprehensive surveys of monastic communities in this period comparable to the panoramic *Status monasteriorum* compiled by the Neapolitan arch-

bishop Filomarino in 1642. Moreover, Florentine tax returns captured only immoveable property and credits in the public debt, excluding both the earned
income and dowry revenues so crucial to balancing convent budgets. Still, despite
these limitations, tax reports afford an extraordinary overview of corporate finance while giving glimpses into nuns' spending habits and styles of financial
management.

The 1427 *catasto* reveals stark economic differences between institutions — rich
and poor, old and new, thriving and declining — that fueled monastic volatility.
Building on Gene Brucker's earlier assessment of monastic wealth, table 3.1
provides a revised ranking of convent assets for the forty-nine female religious
communities reporting holdings in 1427.[6] For purposes of analysis, these communities can be clustered into five groups ranked in descending order of wealth, as
illustrated in graph 3.1, starting with the ten richest convents (group 1) and
proceeding down the list (groups 2–4, ten convents each) until reaching the nine
poorest houses (group 5). Mean assets of all forty-nine institutions stood at 2,844
florins.[7] Comparing this baseline with assets held by the ten wealthiest houses
reveals the wide spectrum of convent finances: top-tier Florentine houses enjoyed
assets more than 2.25 times greater than the norm (6,419 florins). With the
exception of the Paradiso, all of these affluent convents were well-established
institutions with sizeable endowments that had been built up over time, which
translated into high living standards. Members of wealthy convents generally
wore wool or fur-lined cloaks in winter, deliberated in heated common rooms
decorated with frescoes, performed the divine office using magnificent liturgical
books, and nourished sick brethren back to health with delicacies like sweets and
extra meat.

Corporate wealth dropped off steeply below this top bracket. Assets of top-
tier convents were double those in the second group (3,217 florins) and almost
three times greater than convents in the third cluster (2,264 florins). Most of
these middling houses survived on endowment income supplemented by gifts
and earnings but had few buffers against unforeseen events. A few communities
like S. Verdiana and S. Apollonia flourished over the long term thanks to wealthy
patrons or papal favor, but most did not change status appreciably over the course
of the fifteenth century. Houses situated in the lowest two rungs were the most
vulnerable to dire poverty or suppression. Mean assets for the fourth cluster were
1,332 florins — about a fifth of top-tier houses — while convents in the lowest
bracket commanded only one-eighth the assets of the top group (784 florins).

Table 3.1. Gross Assets of Florentine Convents, 1427 (in florins)

Inside Walls		Outside Walls	
1. S. Pier Maggiore	9,658	1. S. M. Monticelli	8,286
2. S. Felicita	9,423	2. S. Gaggio	7,022
3. S. Jacopo di Ripoli	5,715	3. S. Brigida del Paradiso	5,372
4. S. Domenico nel Maglio	4,765	4. S. Donato in Polverosa	5,233
5. S. Pier Martire	4,615	5. S. M. Montedomini	3,927
6. S. Ambrogio	4,108	6. S. Marta a Montughi	3,200
7. S. Caterina al Mugnone	3,536	7. S. M. Disciplina al Portico	3,159
8. S. Agata	3,290	8. S. G. B. detto Faenza	2,990
9. S. Verdiana	3,186	9. S. G. Evangelista (Boldrone)	2,529
10. S. Giuliano	3,086	10. S. Matteo in Arcetri	2,409
11. S. Niccolò Maggiore	3,015	11. S. Piero Monticelli	2,243
12. S. M. Maddalena Cestello	2,785	12. S. M. Fiore detto Lapo	2,089
13. Pinzochere S. Croce	2,735	13. S. Martino al Mugnone	1,693
14. S. M. Candeli	2,314	14. S. Martino a Mensola	1,629
15. S. Onofrio detto Foligno	2,251	15. S. Baldassare a Coverciano	1,362
16. S. Apollonia	2,202	16. S. Giusto fuori le Mura	1,352
17. S. Maria in Verzaia	1,940	17. S. Martino a Maiano	869
18. S. Francesco	1,928	18. S. Miniato/Nuns S. Baroncelli	322
19. S. Orsola	1,761		
20. SS. Jacopo e Lorenzo	1,570		
21. S. Maria in Querceto	1,429		
22. Regina Coeli (Chiarito)	1,312		
23. S. M. della Neve	1,215		
24. S. Maria sul Prato	989		
25. S. Luca	950		
26. S. Niccolò dei Frieri	935		
27. S. Lucia	839		
28. S. Anna in Verzaia	759		
29. S. G. B. detto Monna Scotta	592		
30. S. Elisabetta (Convertite)	515		
31. S. Silvestro	286		

Source: ASF, Catasto, vols. 184, 185, 192, 194, 195.

Living conditions for these impoverished nuns contrasted sharply with those of their affluent peers. In place of warm clothing, ample food, and comfortable surroundings, poor nuns made do with a single chalice or altar cloth, wore fraying garments, ate in sparsely furnished refectories, and enjoyed few dietary luxuries even when ill. They lived the realities of monastic poverty, whether willingly or not. The eventual fate of these houses was conditioned by their marginal economic status early in the century. S. Baldassare and S. Miniato became active

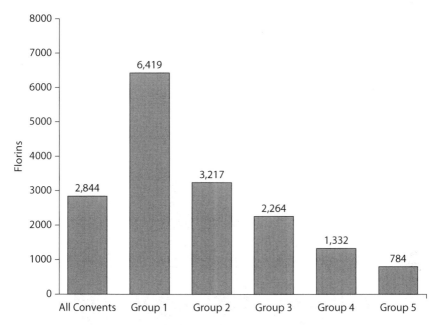

Graph 3.1. Mean Assets of Florentine Convents, 1427 (inside and outside Walls).
Source: ASF, Catasto, vols. 184, 185, 192, 194, 195.

members of the convent labor force supporting the silk industry discussed in the next chapter; the nuns of S. Luca earned their keep by developing a major custodial institution for girls.[8] It was nuns' own labor that kept these convents afloat. The alternatives to work were grim; because the nuns of S. Anna resisted all forms of paid labor in order to avoid worldly exposure, they "lacked half of what's needed to live" by the late Quattrocento, forcing them to endure wretched circumstances "in misery."[9] Other convents in precarious financial condition became targets for papal suppression.

These glaring differences in wealth become more intelligible when figured on a per capita basis. Convents used a baseline similar to the one set by Florentine tax officials, who estimated the annual cost of living at 14 florins. Nuns spent a roughly comparable sum, despite certain economies of scale achieved in running any sizeable institution. As several tax reports stated, it cost between 12 and 15 florins annually "to clothe and shoe" each nun; similarly, boarding fees for young secular girls typically cost 1 florin or more per month.[10] Everyday living expenses for food, clothing, and habitation were increased by the costs of structural repairs to nuns' living quarters, their convent church, and any rental properties, which provided no formal tax exemptions. Figuring corporate assets on a per person basis, it becomes apparent that monastic poverty rather than excessive wealth was the more pressing problem in fifteenth-century Florence: three out of four nuns lived at or below the threshold marking the official cost of living in 1427, at least when calculated in terms of reported endowment income. As Denys Hay suspected some years ago, Italian female religious institutions were severely under-endowed.[11] Generally low levels of endowment support not only impacted nuns' standard of living but also affected their ability to be self-sufficient and voluntarily reclusive. Income from monastic endowments was used to make withdrawal from the world possible; hence the fact that Florentine convents had such limited endowments made it difficult to achieve full reclusion.

This picture of pervasive monastic poverty is modified somewhat when one considers additional sources of income that were not captured by the *catasto*. Like lay households, convents were taxed only on certain fixed assets such as property holdings and *monte* credits. In assessing nuns' living standards, we must also take into account other revenues, however episodic in nature. Chief among these were spiritual dowries that provided the financial lifeblood of female religious communities. Although nuns assiduously recorded dowry payments in their account books, these monies figured into tax assessments only if they underwrote purchases of real estate. Throughout the fifteenth century, such cash infusions often failed to advance the endowment because they were used instead to pay outstanding debts or to make urgent structural repairs. Occasional gifts from patrons or nuns' family members, whether in the form of cash or foodstuffs, also supplemented living standards. Many donations, however, came with strings attached — requiring that the nuns, for example, perform liturgical services or purchase religious objects — that undercut their value, at least according to convent supervisors. Income from work compensated for inadequate endowments to varying degrees, yet threatened nuns' reclusion. Private living allowances provided still other funds to the lucky few; rather than enhancing communal well-being, however, annuities generally supplemented individual diets, paid personal medical expenses, or refurbished a nun's aging wardrobe. On occasion, privileged nuns loaned or donated part or all of their allowances to the community to relieve cash-flow problems, but these monies functioned primarily as stopgap measures rather than long-term solutions to deeper structural problems.

Although these additional funding sources collectively gave Florentine nuns a higher standard of living than suggested by tax returns, they also promoted engagement with secular society rather than encouraging reclusion. Monies derived from work, patrons, or family perpetuated relations with laity instead of releasing nuns from worldly affairs. The inadequate endowment revenues captured in the *catasto* indicate why, from an economic standpoint, Florentine nuns remained so fully immersed in urban life. These data also suggest the precarious position in which some convents found themselves. Business contractions or calamities like fire and flood could easily push the majority of nuns into dire straits. Judging from economic data, polemics linking monastic wealth to lax discipline, whether taking the form of religious critique or literary entertainment, applied to very few Florentine religious women.

A closer look at portfolios in each of the five wealth clusters reveals important differences in the type of assets that conditioned nuns' lives. Topping the wealth pyramid in 1427 were the old Benedictine convents of S. Pier Maggiore and S. Felicita, whose financial backbone consisted of extensive landholdings. As mentioned in chapter 2, S. Pier Maggiore's portfolio was massive, and it was even more extensive in 1427 than a half century later: forty-six houses and four shops in the city, twenty farms, and sixteen pieces of land in the countryside.[12] The convent had acquired most of these holdings by 1400, although the chapter occasionally bought and sold unencumbered properties to manage its patrimony more efficiently. Annual income from this portfolio stood at 676 florins, which provided 25 florins apiece for the community's twenty-seven inhabitants (including male clergy). No income came from investments in the public debt. The nuns of second-ranked S. Felicita also lived off a generous endowment yielding 522 florins annually in 1438. The lion's share (91.2 percent) came from rents, the rest from *monte* credits. Like its counterpart across town, S. Felicita aggressively concentrated its local patrimony; its twenty-one houses and shops ringed the convent. The house was similarly well stocked with "books, chalices, and other liturgical furnishings."[13] However, these assets masked hidden financial problems. Annual expenses totaled 679 florins, leaving a shortfall of 157 florins that tax year. Even discounting this debt, S. Felicita was less robust than first appears, since per capita income stood at 15.3 florins, just slightly above the official cost of living.[14] Whatever amenities these nuns enjoyed came from private discretionary funds and financial windfalls.

This property regime based on real estate holdings was central to the practice of open reclusion. Nuns in affluent houses decided whether and when to re-negotiate rents, extend credit based on clientage, realize major gains through sales, or concentrate holdings in a locale. Property holdings also kept nuns in touch with neighborhood dynamics via tenants who provided important conduits for the two-way flow of information. The lively social contacts embedded in this system probably made religious life more palatable to women lacking vocation. Other top-tier Florentine convents worked from a similar property base, having limited investments in the state-owned public debt. Only four of the ten wealthiest Florentine convents in 1427 derived any corporate income from *monte* credits.[15] Some of these interest-bearing credits resulted from communal restitution of confiscated properties launched by the proaristocratic regime in 1382, which proceeded fitfully until the 1420s.[16] Although convents profited from a spurt of benefactions as citizens divested declining credits in the 1420s and 1430s, this revenue stream remained comparatively small. In 1438, convents in the top bracket still drew only 8–13 percent of corporate income from liquid investments.[17]

Comparing S. Pier Maggiore and S. Felicita with male religious houses shows that top-ranked monasteries and friaries far outstripped these convents in wealth. In 1427 the two richest monasteries in the city and environs — the Florentine Badia and the Certosa of Galluzzo — each claimed over 20,000 florins in corporate assets, more than double the holdings of either convent. The portfolio of fourth-ranked S. Salvi provided each monk with roughly 65 florins annually, a sum 2.5 times greater than per capita income at S. Pier Maggiore.[18] Viewed in more general terms, male religious communities enjoyed mean assets (6,223 florins) more than double that of women's houses.[19] Convent wealth looks especially small compared to other prominent ecclesiastical institutions and personnel. Archbishop Amerigo Corsini claimed an episcopal endowment of 21,142 florins, while the hospital of S. Maria Nuova — the city's dominant ecclesiastical brokerage — weighed in with 42,507 florins. One other comparison is worth making to round out this picture. Convent wealth was greatly overshadowed by the resources commanded by Florence's greatest citizens. In 1427 eight convents claimed assets over 5,000 florins, whereas 224 private citizens were worth that much or more.[20]

A different perspective on Florentine convent wealth emerges from a comparison with affluent Venetian convents. Simply put, rich Venetian nuns were richer than Florentine ones. The two wealthiest Venetian houses, S. Zaccaria and S. Lorenzo, showed a comparable revenue structure to top Florentine convents; they also had accumulated the bulk of their patrimonies before 1400, with subsequent purchases deepening property holdings in particular areas. Yet their assets significantly exceeded those of their poorer Florentine sisters in religion. In 1452

S. Lorenzo registered annual rents of 1,939 ducats, most of which (93 percent) came from urban holdings.[21] To achieve comparable income, S. Pier Maggiore would have needed a 20 percent return on its assets in a period when most stable investments yielded only 3–5 percent. Even at a self-reported low in 1472, S. Zaccaria enjoyed an annual income (1,353 ducats) double that of S. Pier Maggiore and 2.5 times greater than that of S. Felicita. By 1534, a decade after S. Zaccaria had split into two branches, the conventuals claimed per capita income of 36 ducats, the Observants 17.[22] Wellborn Venetian nuns also benefited from higher dowries and more ample personal wealth. Each nun at S. Zaccaria had a personal servant; more generally, top-tier Venetian convents had a higher ratio of servants to choir nuns. After 1458 the nuns of S. Zaccaria disposed of their private rooms as they pleased, a practice unknown in Florence until the sixteenth century.[23] Joining their large personal patrimonies to corporate assets, the nuns of S. Zaccaria spent impressive sums to decorate their convent church, aided by the official organs of church and state. In 1462 the Venetian Senate generously donated 1,000 ducats to rebuild the convent church following a fire; the Venetian patriarch issued an indulgence to raise funds for this purpose. Reflecting a sense of patrician grandeur, the S. Zaccaria nuns retained their given names throughout the fifteenth century rather than adopting new religious identities. Their lavish consecration ceremonies captivated onlookers, outstripping similar Florentine ceremonies in both cost and splendor.[24] These disparities speak to the greater control of wealth exercised by Venetian patrician women, as well as to the special place occupied by Venetian convents in civic religion and ideology.[25]

To understand the structure of Florentine convent portfolios in other tiers, a fuller explanation of the civic *monte* is in order. The establishment of communal public debts in north-central Italy in the fourteenth century offered new investment outlets for noble landholding families, foreign mercenaries, church officials, and entrepreneurs with surplus capital.[26] Founded in the 1340s, the Florentine *monte* created a flexible financial instrument that allowed private and institutional investors to hold interest-bearing credits in what amounted to a state-run bank. The *monte* represented an innovative, mutually beneficial financial scheme. The commune sought cheap credit, mainly to finance its territorial ambitions and defensive military campaigns; investors sought a safe place for savings. Before its mid-fifteenth century decline, the *monte* was considered "part of Florentine patriotic tradition," a mechanism that gave the republic much of its financial potency.[27] Credits in the public debt had numerous advantages, especially for a commercial society that practiced partible inheritance. They were negotiable on the open market, divisible among several stakeholders, and transferable between generations; they also could be used to pay communal taxes. Interest-bearing government funds were a relatively stable source of income, especially in an age of rampant political exile, since they could not be confiscated for any reason. In the mid-1420s, credits were concentrated in relatively few hands; 10 percent of the city's households owned more than 90 percent of *monte* credits.[28]

Nonetheless, *monte* credits also had several drawbacks as investments. Despite yielding a reasonable return, their payout fell short of results expected by more entrepreneurial investors. Most credits were scheduled to pay 5 percent annually; special *monti* established after 1390 carried higher annual interest rates of 8–10 percent. In practice, however, *monte* credits yielded closer to 3.75 percent and were not always paid on time.[29] Credits traded well below face value on the open market, generally between 25 and 50 percent of par. Moreover, it was often difficult to find buyers, especially during fiscal crises, such as those of the 1420s and 1430s. As new Florentine currencies were issued in the fifteenth century, government funds lost real value over time. Citizens forced to advance loans to the government were unable to redeem credits received as compensation because cashing them out would have threatened the communal treasury with bankruptcy.

Although top-tier Florentine convents had limited *monte* investments in 1427, several houses in the middle ranks (groups 2–4) held a larger fraction of assets in this form. They acquired *monte* credits mainly through donations in the 1420s and 1430s, as patrons began using these rapidly declining credits to subsidize family chapels or schemes for remembrance. Convents also accumulated credits piecemeal through legacies earmarked for nuns' living allowances, which disguised the transfer of wealth from laity to ecclesiastical institutions at issue in civic discourse. Topping the list of *monte* stakeholders was S. Apollonia, one of the city's great success stories. In 1438, 61 percent of its income nominally came from *monte* credits, thanks to the largesse of donors attracted to the nuns' asceticism and papal favor.[30] Only three of the twenty-nine nuns had living allowances, all in the form of *monte* credits yielding 2 to 10 florins annually. No other convent remotely approached this level of investment in the public debt. What most likely accounts for it is the chapter's active pursuit of lay patronage, especially among political families. Unlike S. Pier Maggiore and S. Felicita, this house did not enjoy parochial status. Its location on Via S. Gallo — the urban corridor most thickly populated with female religious institutions — placed it in heated competition for funds, especially from patrons normally attracted to mendicant institutions.[31] In 1438, S. Apollonia also owned a couple of farms, three small houses contiguous with the cloister, a residential property across the river, and "a few other small houses" on Via S. Gallo that were later incorporated into the complex. Income from taxable sources — rents, yields, *monte* interest — was less than 8 florins for each of the forty-seven inhabitants, well below the standard cost of living. This figure did not include income from dowries, earnings, and gifts, but it did encompass the three living allowances invested in the *monte*. Most likely, the nuns of S. Apollonia lived a fairly comfortable but ascetic lifestyle. The nuns implored tax officials to bear in mind their small taxable income, "to consider our state and treat us so that in future we are able to serve God and expand his house, yours, and ours."[32] After the midcentury mergers discussed in chapter 2, the convent portfolio more than tripled in size, and its asset mix took on a more conventional form.

Florentine convents situated in the bottom group reported no income from *monte* credits in 1427, indicating that they neither excited the religious imagination or social ambitions of prospective donors nor were tied to civic accounting schemes. Instead, these communities lived off meager property endowments, supplemented by earnings and a few personal stipends. These institutions represented a highly mixed group. Some houses remained deeply committed to ideals of voluntary poverty; others were forced into involuntary poverty when patrons found fresh sources of inspiration elsewhere. Most housed a tiny complement of nuns, often fewer than ten women. Not surprisingly, only two of these communities maintained a salaried chaplain, who probably lived no better than the nuns.[33] When Corsini made pastoral rounds in 1422, he worried halfheartedly about mismanagement and the spiritual dangers of property demands, but neither he nor his successors tried to remedy the inadequate pastoral care poor communities typically received.[34] These convents were left to fare for themselves both spiritually and economically.

Beyond providing essential economic data, this overview of convent wealth points to several distinctive features of Renaissance female monasticism. Significant property holdings not only generated a high standard of living for affluent nuns but also allowed them to exercise corporate autonomy and maintain layered connections with the secular world. Conversely, poorly endowed convents came to depend heavily on civic charity and manual labor. In the early Quattrocento, female religious communities situated at either end of the economic spectrum had not yet developed significant investments in the public debt — a fact that distinguishes their economies from early modern ones. By 1600, virtually all Italian convents held a high proportion of assets in the form of liquid capital, primarily as investments in state-owned credit markets. Liquid capital investments accounted for 25–79 percent of convent revenues in seventeenth-century Naples, while most midlevel convents in post-Tridentine Venice lived off interest-bearing securities such as government bonds, private contracts, and trust funds.[35] Similarly, religious women in seventeenth-century Valladolid relied extensively on liquid capital investments and new instruments of public finance, which enabled them to vigorously participate in the state-run local credit market and to eventually assume their position as creditors to the Spanish crown.[36] Although this trend is partially attributable to the continued development of innovative financial instruments, it also points to changing inheritance strategies among elites, the shift to a more centralized administration of public finance, and the growth of collaborative efforts between church and state to regulate female religious communities in post-Tridentine Europe.

The Paradox of "Private" Wealth

The mixed Renaissance convent economy described above depended to a significant extent on "private" maintenance allowances, which had a long-established place in female monasticism. Nuns in both conventual and Observant communities enjoyed personal discretionary funds, usually in the form of lifetime annuities, that enabled them to improve their diet, replace necessary clothing, purchase books and devotional objects, pay medical expenses, establish mass programs, and become small-scale patrons both within and outside the convent. In 1431 the Benedictine nun Lena Barbadori explained to tax officials the uses to which she put her annuities. Writing in a gorgeous Gothic book hand, she listed various legacies from kin in the form of *monte* credits, some of which yielded nothing; others were so heavily encumbered by religious offices that they provided little income. "In addition," she wrote, "I have to support every expense that might be incurred in illness and other personal needs, beyond what my convent gives me, such as [buying] bread, wine, and meat, three times a week; and every other necessity I draw from this substance."[37] Allowances enhanced nuns' quality of life both by improving material well-being and by creating an important psychological distance from poverty. Although intended for personal use, living allowances frequently complemented corporate revenues, allowing the community to cover cash flow problems, pay taxes, or complete new decorative schemes. At S. Niccolò Maggiore, Suor Lisabetta Marignolli helped subsidize the new altarpiece and tabernacle for the high altar commissioned from Bicci di Lorenzo in 1433. Since the convent could not meet the full cost of 186 florins on its own, she contributed 44 florins from her annuity over several years to help foot the bill.[38] Having several nuns who could readily tap into private cash reserves plainly worked to communal advantage.

At first glance, maintenance allowances appear to violate monastic rules against personal property. Over time, however, religious women and laity alike reinterpreted these stipends in various ways. They might be considered as gifts or alms enabling institutions to balance their budgets, as enhancements supporting the special needs of nuns infirm in mind or body, or as reflections of the distributive principle "each according to need" that remained in tension with strict egalitarianism. Although Renaissance Florentines exploited this practice, they did not invent it out of whole cloth; nor were fifteenth-century monastic records coy about discussing personal allowances, in contrast to post-Tridentine accounts.[39]

Nonetheless, private wealth presented several paradoxes for monastic life. It undercut the spiritual equality and common material life at the heart of monasticism, which might activate the potential for divisiveness, instigate corrosive feelings of envy, and reproduce class distinctions inside convent walls. Deepening the paradox was the fact that maintenance allowances drew nuns into relations of dependence on family and state rather than making them more self-sufficient. Further amplifying these paradoxes was the impediment that private wealth posed to religious vocations. Gabriella Zarri has argued persuasively that pious women in sixteenth-century Italy often resisted taking formal religious vows in order to conserve individual property rights and remain independent from ecclesiastical jurisdiction.[40]

These paradoxes both animated and complicated fifteenth-century Italian female monasticism. Legally, nuns ceded the right to own property outside the convent when they took solemn vows, but there was great variation among orders and even individual houses in the ways they organized and interpreted property relationships.[41] Nuns belonging to the Benedictine "family" enjoyed the greatest latitude in property rights. After taking vows, these religious women legitimately managed the usufruct of personal goods, whether in the form of rents or *monte* interest. This distinction between usufruct and ownership is an important one, because it allowed Benedictine nuns to administer personal patrimonies without violating monastic injunctions — at least in their own eyes. Hence the abbesses of S. Felicita and S. Pier Maggiore could claim with a clear conscience that there were "no proprietors" among them when Corsini visited in 1422, despite the fact that many nuns had personal income.[42] Augustinian nuns followed a similar model in practice. By contrast, Franciscan nuns renounced property interests, although some Poor Clares had permission "to retain in their own name all possessions, goods, and rights which came to them by inheritance and which they would have enjoyed had they remained in the world."[43] Dominican nuns organized the relationship between personal and communal finances in yet other ways, often developing creative solutions that allowed them to transmit personal legacies. Similarly, ownership of personal goods — books, clothing, cells, furnishings, devotional objects — varied according to house constitutions. There was no neat divide between conventual and Observant branches, even within the same order. The Observant Benedictines of S. Apollonia could retain possessions with the abbess's permission; conversely, the Observant Benedictines of Le Murate stressed both the absolute and voluntary nature of their poverty to ecclesiastical visitors, probably to avoid questions about collective property ownership that might arise in future visitations.[44] These variations map the hybrid nature of monastic organization in the fifteenth century, highlighting the extent of the control nuns themselves wielded over key areas of religious life.

An emerging flash point was the status of individual earnings, especially once paid work took firm root in Florentine convents by 1450. It was not uncommon for some nuns in houses with active textile workshops or conservatories to accept extra piecework for cash or to receive tips for custodial services well rendered. Allowances were considered a normal part of family relations; personal earnings, however, sparked quick reprimands from reforming bishops. Dependence on family might be accommodated within an Italian monastic framework, but personal savings from market work were frowned on except at institutions designed to rehabilitate fallen women. In 1509, Cosimo Pazzi reminded the nuns of S. Maria di Candeli that "one's personal earnings should be given immediately into the hands of the abbess," reiterating that one nun should not have more than another. The archbishop adopted a harsher tone with the Chiarito nuns, admonishing them to deposit any private property along with their earnings at the abbess's feet. Taking a middle route, these women devised a system by which choir nuns, novices, and servants paid a fixed portion of their earnings to the communal treasury on a quarterly basis.[45] In issuing these reprimands, Pazzi embarked on a collision course with the realities of convent finance and market incentives. The next chapter makes clear that the marketplace won out, although church officials continued their campaign against this mode of creating personal wealth. The apostolic visitor to Pisan convents circa 1576 reiterated that all earnings should be turned over to the *maestra* of the workroom for common use; he even prohibited keeping records of individual earnings in account books.[46]

In the fourteenth century, nuns' annuities customarily came from property rents, which gave religious women considerable latitude in managing their use. At S. Pier Maggiore, Suor Francesca Albizzi enjoyed the usufruct from several nearby residential properties, and she stewarded these properties prudently enough to accumulate significant savings. In 1385 she donated 50 florins in cash toward the convent's purchase of a large rental property in exchange for an 11-florin annuity, which she received regularly for forty years. As she grew older, Suor Francesca added other layers to these arrangements. In 1402 she assigned rental income from another property, topped off with a gift of 20 florins, to establish a perpetual mass program benefiting her soul.[47] Similarly, Suor Laudomina Rinuccini, granddaughter of the rich, politically liberal knight Messer Francesco, negotiated various property-based annuities with aplomb. In 1412, the chapter of S. Pier Maggiore compensated her for several gifts and loans totaling 100 florins with a single large annuity paid from rents. She collected this money for at least fifty years, all the while exercising her preference for particular tenants and leasing terms. Given her business skills and social contacts, it is not surprising that this nun served multiple turns as convent treasurer or that her name was "remade" frequently after her death in 1463. Hailing from another local family of consequence, the middle-aged nun Felice Bonafede made comparable arrangements for a lifetime annuity based on rents, which was paid until her death in 1438.[48] At nearby S. Ambrogio, Abbess Niccolosa Buonaccorsi drew revenues from a neighboring residential property. "Because she purchased that house with her own money," the convent rent book stated matter-of-factly, "she collects the rent." Her sister Suor Caterina Buonaccorsi owned one-third of a house a block away, from which she collected a lifetime annuity starting in 1423.[49]

The combination of property assets and local neighborhood brokerage gave these women a powerful set of tools, including financial security and easily leveraged resources. Property-owning nuns at similar institutions developed multilayered social relationships with tenants, who frequently paid their rent to nunproprietors in person. Annuities derived from real estate enabled nuns to stay connected to their neighborhoods, to family property, and to the family itself. Families and households benefited from these arrangements as well, particularly in an age marked by extortionate taxes and political exile. Transferring small properties to convents and attaching annuity income to their daughters offered local families secure tax shelters; these gifts also guaranteed safe havens for kins-women and rewarded loyal nun-guardians for watching over the family dead. At the same time, however, these property transfers invited fraud and swelled ecclesiastical property holdings — two thorny issues in church-state relations. Throughout the first half of the fifteenth century, the vast amount of property under ecclesiastical control animated a series of conflicts between church and state. The commune tried to check the flow of lay property into clerical hands through various administrative measures, but solutions were never very stable.[50]

The 1427 *catasto* allows us to gauge the prevalence and distribution of nuns' annuities, albeit imperfectly, since tax returns consistently noted income from *monte* credits but were less diligent in recording rents and yields earmarked for individual nuns. Twenty-four detailed tax returns spanning the wealth spectrum show that 67 of 434 nuns (15.4 percent) claimed some form of private income, but the recipients lived in just thirteen of the twenty-four communities.[51] These figures do not include S. Pier Maggiore and S. Felicita, which would increase the total percentage slightly. The 1438 *catasto* adds interesting details but does not alter this picture significantly.[52] An informed estimate thus indicates that 15–20 percent of Florentine nuns in the city and environs enjoyed private income in the early Quattrocento. These allowances varied considerably in value and internal distribution; as individual supplements, annuities did not free up communal re-sources for poorer nuns lacking independent income, although they often bene-fited the whole community by providing emergency cash. At the austere Domini-can house of S. Pier Martire, only one of nineteen nuns — Suor Piera, the infirm, fifty-four-year-old widow of a bone doctor — had personal income. She received a meager stipend of grain, oil, and wine supplied by a nearby monastery, probably as part of her late husband's bequest. More evenly dispersed were annuities at the Cistercian foundation of S. Donato in Polverosa, where seven of twenty nuns received annual living allowances ranging from 2.5 to 9.5 florins annually. Be-yond the two wealthiest Benedictine houses, the densest concentration of pri-vate subsidies was found at Dominican convents like S. Domenico nel Maglio, S. Jacopo, and S. Giuliano, where more than half of the nuns claimed private income in 1427. At S. Domenico, almost all annuities came from *monte* credits nominally accruing 10 to 15 florins annually.[53] Two nuns reaped more than twice that amount. Hailing from one of the city's most distinguished families, Suor Ghita Capponi received an annual total of 36.5 florins from six different sources. Her portfolio included rents from a small house abutting the convent, two *monte* accounts inscribed in her name, and three other *monte* accounts held jointly with other nuns and a friar. These diverse funds allowed her to engage in property transactions mutually beneficial to self and convent.[54] Similar patterns of joint ownership, mainly of liquid investments, obtained at S. Jacopo.

What accounted for the prevalence of subsidies at Dominican convents was the unique relationship these houses established between personal and corporate finance whereby nuns underwrote some essential expenses that were absorbed communally elsewhere. Dominican nuns in fifteenth-century Augsburg developed similar financial arrangements. The tax report for S. Domenico noted that "these nuns have many encumbrances on the above income: for instance, to clothe themselves, to pay their own expenses when ill, to care for their young charges, and to make annual commemorative masses for the souls of those who left them legacies. From the above monies, there is little 'profit.'"[55] Dominican constitutions mandated that nuns and friars should hold property in common, but these rules were officially relaxed for women because they were prohibited from standard mendicant activities like preaching and begging. These internal contradictions in mendicant organization blurred the line between personal and corporate finance; consequently, bookkeeping practices at Florentine Dominican convents were unusually complex. Because they had to offset many personal expenses, Dominican nuns often reserved portions of their annuities for emergencies. Thus when Suor Alessandra Attavanti died in 1490, her sister-nuns at S. Domenico found 29 gold florins tucked among her books and linens. Similarly, four of the five nuns who succumbed to plague in the wretched summer of 1528 had reserves of 3 to 20 florins stashed away.[56] These savings were entirely licit within the context of house practices, at least as interpreted by generations of religious women themselves.

The prevalence of annuities is deceptive, however, since in many cases they failed to yield expected funds or went unpaid for long periods. Again the 1427 *catasto* affords a good index to the problem. At S. Giuliano, nine nuns ostensibly enjoyed personal supplements. However, Jacopo Giugni was four years behind in paying the annuity he owed his sister, putting him 20 florins in her debt. Giovanni Bartoli had not paid his middle-aged sister's small annuity for almost nine years, while his brother hadn't paid his share for ten. The brothers of another nun owed her 45 florins "from times past." At S. Marta, Suor Caterina da Sommaia was owed a 10-florin annual allowance by her brother; "it has yet to be paid," wrote the convent scribe. Another nun had been assigned 25 florins annually by her father's testament, but the convent had had "nothing" from his heirs over the years.[57] By 1435, Luigi and Paolo Soderini owed S. Gaggio a hefty sum of 190 florins — the equivalent of two monastic dowries — for unpaid maintenance allowances to their two sisters, who died before collecting a penny from their father's legacy. At the same house, the Gianfigliazzi brothers were 95 florins in arrears on their sisters' annuities.[58] Late payments and the extension of credit were common facts of life in Renaissance Italy; yet the fact that nuns frequently did not receive maintenance allowances on time meant that their purchasing power was more robust on paper than in practice. Family legacies, especially those entrusted to nuns' brothers, were often in arrears. This evidence suggests not only the financial complications surrounding bequests but also the structural weakness of ties between brothers and sisters.[59] By contrast, nuns receiving annuities in the form of rents or *monte* interest claimed their stipends in more timely fashion. Tenants behind on rent might enjoy a grace period of six to twelve months, but delinquent leases could be terminated or renegotiated in the convent's favor. Although *monte* payments lagged periodically in the late Trecento, after 1400 the *monte* paid more punctually, rarely falling behind more than a year in paying interest to nuns.[60] In fact, it appears that in the first half of the fifteenth century the public debt had a better payment record to religious women than to other private investors.

Because private wealth was so crucial to their well-being, Dominican nuns exercised an unusually strong sense of proprietorship over annuities. Silvia Evangelisti has shown how nuns in early modern Italian convents used personal goods, money, and objects to regulate their social networks within convent walls.[61] Although nuns in fifteenth-century religious communities enjoyed fewer material possessions, they too mapped out personal relationships through the transmission of annuities. Nuns honored friendships formed over decades spent together in work and prayer, rewarded the loyalty and affection of young nuns they had mentored, and gifted kin and others sharing pious preferences or political standpoints. In using annuities to articulate social networks and ensure their own remembrance, nuns left a lasting imprint on convent finance. At the same time, the favoritism reflected in personal legacies to other nuns posed inherent risks to communal harmony.

Evidence from S. Jacopo puts a human face on these practices. By the early 1420s, Suor Tommasa Cini owned a lifetime interest in three-quarters of a sizeable farm, from which she drew proportional yields and rents; the convent owned the remaining share. In 1425 she and the chapter agreed that, after her death, one of her three shares would revert to the convent. The remaining two shares were to be distributed to other nuns she selected. "With the approval of the convent and chapter of nuns," Suor Tommasa could grant her shares "to two nuns for their lifetime with this condition: that these two nuns are committed and obligated to make an annual celebration for the feast of San Lorenzo and to make arrangements to have the Office of the Dead recited at the convent for the benefit of Suor Tommasa and her mother." When those two nuns died, their shares would revert to the convent with the same obligations attached to them. As Suor Tommasa lay dying some years later, "she declared that one share should be left to Suor Costanza Barucci and the other to Suor Niccolosa Barucci." The chapter honored her dying wishes, assigning the income to these blood sisters, who quickly became a force to be reckoned with. *Monte* credits could be disposed along similar lines. In 1437 Suor Giovanna Masi pooled some cash with the corporate *monte* account from which she drew a lifetime annuity. Her pact with the house stipulated that she "could leave [the annuity] to another sister in the convent for her lifetime," who in turn was obliged to sponsor various religious feasts.[62]

Transmitting annuities was so pervasive at S. Jacopo that even servant nuns circulated small legacies. In 1454 the *conversa* Jacopa secured a small annuity (roughly 1 florin) from the convent, which she used to initiate a chain of legacies among the serving sisters. After her death, she wanted the annuity transferred to another nun; when that nun died, the income would devolve on a third nun. "And in this way one succeeds the other for their lifetimes," explained the convent account. Simultaneously, the third nun made a pact with the convent that redirected the annuity to the previous two nuns should she predecease them.[63] Perhaps motivated by a sense of trust and affection, these women looked out for each other's welfare while fixing their own memory in the community. Annuities were so deeply embedded in S. Jacopo's complex organizational culture that they survived two successive waves of religious reform: the introduction of Observance (1459) and the convent's entry into the Savonarolan fold (1507). Private wealth no doubt perpetuated inequalities within this small world, but eliminating it would have compromised the viability of common life. To dismiss such "private" income as one of the many abuses riddling the pre-Tridentine church would be to miss a crucial feature of contemporary religious understanding and to overlook monastic necessity. The S. Jacopo nuns held strong religious convictions — attested by asceticism and prayer vigils — in tandem with these financial practices. At the same time, they recognized the compatibility of means and ends: it was private income that enabled them to live a common life.

Balancing the Budget

Florentine tax records also document the regular expenses encumbering convent budgets, ranging from food, clothing, and medicine to salaries, building maintenance, and taxes. These institutional expenditures are thoroughly detailed in the 1438 report filed by S. Felicita and are grouped by category in graph 3.2.[64] Comparing this pattern with other convents shows that this breakdown was more or less the norm, despite slight individual variations. At 308 florins, the single largest expense incurred was food, representing almost half (45 percent) of regular expenditures. This proportion parallels that of seventeenth-century Neapolitan convents, which also devoted about half of their budgets to food.[65] With a per capita income of 15 florins supplemented by private stipends, the nuns of S. Felicita enjoyed a fairly rich, varied diet consisting of fresh meat, salt pork, game, eggs, fish, beans, cheese, wine, oil, fruit, and vegetables, with special treats like marzipan and pastries reserved for feast days. Top-notch Venetian convents spent even more on comestibles; in 1534, S. Lorenzo allotted 20 ducats apiece to its inhabitants for food alone.[66]

In reality, S. Felicita's food budget was certainly greater. Reported costs did not include gabelles and portage fees; more importantly, tax returns mask the traffic in foodstuffs given or received as gifts. Jane Bestor has argued convincingly that gift giving in Italian Renaissance society was a communicative, socially productive act.[67] Nuns engaged in gift exchange primarily using foodstuffs and religious objects, whose social and symbolic meaning exceeded their market value. Small gifts of fruit, wine, and sweets were literally the food of friendship, used as tokens of affection to cement social alliances. Throughout the 1450s, Piera de' Medici, the well-connected abbess of S. Verdiana, sent sugared pine-nut cookies and sweet wine to the *signoria* as a breakfast gift reminding the priors to celebrate festivities honoring the convent's patron saint. The chapter of S. Pier Maggiore congratulated newly elected abbesses at neighboring S. Ambrogio by sending hundreds of little cookies for the nuns' pleasure and also gifted the cathedral canons with forty oranges before every Easter procession.[68] In the 1490s and early 1500s, Le Murate participated in an international exchange with the Duchess of Ferrara, the queen of Portugal, and other noblewomen by trading small ephemeral items — fruit, marzipan, sweets, handiwork, devotional objects — for assorted commodities and favors.[69] Conversely, laity often gave nuns fruit, nuts, and good Trebbiano wine on religious feast days to make these occasions still more festive.

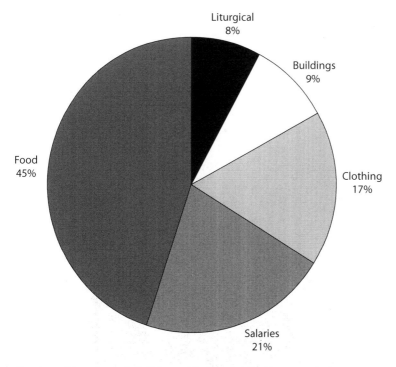

Graph 3.2. Expenses at S. Felicita, 1438. *Source:* ASF, Catasto, vol. 602.

In many ways, food stood as a metaphor for the larger challenges nuns confronted in dealing with gendered issues of monastic wealth. Like their medieval counterparts studied by Caroline Bynum, Renaissance nuns used food to find the sacred in the everyday.[70] Tensions regarding appropriate levels and types of food consumption mapped out different religious visions, both between nuns and clerical officials and among religious women themselves. When enacting Observant reforms in mid-fifteenth century Europe, for instance, the Dominican general Auribelli expressed ambivalence about the severe fasting of some religious women, who took this practice to unacceptable extremes.[71] He advised Dominican nuns not to undertake such abstinence without appropriate clerical supervision on the grounds that it might provoke pride or devilish visions; later in the century, Savonarola preached in a similar vein that nuns' excessive fasting was a vice. Food also acted as a lightning rod for internal frictions surrounding financial management. Because food was an integral part of traditional monastic hospitality, resources wasted on "unnecessary" banquets provoked quarrels. As the

Florentine bishop discovered during his rounds in 1384, the nuns of S. Ambrogio were bitterly at odds with their abbess Francesca Guadagni, in part because she regularly offered "large lunches and dinners" to the two convent chaplains beyond what protocol required, thereby dissipating convent patrimony.[72]

Convents also paid a range of salaries, which comprised the second largest expense (21 percent) in S. Felicita's budget. Although all urban religious institutions used auxiliary personnel, the extent to which they relied on such staff was determined by whether the community was male or female. Unlike monks, who handled religious duties themselves, convents depended on salaried male clerics for cult life; they also had to hire laymen to conduct worldly business.[73] The requirements imposed by reclusion meant that convents supported larger auxiliary staffs than monasteries, which formed part of their household for tax purposes. Not surprisingly, disparities in wealth between Florentine convents were reflected in staff size. S. Felicita supported a salaried retinue of eighteen men: six chaplains, three clerks, and a preacher, who staffed the convent and church year round; a barber, who shaved and tonsured these clerics; three factors, who helped manage convent property, along with a rent collector, greengrocer, doctor, and lawyer. The highest salary (15 florins) went to the preacher selected annually by the nuns, who usually rotated among different mendicant orders. Each chaplain earned 10 florins annually, but he often supplemented his income by performing additional masses or ceremonies. Other annual salaries ranged from 4 to 12 florins. By contrast, the working nuns of S. Luca employed only one layman to conduct business for them. Since they were unable to support a regular chaplain, they borrowed a priest from a neighboring hospital when occasion warranted.[74] Salaries paid to auxiliary staff also figured as the second largest expense at early modern Neapolitan convents, although their support teams were necessarily larger given their greater populations.

Clothing and other personal maintenance formed the next major group of expenses at S. Felicita (17 percent). In the proportion it budgeted for clothing, S. Felicita was representative of other convents, but it organized expenses somewhat differently. Each of the seventeen nuns received an annual prebend of 5 florins. Prebends were an older medieval way of bundling corporate revenues, in which nuns contributed to a common fund from which each member of the chapter then drew equal shares. S. Pier Maggiore also distributed prebends of roughly 2 florins. The papacy discouraged this practice, even though prebends assured a common economic baseline among members of the community.[75] Like private maintenance allowances, these stipends helped nuns replenish or upgrade their stock of personal belongings. Although every nun brought various "extras" to the convent as part of her monastic trousseau — cloth for tunics and mantles, beds and bedding, towels and handkerchiefs, veils, nightcaps, socks, clogs, undershirts, aprons, candles, books — these items had to be replaced periodically.[76] Nuns frequently purchased whatever serviceable items remained when a member of the community died, creating a transgenerational circulation of goods within the house. This practice continued with far greater elaboration in the early modern period, partly because monastic trousseaux themselves grew in size and value as the culture of consumption took hold. At the height of female monasticism in late sixteenth- and seventeenth-century Italy, full inventories of nuns' belongings were taken at death for both administrative and commemorative purposes; the subsequent dispersal of goods was codified within each house and officially supervised by the abbess and other officers.[77] This important subject for understanding both the material culture and social relations of Renaissance convents awaits fuller study.

At S. Felicita, nuns' prebends also supported medical care, which tax reports did not break out as a separate category. Florentine convents organized the economic relationships around health issues in various ways. As noted earlier, nuns in Dominican communities paid for their own medicines. Girls entering religious life with physical or mental disabilities always required additional stipends over and above their dowries to underwrite their special needs. Aging nuns in declining health also benefited from supplementary income, which family members might provide in the form of *monte* credits. Around 1430, for example, the father and uncle of Suor Francesca Bartoli at S. Marta directed the interest payments on two small *monte* accounts to her; "this money was left to her because she is infirm, so that she can be looked after." Similarly, Suor Taddea Ridolfi, a forty-year-old nun in S. Niccolò Maggiore who was "ill and permanently blind in one eye" and had "difficulty seeing with the other," had a *monte* annuity that supported her medical needs.[78] More commonly, medical expenses came out of the communal treasury. Convent tax reports frequently appended pleas lamenting the burdens of illness and the resulting budgetary strain, since infirm nuns not only required expensive care but also were less productive. In 1438 the nuns of S. Pier Maggiore owed 100 florins — the equivalent of one monastic dowry — to their apothecary, the humanist and local parishioner Matteo Palmieri, for various syrups, ointments, and other medical supplies.[79] Convents practicing rigorous asceticism or situated at an unhealthy site incurred especially heavy medical expenses.

Other significant costs included maintenance and repair work on the convent and its properties. This category probably showed the greatest variability among women's religious houses. Nuns' social reputations as well as their financial interests were at stake in maintaining the structural integrity of convent properties. Victoria Primhak has argued that Venetian convents showed particular sensitivity to the condition of buildings adjoining or overlooking their grounds, since their appearance reflected on nuns' status. In 1472, the affluent Venetian nuns of S. Lorenzo explained to tax officials that on account of late rent payments and high maintenance costs, their actual annual income was less than the sum reported. Since "a good part" of their rental properties were "old and in very bad condition," their upkeep cost the nuns 10 percent a year, "which they discount from the rent of the said buildings." Although "one could say in theory" that income was 2,500 ducats, the nuns argued that "in reality it is not [even] 2,000."[80]

Because it was so costly, structural work on convent buildings and rental properties was often deferred until a chapter could earn, save, or borrow enough money. By 1438, the Poor Clares of S. Matteo in Arcetri had no choice but to proceed with expensive reconstruction on their church and refectory, the latter of which had "collapsed" and wouldn't be "habitable without making these repairs." The nuns of S. Maria di Candeli complained that their residential properties cost more to maintain than they earned and further grumbled that, although tenants did not pay on time, they were too poor to make litigation worthwhile. At S. Giusto, the nuns judged that their buildings "were in ruins and for the most part propped up, ready to fall down," yet renovating them would cost more than 200 florins, well beyond their means.[81] Neglect of rental properties or inability to repair dilapidated houses sometimes made them uninhabitable, thereby reducing income. Even wealthy S. Pier Maggiore could not fully maintain its patrimony. Seven of its thirty-four residential properties went unrented in 1438 because they were "pitiful, sad, and falling apart." These laments were commonplace and must be assessed critically, as convents in both Florence and Venice looked for ways to lighten tax assessments. Still, these comments accurately captured the expensive nature of structural work. In 1438, S. Pier Maggiore was indebted for 141 florins, or 42 percent of its debt load, to various workmen who had recently repaired the site as well as to kin and patrons who helped finance construction.[82]

The last major item in S. Felicita's 1438 budget supported religious feasts and liturgical ceremonies. There were few margins in this category, since bequests were heavily encumbered by donors, who often spelled out their wishes in painstaking detail. Obligations at S. Pier Maggiore were probably even heavier than at S. Felicita: it administered forty-four mass cycles annually, at an estimated cost of 3 florins each.[83] A substantial number of legacies made nuns' annuities dependent on the cult of the dead. When revenues consistently fell short of expenses, either because of declining rents or default, convent chapters used their discretion to scale back liturgical programs either by substituting low masses for sung ones, reducing the number of candles or reusing them, or employing fewer priests. Virtually all convents bemoaned the fact that they gleaned little profit from bequests, even though praying for the dead represented a fundamental source of nuns' power. Seventeenth-century Neapolitan convents likewise allocated relatively meager funds to church ceremonies. These modest costs might seem to vary sharply from 1564 Venetian convent tax reports, where church functions topped the expense list, but this discrepancy disappears when priests' salaries are shifted to a more appropriate category.[84]

State and clerical taxes, which often took a huge bite out of convent budgets, only appeared in Florentine tax reports if they created a specific debt. Like other religious institutions, convents were caught up in larger jurisdictional battles between church and state sparked by or resulting in taxation. Communal levies on ecclesiastical institutions in the late Trecento were especially onerous. S. Felicita paid over half its annual income to communal taxes in the few short months between August 1390 and April 1391, then met a similar exaction later that decade.[85] Despite maintaining an aggressive foreign policy, the commune lightened the tax burden on ecclesiastical institutions in the early Quattrocento in response to influential convent "friends" and direct papal intervention on behalf of certain clients. The 35,000 florin communal impost levied on religious institutions in 1426 was soon reduced by 10,000 florins as a result of diplomatic mediation.[86] S. Pier Maggiore used its political connections to win exemption from future state imposts on clergy after 1420, although this immunity only stuck for the short term; in 1440 the convent was hit with a tax payment of 64 florins.[87] Just as communal taxes were lightening, however, papal assessments began increasing. In his desperate search for revenues to rebuild the papacy, Martin V levied a crushing tax of 80,000 florins on Florentine ecclesiastical institutions. S. Pier Maggiore and S. Felicita jointly sought the advice of the noted canon lawyer Lorenzo Ridolfi, one of the regime's leading citizens, who advised them not to pay their assigned share.[88] Fortunately, Martin's successor, Eugenius, showed his gratitude to his Florentine hosts by modifying taxes and liberally dispensing tax concessions to convents.

To summarize, Florentine convents in the early Quattrocento rested on mixed economic foundations that interwove corporate and personal revenues in varying ways. High-end convents relied primarily on rents, whereas the middle tiers made a more competitive use of liquid investments. Hidden from view is the combination of work and alms supporting convents at the bottom rungs. Nuns' annuities represented an internal, privatized property regime that coexisted in various forms with a collective patrimony. These additional resources helped nuns and nunneries buffer shortfalls, meet unexpected crises, and achieve higher living standards — not without exacting a toll of their own on the small politics of everyday life.

The Medici and the *Monte*

The 1450s opened a new chapter in the fiscal relations binding convents and the state, with the *monte* acting as the key nexus. During the financial crisis of the late 1420s and 1430s, lay donors long on *monte* credits and short on cash shed these funds to endow chapels, altars, commemorative programs, religious feasts, and nuns' annuities. Many convents that held no *monte* credits in 1427 became first-time stakeholders over the next decade. By 1438, S. Pier Maggiore derived 12 percent of its income from the *monte*; additional credits flowed in over the next decade.[89] At S. Felicita, *monte* holdings nominally grew by 30 percent between 1438 and 1445, as parishioners used credits to finance masses for their family dead or to subsidize nuns' annuities. Abbess Brigida Guicciardini inherited a *monte* subsidy from her grandmother; Suor Bartolomea Ridolfi got a similar one from her father, the noted statesman Lorenzo, which the commune paid in timely fashion.[90] Funding annuities with liquid capital rather than property made good economic sense from a familial standpoint. Credits lost one-third of their value between 1425 and 1442, yet kin were still able to turn these declining investments to familial advantage. Moreover, since no immoveable wealth was alienated, this practice favored the retention of family patrimonies. By 1600, it was standard Florentine practice to underwrite annuities using various instruments of credit, granting nuns only the interest with no access to the capital.[91] Although convent holdings still paled in comparison to the vast credits held by rich citizens, they were proportional to the smaller scale on which convent budgets operated. Convent beneficiaries used this new income in various ways. The nuns of S. Niccolò Maggiore spent their first fruits "to decorate their church"; the Poor Clares of S. Matteo supported a madwoman entrusted to their care with credits yielding 25 florins annually; a nun from S. Lucia used interest from a newly acquired account to move to another convent across town.[92]

Some convents proactively grew their *monte* accounts in these decades. The convent syndic of S. Jacopo—a friar with a large appetite for business—aggressively rolled over small bequests, cash gifts, and other assets into *monte* credits, which increased by 36 percent between 1431 and 1437. Credits could be bought on the open market for 20–25 percent of par in these years, making them a good choice for nuns seeking reliable annuities that could be sold, exchanged, or held jointly. The syndic carefully distinguished interest owed to individual nuns, detailed any attached provisions, and assured the transfer of annuities between generations of religious women. His successor continued this investment strategy into the 1440s.[93] Similarly, the nuns of S. Apollonia sustained an active trade in the local credit market in the 1430s and 1440s, appointing procurators to sell *monte* credits or collect complicated interest payments. Suor Maria Macianghini tapped a friar from S. Spirito to broker the sale of her credits in 1434; the following year, the chapter empowered the abbess's brother, Manno Donati, to collect interest from credits belonging to two recently deceased nuns. As a result of his success in that tangled venture, the nuns gave him free rein several years later to broker corporately owned *monte* credits in any amount. In the early 1440s, the chapter and various nuns appointed one of their *converse* to collect interest payments, sell credits on the open market, and transfer credits formerly held by a deceased nun to a new member of the community.[94] In all of these transactions, the nuns—many of them daughters and sisters of merchant-bankers—displayed a high degree of understanding about how local credit markets worked.

Acquiring a greater stake in the public debt by 1450 had mixed economic consequences for nuns and nunneries. On the plus side, the Florentine commune generally kept its fiduciary promises to nun-creditors, who gained both personal income and prospective legacies to be passed along like heirlooms. *Monte* credits also diversified corporate investments and were taxed at a lesser rate than property assets in 1427 and 1438. Moreover, these investments proved convenient when convents wanted to pay communal imposts, allowing them to move one set of credits to another account.[95] Yet the declining value of credits by midcentury weakened convent portfolios and the buying power of personal annuities. Nuns still had to comply with the details of commemorative bequests that called for hiring priests, having masses said, and buying wax, even though the credits funding these programs effectively yielded only about 2.3 percent interest. The re-sulting financial squeeze frequently forced religious women to compromise on their obligations, potentially jeopardizing the entire spiritual economy. Most importantly, *monte* investments irrevocably tied convent finances to the fiscal structures of the Florentine state. After 1441, Florentines could only open ac-counts in the dowry fund using *monte* credits, which directly linked the payment of both monastic and secular dowries to the public debt. Other legislation inter-wove aspects of civic and convent finance. Beginning in 1447, fines for sodomy convictions were earmarked to support the convent housing repentant pros-titutes, thereby transforming notorious vices into civic virtues.[96]

Growing convent entanglement in the operations of public finance proved decisive in the 1450s, when the city experienced a wide-ranging fiscal crisis. Throughout this decade, the government increasingly used the *monte* to shore up communal finances. Civic officials raided its coffers to cover shortfalls in a new war against Alfonso of Aragon (1452–54) and to safeguard the viability of the dowry fund. In 1453–57, *monte* values dipped to a record low — 14 percent of par — a decline recognized in the 1458 *catasto*, which valued credits at 20 percent instead of 50 percent.[97] Facing a stark liquidity crisis, the *monte* began withhold-ing interest payments on an ad hoc basis, paying only one-third of interest in 1457–59. Sometimes it issued additional credits instead of cash. These fitful moves threw the *monte* into grave "disorder," as Florentines complained loudly. Attempting to remedy the situation over the longer term, *monte* officials greatly expanded their sphere of influence by assuming supervision over all fiscal mat-ters, ranging from the collection of import duties to the licensing of Jewish pawn-brokers. An appointed chancellor coordinated the work of the various scribes, notaries, clerks, cashiers, and errand boys employed by the *monte*'s many of-fices. By the late 1470s, the *monte* reigned supreme over all elements of public finance.[98]

This fiscal crisis opened a window of opportunity for the commune to extend its oversight of convents and to consolidate state power at the expense of the church. Capitalizing on the civic nature of Florentine convents as institutions serving the city both spiritually and economically remained an unmet challenge for the commune. Nuns' spiritual power had not been automatically harnessed to civic goals but had to be integrated into the workings and ideology of the Floren-tine state. The 1450s proved pivotal in meeting this challenge. By drawing con-vents into formal relations of dependence, the city began to exercise an effective grip on religious women, finalizing a long, strategic process of political consolidation. The sacralization of the Renaissance city was the result not only of ritual processes but also of practical state-building activities that redefined relations between convents and the polity.

In January 1452, at the outset of this crisis, *monte* officials were authorized to withhold interest payments to religious institutions and personnel and to explore other avenues for payment.[99] Most often, they diverted interest payments to convent salt taxes or other salt provisions, enmeshing nuns and nunneries in complex state accounting schemes. Salt was an essential commodity used to preserve foodstuffs; long-standing communal policies, enforced unevenly, mandated that each household and institution purchase a certain quantity based on head count. The attached salt taxes provided a reliable source of communal income that buffered other fluctuations, especially after the gabelle was reinstated in 1440. *Monte* interest was generally applied against convent salt taxes, although sometimes convents were paid in kind.[100] Compensation was trickier for individual nun-creditors, since they did not pay indirect taxes on commodities and their finances were conjoined with other persons and groups. Owing to the many variables in ownership, it was difficult to standardize solutions. The *monte* experimented with different payment methods, some of which quickly proved untenable. In the mid-1460s, the abbess of S. Ambrogio and her sister, a nun at S. Apollonia, were compensated on their joint *monte* account with vast quantities of salt well beyond their needs. Faced with a huge surplus of this foodstuff and no cash, these two women sold the salt that "they got from the *monte* officials" to the nuns of S. Ambrogio for collective use.[101] Similarly, two nuns in S. Domenico nel Maglio, who normally shared the proceeds from a 200-florin *monte* investment, were compensated with other credits that could only be used to purchase salt. Since many nuns in S. Domenico had *monte* annuities, the house amassed a backlog of salt credits worth almost 900 florins by 1494. When these nuns found themselves with an unusable surplus and limited cash, they starting selling their salt credits to private investors on a secondary credit market.[102] Although Florentine religious women were no strangers to business innovations, public policies paradoxically immersed them more deeply in worldly affairs after 1450.

These changes in fiscal policy intersected with other developments reshaping the Florentine political landscape. The growth of Medici power after 1434 needs no rehearsal here, but the family's role in ecclesiastical affairs warrants a closer look. Natalie Tomas has shown how Medici patronage of religious institutions was part of a general strategy to shore up familial support in Florence and surrounding territories. Under Medici influence, the commune began extending charity in the form of grain and salt subsidies, cash payments, and tax exemptions to unprecedented numbers of convents. Especially favored were houses that were poor, pious, and pro-Medici. Similar favors were extended to convents outside Florence that fell within the orbit of Medici patronage, particularly institutional clients in Pisa.[103] In the early Quattrocento, the commune had granted subventions to numerous male-run institutions — churches, monasteries and hospitals — that both identified the kinds of religious foundations the commune favored and allowed it to exercise fiscal control over them. However, convents remained on the periphery of this charmed circle, garnering only 39 percent of the financial support to religious institutions codified in the 1415 communal statutes.[104] Corporate groups like the Parte Guelfa and various guilds sometimes gave nuns alms to mark honorific occasions or to launch a promising new community, but these small donations offered "for the love of God" were both episodic and undifferentiated from other charity. By contrast, tax concessions and official exemptions offered a "singular grace," as the nuns of S. Luca called them — a centralized charity that only the state could give.[105]

By 1470, the government had begun exempting dozens of convents in the city and suburbs from major gabelles on salt, wine, gate tolls, and contracts, both as a means of showing civic support for these institutions and exercising fiscal authority over them. Individual convents still had to petition for these favors, outlining their rationale for seeking charity and listing the number of nuns who would be assisted. This detailed information enabled both the *signoria* and the Medici to track internal convent dynamics across Florentine territory, which probably informed other regulatory decisions. By 1480, charitable measures intersected with *monte* offsets to form a coherent fiscal policy that drew convents into a broad network of fiscally dependent civic institutions operating under the umbrella of Medici patronage.

The first convent to receive sustained civic charity was Le Murate — a Medici client and the city's fastest growing convent that had been headed by the savvy abbess Scholastica Rondinelli since 1439. F. W. Kent has shown how this religious woman used her remarkable powers of persuasion with various city fathers, including the young, impressionable Lorenzo de' Medici, to secure the return of her exiled kinsmen and obtain favors for her community.[106] She enjoyed the good graces of wealthy bankers like Giovanni Benci as well as Medici benefactors like Cosimo, his sons Piero and Giovanni, and Giovanni's wife Ginevra Alessandri, all of whom made a habit of cultivating clients within the Florentine church.[107] To this list of achievements must be added her business acumen in developing the silk workshops that gave backbone to her political requests. In 1442, Abbess Scholastica began issuing a stream of petitions to the *signoria* for assistance. Describing her nuns as "little paupers," she requested and received a small annual subvention (30 lire) in perpetuity to pay communal gabelles. Several years later (1450), she petitioned again, boldly asking that this subsidy be increased fivefold.[108] These grants were essentially paper transactions that moved funds from one communal account to another under the auspices of the *monte*. Soon after, however, Le Murate began receiving real gifts. In 1458, the commune granted her request for an annual gift of 10 *staia* of salt (720 pounds), which she explained was necessary because the convent had expanded from 84 nuns in 1449 to 124 nuns a decade later. In subsequent petitions — all successful — the abbess cited continued growth (to 151 nuns by 1465) along with rigorous asceticism, prayerfulness, reliance on alms and manual labor as the principal reasons why the convent was seeking charity.[109] These favors were not insignificant gestures, since gabelles reached new heights in the last quarter of the Quattrocento. In 1479 Le Murate estimated that it spent 155 florins annually on gabelles alone.[110]

To advance her cause, Scholastica supplemented petitions to the *signoria* with personal letters to Lorenzo and other Medici family members. Letters were "the lifeblood of Renaissance patronage," as Vincent Ilardi has called them, and convents across the Florentine dominion were not shy about making their needs known to the city's ruling family through correspondence.[111] Lorenzo's grandfather Cosimo had received many dozens of letters from nuns across Italy asking for favors or assistance, ranging from small gifts and tax reductions to substantial building expenses. "Once again we put ourselves forward . . . to have recourse to your charity," wrote the Florentine prioress of S. Francesco to Cosimo, "not for living costs or for our own sake, because we are content with only what is necessary, but to rebuild the house of S. Francesco which is very small and in bad condition. We don't see another way to be able to live, even with difficulty, without rebuilding. The place where we sleep is so small that we can't put in enough beds for everyone."[112] As patronage became one of the dominant social processes in Laurentian Florence, the number of convents drawn into clientage relations with the Medici proliferated. Especially numerous were requests asking the Medici to intervene with tax officials, where their subtle suasion was felt most keenly.

Coupling formal petitions to the *signoria* with informal letters to the Medici became a common strategy by which convents secured civic support in the second half of the Quattrocento. The letters flowing from Scholastica to Lorenzo provide a good case in point. As Lorenzo grew to manhood, the abbess's letters to him commingled maternal intimacy with a clear recognition of power differentials. She chided him gently, offered spiritual advice, and pleaded her case with economy and deference; she also showed a fine-tuned understanding of how Florentine politics worked.[113] One outgrowth of this relationship was that Lorenzo developed a particular affection for Le Murate, which he aided out of his own pocket. Besides making regular gifts of grain, wine, and oil, he supplied special Easter meals and reportedly sent marzipan and other confections to sick nuns.[114] Although it is difficult to assign a precise economic value to these gifts, they probably remained within modest bounds, since Lorenzo preferred not to call public attention to his patronage at the convent. These personal gifts ceased after his death (1492), but Lorenzo left a lasting legacy in institutionalized civic patronage of the Murate achieved through his influence over aspects of public finance. By the time Scholastica died in 1475, the convent was receiving three forms of civic charity concurrently, all administered through the *monte*: gifts of cash, gifts in kind, and tax concessions.

In the 1470s, other convents secured civic and Medici patronage by deploying similar rhetorical strategies to those used so successfully by Scholastica Rondinelli. In petitions and letters, Florentine nuns highlighted the rapid growth of their communities, their poverty and piety, and above all their willingness to trade prayers for favors. Nuns' intercessory prayers were the crux of their social and spiritual power, and they leveraged this point to full advantage in soliciting patronage. Religious women might request anything from sufficient yardage for a single monastic tunic to extensive construction funds, but one of their most frequent targets was tax relief. Writing to Lorenzo in 1479 to obtain help with salt taxes, the abbess of S. Chiara assured him that, if her request were granted, she would be "forever most obligated to make and have made special prayers daily for the preservation of your well-being."[115] Local nuns supplicated not only Lorenzo but also the Medici women—Contessina de' Bardi, Lucrezia Tornabuoni, Clarice Orsini, Maddalena Cibo and later Alfonsina Orsini, Lucrezia Salviati, Maria Salviati—to obtain favors outright or to enlist their influence in a kind of "matronage" system. The prioress of S. Domenico in Pisa was only one of many convent leaders who implored Lucrezia to intercede with her son Lorenzo on behalf of her convent. Noting that their salt duties had been reduced in the past through Medici favor, the prioress assured Lucrezia that "we are most obligated to pray God for the souls of the Medici dead and thus we do. Likewise, we pray for your well-being and for the well-being of your magnificent sons that they may always have happiness and good health."[116] Dozens of nuns' letters traded on this spiritual economy in which nuns positioned themselves as needy, deserving clients gratefully offering prayers on behalf of generous patrons.

Although nuns obviously knew the rhetoric of supplication well, there was a grain of truth in their claims of poverty. As noted earlier, three out of four Florentine nuns lived at or below the official poverty threshold in 1427, with various enhancements lifting their standard of living. Although scholars disagree about whether the economy of Laurentian Florence remained vibrant or not, convents showed several signs of increasing distress in the 1470s and 1480s.[117] Paradoxically, by standard measures, convents were wealthier institutions in the late Quattrocento than they were a century earlier. They profited from greater human capital in the growing population of nuns; their expanding physical complexes dominated the cityscape; and the material contents of convent churches, chapels, refectories, libraries, and monastic cells gave institutions tremendous financial heft when considered in the aggregate. Yet these corporate assets did not necessarily translate into higher income levels or elevated living standards. Many convents felt the pinch of expanding numbers, insufficient revenues, renewed taxation, and short-term disruptions induced by war, inflation, and plague. Anthony Molho has calculated that Florentine property values declined by 3.1 percent between 1427 and 1480; when adjusted for inflation and for the greater gap between the relative value of the florin and lira, the drop would likely be even more significant. Convent rents based on long-term leases declined in real value over the fifteenth century due to currency depreciation, although the precise impact on convent income is unknown.[118] Lorenzo de' Medici's fight with Sixtus IV in the late 1470s did little to improve the general economic climate; in fact, it prompted yet another tax levy on local religious institutions to finance war against the papacy.

What pushed many convents into serious financial trouble was the disruption of local business arrangements by plague and warfare in the summer and fall of 1478. Although this conjunction probably represented a surface disturbance in the long-term economic cycle of the fifteenth century, it significantly impacted convent budgets. The plight reflected in the 1478 *catasto* was no less real for being short term. Because this tax survey assessed institutional wealth differently from earlier ones, its primary value lies in the powerful narratives attached to returns, which included an exceptional number of pleas to reduce taxes. S. Jacopo, one of the ten wealthiest convents in 1427, offers one example of an established house that found itself in trouble a half century later. The nuns were deeply indebted to local merchants, bore taxes supporting the Pisan Studio and the Misericordia, and incurred "many small expenses that would take too long to tell." The recent outbreak of plague pushed them over the edge. Since they relied on silk work to make ends meet, the loss of commercial revenue hit their treasury hard. "We plead for your charity, lord officials . . . because here we are abandoned by everyone due to war and plague. We can't earn anything more because the shops don't want to send us anything on account of the plague, which lies right outside our door. It wouldn't be so hard to pay if we could earn something. This will force us to go out begging in search of alms." This desperate plea concluded on the plaintive note: "Do us the least harm that you can."[119] The nuns of S. Niccolò de' Frieri faced a more serious crisis. They suffered from chronic health problems, reportedly due to poor air circulation at their site under the city gates. "Half the nuns are sick continuously," their report maintained. "Even the physician wants to draw blood from them regularly every year." In October 1478, plague struck the house. Several inhabitants died; the nuns "were abandoned by friends and kinsmen" and lived in such an impoverished state that "God should guard every person from such a fate." Because of their "small income for sustenance, the many debts they have, and their bad fortune," the nuns begged tax officials to retain their exempt status. In fact, the inventory of convent holdings listed few properties, although the convent had acquired 2,000 florins in *monte* credits by this time; in 1427, it had none. The nuns responded to these dire straits by enlisting new recruits; "with the monies gained," they tried "to refurbish themselves as best they c[ould]." Although this strategy solved immediate cashflow problems, within a generation it merely diluted per capita income. To gain solvency over a longer term, the nuns developed a vernacular school and took in boarders.[120] Other convents sold some of their assets to meet immediate needs, which created a vicious cycle by diminishing endowments.

Although the economic impact of the troubles dogging convents in the 1470s cannot be established precisely, these tales of woe certainly helped enlarge the circle of civic charity over the next decade. The first big wave of civic support came in the 1480s, when the government granted tax exemptions or cash subsidies to a wide range of convents irrespective of order. Another attempt to reform the *monte* in 1481–82 resulted in a more consistent application of *monte* interest to various import duties. These two tactics—applying *monte* payments to gabelle accounts and extending civic charity—intersected in complex ways tailored to each convent's needs and circumstances. The commune supported tertiary communities (Annalena, S. Orsola, S. Giorgio); poor or declining Benedictine houses

(Le Murate, S. Niccolò Maggiore, S. Agata, S. Maria a S. Miniato, S. Anna); middling Augustinian convents (S. Maria di Candeli, Lapo, the Chiarito); mendicant affiliates (S. Chiara, S. Maria a Monticelli, Montedomini; S. Lucia, S. Domenico nel Maglio, S. Jacopo); and assorted others (S. Brigida del Paradiso, S. Giovanni Laterano).[121] Each convent negotiated a different arrangement depending on the number of "mouths" and *monte* credits involved. But even convents with significant assets won concessions as the century waned. In September 1492, S. Apollonia received its first free ten-year salt subsidy. By February 1495, the commune had more than doubled its grant, "there now being seventy or more mouths" to feed. This gift continued until Duke Cosimo's massive reorganization of convent administration in 1545.[122] However individualized the outcome, the steady stream of convent petitions begging for subsidies or tax concessions permitted officials to monitor the economic condition of the city's religious women and control their fiscal status. These grants reversed civic policy of a century earlier: instead of treating convents as a source of fiscal exploitation, the commune subsidized them heavily.

By 1510, virtually every convent in the city and dominion was receiving some form of public assistance. Convent petitions rolled in year after year, creating an ongoing cycle of civic support. Among the last to solicit aid was S. Monaca, one of seventeen convents that petitioned successfully in 1508 either for tax relief or gifts in cash or kind. Using familiar tropes, the nuns of S. Monaca played up their expanding numbers and deepening poverty. "Since they are about fifty or more in number, are very poor, and live on alms, they would like to have some public subsidy for the tax account they pay at the gates of our city, as has been conceded to many other convents."[123] By contrast, only one monastery (S. Spirito) won a similar subsidy that year. Another wave of tax concessions passed in 1515 favored fifteen major convents housing close to fifteen hundred nuns, more than half the city's religious women.[124]

Medici patronage continued to play an important role in the distribution of tax favors after the family's restoration to power in 1512. Writing to Goro Gheri, secretary to Lorenzo, the Duke of Urbino, the abbess of the Paradiso asked him to intervene with civic officials on their behalf. "We get sixteen *staia* of salt every year from the Florentine commune by reason of 2,233 florins [invested] in the *monte*," the abbess explained in 1519. "Because our numbers have increased by about thirty people . . . we were compelled to use more of the said salt and are now in debt. We understand that the official in charge doesn't want us to incur further debts, since we already had eight *staia* in advance. But we need it," she concluded emphatically.[125] Alfonsina Orsini Medici — a formidable patron in her own right — received numerous requests from nuns asking for tax exemptions, which she forwarded to her son Lorenzo with various recommendations.[126]

Nuns reciprocated these gifts and favors with prayers made on behalf of the city and its governors, whether Medicean or republican. The Observant Dominican nuns of S. Pier Martire had stressed the civic value of their prayers early on when filing their 1478 tax return: "In this convent, prayers are offered for the good state of this city; which prayers, coming as they do from persons of such great piety, are worth more than two thousand horses." Similarly, the diarist Benedetto Dei reminded fellow citizens of the enormous spiritual work nuns undertook on their behalf: "They spend day and night praying for the most worthy *signoria* of Florence. Open your eyes and appreciate that!"[127] Exchanging civic gifts for spiritual intercession, which became fairly commonplace in French cities around 1500, represented an important intersection between the late medieval spiritual economy and urban polities in the process of consolidating political power.[128]

Yet the extension of civic patronage must also be gauged against the more particular backdrop of political turmoil that wracked Florence and the Italian peninsula after the French invasion of 1494. Political instability highlighted nuns' invaluable role in the desperate search for safety and salvation. In the aftermath of invasion, the republican *signoria* sent "copious alms" to the city's most Observant nuns living in Le Murate, S. Orsola, S. Chiara, and S. Giorgio "for the remedy of the Florentine citizenry and populace and to placate the wrath of God."[129] Although political factionalism had permeated convents — some houses, like S. Apollonia and S. Verdiana, were vigorously pro-Medici, while others were notorious Savonarolan hotbeds — all of them continued to receive state support regardless of political allegiance.[130] The Pisan house of S. Domenico was one of the few convents punished by the withdrawal of tax exemptions after the Medici ouster, probably as a way to discipline the periphery of the Florentine state.[131] After Savonarola's execution in 1498, convents adhering to his movement did not find their tax privileges withdrawn, despite the hostile political climate. In fact, the brand-new Savonarolan foundation of S. Caterina da Siena successfully petitioned for gabelle exemptions in 1505, and the nuns easily won enlargement and extension of these privileges three years later as their numbers multiplied. Similarly, S. Jacopo suffered no reduction or withdrawal of charitable assistance during various regime changes.[132] Convents expressing *Piagnone* allegiances faced other kinds of challenges as civic and church officials tried to eradicate the preacher's memory, and the movement itself was riven by internal strife in the early sixteenth century. But the continued extension of public funds to convents irrespective of political ties underscores the extent to which nuns were perceived as belonging to the city writ large.

Financial arrangements instituted in these decades conditioned the operation of convent budgets well into the early modern period. We can trace this long-term trajectory at S. Jacopo, one of many houses that gained civic support in the form of charity and *monte* offsets. By 1485, the sixty "pauper" nuns "living as they can" were already receiving annual gifts of salt. That year, the nuns petitioned successfully for a ten-year exemption on the salt gabelle. This grant was renewed decennially in 1489, 1499, and 1509, the value of the salt being charged against their *monte* interest. Running concurrently was a ten-year exemption from the gate gabelle on convent provisions, which was reissued in 1501 and 1511.[133] House records noted that S. Chiara, S. Maria di Candeli, and "many other convents and pious establishments" made similar arrangements with *monte* officials. In return, the nuns were obliged "to pray to God continuously, both in common and private prayer, for the sublime Florentine republic and for the citizens who supported them and from whom they received so many and such great benefits."[134] In 1545, shortly after Cosimo I took the helm, S. Jacopo rationalized its arrangements with the *monte*. The nuns charged their salt consumption and gate tolls against *monte* credits, remained exempt from the salt gabelle, and received an annual cash subsidy of about 60 scudi to pay other gabelles. However, these arrangements, which permitted more rational financial planning, were only valid for five years at a time. The nuns had to petition Cosimo and his successors for renewal at regular five-year intervals, ensuring continued ducal oversight. As late as the 1770s, S. Jacopo was still receiving tax offsets attached to *monte* credits it had acquired three and a half centuries earlier. In return for these concessions, the nuns shifted the focus of their prayers to the grand dukes as peacemakers and rulers of the city.[135]

Through the instruments of public finance and the extension of civic charity, the Florentine commune redrew political relations between convents and the state. Public subsidies and *monte* transfers were not simply a way to support financial needs; they also enabled republican and Medicean regimes first to identify and then regulate convents as civic institutions. In turn, these repositories of sacred virgins helped sacralize the state, much like their Venetian counterparts.[136] The mid-fifteenth century marked a decisive turning point in church-state relations when this ecclesiastical sector, so crucial to political consolidation, was finally tamed. Following the *monte* reforms of the 1450s, convents were entangled in a vast civic bookkeeping operation and further woven into the political fabric through Medici patronage. By the twilight years of the Florentine republic, these religious institutions had been irrevocably impressed into spiritual service to the state, transforming brides of Christ into daughters of the city.

CHAPTER FOUR

Invisible Hands

Renaissance Nuns at Work

One of the primary revenue streams supporting the mixed Renaissance convent economy was paid labor. Although scholars have long noted nuns' engagement with economic activities such as handiwork, teaching, and property management, we lack a clear understanding of the prevalence and significance of work to female religious communities across medieval and early modern Europe.[1] Several factors account for this elusive picture, especially in urban Italy. First, our overall grasp of women's work remains impressionistic, in part because tax returns neither captured earnings nor recorded occupations consistently. More crucial is the fact that Italian guild sources, such as statutes, matriculation lists, and electoral scrutinies, mask the nature and extent of women's contribution to the local economy. The weak female presence in these otherwise bountiful records stems primarily from the early political development of Italian city-states. As communes took shape in the twelfth and thirteenth centuries, guild membership became an essential requirement for political participation. Identifying female workers as subordinate guild members, or omitting them altogether, helped restrict their role in formal political affairs.[2] This link between economic and political marginalization was especially strong in Florence, whose structure as

a guild republic took root in the 1280s. Not surprisingly, the two female occupations in Renaissance Florence that have been studied most extensively —
domestic service and prostitution — fell outside the realm of guild regulation.[3]
Despite this source bias, recent studies have shown that fifteenth-century Florentine women were distributed throughout the workforce rather than being
clustered in low-wage jobs as previously thought.[4]

The second obstacle to understanding the scope and significance of nuns'
work has been the reluctance to take nunneries seriously as sites of commercial
production. Traditionally, convents have been viewed as spiritual entities whose
main economic role was linked to the marriage market, not the urban marketplace. Whatever nuns accomplished when not engrossed in prayer has been
considered either as mere pastimes occupying intervals between spiritual offices
or as small-scale ventures exerting little impact on broad economic trends like
the development of early modern capitalism. Recently, feminist scholars have
pointed to a more robust economic role for nuns as property managers and
influence brokers in the courtly societies of early modern Europe.[5] Although
we still know relatively little about the multifaceted relationship between nuns
and work, especially in the vibrant economic sectors that distinguished Renaissance Italy, previous conceptions of nuns as primarily consumers producing little
for the market cannot be sustained.[6] Throughout the Quattrocento, religious
women had significant work lives that intersected with their spiritual and social ones.

This chapter offers new angles of vision on the Renaissance convent as an
economic institution oriented toward market production, focusing on the contributions that nuns' work made to convent finance and the urban economy. Based
on extensive business records kept by nuns and their supervisors, I argue that
work formed both a crucial source of revenue and a key element in convent
economic policies. In light of the generally poor endowments documented in
chapter 3, work was a necessity of everyday life for most Florentine nuns. Since
convents lacked sufficient income from other sources to provide an adequate
living, religious women had to supplement their income through paid labor. As
one abbess claimed in her 1427 tax report, "We use our arms to sustain our
lives."[7] Florentine religious women were quite resourceful in the ways they utilized their own labor, both in diversifying activities in response to changing
market conditions and in training successors to continue various craft traditions.
By earning money for "the many tasks performed by their own hands," nuns
enhanced their quality of life, enabled overdue building repairs to be made, and

embarked on new decorative schemes.[8] Their participation in the world of work was facilitated by the fact that the principal tasks they undertook between 1350 and 1550—textile activities, book production, education—did not require large capital investments. Instead, these activities depended primarily on literate and manual skills, religious and technical knowledge, and significant human capital, which convents possessed in ever greater abundance over the course of the fifteenth century.

Yet the nuns' commercial production was important not only because of the contribution it made to their internal budgets. Florentine nuns also formed part of an invisible labor force constituted by women and children that contributed significantly to the urban economy.[9] In particular, nuns played an irreplaceable role in the expansion of the Florentine silk industry, which established the city as a commercial center of the first order. Religious women furnished a captive labor force on which local entrepreneurs could depend—a fact that gave convents a competitive advantage over other sectors of the labor market. Even in economic sectors where the impact of their work was indirect or indeterminate, Florentine nuns gave the local economy much-needed elasticity by providing a pool of cheap, unregulated labor.

After framing salient issues in the first part of the chapter, I survey nuns' varied roles in the silk industry that lifted Renaissance Florence to international prominence. The participation of religious women in this burgeoning industry—as reelers, spinners, and brokers facilitating more efficient modes of production—was crucial to making the Quattrocento the century of silk. The third section offers three case studies of convent textile workshops, which allow us to gauge more precisely the economic significance of work to convent life. Rounding out the analysis is a look at nuns' activities as copyists and educators. Throughout the discussion, I consider how working for the market amplified social contradictions by pitting nuns' economic needs against gender norms, traditional values of honor, and ideals of religious reclusion.

Economic Strategies and Opportunities

Diversification was a hallmark of commercial activity in Florentine convents, whose economic traditions stretched back to the ninth century.[10] Renaissance religious women commonly cobbled together a patchwork of diverse activities that enabled them to respond nimbly to changing market conditions or to different stages of institutional development. Perhaps most importantly, however, diversification gave nuns greater leverage over their own labor. Since religious women had little invested in equipment or in a physical plant, they could shift easily from one form of craft production to another, which gave them a comparative advantage in the market. Although nuns' work did not require significant capital outlay, it did require certain skills and knowledge as well as considerable human capital. In the way they leveraged these resources, nuns resembled laywomen as "dabblers" in an "economy of makeshift," a trenchant characterization of women's work in premodern Europe that emphasizes their involvement in labor that called for generalized, often low-paid craft skills rather than an investment in a specific product or industry.[11] Given the preliminary state of analysis, the subjective meanings nuns attached to work and the extent to which they claimed distinctive occupational identities must remain open questions.

Each community pursued a particular mix of activities based on its size and physical location, internal craft traditions, business networks, talents of its residents and leaders, religious values, and market opportunities. Typical of Renaissance convent work patterns were the Observant nuns of Le Murate, who copied manuscripts, spun gold thread, made perfume and plaster reliefs, and sewed garments and household linens under the direction of their energetic, well-connected abbess, Scholastica Rondinelli. These various cottage industries brought in 500 florins annually by the mid-fifteenth century. In the absence of convent account books, it is impossible to know what percentage of income this represented, although the sum itself equaled about the annual income of thirteen skilled workers (earning 20 soldi per day) or twenty-six unskilled workers making half that amount.[12]

Although laywomen who worked were often satirized or criticized as dishonorable, work raised distinctive issues for nuns.[13] Producing for the market placed heavy demands on their time and energy, which threatened to distract them from the divine office — the very reason for monastic reclusion. In turn, religious duties limited the volume that could be produced. The S. Gaggio nuns noted in 1438 that reciting "the divine office at all hours" left them unable "to pursue work other than to sew and spin enough for their own needs."[14] This tension was endemic to female monasticism, but it acquired new force in the commercial environment of Renaissance Florence: nuns needed to work, and the urban economy needed their labor. The resulting conflicts put Florentine nuns in a double bind, wedging them between their financial needs and the reclusive demands of female monastic ideology.

While the principal forms of nuns' work were rooted in the development of the Florentine economy, they also described an institutional life cycle to some extent. Generally speaking, textiles provided the common entry point for new convents seeking to jump start endowments or otherwise aggressively boost income. A quarter century after its foundation by the playwright Antonia Pulci circa 1500 on little more than a prayer, S. Maria della Misericordia derived two-thirds of its income from textile work; the remaining one-third came from the alms box.[15] Intensive textile work allowed the disgraced nuns of the Chiarito to recover financially after Pope Eugenius closed the house for twenty years to punish their abbess. Returning to their former dwellings in 1454, the convent treasurer proudly noted that during her year in office, her companions earned enough from "all our manual labor, that is spinning and sewing," to pay their food bill—the single largest item in the budget.[16] As a community became more established or affluent, it often redirected energies from producing textiles to educating young girls, capitalizing on established networks in the process.

Emblematic of this trajectory of development was the Augustinian convent of S. Maria del Fiore (called Lapo after an early benefactor), located on the city's northern outskirts in the diocese of Fiesole.[17] Founded in 1350 with a meager endowment, the Lapo nuns supported themselves by tapping into the new demand for luxury goods that emerged in the late Trecento. These fifteen to twenty women busily occupied themselves making colorful ribbons, silk purses, embroidered cuffs, linen sheets and undershirts, thread, yarn, fine-carded wool, stuffed pillows, and assorted trousseau items that fed a burgeoning consumer market. This handiwork, sold to an overwhelmingly female clientele, garnered annual income of 50 to 60 florins in the late 1360s, with earnings growing in subsequent decades. In addition, the nuns developed a thriving scriptorium that produced devotional and liturgical books for both lay and ecclesiastical clients. In the late Trecento, Lapo regularly sold its books to the highly educated Dominican friars of S. Maria Novella, who may have later illuminated them. These enterprising nuns also branched out beyond conventional book production, offering graphic services to female clients unable to write. Taking advantage of their established client base, they wrote various chits and memoranda for women wishing to retain a written record of informal transactions for safekeeping.

The Lapo nuns built on their clientele for textiles, books, and graphic services when turning to new economic ventures. Although they continued small-scale textile production throughout the fifteenth century, after 1400 they focused their energies on education, which repaid them handsomely in income and social capital. By 1450, the Lapo nuns had developed the premier girls' boarding school in Florence. These diverse activities were crucial to survival, since the house claimed assets of only 1,366 florins in 1438, yielding annual per capita income for its twenty-five inhabitants of under 4 florins—less than one-third of the official cost of living. These nuns needed to work hard because their endowment simply did not yield enough food or money; by 1478, the community "lacked enough grain, wine, oil, and wood every year" to meet basic needs.[18] Because these women sought to maintain strict ideals of poverty, they chose not accumulate a larger patrimony, but their story nevertheless encapsulates the economic policy of diversification common to Renaissance convents.

The Century of Silk: Nuns and Textile Production

It is not surprising that textile production formed the backbone of nuns' work. As the lifeblood of the Florentine economy, textiles were responsible for integrating this landlocked city into international trade networks. Since the arts of sewing, embroidery, and spinning aligned well with contemporary notions of virtuous femininity, many convents across the peninsula were safely able to take them up, and many became renowned for fine needlework.[19] Although Italian nuns often made hefty sums executing piecework for wedding trousseaux, this activity did not require the extensive commercial networks characteristic of industrial production.[20] Nuns participated in all major Florentine textile industries—wool, linen, and silk—but their level of engagement differed according to the structure, organization, and labor demands of each industry. Economically vital since the thirteenth century, wool manufacture was a highly organized, regulated guild industry composed of a graduated workforce whose skills and wages were evenly distributed between top and bottom. In the late fourteenth and fifteenth centuries, nuns played a very limited role in wool production owing to the ready availability of laywomen workers. Franco Franceschi has shown that Florentine laywomen appeared in all segments of the industry in this period, performing heavy tasks like skinning and shearing as well as lighter work like carding and stretching. The majority of wool-working apprentices coming from the countryside were young girls age seven to twelve.[21] Given this supply of female workers, there was little demand for nuns' labor in this sector.

Florentine nuns participated more extensively in linen manufacture, which was less tightly organized than wool production and tied to local and regional markets rather than international ones. The staple cloth of everyday life, linen filled various market niches. Nuns made linen wares ranging from basic household items like sheets, towels, and undergarments to industrial items like the heavy hemp cords that ran the city's wool looms. Flax suppliers were all local; sometimes raw materials were obtained from convent properties, eliminating the need for outside agents. In fact, most of the linen the nuns produced was meant for their own consumption. When nuns produced goods for sale, their buyers were primarily local, although some fine linen articles enjoyed a regional reputation. Budget shortfalls forced convents to engage in commercial linen production to varying degrees, but the homespun nature of linen manufacture carried little social cachet or geographic reach.[22]

It was in the "new" industry of silk production that religious women made their biggest mark. Silk was the ultimate Renaissance luxury cloth, produced in a stunning array of colors, textures, weights, depths, designs, and grades to satisfy a rapidly growing culture of display. Unlike linen, silk production required regional and international links; silk merchants (*setaiuoli*), for example, traversed the map of Europe and parts of the Levant in search of silk cocoons, dyestuffs, and buyers.[23] The Florentine silk industry had a distinctive structure and organization, different from that of either wool or linen manufacture. Richard Goldthwaite has shown that the workforce in this industry "was highly polarized toward extremes," the greatest number of workers being concentrated at the bottom end.[24] In Florence, silk merchants organized and controlled the entire production process. Having fronted the capital for long-distance trade, these entrepreneurs constituted the only full-fledged guild members. Silk weavers (*tessitori di drappi*) had to obtain materials exclusively from them and remit finished products into their hands. Still, silk weavers earned high wages that accounted for two-thirds of the labor costs involved in making silk fabrics.[25] These two groups — silk merchants and weavers — stood at the top end of the wage scale. Most silk workers collected at the opposite end, especially those engaged in preliminary production stages like reeling and spinning. The bulk of this labor force consisted of women and girls, who often earned less than the minimum wage paid an unskilled male laborer.

The growth of the Florentine silk industry in the fifteenth century profoundly impacted nuns' labor patterns. In contrast to other renowned Italian centers of silk production like Lucca, Genoa, and Venice, Florence came relatively late to this enterprise. Although the Florentine silk industry got underway in the late fourteenth century, it only developed real dynamism after 1400, spurred by the immigration of more technically advanced artisans from Lucca.[26] By 1420, more effective coordination between the production of silk cloth and metallic thread propelled the industry into new competitive markets. Enriched by entrepreneurial merchant capital, this sector saw investments almost double over the fifteenth century, from 230,000 florins in 1436 to 400,000 florins in 1490.[27] The ascent of the silk industry, which complemented a still vibrant wool sector, transformed Florence into one of the principal textile centers of Western Europe.

This ascent opened up new opportunities for nuns' work in three main areas: reeling and spinning silk from cocoons (*incannatura di seta*), which was a delicate but low-wage task; making metallic threads of gold and silver (*filatura d'oro*), a craft well known to thirteenth-century Genoese noblewomen, who engaged in both its manufacture and export;[28] and embroidering finished products with multicolored silk, gold thread, and pearls and other jewels that further embellished them. Florentine nuns engaged in all three activities. Except for making ribbon on narrow ribbon looms, they did not weave silk cloth, since that was a protected craft activity. All three types of silk work required backward and forward linkages with commercial suppliers, who provided raw materials and to whom nuns consigned finished products. *Setaiuoli* sometimes marketed embroidery pieces made in convent workshops, but more frequently these expensive projects were commissioned by individual buyers. Although many abbesses aggressively pursued business relations in order to launch or expand production, they were not entrepreneurs in the classic sense, since there was little risk or capital outlay involved. Still, silk production exposed religious women to all aspects of commercial culture. Through regular contact with suppliers and brokers, nuns gained important commercial and technical knowledge that enabled them to make informed decisions about the market value of their handiwork relative to other producers. In turn, this knowledge heightened their ability to appraise the quality of their workmanship, especially in the medium of embroidery, and to estimate the value of liturgical goods donated to them.

Each of these activities — reeling, spinning gold thread, and embroidering — involved nuns in a different set of labor processes and in different organizational roles. From the 1440s onward, nuns contributed to the preliminary production processes of reeling and spinning silk as workers and supervisors and also played a critical role in the industry's delivery system. Convents acted as distribution points for raw materials, which expedited delivery and pickup of products by female workers. Instead of dispersing raw materials to many individual residences and then collecting the products, silk dealers used the institutional spaces of convents as way stations. As industry volume grew by the mid-fifteenth century, *setaiuoli* also began employing nuns to organize and manage larger manufacturing networks of laywomen. Nuns consigned reeling and spinning jobs to wives, widows, and girls working at home for a pittance — brokerage tasks for which nuns were ideally suited since they already had extensive contacts with neighborhood women. By relieving dealers of these duties, religious women formed an important link in the manufacturing chain. Not every house filled this operational niche, but convents' organizational capacity was clearly instrumental to fifteenth-century industrial development.

S. Domenico nel Maglio offers early evidence of how convents functioned as key organizational nodes for preliminary production processes. Located on modern-day Via Venezia, this Dominican convent stood at the center of a local production network. In 1441, these nuns were already reeling silk for two *setaiuoli*, Francesco Martini and Michele di Giovanni, who sent them cocoons of varying types and grades in marked batches weighing four to fourteen pounds.[29] Reeling silk entailed boiling cocoons to remove the gummy substance binding the filaments (which typically reduced the original weight by 25–30 percent) and then winding the rough, loosened filaments around a cross-shaped spindle; the filaments would then be ready to be spun into thread. Like other textile products, the weight of the finished product determined payment. The nuns earned 18 soldi for each pound of spun thread, which still required further processing, such as doubling, twisting, and dyeing, beyond convent walls. By 1446, the community had expanded its business, establishing regular partnerships with six silk dealers; by 1450, it had entered into a new business relationship with the firm of Cosimo de' Medici.[30] Source variations make it impossible to reconstruct total output, but we know that the nuns produced 750 pounds of finished silk thread in 1443–44 for one of their dealers, Domenico Borghini. The 153 florins earned from this partnership translated into per capita earnings of about 5 florins, from which secondary labor costs were deducted.[31]

From the outset, the thirty or so nuns of S. Domenico consigned supplementary work to laywomen living in nearby Via S. Gallo, and over the next decade they enlarged the size, reach, and production volume of their manufacturing network. Within two years, they were managing a putting-out operation involving at least twenty women scattered across the city. Every one or two months, individual reelers remitted batches of semifinished product weighing nine to eleven pounds, for which they earned 8 soldi per pound. This arrangement allowed nuns to focus on the higher-paid activity of spinning, which netted them 10 soldi per pound.[32] As brokers employed by silk firms, the nuns were responsible for managing all aspects of commercial exchange with reelers, from consigning batches to conducting the final weigh-in and paying the reelers for their work. Reelers picked up cocoons from the convent or had them delivered via porter, then returned full spindles the same way; upon receipt, the nuns paid them on the dealers' behalf. We know little about the identity of these working women, although their limited volume and small earnings make it likely that they worked for other convents and dealers as well. Several reelers were identified as widows; one was a barber's wife, another a hospital warden. More frequently reelers were identified in convent accounts by place of residence. Although initial consignments were made within the neighborhood, the nuns quickly expanded their outreach, probably tracing the footprint of citywide recruitment patterns as well as dealers' recommendations. Two reelers working for them lived across the river; another resided at Ponte alla Carraia. At least four reelers lived in the heart of the old city.[33] Their geographical dispersion highlights the crucial role convents played in making the industry's delivery system faster and more efficient. One of the most surprising features of these accounts is the inclusion of about a dozen signatures by reelers themselves in unpracticed hands, attesting to payment in the 1450s and 1460s.[34] Since graphic competence was even less prevalent than reading ability at all levels of Florentine society, these signatures provide unexpected evidence for a wider dissemination of rudimentary writing skills among women than previously thought. The nuns managed this putting-out operation at least through the 1460s.

Among nuns' silk-working activities, the production of gold thread was the most economically significant for both convents and the industry itself. The luxurious shimmer of gold thread was essential to the "look" of high-end Renaissance clothing and decorative arts. Before Florence launched its own industry in earnest, silk dealers bought gold thread made in Lucca or Venice. In 1427, there were still only two shops in Florence producing metallic thread; thirty years later, that number had grown to six.[35] Since the city lacked a long tradition in this craft, a new workforce had to be created and sustained. The rising demand for cheap labor in this stage of production, which held down the overall cost of luxury goods and increased profitability, could only be met by employing hundreds of religious women living behind convent walls. By 1470, at least twenty convents produced metallic thread; by 1500, virtually every convent in the Florentine dominion made gold thread, with production concentrated in the largest, poorest communities. The size of the available workforce can be gauged from the expanding female monastic population. In 1500, nuns in the city and environs numbered approximately 2,000, with that figure approaching 2,500 by 1515.

Even if only 50–70 percent of nuns participated in production (allowing for age, disability, and other work assignments), it is apparent that convents supplied the single largest, most concentrated labor force in the silk industry.

Given the economic importance of metallic thread, it is useful to review the major steps in its manufacture. Making gold thread required good eyes, sharp scissors, and skilled hands, all of which took a beating in the course of work. The procedure was not especially complicated, but it did require specialized skills and tools. Apprenticeships for secular girls learning this craft in late medieval Montpellier lasted four years.[36] Nuns obtained raw materials from silk dealers and goldbeaters (*battilori*), whose functions were often combined within the same firms after midcentury. Silk dealers furnished spun, dyed thread — white silk for the core of silver thread, yellow silk for gold — along with the wooden spools used to store the finished product. *Battilori* supplied the thin, foil-like sheets of gold leaf, made by smelting gold coins in small batches. With these materials in hand, nuns cut the tissue-paper-thin sheets of gold leaf into very narrow strips with long, flexible scissors, then delicately wound the strips around a core of silk thread. The finished thread remained supple enough to be worked into sumptuous brocades on a loom.[37] Winding the precious thread around spools, they returned completed batches to the supplier, who priced it by weight. Nuns took their earnings by subtracting the cost of raw materials from the price of the finished good paid by the supplier. Like other textile workers in the putting-out system, nuns were paid for the product, irrespective of time worked; their production practices were consonant with industrial organization at the time. Proceeds went into the convent treasury via the abbess, treasurer, or other representative; unless a nun accepted additional piecework, she usually was not paid directly. However, because many convents had idiosyncratic financial arrangements, some nuns earned money individually. Each of the dozen nuns of S. Jacopo — a convent that was among the earliest to participate in this craft — who spun gold thread had a personal account with her dealer; all were young to middle-aged women in the bottom half of chapter seniority.[38]

The first Florentine convent to manufacture gold thread was Le Murate, whose population already topped 150 nuns by midcentury. In 1447 the silk entrepreneur Tommaso Ridolfi reached an agreement with Abbess Scholastica Rondinelli, the enterprising religious woman who guided the community's rapid ascent. Apparently the Murate nuns were already acquainted with the craft.[39] Upon receipt of the first finished spools, Ridolfi immediately sold them to the Medici silk firm for 14.5 florins per pound, which included his markup. Because of the precious metal used, this price was seventy-five times higher than what the S. Domenico nuns earned for spinning basic silk thread. Searching for a larger workforce, Ridolfi contracted a month later with the Convertite, the house for reformed prostitutes. As this entrepreneur himself noted, "We undertook to teach the women of the Convertite how to spin gold thread." He sent several laywomen instructors along with the necessary tools and supplies, and shortly afterward arranged for a scissors master (*forbiciaio*) to give hands-on help to nuns employed by the firm. Bruno Dini speculates that Ridolfi sought out nuns for this new labor force because their dedication to work and prayer guaranteed a superior product and shorter production time.[40] Whatever the case, Ridolfi's approach to these two houses surely was not accidental. Le Murate and S. Elisabetta delle Convertite were among the largest convents, whose tiny patrimonies rendered them tax exempt. Living on the edge, their members probably were quite receptive to new wage-earning opportunities.[41]

From 1447 to 1456, the Ridolfi firm established agreements with eight convents to produce metallic thread. As Dini has shown, these communities accounted for 79.2 percent (675 pounds) of the company's total production figure; individual laywomen spun the rest. Included in this labor vanguard was Le Murate, responsible for 33 percent of total output, along with S. Monaca, S. Elisabetta delle Convertite, S. Jacopo, the Portico, S. Miniato, S. Martino, and S. Gaggio.[42] These convents seamlessly maintained production when Lorenzo Neroni picked up Ridolfi's business in 1457. Neroni became the principal agent for Le Murate and the Portico but still partnered to a lesser extent with the other houses. In the late 1460s, the young, intrepid *battiloro* Giuliano Gondi—dubbed the "most ambitious, most audacious" of the midcentury silk entrepreneurs—became one of the principal dealers for S. Gaggio, which did business with the firm until at least 1520.[43] As convent production proliferated, so too did the number of suppliers active at any institution.

Florentine civic officials quickly recognized the significance of nuns' manufacturing activity to the commercial life of the city. Luca Molà has argued that early modern governments "paid particular attention to the creation of a female labor force," since they were acutely aware that women were indispensable to the entire production cycle.[44] In the Florentine case, state intervention focused on protecting business relations between nuns and their associates, not on women themselves. High-volume production necessitated that scissors masters, goldbeaters, dealers, estimators, and other men have ready access to religious women and their spaces. To protect its nascent silk industry, the Florentine commune put itself in a paradoxical position vis-à-vis other civic initiatives. Since the 1420s, city fathers had voiced determination to shield convents from worldly matters by policing enclosure. Yet when industrial production was at stake, magistrates ignored these vaunted principles to advance the fortunes of leading citizens. The city's business-minded governors created a statist model of economic protection that was deeply at odds with an avowed moral framework, riddling their oversight with hypocrisy.

Convent entry permits issued by the civic magistracy of the night officers afford a quantifiable perspective on interactions stimulated by silk work. One of several innovative mechanisms developed in the 1420s, the night officers acted as a kind of moral police force. These six sage, older men were charged with vetting lay visitors to female religious institutions within the city and a five-mile radius.[45] To enter a convent legitimately, laymen who were not kin needed a permit issued by this group, which also prosecuted sodomy cases. In the 1450s, the magistrates consolidated procedures that made licensing more systematic. By 1470, annual permits issued to artisans and tradesmen involved in silk production abounded. For instance, in 1469 the night officers licensed two scissors masters and their assistants to enter twenty convents at any point during the year to keep nuns' tools in tip-top shape. In 1472, magistrates granted a similar license to another scissors master enabling him and a companion to enter "each and every convent within the jurisdiction of these officials" — about fifty communities — during the year.[46] From the mid-1470s until 1502, when the magistracy transferred its administrative competencies to another agency, officials permitted these artisans to enter convents across the dominion every year without exception. At S. Maria sul Prato, one of the most active production centers, they extended annual permits to three different *forbiciai* and their assistants in the same year (1492).[47]

These tradesmen represented only a small fraction of laymen who accessed Florentine convents in the course of carrying out normal business. Around 1480, the night officers began authorizing individual silk dealers and *battilori* to enter convents with which they did business. Transactions normally took place in the convent parlor or abbess's quarters but may have reasonably extended to workrooms as well. With gold thread production in high gear by the 1490s, the traffic between convents and suppliers became so frequent that magistrates simply issued generic permits to "*battilori* who give gold for the nuns to spin" and to "masters who evaluated" their products.[48] Although civic authorities initially seized the moral high ground, they flagrantly violated church decrees and threatened the very ideology of female enclosure to assure the success of the silk industry.

The expansion of female monasticism created a highly favorable situation for the silk industry by providing the necessary scale and stability of a new workforce. By 1450, numerous convents had achieved the size needed to run a commercial workshop and at the same time attend to communal life. The tipping point hovered at twenty-five nuns; most convents that engaged in substantial commercial output housed considerably more. Although convents were not necessarily surrounded by massive walls in this period, their physical enclosures and on-site residents helped protect expensive raw materials, which eliminated the need to hire young boys to sleep overnight in the workshops as watchmen, a common practice among commercial silk workshops. Other features gave the convent workforce both a comparative advantage and a distinctive profile. There was tremendous turnover in the ranks of the young boys and adolescents at the bottom rungs of the industry. These youths were often unreliable employees working on short-term contracts; they tended to be restless adolescents, always on the lookout for more advantageous terms of employment.[49] The contrast with the convent workforce could not have been greater, since nuns lacked the commercial freedom enjoyed by young male silk workers, however poorly paid. Both their gender and institutional situation discouraged physical mobility: once novices took final vows, they became members of the community for life. Only death, disability, or flight could remove them from the convent labor force.

This stability translated into continuity of craft training within and across generations at no cost to the industry. Silk dealers not only controlled access to raw materials; they also controlled a subordinate labor force that assured regular production schedules and that reproduced itself over time in the form of novices. Taught by older, more skilled nuns, novices between ages five and sixteen learned and perfected graduated skills. As they gained experience using cheaper materials or performing light tasks like carrying spools, reeling silk, moving shuttles, and cleaning the workroom, they acquired craft training while contributing to production. In the fifteenth century, however, convent workshops still utilized classic apprenticeships, which distinguished convent work arrangements from technical training schools or workhouses.[50] As best we can determine, these textile workshops provided individual instruction through which a personal relationship between "master" and "pupil" developed; the transfer of craft skills between generations remained the key nexus rather than cash remuneration. Moreover, nuns' long-term coresidence in a structured environment enabled convents to ensure the global formation of an "apprentice's" character. The record books of several convents with recognized workshops frequently refer to young nuns as *discepole*, a term commonly used by Florentine guildsmen in the thirteenth and fourteenth centuries to refer to apprentices.[51] Further, unlike many Italian custodial institutions such as orphanages and conservatories after 1550, Renaissance convents did not house dense concentrations of children working under sweatshop conditions that led to high death rates.[52] The Portico, which had two thriving textile workshops, offers a valuable data point in this regard. In 1509, only two of the forty-four choir nuns were twenty years old or younger; the single novice was age eleven. The fifteen servant nuns showed a similar age profile; only one was under twenty years old.[53] The community also housed four young pupils who received religious instruction and learned how to sew and read, but there is no evidence that they were used as apprenticed workers.

The centrality of nuns to the silk industry raises the question of the extent to which silk production stimulated monastic expansion. Contemporaries invariably situated the growth of female monasticism within the discourse of marriage, making no mention of market production. These perceptions notwithstanding, however, there was no consistent relationship in this period between celibacy, on one hand, and women's participation in the workforce, on the other. Nonetheless, silk production certainly figured among the several factors that enabled the breathtaking pace of monastic expansion in the later Quattrocento. Poorly endowed convents surrendered most quickly to market forces. The Convertite, which rehabilitated repentant prostitutes through a stringent program of work and prayer, could only survive through silk work. Paradoxically, this industry permitted some nuns greater personal agency. The determined Convertite nun Agnoletta Soldani amassed the considerable sum of 55 florins "with her hard work at spinning gold thread," which she exchanged in 1511 for a 5-florin lifetime annuity "to clothe and shoe herself and provide for other needs."[54]

While the advent of silk opened up new work opportunities, it also sharpened class distinctions within convents. After 1450, it was not uncommon to run linen and silk workshops in the same convent, although it required a complex management system that was overseen by the abbess. Textile materials mapped out status differences within a house: servant nuns continued to spin linen while choir nuns shifted production efforts to silk. These distinct work patterns were not accidental. In 1466 the Paradiso accepted the daughter of a linen weaver as a servant nun, with the proviso that she continue to spin linen for the convent.[55] More comprehensive evidence comes from the Portico. In 1509, this austere Augustinian convent supported two profitable enterprises: a thriving linen workshop run by *converse* that used three hundred pounds of flax harvested annually from its properties and a gold thread workshop that presumably employed most of the forty-four choir nuns. The number of Portico nuns engaged in making gold thread made its silk workshop one of largest manufacturing enterprises in the city. In 1525, the largest secular silk weaving workshop employed thirty-two workers, while the next two largest had only sixteen workers each.[56] Unfortunately, the nuns did not stipulate how much they earned, except to note that each activity was "profitable." However, they did note that their property holdings rendered only 200 florins a year, giving an annual per capita income of 3.3 florins — far short of the baseline essential for survival.[57] The nuns earned an additional 40 florins from educational tasks. Although no single activity provided enough income to meet basic needs, the lucrative nature of silk work gave it high standing within the mixed convent economy.

Making metallic thread also introduced new forms of spatial segregation that reinforced internal convent hierarchies. Silk production forced a greater differentiation of work spaces, since silk and linen workshops had to be physically separated to avoid contaminating expensive materials with coarse linen filaments and by-products. S. Gaggio constructed a new room solely for silk work as early as 1450, and ledgers kept by S. Orsola indicate that it also effected this kind of spatial division. Silk production was situated in the main room (*sala*), while spinning and weaving linen took place in another space (*telaia*); each workshop had its own set of accounts. The architectural plan for remodeling S. Jacopo made sometime after 1550 clearly shows a room for making gold thread separated from the general workroom.[58] Besides putting additional pressure on the disposition of internal space just as convent populations were climbing, silk work split off choir nuns from *converse*. Although these two groups never recited the liturgy together, they did spend several hours a day toiling and chatting in each other's company. Thus instead of promoting greater cohesion and sociability, this new mode of production pushed convents toward greater social stratification — another hallmark of early modern female monasticism.

Three Case Studies in Textile Work

The evidence for nuns' textile activities marshaled thus far demonstrates that religious women were fundamental to the development of the silk industry, both for the labor and organizational resources they provided. Unfortunately, sources do not permit a macroanalysis of their overall economic contribution in terms of volume or earnings. Tax reports, which normally provide the best avenue for systematic analysis, captured only fixed assets, not earned income. Hence we must turn to individual case studies to clarify aspects of the production process and to gauge the scale of convent operations. A closer examination of three major silk workshops located at S. Gaggio, the Paradiso, and S. Maria a Monticelli offers insight into the organization of labor, internal work rhythms, marketing patterns, and types of commodity production. The S. Gaggio workshop reveals the dynamics of gold thread production; the Paradiso shows an active embroidery workshop catering to the upper reaches of Italian society; the Monticelli workshop documents the shift to lace making in the sixteenth century. Given the variation in convent size and wealth, it would be imprudent to project comparable output or activities for all houses. Instead, these stories describe a range of economic strategies and experiences that reflect the hybrid nature of fifteenth-century female monasticism.

S. Gaggio was located about a kilometer beyond the southern gate, allowing easy access to suppliers and brokers in both city and countryside. In the early Quattrocento, the fifty-one nuns living "completely in common" began marketing linen wares on a small scale. Their scribe noted that the nuns "perform a great duty in serving God, except that they wear themselves out in the task of spinning linen." Despite being one of the wealthiest suburban convents, income was insufficient to meet regular expenses and fund new capital projects simultaneously. Probably the motivation to market on a larger scale stemmed from plans for new building and decorative projects carried out between 1438 and 1441.[59] The workshop produced various linen wares aimed at different market segments, such as vast quantities of sturdy cord intended for wool looms as well as coarse linen thread used to make the warp for less expensive grades of silk velvet. The nuns made large bolts of linen cloth that sold for 1 to 2 florins apiece but also produced some finer linen articles that commanded high prices because of their regional reputation. In 1450, the witty cleric Piovano Arlotto purchased a "new, soft, fine handkerchief" costing more than 1 florin, "which he said was to be sent to a citizen of Livorno, who was searching for a kerchief of this price and quality for his wife."[60]

In 1450, the S. Gaggio nuns shifted focus to the more lucrative production of gold thread. They set up a new work space (*sala dell'oro*) specifically for spinning gold thread and improved its lighting conditions by covering the windows with sheer white linen, a tactic that served to admit maximum light into a room. At the same time, the chapter purposely limited its numbers to achieve a higher standard of living. Between 1427 and 1438, the convent population fell from fifty-one to forty-four nuns, and by the early 1470s, that number had declined to roughly twenty-five, as members were drawn increasingly from high-status families instead of from across the class spectrum.[61] Unfortunately, early ledgers documenting the first fifteen years of workshop operation are seriously damaged. Good records resume by the mid-1460s, when the workshop was turning out an impressive volume of gold thread despite its modest size. Much of this ambitious production schedule stemmed from the energetic efforts of Abbess Elena Guasconi, who opened a new ledger kept on facing pages (*alla veneziana*) in 1466. Any authorized nun could make entries in this bilateral format, which demonstrated both the nuns' graphic competence and economic sophistication.[62] Her successor, Angelica de' Pilli, changed accounting practices but not the overall economic or social direction of the house. Between 1469 and 1480, the nuns meticulously cut 6,777 ounces of gold leaf (about 565 Florentine pounds, or roughly 192 kilos), which they transformed into gold thread.[63] In eleven years, this modest-sized workshop produced the equivalent of 83 percent of the total spun by eight convents for the Ridolfi firm from 1447–56. The workshop hit peak production from 1471 to 1475, increasing volume by one-third and wearing out three pairs of scissors in the process. Total earnings for the eleven-year period were just over 900 florins, with average monthly earnings equaling just over 38 lire. By comparison, the Murate workshop earned a monthly average of 65 lire in 1457–58 because it was so much larger.[64]

To meet their increased production schedule in the mid-1470s, the S. Gaggio nuns took on new suppliers of gold leaf. Their principal dealer was the enterprising Giuliano Gondi, to whom they consigned seven batches of thread in 1469–70 netting 14 soldi per ounce — seventeen times more than the net earnings reeling and spinning silk yielded. Gondi handled these transactions with several nuns beside the abbess, attesting to the distributed nature of commercial knowledge at S. Gaggio. In 1471 the nuns established a partnership with the silk firm of Tommaso Capponi; a third firm, run by the *battiloro* Giuliano di Ser Simone, came on board in 1475. Over the next decade, the nuns entered into business relations with eight other firms.[65] Throughout this period, the nuns continued to produce linen, in part by consigning some work to poorer female tenants.

The goal of this stepped-up operation was the expansion, repair, and decoration of the physical complex. Beginning in 1471, the nuns enlarged and remodeled the dormitory, repaired the refectory roof, added space in the infirmary, purchased liturgical items for the sacristy, and placed new, white glass windows in the exterior church and refectory.[66] The correlation between spikes in production and subsequent building projects indicates that the nuns had a clear idea of how much money and work were needed to underwrite projects. At S. Gaggio, making gold thread was a means to a well-defined end. Once new construction was complete, they turned to decoration, commissioning from the renowned artist Antonio Pollaiuolo a "large crucifix of brass and gilded silver, with enamel" for the convent church worth 45 florins (now conserved in the Bargello Museum). When striking this agreement in 1476, the nuns' hands-on experience with gold work heightened their effectiveness as informed art patrons. At the nuns' insistence, Pollaiuolo agreed to submit the final work to them for their evaluation so they could make sure it was "well furnished with gold" before they made payment.[67] Their counterparts at Le Murate invested the fruits of their labors in similar ways. Abbess Scholastica Rondinelli used 100 ducats gleaned from the nuns' earliest spinning efforts to buy liturgical books for the convent church. As several scholars have argued, fifteenth-century Italian nuns exercised remarkable autonomy in making artistic choices about the form and decoration of their living environments.[68] Sadly, the results of the S. Gaggio nuns' prodigious efforts were destroyed during the 1529–30 siege, which reduced their buildings to rubble.

These manufacturing activities also spun a tangled web of social relations between nuns and dealers. Giuliano Gondi bought wine on the nuns' behalf to offset partial earnings; conversely, he acted as their creditor to assure continued production, paying off the scissors masters to whom the nuns owed money. Tommaso Capponi extended his role as supplier when he paid the gold gabelle for the nuns. More tellingly, Capponi fronted dowry funds on behalf of his father-in-law, Antonio Alessandri, who enrolled his daughter Felice at S. Gaggio in 1477. Four years later, this new nun's brother became a regular supplier of raw materials for spinning gold thread.[69] In later decades, silk work increasingly took on features of family businesses. One of the convent's main dealers in the 1490s and early 1500s was Piero Squarcialupi, whose sister Suor Margherita undoubtedly was instrumental in securing this mutually beneficial business relationship. In turn, Piero rented a farm and bought livestock from the convent, commissioned a religious feast at the convent church, and placed two of his own daughters as nuns in the house. Suor Margherita was still looking after her brother's intertwined accounts in 1515.[70]

The intensified work campaign begun in the 1470s only heightened perennial tensions between the dictates of monastic reclusion and the demands of business. In 1475, Abbess Angelica de' Pilli asked the convent syndic to keep business records in a different fashion, using him as a buffer to preserve spiritual tranquility and social distance — a decision made internally rather than imposed by officials. The desire to moderate growing family pressures may also help to account for the nuns' decision. As this syndic explained, he was tasked with "securing payment from whoever owes money and paying those who are owed. Then the nuns will extract [accounts] from this ledger and enter them in their own ledgers kept inside the cloister. They wanted this done in order to serve God with greater repose and peace of mind, and not be troubled by so many people from the outside." To avoid confusion, the nuns agreed to mark off accounts when transferring them from external to internal ledgers.[71] The nuns sustained an active production schedule through the end of the century, adding new accounting features like the "book for gold leaf" (*libro della foglia*) to track their many business partnerships. The political crises of the 1490s did not disrupt production noticeably, but volume tapered off by about 10 percent in the 1510s, probably in response to changing fashions that resulted in lower demand.[72]

The siege of Florence, on the other hand, radically altered production patterns as well as the convent's economic direction. This evidence supports Goldthwaite's contention that the silk business went on as usual despite political turmoil, except during the crisis of 1527–31.[73] Forced to abandon their dwellings in October 1529, the nuns took shelter in kinsmen's homes while their convent was sacked. Returning in May 1531, they attempted to repair a couple of still habitable rooms, but the devastation was extensive.[74] Confronted with rebuilding their convent and restoring rental properties in an inhospitable economic climate, the nuns resumed spinning almost immediately but never reached former production levels or fully reconstituted their business networks, despite the fact that the convent ran an annual deficit into the mid-1540s. By 1540, they produced gold thread for only two dealers; volume had declined by 50 percent from the 1470s.[75] Instead of rooting recovery in their own labor, the S. Gaggio nuns turned to dowries to raise capital more quickly, doubling them for new nuns, who also brought more extensive furnishings. They also turned to education and guardianship as their principal economic activities, which solidified patronage relationships. Further subsidizing reconstruction were donors, corporate patrons, and their own families, all of whom demanded a voice in convent affairs.[76] Although many elements of monastic life survived the crisis of 1529–31, it marked a turning point for Florentine female monasticism; it scrambled established work patterns, reorganized monastic topography, and destroyed valuable physical plants. The recovery process only heightened relations of social and economic dependence between nuns and their families — yet another characteristic of early modern convent experience.

The second major textile workshop analyzed here, located at the unusual Brigettine house of the Paradiso, enlarges our view of nuns' textile work in two ways. First, its records are more comprehensive than those of S. Gaggio over a longer period; second, the Paradiso not only produced gold thread but boasted one of the city's premier embroidery workshops. Although the nuns' early Quattrocento account books are sketchy, their records became quite rich after 1450, by which time the textile workshop had already established a regional reputation. Further workshop expansion suggests that this mixed house of nuns and monks under the direction of Abbess Tommasa da Diacceto developed deliberate strategies for market production. Like S. Gaggio, the Paradiso embarked on commercial ventures both to provide basic support and to fund more expensive projects. In 1438, the convent claimed assets of 8,299 florins, which, when capitalized at the normative rate of 7 percent, gave a per capita income of 11.6 florins for the fifty inhabitants.[77] While probably providing enough for the basic necessities of life, this sum certainly did not permit costly building projects. As soon as revenues from textile production began flowing in, the convent directed monies toward the expansion, repair, and decoration of the complex, renovations that included the installation of new windows "in the place where the nuns embroider."[78] In the later Quattrocento, convent finances profited from the talented leadership and wide connections of Abbess Eulalia Buondelmonti, who took the helm in 1458 and supervised workshop expansion until her death circa 1481.[79]

The Paradiso pursued economic diversification, keeping textiles at the core of its enterprise. Besides weaving linen cloth and taking in sewing, the nuns also spun and reeled silk, which paid poorly but consolidated relationships with various silk dealers. More lucrative was the production of gold thread, which spawned long-term relationships with suppliers like Bartolomeo Peruzzi, Pierozzo Banchi, Giovanni Federghi, Tommaso Ridolfi, and the omnipresent Giuliano Gondi.[80] It was this latter activity that launched the development of the embroidery workshop. The Paradiso nuns purchased silk and gold thread used for embroidery from the same dealers for whom they produced it; in turn, these dealers offered additional outlets for finished pieces. Because the volume of work necessitated extensive supply channels, at any given time the nuns managed five to eight business relationships, although they usually identified a principal dealer.[81] Moreover, the nuns were able to alternate between spinning gold thread and embroidering — once they received a major embroidery commission, they would temporarily slow down the production of gold thread and then increase it again upon completion of the embroidery. Sustaining this diverse activity was a medium-sized workshop; the Paradiso grew from thirty-one to fifty-six nuns between 1443 and 1478. By 1509, the convent hit its peak population of sixty-three nuns, which represented three more than the "perfect" number prescribed by their rule.[82]

Among the diverse products manufactured were eyeglasses, which fell in the monks' domain (as noted in chapter 3, the Paradiso housed both male and female religious). Vincent Ilardi has shown that fifteenth-century Florence was "the optical capital of the world" and that the Paradiso figured as a major production site of sophisticated optics.[83] These new, affordable reading aids quickly found a receptive audience across Italy. The Paradiso wares were marketed in Florence, Mantua, and Rome; dozens of pairs of spectacles were given as gifts at the Sforza court of Milan in the mid-Quattrocento as a kind of status symbol. Ordinary users of eyeglasses included nuns working in the Lapo scriptorium, the nuns of S. Pier Maggiore (who purchased five pair from the Paradiso), and laywomen like the letter writer Alessandra Macinghi Strozzi.[84] Despite its enormous technological significance, the production of eyeglasses at the Paradiso yielded comparatively little income. From 1453 to 1463, sale of eyeglasses brought in only 1.8 percent of total convent income, while textile earnings yielded 12.5 percent for the same period.[85] Granted, the monks' workforce was smaller, but it was still substantial. In 1478, the convent housed forty-two men — twelve monks, twelve servant monks, twelve annuitants, and six chaplains — although it is unclear how labor was allocated among them. By 1509, the number of male clerics had fallen to sixteen.[86]

The richness of the Paradiso's business records permits a comprehensive picture of convent textile income between 1451 and 1498. These data allow us to trace the trajectory of economic development and workshop output over a critical half century. The bulk of convent income came from a combination of rents, dowries, gifts, and bequests and is not differentiated here. Over this forty-seven year period, textile production represented 10.1 percent of all convent income, ranging from a high of 15.1 percent in the 1450s to a low of 5.5 percent in the 1490s. As illustrated in graph 4.1, gold thread production and embroidery brought in roughly equal sums over time, with linen production running a distant third. In any given year, the percentage yielded by textiles fluctuated

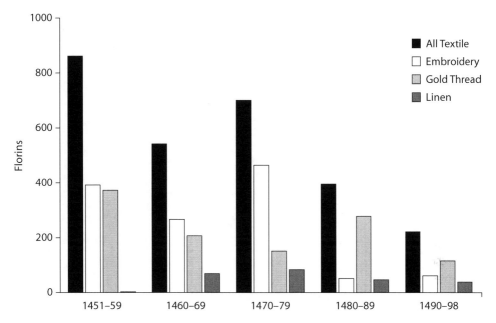

Graph 4.1. Textile Income, S. Brigida del Paradiso, 1451–98. *Sources:* ASF, Mon.
S. Brigida, vols. 147, 148, 149, 152, 154; ASF, Mon. S. Luca, vol. 79.

dramatically, from a high of 53.1 percent in 1453 to a low of 1.04 percent in
1495–96. This variation owed less to irregular production patterns, however,
than to the fact that dowries, land sales, and large embroidery commissions
episodically swelled the treasury. It becomes difficult to measure and differentiate
nuns' textile production after 1498 owing to changes in accounting practices, although these activities continued well into the 1540s.

Several points are worth highlighting in connection with these data. First,
although the highest earnings derived from luxury wares, the nuns did not produce exclusively for that market. The Paradiso retained its foothold in the everyday world of linen, a strategy that diversified both its production portfolio and
the social range of its customers. Second, although the volume of embroidery
pieces was necessarily small given their steep prices and labor-intensive facture,
the convent earned as much from customized luxury production as it did from
more generic manufacture of metallic thread, and required the participation of
fewer nuns. In the mid-1480s, the embroidery workshop numbered at least nine
nuns, but probably not very many more than that.[87] Third, by 1500 textile in-

Fig. 4.1. Chasuble (late fifteenth century), with embroidered orphrey band (late fifteenth to early sixteenth century), Italy or Spain. Silk and gilt-metal-strip-wrapped silk. 131.8 × 73.4 cm. Gift of Mrs. Chauncey McCormick and Mrs. Richard Ely Danielson. 1948.129a. The Art Institute of Chicago.

come made a smaller contribution to convent finances. Although changing consumer tastes accounted for part of this reduction, the main driver was increased property income that allowed the nuns to step back from the marketplace.

Having already examined gold thread production at S. Gaggio, we can turn immediately to embroidered wares, which stood at the pinnacle of luxury goods manufactured in silk. Unlike plain sewing, which had obvious functional value, embroidery carried noble associations with leisured aristocratic women. As a creative, expressive exercise often called "painting in silk," embroidery was a "source of power and pleasure" for nuns and laywomen alike. Elaborate stitching required considerable technical skill as well as a meditative patience that fostered devotion. The development of the new technique called *or nué* allowed Florentine embroiderers to achieve perspectival effects similar to painting.[88] Like professional male embroiderers, the Paradiso nuns collaborated with several noted Renaissance painters — Antonio Pollaiuolo, Botticelli, Perugino, Neri di Bicci, Raffaellino del Garbo, and Andrea del Sarto — who developed project designs illustrating familiar religious subjects.[89] Close collaboration between painters and embroiderers vaulted Florentine embroidery to the height of European fashion after 1450. Such collaboration both speaks to the unity of the visual arts in the fifteenth century before restrictive specializations set in and signals the creative translation fundamental to production. Even though art historians have valorized design over execution, embroiderers were not mere technicians but skilled artisans in their own right who adapted elements of the painter's cartoon to a new medium.

The Paradiso nuns specialized in the production of fine embroidered liturgical vestments and furnishings — copes, chasubles, dalmatics, altar frontals — made mainly on commission for other nuns and clerics. Table 4.1 lists all major embroidery projects costing 10 florins or more completed by the workshop between 1451 and 1511. These aesthetically refined pieces combined a taste for the pictorial with the sumptuous; their style was similar to that of the velvet chasuble with embroidered orphrey band shown in fig. 4.1. The nuns were not responsible for making the exquisite cloth from which these items were fashioned. Rather, they crafted the final decorative elements that embellished vestments or frontals in the form of orphreys or figured borders telling a religious story.[90] Viewed within a Renaissance aesthetic, these jewel-like ornaments perfected a sense of the whole by harmonizing all of the constituent elements. Embroidery work also made each piece unique, which satisfied the taste of high-end buyers who wanted to customize furnishings according to liturgical season or spiritual preferences.

Unfortunately, few of the nuns' products survive today. Over the centuries, liturgical furnishings were either destroyed to recoup precious metals or cut into smaller pieces to satisfy collectors. One impressive survival securely identified with the Paradiso workshop is the altarcloth destined for the high altar of S. Maria Novella, the city's principal Dominican church.[91] Commissioned in

Table 4.1. Major Embroidery Commissions at S. Brigida del Paradiso, 1451–1511

Year	Item	Imagery	Client/Broker	Price (in florins)
1451	2 altarcloths	Lives of Christ, Virgin	Pierozzo Banchi, *setaiuolo*	80
1451	Altar frontal	Life of Virgin	Nuns of Montevarchi	20
1451	Altarcloth	Life of S. Donato	Clergy of Arezzo	60–70
1451	Border for cope	Life of Christ	Fra Zanobi, syndic of the Paradiso	80
1452	Altarcloth	Nativity of Christ	Mariotto Banchi, *setaiuolo*	42
1452	Chasuble, other vestments	Virgin and Christ child	Friars of Scopeto in Florence	over 47
1453	Altarcloth	Life of Virgin	Gherardo di Pagolo, *setaiuolo*	46
1453	Altarcloth	Life of Virgin	Sold via Fra Zanobi	48
1462	Border for chasuble	Life of Virgin	Archbishop of Florence	40
1463	*Fregio*	Nativity of Christ	Cardinal of Spoleto	50
1463	*Fregio*, cope hood	Life of Virgin; coronation of Virgin	Lorenzo d'Alcieri Biliotti	59
1465	Border for cope	Nativity of Christ	Piero d'Antonio, merchant in Arezzo	55
1466	Altarcloth	Life of Virgin	Friars of S. M. Novella	30
1466	Altarcloth	Unknown	Gesuati friars of Siena	11
1467	Altarcloth	Unknown	Gesuati friars of Florence, on behalf of nuns of S. Marta in Siena	22
1468	Altarcloth	Unknown	Nuns of S. Niccolò in Pisa	17
1470 –72	Full liturgical garb	Various	Don Gratia, papal cubiculary	382
1475 –76	Altarcloth	Unknown	Nuns of Monticelli	62
1477	Altarcloth, cope hood	Unknown	Francesco Sassetti, gift to friars of S. M. Novella	48 sugg.
1484	Altarcloth	Life of Virgin	Alessandro di Giovanni della Magnia	43
1494	*Fregio*	Unknown	Francesco and Giovanni Pandolfini, *setaiuoli*	40
1496	*Fregio*	Life of Virgin	General of Franciscan order	44
1500	*Fregio*	Unknown	Francesco Marsuppini	40
1511	Cope hood	Annunciation	Purveyor of Merchants' Guild Court	11

Source: ASF, Mon. S. Brigida, vols. 147, 148, 149, 152, 154, 155, 158.

1466, this monumental piece depicts fifteen stories from the life of the Virgin, following a design by the painter Paolo Schiavo (1397–1478). In the 1450s and 1460s, Paolo Schiavo was the convent's chief collaborator on embroidery designs, establishing a niche market for himself despite the fact that his graceful but austere classicism may have seemed somewhat antiquated by midcentury. Nonetheless, his style was diffused to a wide, mixed audience across Tuscany through the capillary reach of the decorative arts. Clearly the Paradiso nuns appreciated his artistic vision, since in 1463 they commissioned him to paint their new refectory, whose images are now lost.[92] Paolo also collaborated with the nuns of S. Verdiana, known for their exquisite workmanship, although they did not embroider for the market. The *tondo* depicting the coronation of the Virgin, executed circa 1459 by one or several nuns based on his design, became an object of cult worship within S. Verdiana after the resplendent face of the Virgin was miraculously completed "by the hand of an angel."[93]

The first documented embroidery commissions at the Paradiso date from early 1451, when two historiated altarcloths (*fregi*) were sold through the convent's main silk dealers, Pierozzo and Mariotto Banchi, for 80 florins.[94] These pieces, illustrating the lives of Christ and the Virgin, probably shared the lively chromatic quality and dynamic figural composition characteristic of liturgical furnishings made in this decade. In the spring of 1451, the nuns began work on three additional pieces based on Paolo's designs. The concurrent work on three major projects indicates that this was a vibrant workshop aggressively pursuing local and regional clients. Since large projects like altarcloths required the supporting work of many hands, the product itself became a reflection of religious women's lives together. One of their initial clients was a group of nuns in the neighboring town of Montevarchi. The choice of subject matter and the selection of particular hands for facture underscore once again the extent to which groups of religious women made their own aesthetic decisions about the visual embellishment of their community. Another hanging illustrating the life of S. Donato was made for clergy in Arezzo, valued at 60 to 70 florins when finished. Subjecting nuns' wares to the same scrutiny as those produced by secular artists showed the extent to which religious women had entered the marketplace. A third piece of embroidery depicting the life of Christ went to an unnamed client.[95]

By the 1460s, the Paradiso nuns were attracting high-status clients looking for refined workmanship and tasteful, classicizing designs. Among them was the archbishop of Florence, Giovanni Dietisalvi, for whom they embroidered a chasuble in 1462 "with silk of different colors, gold, and silver, showing the story of

Our Lady," costing 40 florins. The following year, the nuns sold a similar piece to the cardinal of Spoleto, this time illustrating scenes from Christ's nativity. Other important commissions in the 1460s came from the Gesuati friars of Siena, whose patronage marked the workshop's regional prestige given the many Sienese workshops renowned for similar work. In the same years, the nuns embroidered liturgical furnishings for their own sacristy. They continued to make sumptuous pieces through the Quattrocento, occasionally working with private patrons like Francesco Sassetti, who bought vestments for S. Maria Novella; Sassetti's kin were the original patrons of the high altar there.[96] More commonly, commissions issued from high-ranking ecclesiastical officials like the general of the Franciscan order as the nuns' reputation spread by word of mouth through clerical networks and was promoted by Paradiso monks.[97] Although the nuns continued to manufacture various textiles through the 1540s, their last significant embroidery commission dates from 1500. One additional, less substantial job was undertaken in 1511.

The Paradiso workshop reached its zenith in 1470, when it was commissioned to embroider a full set of liturgical vestments for Don Gratia, Benedictine abbot of Léon and papal chamberlain to Paul II.[98] This crown jewel of workshop production, consisting of a chasuble, dalmatic, cope hood, and several smaller items, took eighteen months to complete and carried a price tag of 382 florins. A project of this magnitude not only required an extensive, reliable network of suppliers but also an internal management system of some complexity. Work began in October 1470 and proceeded apace; to speed completion, the nuns consigned smaller decorative elements such as fringes to other religious women and hired a goldsmith to make various ornaments for the cope hood.[99] Consigning parts of large embroidery pieces was not uncommon among convent workshops. The Paradiso nuns reserved the primary figural elements for their own hands, however, thus paralleling the practice in painters' workshops whereby the master assumed responsibility for the most important work. Paolo Schiavo designed several of the pieces and probably coordinated the overall project design. Other painters involved in the project included Antonio di Boldoro and Domenico di Michelino, both commonly identified with the circle of Filippo Lippi. Because the capital outlay for raw materials was substantial, Don Gratia arranged seven installment payments, two via the Medici bank.[100] As work progressed, Abbess Eulalia Buondelmonti shrewdly gifted their patron with a pair of the convent's famed eyeglasses and other tokens of friendship. In July 1471, the abbot himself visited the house to check progress and attended the convent banquet held in his honor. He and his entourage returned once again in April 1472 to pick up the outfit.[101] This stunning ensemble required coordination with local painters, artisans, and other nuns and also drew the Paradiso nuns into business relationships with international bankers and members of the papal court.

Interspersed with these costly, large-scale commissions were smaller projects undertaken for other religious houses or consigned by professional lay embroiderers. These items are of particular interest for the history of material culture and devotional practices. Instead of catering to affluent patrons with a penchant for display, these little embroidery pieces formed part of an everyday visual culture centered on affective piety. The Paradiso nuns embroidered a little tunic for a statuette of the Christ child exhibited by the monks of S. Salvi, embellished a small pouch for the Gesuati friars of Siena showing a Pietà flanked by two diminutive angels, and made tabernacle cloths and a Gospel book cover for the nuns of Monticelli, themselves renowned for silk work. In the 1460s and 1470s, the workshop embroidered small faces of saints for S. Pier Maggiore; several were incorporated into an altarcloth for the convent church, while others apparently were independent devotional objects.[102] These unassuming commissions formed part of a monastic network of commercial exchange that has yet to be recovered fully. In the case of S. Pier Maggiore, kinship ties facilitated transactions with the Paradiso. In the later fifteenth century, each convent housed two pairs of talented sisters from respected notarial families. Most likely Margherita Riccoldi — a known scribe, embroiderer, and frequent second in command at the Paradiso — settled business arrangements with her sister Benedetta, who headed S. Pier Maggiore from 1474 to 1489. The Paradiso nuns developed yet another set of business contacts with professional embroiderers, for whom they made complex elements like faces and figures rather than simpler decorative ones like fringe. Depending on the number and size of objects produced, each minor commission fetched between 1 and 7 florins.

Despite its religious subject matter and liturgical uses, convent embroidery came under censure by reformers for its "vanity" and worldliness. Spearheading this crusade was the Dominican preacher Savonarola, who aimed his invectives primarily at the Murate nuns internationally recognized for both embroidery and manuscript illumination. In a scathing sermon delivered in May 1495, Savonarola recalled that he had admonished the house a few days earlier to stop producing such vanities. In a public tongue-lashing, Savonarola scolded the nuns and urged them "to put aside the splashes, patterns, webs, and olive trees that they make in gold and silver" and further instructed them to throw away their choral books written in the new polyphony, which he viewed as "satanic."[103] At stake in these critiques was a competing vision of monastic life defined by austerity, even though these products were not intended for convent consumption. With his usual dramatic flair, Savonarola positioned illuminated manuscripts, polyphonic music, and embroidery pieces as religiously contested objects whose sensuality polluted convents and whose glitter distracted nuns from divine illumination. Although the preacher enjoyed a devoted following at Le Murate, economic needs trumped his objections. Savonarola's followers had more success in restricting luxury production at convents under their tutelage. In 1514 the staunch Savonarolan and Dominican general Tommaso Gaetano forced the nuns of S. Jacopo to limit earnings from gold thread production to 8 florins per month, to be put toward communal expenses; any excess had to be deposited with their supervisors.[104]

In the 1490s, income from the Paradiso embroidery workshop began to taper off in response to changing consumer tastes rather than reforming zeal. Under the guidance of Abbess Eufragia Biliotti, the workshop shifted to a midrange niche in fine linen wares.[105] Although priced far below ornate liturgical furnishings, fine linen goods were still expensive items; the handkerchief Piovano Arlotto bought in 1450 for 9 lire represented more than three weeks' earnings for an unskilled laborer. These articles were dispersed along different pathways from those of embroidery and put a different social face on commercial transactions. Fine linen goods were sold directly to individual customers at the convent turnstile; the nuns probably kept a small ledger nearby to record purchases, as did the Monticelli nuns for the sale of foodstuffs. Clients included nuns' friends and families, their tenants, the wives of Paradiso business associates, and other Florentines seeking quality wares, like the bookseller Vespasiano da Bisticci.[106] Handkerchiefs were also marketed in lots of ten at the Arezzo textile fairs by convent linen suppliers.

Around 1500, the Paradiso nuns began to scale back market production as their portfolio took on more traditional features based on rents. After completing their last embroidery commission in 1511, the nuns continued to spin gold thread in lesser quantities and to sell fine linen handkerchiefs through the 1540s. Workshop production may have slowed in connection with internal dissent between monks that factionalized the nuns in the first two decades of the century.[107] But the primary impetus behind shrinking volume was probably economic in nature. The Paradiso assiduously purchased residential and commercial properties with surplus earnings and dowries, but their endowment only stabilized after it absorbed the patrimonies of several smaller male houses. In the last quarter of the fifteenth century, the convent integrated an extensive, far-flung rural patrimony in Montevarchi, Poggibonsi, Monte Marciano, Castelfranco, Empoli, and Montelupo into its portfolio. The nuns also developed a much stronger presence in Florence as urban landlords, inheriting properties scattered throughout the city from these smaller male houses.[108] These acquisitions paid tribute to the nuns' religious merits and political acumen. Political dynamics favored large, female monastic institutions over less robust male houses in the territorial periphery; no doubt the influence of Lorenzo de' Medici as a convent *operaio* also made itself felt in high ecclesiastical circles.[109]

After 1500, the Paradiso profited still further from ongoing suppression of small male houses as distant as Volterra. When the convent undertook a full-scale inventory of holdings in 1538, it claimed an enormous patrimony comprised of at least 497 properties, ranging from small vineyards and mills to profitable farms, shops, and houses with balconies.[110] This portfolio probably made the Paradiso the wealthiest suburban convent at the start of the Medici principate, with real geographic reach as a landowner. Like S. Gaggio, the house faced expensive reconstruction after the siege, but unfortunately accounts are too sketchy to document the process in detail. The convent economy remained a mixed one, however, and the nuns never withdrew completely from the market.

The third and final case study presented here concerns the Franciscan nuns of S. Maria a Monticelli, which takes the story of convent textile production forward in time and illuminates responses to changing demand and new fashions as well as to contracting work opportunities after Trent. By 1500, this venerable convent south of the city was already an active player in the silk industry. The nuns raised mulberry leaves, which they sold to various buyers, including the Portico nuns, as part of a broader attempt to establish a native sericulture in Tuscany.[111] Like some of their urban counterparts, they also organized a local network of reelers on their dealers' behalf. In the 1510s Suor Piera Pitti, "our mistress for reeling silk," worked closely with the *setaiuolo* Giovanfrancesco Infanghati, who also employed laywomen reelers directly.[112] Although their textile work ran the gamut, by 1500 the nuns' most lucrative product was decorative tassels (*nappe*) made of silk and gold, produced mainly for the Gondi and Capponi silk firms. These generic luxury items found a wide range of applications on high-end clothing, liturgical furnishings, household goods, and decorations. From 1500 to 1520, textile manufacture consistently represented 10 percent of convent income, on par with earnings at the Paradiso in the second half of the Quat-trocento.[113] Commercial knowledge at Monticelli was thoroughly distributed throughout the senior ranks. Abbesses, as they were called by house tradition, served three-year terms and often rotated in and out of other important offices. In the first half of the sixteenth century, the sixty nuns were led by women from the city's principal families, such as Cecilia Niccolini, Lucrezia and Paola Cinozzi, Battista Corsini, and Chiara Baroncelli.[114]

Around 1510 the Monticelli nuns adopted lace making as a commercial activity. The impetus behind this decision is unclear, although their extensive business connections surely alerted them to new market trends. Other convents adjusted production around this same time to conform with changing fashion and patronage arrangements. The tertiaries of S. Orsola added lace making to their wide-ranging repertoire by 1520; by midcentury it had become their principal textile activity. Around 1500 the nuns of S. Monaca, among the earliest commercial spinners of gold thread, began selling their product directly to wealthy private patrons, like the wife of Lorenzo di Pierfrancesco de' Medici, who they also provided with finished goods. Rather than producing for the open market, these nuns later became principal furnishers for the Medici court and other private consumers.[115] In 1507 the Monticelli workshop began producing *reticella*, one of the earliest needlepoint laces featuring geometric designs.[116] Using fine white linen thread, they made lace for delicate cuffs, collars, and trimmings and used metallic thread for the heavier, more sumptuous lacework embellishing women's snoods and garments. The fashion for lace expanded rapidly, becoming more varied, complex, and delicate. Pattern books soon appeared, like the one printed by the Venetian Alessandro Paganino in 1527, to satisfy "the virtuous desire shown by astute, clever women" pursuing this elegant needlecraft.[117]

By 1550, the new vogue for lace and changes within the silk industry itself had displaced gold thread production and embroidery in convent workshops. Faced with increased competition in foreign markets and rapid product innovation, *setaiuoli* redirected production around midcentury toward less expensive fabrics like plain silks and taffetas to secure a niche market. Dominated by male weavers, this production afforded nuns little role; to adjust to this development, convents deemphasized the production of gold thread and embroidery and focused on fine lace instead.[118] In the mid-1540s, the nuns of S. Piero a Monticelli manufactured over 1,000 *braccia* (over 580 meters) of lace annually for customers ranging from court attendants to Duchess Eleonora of Toledo to the convent of S. Jacopo, which probably resold these wares. Ironically, one of the textile activities under-

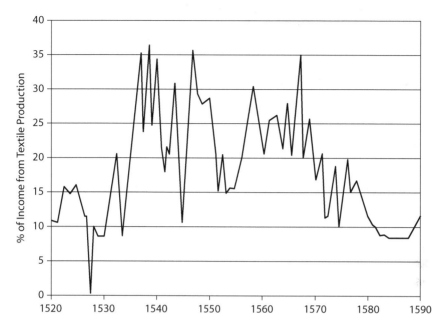

Graph 4.2. Monticelli Textile Income, 1520–90. *Source:* ASF, CRSGF, 98, vols. 27, 28, 29, 30.

taken by S. Orsola for the Medici court in the mid-sixteenth century was burning down metallic thread to recoup the precious metals.[119] After 1550, Monticelli's nun-treasurers grouped annual textile revenues under a single heading called "lace and other handiwork." They probably kept secondary ledgers for various workrooms, but the disappearance of these ledgers makes it impossible to recon-struct marketing patterns and relative volume.

Still, the Monticelli business accounts document the trend line for textile income over the century, which is summarized in graph 4.2.[120] The nuns consis-tently drew 10 percent of income from handiwork between 1500 and 1520 but were plunged into crisis after 1527 when plague, quarantine, and foreign troop movements severely disrupted trade. The siege of 1529–30 brought about the complete destruction of their site and their permanent relocation within city walls. Taking up temporary residence in private houses near S. Spirito, the nuns continued to reel and spin silk "for various workshops" under the "charitable and prudent" governance of Abbess Chiara Baroncelli.[121] In 1534, they moved into new quarters, an adapted plague hospital behind S. Croce, and embarked on an intensive work campaign to remake their fortunes. Textile earnings represented

31 percent of total income from 1534–40; lost rents were partially offset by gifts and loans from "many people" eager to see the convent flourish. In the following decade, raw earnings increased but fell proportionately to 26 percent because, like S. Gaggio, these nuns also doubled monastic dowries and alienated property for quick cash.[122] Work continued to offer a dependable means of regaining solvency, with textile manufacture generating 21–26 percent of convent income in the 1550s and 1560s; the primary product was lace. Although the nuns worked with other materials, they consigned low-paying tasks like carding and spinning to "various women," just as nuns in the silk industry had done a century earlier.[123]

In the 1570s and 1580s, however, textile income declined consistently, representing only 17 percent and 10 percent of income in those decades. Although the nuns continued to tally annual sales of lace, new enclosure rulings enforced after 1575 negatively impacted production. Silvia Evangelisti has shown that Florentine nuns resisted the imposition of *clausura* in part because it undercut business activities and support networks. Convent businesses, like the flourishing apothecary shop at S. Orsola, suffered when laity could no longer visit freely and buy their products.[124] The Monticelli case affords more concrete evidence of the contraction of nuns' work after Trent, which thus far has been impressionistic. Textile production did indeed decline by the 1580s, forcing nuns to depend more completely on their families and state subsidies. Reduced income from handiwork was felt keenly, especially when it was accompanied by the loss of autonomy and other forms of retrenchment. The full emergence of a post-Tridentine monastic system hinged not only on the institution of enclosure but also on the subsequent displacement of an economic regime more than a century in the making.

Books and Educational Activities

While textiles dominated nuns' work, the time-honored monastic activity of copying and illuminating books constituted a secondary revenue stream at some houses. At least seven Florentine convents produced books for the market in the fifteenth century: Le Murate, the Paradiso, S. Gaggio, Lapo, S. Jacopo, S. Francesco, and Monticelli. There was a strong correlation between book production and embroidery, which sometimes were executed by the same nuns. Although the arts of pen and needle produced different classes of objects with a different standing in the art historical canon, embroidery and copying required similar manual dexterity, shared similar aesthetics and narrative subjects, and entailed similar repetitive demands that furthered spiritual maturation through discipline and concentration. These activities were easily absorbed into convent rhythms; the work was easily taken up or put down in tandem with the liturgical hours. Such quiet, sedentary activity suited the health needs of women's communities, which invariably supported several nuns with chronic health problems or other disabilities.[125] Importantly, nuns' scribal activities frequently inverted customary power relations between the sexes. The literate, well-born nuns of the Monticelli produced breviaries and other *scritti* for Franciscan friars who lacked both their social rank and graphic abilities.[126]

In fact, the Paradiso had a significant, unrecognized influence on the Florentine book trade throughout the Quattrocento. Encouraged by their rule to read, these nuns displayed an "appetite for books" that rivaled their noble English counterparts at famed Syon Abbey.[127] The nuns reportedly read aloud at every meal and owned various works of vernacular religious literature "in good condition." Soon after the community's refounding in 1401, the Paradiso began producing books on commission and marketing them directly to clients.[128] Focusing exclusively on the monks' activities, Renato Piattoli has argued that the Paradiso functioned more as a distribution center than as a node of production in the early Quattrocento. Although they worked for various clients, the monks established their principal relationship with the Franciscan order, procuring books for convents and friaries throughout Tuscany and Italy. Among their customers was the renowned Franciscan preacher Bernardino of Siena.[129]

By midcentury, Paradiso nuns also produced books for the market, which generated 1–2 percent of convent income, but they cultivated a more ordinary lay clientele for these items. Throughout the 1450s, the scriptorium regularly turned out standard religious books, "that is, breviaries and books of hours written and produced by our monks and nuns for sale," although we do not know the size of the scriptorium or its annual output. Books of hours were among the most popular items of vernacular religious literature throughout Italy, especially among women readers. Each volume was produced by a single scribe working independently.[130] Probably only a small number of nuns worked as copyists; eight to ten nuns staffed the commercial scriptorium at Le Murate in the late 1480s. Nuns at Monticelli and S. Gaggio also produced books of hours for commercial sale in small quantities, while other convents regularly sold their products to religious houses via networks whose contours we are only just beginning to discover.[131] Scholars may have underestimated the scope of the Florentine book trade by discounting these secondary centers of production and distribution.

Like silk work, book production occasionally drove changes in the physical complex. In 1465 the Monticelli nuns installed a new glass window to improve lighting conditions "for the writing" of their principal scribe, Suor Filippa de' Medici, while the Murate nuns re-sited their scriptorium to a well-lit upper loggia following a disastrous fire in 1471.[132]

This evidence should be read for its cultural significance as well as its economic import. Although our understanding of the scope of convent book production remains impressionistic, it is clear that nuns played a critical role in the diffusion and expansion of literacy throughout the Quattrocento, especially among urban women. Monastic women not only penned hundreds of letters in search of favors, gifts, and loans; they also authored a wealth of literary texts, including poems and plays. In addition, Judith Bryce has shed new light on patterns of book ownership among fifteenth-century Florentine laywomen, many of whom profited from convent education.[133] Even the transition to printing involved a few nuns in its early stages. Several nuns worked as typesetters for the short-lived press established in 1476 at S. Jacopo, the second such enterprise in the city; Suor Marietta Bellacci earned 3 florins for her work as a compositor on Pulci's *Morgante*.[134] During its eight years of operation, the press printed some twelve thousand volumes and thousands of religious images and saints' lives. Although the majority of named clients were clerics, customers included the nuns of S. Lucia, S. Jacopo itself, and the Annalena, well known for educational activities that redistributed texts and knowledge.[135]

Although not all graphic activity was geared toward commerce, copying had second-order economic effects that aided self-sufficiency. Houses with active scriptoria produced liturgical books for internal use, thus eliminating the need to purchase them. At S. Gaggio, nuns copied breviaries and psalters for their new sisters, the raw materials for which were often supplied by the novices' kinsmen.[136] These books might later be sent out for illumination by a lay miniaturist. Before the advent of printing, liturgical books, ranging from small breviaries and psalters for daily use to large, ornamented choir books, often carried high price tags depending on materials and craftsmanship. Breviaries written on paper could be found in numerous stationers' shops, but more durable versions were made of higher-priced parchment. The breviary purchased in 1471 for Petronilla Bini, a young nun in S. Pier Maggiore, cost 25 florins; antiphonaries and other choir books cost considerably more.[137] Some of the works nuns copied for their institutions were of exceptionally high quality. Although monastic humility discouraged claims of authorship, a few examples can be attributed to individual hands. In the mid-Quattrocento, Piera de' Medici, the accomplished abbess of S. Verdiana, put her graphic talents to convent use by copying a missal in her elegant, modified Gothic book hand. Suor Angelica Rucellai, an active scribe at S. Jacopo, signed the copy she made of Domenico Cavalca's *Specchio di croce* in 1460, while another copyist in the same house, Suor Lucrezia Panciatichi (d. 1535), was praised in her obituary for her tireless efforts "in copying and notating books retained by the convent choir."[138] Other nuns excelled as miniaturists as well as scribes, and occasionally the miniaturists partnered with the scribes to create the finished product. Suor Agnola da Rabatta and Suor Gostanza Cocchi of S. Ambrogio collaborated on a breviary for the convent in 1518 (fig. 4.2); Suor Gostanza copied the text, Suor Agnola illuminated it. Both nuns autographed their work.[139] Occasionally, these precious volumes found their way into the gift economy that enriched Florentine social and political relations. Several years after Suor Battista Carducci illuminated a lavish missal at Le Murate circa 1509, the convent presented it to the visiting pope Leo X, who reciprocated with a stunning countergift of 200 scudi.[140] Florentine nuns also reproduced books of sermons, moralizing tracts, compilations of saints' lives, and other works of vernacular religious literature. In this way, they enlarged their convent libraries and expanded the cultural reach of their institutions.

The combination of nuns' literacy and textile skills provided the foundation for activities centered on the education and moral formation of young girls. Custodial and educational services were second in economic importance only to textile work, although it should be noted that female religious orders in this period were not specifically charged with educational duties. Only with the growth of the Ursulines (approved 1544) and Tridentine enclosure provisions did religious women adopt primary responsibility for female education. In Renaissance Florence, convent schooling blurred the distinctions between guardianship and education. Having discussed these subjects elsewhere in print, I highlight only the basic points here.[141] Florentine girls from the commercial and professional classes could acquire vernacular literate skills in one of several convent schools scattered throughout the city. Although there was no fixed curriculum, these boarding schools instructed girls in reading, sewing, and "the virtues," which formed a unified ensemble geared toward individual moral formation. Since the idea of women's reading still engendered social anxieties in the Quattrocento, embedding the acquisition of literacy in a holistic religious program lessened its dangers. Nuns not only gave girls an elementary religious education but also taught them the core values of female deportment — silence, modesty, disciplined use of the

Fig. 4.2. Suor Agnola da Rabatta (miniatures) and Suor Gostanza Cocchi (text), breviary from convent of S. Ambrogio, Florence, 1518. Photo: Kunsthistoriches Institut in Florenz — Max-Planck-Institut.

body — through a complete, round-the-clock immersion. Convent education re-volved as much around inculcating gender norms as it did around teaching prac-tical skills. Over the course of the Quattrocento, hundreds of young girls who spent between one and two years in convent schools came to embody important gender expectations, which they then carried over into secular culture. Some girls may have learned how to write as well, although it remained morally prob-lematic for laywomen to acquire graphic skills. From an economic standpoint, the fees, tips, and other markups attached to "learning the virtues" offered female religious communities a significant income stream that could be leveraged ac-cording to circumstances.

Besides providing formal education, convents frequently accepted young girls as temporary boarders when family circumstances warranted. The practice of placing girls in convent care (known as *serbanza*) was widespread and served as a way to protect their honor and marriage prospects. This practice became in-creasingly prevalent in the politically turbulent years from 1480 to 1530, with spikes in guardianship correlating to the movement of foreign armies and other dangers to girls' physical integrity. Prior to the development of large-scale cus-todial institutions in Florence circa 1550, *serbanza* was the major form of extra-familial care for girls of the middling, artisan classes as well as for the vul-nerable rich.[142] Even S. Pier Maggiore, possibly the only Florentine convent that did not produce marketable goods, occasionally took in girls and adult women as boarders. By 1500, an informal urban geography of girls' conservatories had a-lready emerged, concentrated in three zones: the northern sector on Via S. Gallo, especially at S. Luca, S. Apollonia, and S.Agata; the southern edge, mainly at S. Niccolò dei Frieri; and outside the walls, at Lapo, S. Piero a Monticelli, S. Martino al Prato, S. Maria al Vergine, and the Portico. Interestingly, the Paradiso nuns never embarked on this path, despite their commitment to literacy and female clients, because other elements of their value system precluded such distractions.[143]

At the most basic level, taking girls into custody was another strategy for economic survival, especially at houses with small patrimonies. The assertion made by the nuns of S. Luca that they lacked sufficient endowment income was confirmed by their 1509 balance sheet. When Pazzi made his pastoral rounds that year, the annual fees paid by four young boarders at this major conservatory — 52 florins — equaled all combined convent rents. That same year, the Portico nuns netted 40 florins from boarders, a sum that exceeded rents by roughly 5 flo-rins. In other words, these two convents were more dependent on teaching fees than on their property endowments. Beyond offering these immediate economic gains, however, *serbanza* figured as the leading edge of future patronage. Nuns' work as caregivers and teachers made vital contributions to both convent finances and the urban social order, but guardianship did not turn solely on economic issues; it also was a political strategy, providing a means of sustaining social influence through clientage.

Several smaller sources besides textiles, books, and education fed mixed convent economies. The demand for art that helped define Renaissance Italy dovetailed with forms of late medieval piety stressing material aids to devotion. Nuns seized the opportunities created by this intersection by marketing items such as rosaries, which enjoyed an explosive popularity in the late fifteenth century under Dominican promotion. They also made inexpensive figurines of saints, angels, and the Virgin using ephemeral materials like glass, paper, and plaster that had a short life span. In the 1490s, the nuns of S. Domenico, who ran a successful putting-out operation earlier in the century, also gilded and decorated small devotional items probably constructed out of papier-mâché or gesso. Fifteen nuns, each identified by name in convent accounts, painted rosaries and figurines in a workshop arrangement.[144] Each nun earned 7 soldi for painting a rosary, 3 soldi less than what an unskilled laborer earned in a day; making and embellishing a figurine earned 18 soldi. The mass production of such devotional objects helped fuel the expanding market for religious artifacts and worldly goods.[145] Although similar items were produced in lay workshops, the ones produced by religious women probably gave them a special cachet. These workshops formed the historical backbone of later monastic craft collaborations, like the one organized around Suor Plautilla Nelli, "the first woman painter of Florence."[146]

In addition to these income-producing activities, Florentine nuns also engaged in various brokerage functions that gave them standing in the local economy. They retailed used goods acquired through death or donation, purveying burial palls, wax, books, household linens and furnishings, and used clothing in the city's thriving secondhand markets. In times of plenty, nuns retailed foodstuffs from their farm holdings and sold or exchanged goods in kind received as rents or gifts. Protecting the integrity of these business transactions made convents frequent litigants in the archbishop's court throughout the fifteenth century.[147] At more richly endowed institutions like S. Pier Maggiore, religious women directly controlled capital that enabled them to broker credits and debts with neighbors; they also put their business savvy to work as appraisers in property disputes. Even if we cannot assign a precise monetary value to these transactions, they nonetheless illuminate the extent to which nuns were involved in the economic culture of their day.

In conclusion, the evidence presented here offers new perspectives on commodity production, the scope of nuns' work, and the behavior of convents as economic institutions in Renaissance Florence. Convents pursued an intentional policy of market diversification that rendered them more nimble and gave the Florentine economy much-needed elasticity, providing cheap labor reserves situated outside regulated guild structures. Wide-ranging commercial activities not only put nuns in contact with buyers, suppliers, and distributors, but also spun a web of other kinds of relations — ones of dependence, patronage, and exchange — around religious women and their institutions. Economic activities restructured cloisters, prompting the installation of new windows and the allocation of separate spaces for workrooms.

Moreover, convent records document the essential yet unrecognized role nuns played in the development of the Florentine silk industry. Tucked away behind convent walls, the nuns helped advance the city's growing international stature grounded in this entrepreneurial industry. The vital role of the Florentine state in protecting private business interests maps out a statist model of economic development, illuminating the profound contradictions inherent in civic policies. Having seized the moral high ground as protectors of convent purity, the commune then proceeded to utterly contradict itself by permitting the easy flow of male business associates into convent precincts. These official actions cast new light on the cyclical calls for monastic reform as well as point to the dim likelihood of success. With so much at stake economically, reform efforts and civic control seemed destined to fail.

Finally, this robust evidence provides insight into what motivated nuns to work, a complex matter. Beyond meeting basic needs, paid labor was a means to various ends. Earnings not only improved nuns' living standards but helped them launch capital projects over which they exercised considerable decision-making power. Work further extended nuns' social reach by drawing them into interconvent commerce and broad-gauged clientage relations. Despite their celibate status, Florentine religious women played an irreplaceable role in the reproduction of society through education and the dissemination of texts. Regardless of monastic order or level of affluence, virtually all Florentine nuns can be considered working women who regularly engaged in market activities.

CHAPTER FIVE

Contesting the Boundaries of Enclosure

For centuries, the literary figure of the wayward nun has dominated views of Renaissance convent life. Whether intended to titillate readers or condemn clerical hypocrisy, ribald stories of bawdy nuns and their daring lovers reflect a deep-seated fascination with what one scholar has called "eros in the convent."[1] These imaginative tales depict Renaissance convents as sexual hothouses akin to brothels — a seductive depiction but one that nonetheless distorts our understanding of Italian religion and society in important ways. Convent licentiousness has been proposed not only as fact but as explanatory fact, especially for the momentous religious reforms of the sixteenth century. Early modern religious polemics designed either to discredit female monasticism as a way of life or to discipline it entrenched this view of promiscuous nuns running rampant in poorly governed houses.[2] Ironically, recent studies that open valuable windows on the history of sexuality have further strengthened the link between sex and "scandal" in the convent.[3]

Scholars are just beginning to assess the extent to which this view of sexual dissipation accurately reflects historical conditions. Elizabeth Lehfeldt has shown that the permeable cloister characterizing pre-Tridentine Spanish convents more commonly generated legal literacy among nuns than sexual adventures. Similarly, Katherine Gill has argued that convent scandal resulted less from nuns' promiscuity than from the often incompatible political, social, and institutional views held by Italian religious women and their supervisors. As nuns engaged with difficult issues — self-governance, collective organization, political presence, sheer survival — they asserted their own sense of the priorities ordering their lives. Other studies have established that in Europe, celibacy was neither the centerpiece of female religious life nor the end goal pursued by many religious women.[4] Indeed, the very concept of virginity itself was open to contestation among canonists and hagiographers, who considered wives and widows capable of retaining the more significant virtue of "integrity" or of preserving their "true" virginity through scrupulous purity.[5] In other words, meanings of female virginity were part of a larger process of social negotiation both inside and outside the convent.

Rather than accepting sexual suspicions at face value, we need to consider how and why nuns' sexual behavior — imagined and performed — constructed previous historical accounts and continues to shape explanatory schemes. Because sexuality itself is so potent, it helps mask other circumstances through invocation or proxy. Assertions of licentiousness, for instance, obscure the inadequate level of pastoral care generally afforded religious women and hide the state-building agendas so evident in Italian Renaissance cities; moreover, scurrilous charges deflected attention from who had power to assign female celibacy in the first place. Simply talking about sex was a political act with real power to harm, making sexual defamation one of the most powerful tools for regulating behavior in late medieval and early modern Europe.[6]

This chapter investigates the religious discipline of Florentine convents by critically addressing issues of nuns' sexuality and reclusion. It places questions of monastic discipline on a more complex footing by exposing the competing interests in organized religious communities held by civic magistrates, ecclesiastical officials, kin, patrons, and nuns. Many of these conflicts were played out around enclosure, which often figured as a stand-in for general convent discipline among contemporaries and historians alike. One scholar directly attributes the infamous moral laxity of Venetian convents to failures of *clausura*.[7] Prior to the imposition of mandatory enclosure by Tridentine reformers, however, enclosure functioned as a politicized concept that was only partially concerned with women's physical reclusion.[8] Instead, what stood at the heart of enclosure controversies in Italian Renaissance cities was a battle for control of religious resources. Enclosure served as a lightning rod for jurisdictional disputes as well as for broader tensions surrounding female agency, male sexuality, divergent religious values, and familial claims on local institutions. The multiple roles created by and imposed on nuns—whether as vulnerable virgins, textile workers, purveyors of crucial goods and services, political clients, family members, spiritual friends—only deepened these tensions. Whatever type of enclosure nuns practiced, they inevitably irritated one segment of society or another since they served many masters with differing points of view.

The first part of the chapter surveys the prescriptive framework of enclosure from 1300 to 1450 as well as the social expectations that established open reclusion as the norm for Florentine convents. The second section tracks attempts by reformers and ecclesiastical officials to enforce tighter enclosure in the mid- to late fifteenth century—attempts that paradoxically consolidated the hold of lay patrons and kin on Florentine religious communities. The third section analyzes the civic regulation of convents using previously untapped records kept by the innovative Florentine magistracy charged with policing nuns, prostitutes, and sodomites. Because the Florentine state lacked a well-developed coercive apparatus, efforts at civic control relied heavily on street gossip and formal denunciations that provide a unique window on the urban discursive landscape. The final section takes up the more concerted implementation of enclosure in the early sixteenth century. New mechanisms to enforce *clausura*—licensing visitors, censoring letters, encasing nuns in a multitude of restrictions—catalyzed the growth of both civic and ecclesiastical power. Although claustration proceeded fitfully, there was a clear movement toward greater uniformity and discipline at least a century before the Catholic Reformation reached its peak. In other words, Tridentine enclosure decrees represented only the culmination of earlier Italian trends, much as they did on the Iberian Peninsula.[9]

The Practice of Open Reclusion, 1300–1450

Medieval religious women pursued a wide spectrum of religious practices, ranging from extreme asceticism and withdrawal to an active apostolate among burgeoning urban populations. These many variants of female religiosity worried thirteenth-century church prelates concerned about the financial stability of traditional monastic institutions, the role of new groups in advancing heresy, and loss of organizational control over uncloistered holy women. Boniface VIII responded by issuing the directive *Periculoso* (1298), which established the canonical framework for enclosure until the Tridentine era.[10] Although flight from the world had long formed part of monastic ideals, *Periculoso* transformed reclusion from a religious choice into an institutional imperative. This sweeping directive announced that all nuns, regardless of rule or location, were to be continuously and perpetually cloistered.[11] *Periculoso* embodied a paradoxical, gender-specific ideology that represented religious women as weak-willed yet powerful beings who needed protection from both the world and themselves. Professed nuns were directed not to leave the convent nor to allow unauthorized persons to enter. The directive thus distinguished between active and passive enclosure, although it did not use those terms explicitly. Certain loopholes remained. *Periculoso* permitted abbesses to conduct convent business outside the cloister and allowed lay entry for "reasonable and obvious cause." This legalistic safety valve opened the ruling to interpretation by nuns seeking greater engagement with the world as well as by sympathetic supervisors looking for reasons to grant it. Members of tertiary communities, who took simple rather than solemn vows, were exempt. Local ordinaries — in essence, bishops — were responsible for enforcing enclosure throughout their diocese, even at institutions otherwise outside their jurisdiction.

While *Periculoso* firmly linked female monasticism to physical reclusion, it was either silent or ambiguous on various points. It did not articulate the "inner" convent spaces forbidden to laity, which in later glosses were considered to be the nuns' choir, refectory, dormitory, chapter house, and workrooms. Nor did the decree seek to control the zones of accommodation mediating secular and cloistered space, such as the parlor, grates, doorways, or turntable used for exchanging goods and money. Questions of visual privacy — the ability of nuns to see and be seen by laity — were not addressed. In contrast to post-Tridentine enclosure rulings, the directive did not emphasize the convent wall as a crucial safeguard of sexual purity; hence the wall did not loom large in either the self-perception or cultural production of Renaissance nuns, in contrast to the sixteenth and seventeenth centuries. Original provisos that enclosure could be broken only if contagion threatened were expanded by the late fourteenth century; nuns were permitted to flee in the face of "fire, ruin, thieves, malefactors, or similar cases of mortal danger."[12] In practice, *Periculoso* was not a single document but an amalgam of ideas that developed over time.

Within a decade of issue, *Periculoso* fell prey to both the jurisdictional battles and special exemptions that characterized the medieval Italian church. Popes and bishops granted exemptions based on local conditions and ecclesiastical favor; enclosure practices thereby became more complex and differentiated throughout the peninsula instead of more uniform. Claustration often activated other conflicts, including struggles related to self-governance. Gill has shown how enclosure controversies galvanized assorted grievances between medieval Italian bishops and the Santuccie (approved 1265).[13] This Benedictine congregation distinguished itself by centralized governance under an abbess general, which allowed adherents to pursue spiritual goals free from politicized meddling by local bishops. Their charismatic founder, Santuccia Carabotti of Gubbio, personally supervised the twenty foundations that sprang up in central Italy before her death in 1305. Shortly after *Periculoso* was issued, Santuccia became embroiled in a fight with the bishop of Faenza over her mobility and supervisory role. To avoid future conflicts, her successor obtained papal confirmation of rights to visit "her convents" with several companions. Later abbess generals periodically visited Santuccie foundations in Italy, including the one in Florence, through the fifteenth century.[14]

Religious women across Europe also lobbied local bishops for greater latitude of movement in order to sustain their economic and political vitality.[15] In Florence, the nuns of S. Pier Maggiore were the first in the city to petition for episcopal enclosure exemptions, winning from Bishop Lotterio della Tosa in 1304 "the power to exit the convent and to speak in the parlor or elsewhere to whomever was necessary for the affairs of the convent."[16] This exemption permitted any nun, not just the abbess, to leave the house on convent business. It did not stipulate that a chaperone was required nor place a time limit on these ventures; it also opened the cloister to persons deemed "necessary" to the full conduct of convent affairs. Several centuries later, in 1526, nuns like Suor Clemenza Tornabuoni merely acted in accord with established privilege in transacting local business outside the cloister by, for example, walking to nearby S. Ambrogio to supervise the pickup of wine dregs. Practically speaking, this privilege had to be exercised regularly for it to retain its effectiveness; nuns' frequent movements throughout the locale reminded neighbors of their special status. S. Pier Maggiore preserved a copy of this privilege in its archive and maintained its viability until the late sixteenth century.[17] Nun-bursars at S. Ambrogio occasionally made the same journey in reverse when delivering payments to S. Pier Maggiore, which enabled them to discuss sensitive matters in person without mediation by male procurators. In Venice, S. Zaccaria was one of at least ten houses practicing open reclusion until the early sixteenth century, much like the nuns of St. Katherine in fifteenth-century Augsburg.[18]

The most remarkable local expression of open reclusion was the ritual marriage between the abbess of S. Pier Maggiore and the Florentine bishop, which formed the centerpiece of episcopal installation rites from 1286 to 1583.[19] Late medieval Italians were on familiar terms with the trope of mystical marriage as an allegorical union between Christ and his church; hence the ironies inherent in the marriage of two avowed celibates could be glossed over. The bishop-groom claimed his see by taking fictive possession of his abbess-bride, who embodied the Florentine diocese. Their ceremonial union closely mimicked lay nuptial rites; it included an exchange of gifts, a ring ceremony, and even a fictive consummation that "perfected" the union. Not only did the bishop's lay guardians attend the wedding banquet in the cloister, but the new bishop himself slept in the convent overnight in a magnificent bed prepared by the abbess and nuns. This extraordinary enactment formally sealed the union between bishop and diocese in ways that made it broadly intelligible to a lay audience. As late as 1567, the abbess personally delivered the marriage bed to the episcopal palace following the ceremony.[20] Since the rite was approved by both civic and ecclesiastical authorities, neither the presence of laity in the cloister nor the abbess's exit vexed onlookers. Indeed, laymen entered female cloisters well into the eighteenth century when it suited political or clerical regimes. At the Venetian convent of Le Vergini, for instance, the doge continued to "marry" the incoming abbess as a demonstration of ducal patronage rights long after the institution of compulsory enclosure.[21]

Open enclosure was not only significant because it enabled nuns to venture out of the cloister to transact ordinary convent business or take various healing cures. It was also important because nuns' visibility on certain festive occasions proved crucial to sustaining a public ritual presence. In the 1450s, the nuns of S. Margherita in Prato joined the throng gathered in the city square on the feast of the Assumption to witness the miraculous relic of the Virgin's girdle being unveiled.[22] Thirty years later, the renowned painter Cosimo Rosselli immortalized the participation of S. Ambrogio nuns in the annual Corpus Christi procession by depicting a cadre of elderly religious women spilling out of the convent church in full view of onlookers (fig. 5.1). Their ability to see and be seen helped them stake a corporate claim to the miraculous relic at the heart of the celebration, which they parlayed over time into other forms of social and economic power.[23] Less frequently, nuns might be seen in transit moving from one dwelling to another; several Florentine communities located outside the walls owned refuges inside the city to which they transferred for greater safety during times of trouble.[24] Physical mobility also enabled nuns to fulfill the spiritual obligations thrust on

Fig. 5.1. Cosimo Rosselli, *Procession of the Holy Miracle.*
Cappella del Miracolo, S. Ambrogio, Florence, 1484–88
(detail). Photo: Kunsthistoriches Institut in Florenz —
Max-Planck-Institut.

them, by which they made a discernable impact on the surrounding community.
Walking through their neighborhoods, they could identify girls who deserved
the dowries testators asked them to administer or judge for themselves which
tenants needed help in the form of an extended grace period on rents. This
hands-on assistance formed a normal part of urban outreach even for nuns who
practiced more traditional forms of monasticism, especially in the absence of
more specialized urban charitable institutions.

Various religious women found a legitimate place on Florentine streets even
after the appearance of *Periculoso*, since new monastic groups often negotiated
modified forms of enclosure as part of their approved charter. Among these local
communities was S. Niccolò dei Frieri, founded in 1392 by five devout Florentine noblewomen under the auspices of the Jerusalemite order. Before taking
solemn vows, these women had remained "completely united" in their goal of
pursuing an active apostolate in which "they visited hospitals and performed
good works."[25] Convent records before 1440 are now lost, but later generations
of nuns reconstructed the community's early history using documents still extant

in the late eighteenth century. Noting with some nostalgia the permeable nature of enclosure throughout the Quattrocento, these nun-chroniclers reported that in 1436 the abbess and two nuns personally accepted several annuitants at a notary's house, which they were able to do because "up to that time one found the nuns without enclosure." Similarly, they cited the fact that profession ceremonies welcomed "many kin of the nuns and servants," leading them to conclude that "the convent still did not have enclosure" thirty years later.[26] However, a rare story of convent escape shows that enclosure could be invoked by the chapter itself when useful to the institution. One night in 1442, three discontented nuns who formed a splinter group within the house fled S. Niccolò "out of malice."[27] The escape must have been planned with outside help, since one nun carried away several expensive prayer books, clothing, linens, a painting of the Virgin, and other things she had kept under lock and key "against the rule." Although full details are unknown, the runaways negotiated individual settlements with the chapter after being apprehended. Instead of rejoining the community, the treasure-laden nun, aided by her brother and a lawyer, reclaimed her monastic dowry plus an annual stipend that would enable her to live independently. A less fortunate companion was imprisoned for several years in a special chamber built "near the oven" as punishment for the failed escape.

Most prominent among the religious women traversing city streets were tertiaries not bound by enclosure rulings. Mario Sensi has shown that these mobile religious women, often equated with the beguines of northern Europe, were commonplace in central Italian towns throughout the fifteenth century.[28] In Florence, the Franciscan tertiaries of S. Onofrio wandered the city seeking alms until the very end of the Quattrocento; the community attended Savonarola's sermons daily as a group to show support. Tertiaries of advanced age or in poor health enjoyed added protection from censure about their mobility.[29] Nonetheless, enclosure surfaced repeatedly as a point of contention. Even before the Savonarolan movement made enclosure a hot-button issue for Dominican women, Antoninus locked horns with Annalena Malatesta, the pious founder of the community bearing her name, when he tried to transform the house into an enclosed nunnery. Working tirelessly to sustain her own vision of religious life, Annalena successfully countered the archbishop through the aid of a powerful lay patron, Lorenzo di Pierfrancesco de' Medici, who used his influence with the papacy to secure judgments favorable to the community. Flourishing through Medici benefaction, the Annalena remained unenclosed until 1586, when Pius III ordered all tertiaries to take solemn vows or leave their communities.[30]

Throughout the Renaissance, female religiosity was enriched by women who lived without a formal rule, unfettered by monastic hierarchy, clerical oversight, property concerns, or mandatory enclosure. Because these alternative modes of religious life lacked a stable institutional base, they tend to be less visible in the historical record. Some communities did not outlive their founders, having exhausted available finances; others simply died out or resurfaced in another form. The spiritual work these groups engaged in spanned a broad spectrum, which placed them in different relationships to enclosure. At one end of the spectrum stood women who valued mobility and lay interaction as an integral part of an active apostolate, like the devout noblewomen who founded S. Niccolò dei Frieri and the Augustinian nuns who ran the hospital at S. Giovanni Battista in the Oltrarno. At the other end were recluses and hermits who sought complete isolation in the liminal spaces of bridges, gates, and walls. Corsini's 1422 visitation turned up two such hermitages on present-day Ponte alle Grazie: one is lost to history; the other was the founding group of Le Murate. What became the largest Renaissance nunnery in Florence had its origins in the spiritual quest of two recluses seeking a simple, penitential life by immuring themselves in a small bridge house. The charismatic pair lived in solitude and poverty, "not wishing to place themselves under another rule than to live peacefully in profound humility as earnest recluses."[31] Scholars have argued that informal groups like these were increasingly regularized by 1500, a claim borne out by the Florentine evidence.[32] The direction of change moved decidedly toward more formal, structured monastic associations that transformed unaffiliated penitents into cloistered nuns. The Italian church proved receptive to charismatic or "irregular" women only to the extent that their spirituality could be harnessed to larger institutional goals. Yet equally striking is the fact that these evanescent associations continued to surface throughout the fifteenth and sixteenth centuries, even if their organizational modes were short lived and their contributions erased from later narratives.[33]

Other uncloistered communities included groups of semireligious women who lived according to a monastic rule but without formal ecclesiastical supervision. These communities were the long-term legacy of the penitential movement that had gripped the Italian religious imagination in late Middle Ages. Unaffiliated congregations were especially widespread in central Italian towns, but Trecento Florence claimed more than thirty groups following some version of the Augustinian rule. One such group was the Gesuate, whose house near S. Croce was established by three Tuscan pious women in 1382 and expanded by them a decade later.[34] In 1422 Corsini found eight women living there without endowment or formal titles, supported entirely by alms. Greeted by the well-born member Maddalena Adimari, the archbishop learned that the women lived "quietly and peaceably," eating and sleeping together in common spaces.[35] The group's social composition resembled the fifteenth-century Roman Oblates of S. Francesca Romana, which brought together spiritually minded noble women with those from lesser backgrounds. Similarities in dress led to frequent confusion between the Gesuate and Franciscan tertiaries, an ambiguity disliked by Eugenius, who also disapproved of their unsupervised lifestyle.[36] Another ambiguous group blurring status boundaries was the early Quattrocento association of Florentine women "devoted to the Virgin Mary" who lived together in Piazza del Carmine. Although their exact number and identity are unknown, their presence nonetheless enriched neighborhood devotional life, perhaps even figuring into the composition of Masaccio's famed Brancacci chapel in the Carmine. These *devote* appeared in the tax records of both laity and religious, confounding even the best efforts of Florentine tax officials to categorize them. By the 1430s and 1440s the group claimed assets of several hundred florins, only to fade from view afterward.[37] Most likely these women were related organizationally to the large "company of women" resembling a hybrid between a consorority and a beguinage founded in the same vicinity a generation later in 1460.[38]

In addition, some uncloistered penitents lived independently, either taking vows as tertiaries or simply adopting a penitential lifestyle in their own homes. A number of fourteenth-century holy women — Catherine of Siena, Bridget of Sweden, Dorothea of Prussia, and a local charismatic, Villana de' Botti — pursued lives of domesticated sanctity outside the cloister. In 1451 the Franciscan minister general John of Capistrano estimated that over six hundred thousand Franciscan tertiaries across the Italian peninsula still lived in their own homes. This figure is surely exaggerated; the 1427 *catasto* recorded only fifty such women in Florence.[39] One was Gentile Guasconi, described as "a fifty-four-year-old woman, infirm and old. She has never had a husband or children because, since childhood, she has worn penitential garb and been devoted to the Virgin Mary." Since her father was long deceased, by 1457 her brother had bought a small house for her use and assigned her life interest in a farm. A certain penitent named Santa resided with Neri Capponi in the 1490s, supported by a 3-florin income from a rental property in Via del Fiore; her host picked up remaining expenses. For over a decade, the widowed playwright Antonia Pulci practiced a penitential lifestyle in a small room in her own house before retiring to a tertiary community circa 1500.[40] Although the number of unattached religious women remained small, the fact that this alternative remained attractive indicates both the ongoing pull of penitential ideals and the ongoing resistance to institutionalization by some Florentine women.

Throughout the Quattrocento, the sheer variety of religious women practicing open reclusion conditioned their own expectations, sometimes leading them to articulate different concepts of enclosure from their supervisors. Circumstances of reclusion were always shaped by local tradition, but breaches of enclosure came to light most frequently when compounded by other problems. Even during the reforming episcopate of Antoninus, breaking enclosure rarely caused a "scandal" in its own right. Investigating the dissent wrenching the Benedictine convent of S. Agata in 1450, the archbishop accidentally discovered that enclosure was not being observed. Abbess Francesca Micucci had authorized several nuns to venture outside the cloister to discuss concerns about an adjoining garden with neighboring friars instead of relying on convent proctors to carry out this task. A few nuns had been sent to monastic churches for unspecified reasons; one was allowed to witness the civic processions for St. John the Baptist without wearing her habit. These were infrequent excursions that undoubtedly retained the taste of forbidden pleasures, but they hardly constituted sexually scandalous behavior. Vigorously defending these actions to the archbishop, the abbess and nuns claimed that they recently had petitioned for papal permission to leave the cloister on occasion and simply were exercising that right while awaiting final approval. Antoninus seemed genuinely dismayed by this arrogation of power, which resembled the prerogatives exercised by medieval abbesses. Yet the other dozen nuns did not find such behavior worrisome. When they roundly criticized their abbess, they highlighted actions damaging to communal well-being such as the embezzlement of convent property and undue favoritism shown toward her niece.[41] From the nuns' perspective, it was mismanagement and poor leadership, not the violation of enclosure, which made the abbess's removal necessary. Despite his different viewpoint, the archbishop gladly obtained her resignation in short order.

The regulation of active enclosure proceeded by fits and starts during the Quattrocento, but nonetheless it was being addressed. Passive enclosure, on other hand, ultimately proved a more intractable problem. Conversations with nuns formed part of the basic fabric of everyday life; kin, patrons, friends, neighbors, clients, tenants, and business associates pressed for continued access to religious women. In turn, most nuns prized these contacts that both nourished economic vitality and enabled them to pursue political objectives from behind convent walls. An early wave of Observance, stimulated by the penitential fervor coursing through Florence and other Italian cities in the late Trecento, had already advanced fuller enclosure by taking a cautious approach to social interactions. New constitutions written for S. Jacopo di Ripoli readily conceded visits by clergy, kings, and patrons, yet took great pains to ensure that nuns did not form intimate or improper liaisons with male visitors, especially clerics.[42] Kinsmen and churchmen alike worried that clergy might abuse their confessional role in private conversations with nuns, and standard fifteenth-century glosses on *Periculoso* remarked that not even monks should enter female cloisters unlicensed.[43] Ironically, the burden of maintaining faultless moral standards fell on nuns, despite their purportedly frail judgment. At S. Jacopo, clerical visitors inside the cloister were accompanied by the prioress and three elderly nuns, who were advised to speak briefly, only when necessary, and in each other's presence. Workmen repairing interiors were chaperoned by three convent officers plus three elderly nuns, whose conversation had to be audible by all present.[44] Illness posed special challenges to passive enclosure. The entire community processed solemnly to the infirmary when a nun lay dying and then sat quietly in prayer or meditation while their dying sister confessed. To avoid repeated intrusions, the sacraments were administered together.

More commonplace exchanges in the convent parlor gave rise to different concerns. Once again, however, nuns' speech was at the regulatory center. The S. Jacopo constitutions punished nuns equally for rebelling against prelates, leaving the convent without permission, and telling secrets or lies about other nuns or the convent to outsiders. Elevating enclosure violations to the same status as flagrant disobedience marked a new seriousness of purpose in enforcing *clausura*. In these rubrics, enclosure signified not merely a physical boundary between worlds but a complete separation of nuns' knowledge and experience from that of the secular world. An offender faced stiff penalties: "Stripped bare to the waist, she is to be whipped at the feet of each nun, starting with the prioress and [continuing] down each side of the chapter."[45] The culprit was forbidden the common table and forced to eat on bare ground in the middle of the refectory; even her leftover bread crusts could not be mixed with others. During canonical hours, she stood at the choir entrance while others filed by silently; she could not take communion or hold convent office while "in penance." These potent rituals of exclusion helped police enclosure from within.

Before 1450, Florentine bishops showed only limited concern with enforcing either form of enclosure, focusing instead on practical issues like finance, internal administration, and liturgical duties. With few exceptions, the Florentine diocese lacked strong episcopal leadership throughout the fourteenth and fifteenth centuries, and diocesan governance was plagued by rapid turnover of bishops as well as by fierce conflicts with the commune over clerical liberties.[46] Yet the low priority accorded enclosure was not simply a result of poor pastoral care. Visitation records show that Florentine bishops often recognized the practical challenges facing local monastic institutions in a way that more distant, or more zealous, mendicant supervisors did not. Of course, convents had a vested interest in putting their best foot forward to ecclesiastical visitors, since airing grievances of whatever sort to the bishop might result in serious censure. Still, the discovery of internal problems by bishops shows that egregious infractions or sexual misconduct did not easily escape episcopal notice. When read with a critical eye, these records provide a reasonably good gauge of monastic discipline when open reclusion was the norm.

The first Florentine visitation in 1384 brought few enclosure violations to light. Of the twenty-five houses surveyed, only one convent was suspected of "dishonest" living because a layman often spoke with one of the nuns.[47] More commonly, this visitation revealed sparse populations, heavy debts, poor administration by convent chaplains, and occasional lapses in communal routines. One house — S. Ambrogio — displayed problems entwined with enclosure, although the nuns themselves identified their main difficulty as failed leadership by Abbess Francesca Guadagni. She reportedly administered convent funds with a free hand; failed to audit accounts; monopolized the convent keys instead of sharing them with other officers; slept apart in her own room; provided badly for sick nuns; and kept a "small girl" in the house at convent expense. These infractions loomed large to the twelve chapter members because they dissipated the endowment and undercut a sense of community. Her failures were compounded by the disreputable actions of two convent chaplains, who threw banquets for outsiders and allowed laity into the convent as they pleased.[48] Importantly, however, the nuns never identified enclosure as a primary concern during the visit but instead focused attention on practical matters such as favoritism, diminished resources, and loss of control over their habitat. The episcopal vicar Francesco Zabarella agreed with the nuns' priorities: he censured the chaplains but allowed the abbess to retain her post despite obvious failings.

Nevertheless, late Trecento bishops monitored passive enclosure when it was politically expedient to do so. As Florentine convents were drawn into an ongoing battle between bishop and commune, passive enclosure came to serve as a politicized lightning rod. In 1392 and again the following year, Bishop Onofrio dello Stecchuto warned the abbess of S. Pier Maggiore, Benedetta Macci, not to speak to "outsiders" or allow lay people into the convent—an injunction that directly contradicted the convent's historic privileges. In 1405, Stecchuto's successor admonished Abbess Lucia Falconieri not to receive any visitors, again ignoring both privilege and practice.[49] Although we lack the nuns' version of the story, the bone of contention appeared to be political in nature. The nuns had entered dangerous waters in these war-torn years by sheltering nonnative noblewomen, including, in 1408, a girl from the renowned Gambacorta family of newly conquered Pisa. Before his death, Piero Gambacorta had been a loyal friend of the republic, and his descendants helped arrange the occupation of their native city by Florentine troops.[50] To reciprocate these favors, S. Pier Maggiore offered asylum to vulnerable Gambacorta women and their circle, which aligned the convent with civic policies. Consequently, the nuns came under harsh scrutiny five years later, when Corsini scathingly told them "they were not to receive people either to dance or to take refreshments." He repeated a similar injunction the following year.[51] Dancing was considered a vanity rather than inherently sinful, and it is not clear whether the nuns participated in or simply allowed this morally ambiguous activity.[52] These unique entertainments may have been prompted by the need to cultivate ongoing contacts between Pisan noblewomen and their Florentine hosts, with the nuns acting as the nexus of social exchange for foreign policy. The extent to which they complied with Corsini's instructions is unknown, but in any event he quickly turned his attention to more pressing challenges posed by local clergy bent on governing the diocese as a corporation.[53]

Despite these frictions, Corsini found S. Pier Maggiore to be a model convent when he made pastoral rounds a decade later—a process by which he reasserted episcopal control over monastic foundations. The timing of this visitation, a year after the commune established a civic agency to police convents, also speaks to his struggle to regain lost jurisdictional ground. Finances at the house were on solid footing; it had acquired new properties and had little debt load. The nuns reportedly slept in a common dormitory, ate together in refectory, cared for their sick, lived "continently," discharged monastic offices diligently, held frequent chapter meetings, and observed silence at appropriate times. In addition, Corsini found that "there was no dissent among [the nuns] but only peace, unity, love and concord." Young nuns like Suor Antonia Acciaiuoli deepened their spirituality by copying sermons, religious tracts, and other monastic compendia.[54] Although they practiced a traditional piety, not a penitential one, the nuns' orderliness demonstrated that open reclusion was indeed compatible with monastic discipline. Corsini did not trouble the nuns again during his remaining twenty years in office.

The archbishop's visitation of twenty-eight other convents revealed no sexual scandals or violations of enclosure, although it did highlight the immiseration of some nuns. Judged by standard monastic benchmarks—sound administration, observance of custom, harmonious group dynamics—Florentine convents stood in relatively good moral order in 1422. The twin evils besetting female communities were underpopulation and underendowment. To gain a better grasp of convent finances, Corsini instructed about half of the communities to furnish a complete inventory of goods and holdings within one month. Despite their poverty, the vast majority of nuns maintained that there was "peace and harmony" among them, asserting repeatedly that they lived "quietly and peacefully" or were "united in peace." Even the disarray exposed at S. Ambrogio forty years earlier had been remedied by the "good, diligent, and careful" leadership of the new abbess, Niccolosa Buonaccorsi.[55]

This overview of open reclusion prior to 1450 simultaneously points to shared expectations among nuns and to the roots of future conflict. Nuns' perceptions of enclosure were conditioned by frequent exemptions and by the exuberant pluralism of female religious life. The ease of exchange between nuns and laity entrenched private claims to convent spaces, ultimately making passive enclosure a thornier problem to uproot. Conflicts between civic and ecclesiastical officials demonstrated how readily enclosure might be politicized by contemporaries seeking to control local convent resources. This is not to say that Florentine nuns led blameless lives or that they did not interpret enclosure to their own advantage. Nonetheless, there is little evidence that open reclusion led to widespread moral laxity.

Privatization, Enclosure, and Reform, 1430–1500

The mid-fifteenth century marked a watershed in attempts to secure the fuller enclosure of monastic women across Europe. What differentiated this push from earlier efforts was that it issued simultaneously from several quarters: monastic reformers, local bishops, the papacy, and city governments. In 1433, as the institutional church tried to restore lost authority after the Schism, the Council of Basel called for the local enforcement of *clausura* by bishops.[56] The goals of

Observance as well as papal reform meshed ideologically with civic interests in governing convent mores, although mechanisms for oversight differed significantly. Nevertheless, this convergence led to a pronounced strengthening of regulatory interests in the second half of the Quattrocento.

The papacy's weakened position in the first half of the fifteenth century forced a piecemeal approach to clerical reform. Upon taking office, Eugenius quickly promulgated new constitutions for the Roman secular clergy—a group not known for its organizational discipline or high moral tenor—that forbade clerics convent entry unless of advanced age and above suspicion, "such as would be expected in an eighty-year-old man." Similarly, he prohibited women of "whatever age, status, grade, authority, or condition" from entering monasteries belonging to the newly formed Congregation of S. Giustina.[57] Eugenius's lengthy residence in Florence already showed his penchant for disciplining. Viewing contacts between nuns and clergy as dangerously prone to sexual misconduct, in 1435, he barred Franciscan friars from "having the temerity" to enter any Florentine house of Poor Clares, citing women's propensity for poor judgment.[58] Even as Eugenius and his successor, Nicholas, rebuilt papal fortunes, however, they continued to issue enclosure privileges to nuns' kin and patrons. In so doing, they worked at cross-purposes to stated reform objectives. These popes directly undercut their own insistence on *clausura* to satisfy lay patrons, whose generosity required reciprocal gestures. The more deeply rooted patronage became as a governing social force, the more influence lay patrons exercised over convent spaces and their inhabitants. By midcentury, these competing claims only highlighted the extent to which Italian female monasticism was rapidly becoming a system at odds with itself.

As the experience of Le Murate illustrates, papal policies sealed the privatization of Florentine convents under the guise of charitable assistance. In 1442, Eugenius, despite his reform initiatives, licensed laity who raised alms for the nuns to enter their premises, speak with them, and share the grace of their plenary indulgence.[59] His successor, Nicholas, amply rewarded the convent's principal patron, Giovanni Benci, who reportedly spent 10,000 florins on construction costs alone, by granting the entire Benci family entry rights on special occasions. These privileges trapped the Murate nuns in a double bind that pitted economic need against their expressed desire for religious reclusion. In 1461, they acceded to patrons' demands by authorizing construction of a private cell where Benci women could retire for extended periods. After 1500, other prominent laywomen like Caterina Sforza and Argentina Malaspina built or stayed in private cells in return for favors and financial support, often negotiated directly with the abbess.[60]

Although patrons enjoyed unusual privileges, even ordinary laity had legitimate access to cloisters, owing to the historically layered nature of these spaces. At S. Pier Maggiore, the tomb of Beato Giovanni da Vespignano (d. 1331) was sited "in the cloister of the convent, along with many other tombs." Because his relics enacted many healing miracles, grateful laity mounted votive images, which in turn attracted still greater popular devotion. Only after Trent was his body transferred to the convent church since, as the hagiographer Stefano Razzi put it, "one could no longer enter women's convents with the freedom and simplicity of old." Tombs of less saintly folk gave grounds for kin to visit their family dead inside cloisters.[61] Nuns' profession ceremonies, funerals, and elections furnished still other occasions when family claims proved irresistible to all. When the abbess of S. Apollonia, Camilla de' Bardi, died in 1515 and Agnesa Gualterotti was elected as her replacement, "all the nuns' fathers and brothers" who "had come to honor the former abbess and congratulate the new one" gathered in the infirmary to hear a sermon. Nuns might be brides of Christ, but they were still the daughters of men.[62]

In the second half of the Quattrocento, the growth of convent populations heightened tensions between reclusion and access, making passive enclosure the principal locus of ecclesiastical concern. Especially pressing was the matter of access by highborn laywomen, who not only visited convent parlors but retreated to cloisters for extended periods to visit relatives or refresh themselves in a tranquil spiritual environment. Although these retreats no doubt satisfied a desire for social interaction and were mutually enjoyable, they also had a certain religious rationale. Silence and prayer were conducive to reflection; edifying images found in oratories and refectories stimulated spiritual growth. Spiritual recreation might also include watching convent dramas and other entertainments for which Tuscan nuns became renowned later in the sixteenth century.[63] These social practices provoked widely varying responses: neither clergy nor laity spoke with a consistent, unified voice. One strand of thought maintained that regular interactions with nuns enhanced the civic good. The humanist bookseller Vespasiano da Bisticci stressed the edifying effects of exposing young girls to role models of modesty and bodily control — the very fundaments of female virtue. He contrasted this laudable mode of Christian character formation with the troubling new fashion for dancing lessons and other "frivolities." Moreover,

Vespasiano posited a seamless continuum between monastic and lay values, noting that good households were run "like a well-ordered convent."[64] Conversely, other laity influenced by Observance emphasized nuns' salvific role, which they felt was best maintained through isolation. In consequence, conflicting views on enclosure played out around the competing roles assigned to nuns by lay society.

Italian ecclesiastical officials adopted a pragmatic, regulatory approach toward passive enclosure that implicitly acknowledged secular claims on nuns. Eugenius devised a licensing process for laywomen wishing to enter or reside in intimate convent spaces, although the papacy did not regulate convent parlors. This was a brilliant compromise that simultaneously satisfied lay demand, buttressed papal authority, and created new patronage opportunities for the institutional church. The extent to which the papacy willingly accommodated lay visits can be gauged from permits granted to visit Poor Clares, who had the most stringent enclosure rules of all female orders. The steep upward trajectory of apostolic licenses granted between 1435 and 1492 demonstrates how laity legitimately gained influence over religious women and their houses. Neither Eugenius nor Nicholas issued permits to enter Franciscan houses anywhere in Europe, but their successors satisfied secular pleas more readily.[65] Calixtus III and Pius II each issued one license to aristocratic women: the first to Isabella, Duchess of Burgundy, and the second to the widowed tertiary Margherita Malatesta of Ferrara. By contrast, the reform-minded Paul II took aim at what he perceived to be a growing problem. In 1470 he released a group of "devout, obedient" Franciscan tertiaries in Arezzo from oversight by a Florentine convent because it harbored numerous lay residents, who were instructed to take vows if they wished to remain.[66]

The pontificate of Sixtus IV (1471–84) represented a crucial turning point in papal policy. This great papal builder and archenemy of Lorenzo de' Medici began trading access privileges as political favors to the Italian and European aristocracy, conceding extensive convent visitation privileges to Italian noblewomen, sometimes in return for donations to his campaign against the Turks. Among the recipients were Leonora, wife of Duke Ercole d'Este of Ferrara; her sister-in-law Ippolita, daughter of the Milanese duchess Bianca Maria Sforza; and Caterina Sforza, Countess of Imola, who later established a personal patronage relationship with the Florentine nuns of Le Murate.[67] Sixtus typically discouraged extensive contact between nuns and noblewomen, who often brought sizeable retinues with them, by building in safeguards against long-term convent residence, limiting the annual number of entries, and forbidding overnight stays.

Visitation permits took on a whole new complexion during the reign of Innocent VIII (1484–92). During his first year in office, Innocent granted all of the thirty-one petitions he received, which represented roughly a tenfold increase over the number granted by his predecessor. In subsequent years, he issued about fifty such permits annually.[68] There was a pronounced Italian character to the distribution of favors, which reflected the papacy's attempt to solidify alliances with local Italian elites. Half to three-quarters of these access permits were issued for Italian convents, with Spanish houses running a distant second and the remainder scattered across Europe. Other trends during Innocent's pontificate included more joint petitions from laywomen, usually related by blood or marriage; larger numbers of permissible companions; and increased frequency of annual visits. In the closing decades of the Quattrocento, intimate convent spaces were regularly opened up to laity with full papal consent. Innocent extended similar privileges to several dozen women of the Florentine merchant elite, including one to Francesca Guasconi in 1489 to take "one or two honest matrons" with her "to converse with the nuns" of several local convents four times a year. Other women garnered more ample favors. In 1490, Innocent approved a joint petition allowing Alessandra, widow of Giovanni Lanfredini, to visit any Florentine convent four times annually, either alone, with a companion, or with her sisters and daughters. Included in this entitlement were the wife of her husband's nephew, that woman's daughters, and other Lanfredini in-laws. Similarly, three Ricasoli sisters, "spurred by zealous devotion and charity," won approval to visit any Florentine convent, accompanied by four or five "honest matrons." Not only could this band of women eat, drink, and converse with the nuns; they might do manual work alongside them, bring supplies, and receive finished goods, almost certainly as brokers for silk shops.[69] Successors to the papal throne extended this practice of convent visitation privileges; indeed, Julius II and Leo X actively promoted these entitlements in their search for new revenues to support military campaigns and build St. Peter's Basilica.[70]

These same decades saw a growing influx of pupils and boarders in response to political turmoil, pinched convent finances, and reciprocal social expectations. As I have shown elsewhere, after 1500 it became increasingly common for young boarders to reside in convents for longer periods of time, often for several years.[71] Older annuitants found congenial, long-term residential options in religious houses, especially if they enjoyed existing ties with the nuns. Nuns anticipated the prospect of both immediate financial gain and future political preferment for the convent when admitting these women and girls. In some cases, legacies hinged on the acceptance of one or more trusted family servants as long-term boarders. Oftentimes, convent residence was payback for favors already rendered. A half century after Lorenzo de' Medici became their protector, the tertiaries of Annalena reciprocated by sheltering his nephew Giovanni for eight months in 1503 during the Medici exile; this young boy stayed in the founder's own rooms.[72] Moreover, as Florence was drawn into a vibrant web of political and diplomatic relationships, visiting dignitaries often accessed the city's most renowned convents. In Laurentian Florence, Le Murate was a regular destination for ambassadors traveling through the city. The Ferrarese ambassador wrote to Duke Ercole d'Este that he visited the "whole convent," and in 1492 the duke himself paid a visit in which he gazed on "all the nuns, which was a beautiful thing to see."[73]

By 1500, both the presence of outsiders and the visual accessibility of nuns were facts of everyday life. The roots of what sixteenth-century reformers considered to be an intractable problem lay in earlier, widespread recognition of secular claims on local religious resources. Indeed, the very willingness of Florentines to support large numbers of celibate women should be linked not only to urban marital strategies, commercial textile production, and spiritual intercession but also to their understanding that convents could be put to a range of instrumental uses. Still, the question of who determined conditions for contact remained contested, and the perceived legitimacy of interactions turned on who had authorized the exchange. State-approved visits by notables like the Este dukes were conceived as expressions of civic pride in nuns' spiritual heroics and in the beauty of their cloisters, not as breaches of enclosure, while stolen glimpses of nuns through windows or doorways elicited sharp disapproval. Contests over the right to see or speak with nuns were fundamentally battles over the right to influence and deploy these important institutional resources. What complicated this scenario still further was the unprecedented role of the Florentine state in policing convent boundaries.

The Florentine "Night Officers"

Around 1400, the Florentine state began to take a more pronounced regulatory interest in the moral status of female religious communities—a potent source of anxiety in the wake of successive plagues. Demographic decline as well as warfare, social unrest, and fiscal problems were interpreted by many Italians as forms of divine punishment. As early as 1349, the Venetian government enacted penalties for both coercive and consensual sex with nuns, which became increasingly draconian over time.[74] But Florence created the first magistracy in Europe expressly dedicated to the task of safeguarding nuns' sexual purity. Worried about the possible correlation between nuns' misbehavior and troubles plaguing the city, the Florentine priors established the Office of Convent Guardians in 1421 to "conserve the morality" of the city's sacred virgins. City fathers considered this oversight necessary "for the honor of the city and its citizens, for the honor and good of religion, and for the utility of the entire Florentine republic."[75] In 1433, this office was folded into the newly created sodomy tribunal charged with containing the "nefarious" sin for which the city was famous. The combined magistracy, generally known in English as the Office of the Night, fleshed out its brief in 1454 when it assumed jurisdiction over prostitutes who lived or worked near convents.[76] Reorganized by 1460, the Florentine night officers continued to serve as sexual watchdogs until its administrative competencies passed to the city's main police force (Otto di guardia) in 1502.

This innovative magistracy formed part of what Michael Rocke has called "a vast, if piecemeal, governmental program to reform and discipline the community's morals and behaviors."[77] Scholars have argued that the early 1400s represented a turning point in the regulation of public morality in Florence and Venice, marked principally by increased civic intervention in sexual conduct. Between 1403 and 1432, the Florentine state began to regulate prostitution, founded civic brothels, placed tighter restrictions on gambling, undertook new sumptuary campaigns, and formed a sodomy commission. The goals of several initiatives echoed the pronatalist aims of the civic dowry fund, which promoted married reproduction while aiding the public fisc. Controlling the volatile potential of sex provided a crucial impetus to the growth of Italian Renaissance states, both princely and republican, throughout the fifteenth century.

In the second half of the Quattrocento, the Florentine commune regulated the diverse challenges of sodomy, prostitution, and nuns' sexuality under a single legal and discursive umbrella. Bundling nuns, prostitutes, and sodomites together made a great deal of sense to contemporaries, since all three groups were central to maintaining the Florentine marriage system: nuns through enforced celibacy, prostitutes through the licit sex trade, and sodomites through nonprocreative sex. It would have been impossible to sustain high levels of marital endogamy or to delay men's first marriage until age thirty or thirty-two without these practices. Other administrative mechanisms linked these disparate groups. After 1442, fines from sodomy convictions directly supported the convent for repentant prostitutes; the abbess herself was drawn into the fringes of civic administration when asked to furnish written proof that offenders had paid their fines. Nor was it coincidental that civic regulatory interests in nuns and prostitutes emerged at about the same time. As Ulrike Strasser has argued for early modern Bavaria, state-sanctioned control of both female celibacy and illicit female sexuality shored up a normative family system.[78]

Still, the Florentine commune took great pains to differentiate "holy" women living in convents from "public" women housed in civic brothels. In 1454, the commune established sanitized zones within the city by prohibiting prostitutes from living within three hundred yards of any convent. This policy resembled earlier Venetian initiatives to localize prostitutes around the Rialto to better supervise their activities and keep male clients away from respectable women and major civic churches.[79] City fathers also sheltered nuns from the "corrupting" influence of secular music when, in 1446, they barred heraldic civic musicians from playing within fifty yards of any convent. Given the growing ceremonial demands of civic life by the mid-Quattrocento, it must have been difficult to enforce this prohibition without distorting honorific practices or time-honored processional routes, especially along the densely packed *via sacra* of Via S. Gallo. Still another law drawn up in 1456 blocked the establishment of inns and taverns near the Annalena, where many respectable citizens placed their young daughters for educational purposes.[80] These measures to sanitize and control the cityscape reveal the impressive breadth of civic regulatory ambitions, whose efficacy nevertheless remained limited in practice.

From its inception, the campaign to police convents was fraught with problems. Unlike other administrative innovations, civic intervention in convent life clearly encroached on ecclesiastical jurisdiction. In 1436, during his residence in Florence, Eugenius tried unsuccessfully to have this function of the magistracy abolished as an infringement of established church privilege.[81] The magistracy's efforts were also confounded by the competing ideological claims that formed part of its brief. Exposing nuns' misconduct was a dangerous proposition for civic well-being because it explicitly risked family honor. These tensions assumed a personal urgency for magistrates, many of whom came from well-heeled political families amply represented among convent populations. In consequence, allegations of illicit sex were treated gingerly, and serious scandals were sometimes hushed up or tried in ecclesiastical courts.[82] Magistrates also wrestled with many of the internal contradictions animating Florentine society: social expectations that demanded both segregation and access to religious women; gender prerogatives that legitimated men as the superior sex and gave them certain entitlements to all women; religious attitudes that simultaneously viewed nuns as potent inter-cessors and weak-willed, lustful beings. These conflicting pulls meant that, de-spite the commune's moral concerns, the night officers were not charged with reforming convents, as were subsequent sixteenth-century magistracies across north-central Italy. Hence the magistracy was able to adopt the "pragmatic flex-ibility" characteristic of local judicial practice.[83]

These tensions created a certain discursive ambivalence about nuns' moral accountability and sexual agency. The 1421 enabling legislation squarely placed the blame for perceived laxity on men; the priors claimed that they had to police convents "because of the frequent harassments meted out by each generation of men to holy nuns day in and day out." As the preamble stated, "due to the excessive conversation of laymen with nuns even under the guise of kinship, almost all of the convents both in the city of Florence and within a four-mile radius suffer from the reputation of being misgoverned, until they are known to be on the brink of ruin."[84] Subsequent legislation used nuns' scurrilous behavior as a political pretext for intervention, although it reverted to familiar tropes about women's gullibility once the grounds for intervention had been squarely established. A 1435 deliberation laid the blame for "the evils of wars, disorders, epidemics, and other calamities and troubles" at the feet of "many nuns" who, "through carnal desire, have failed in their reverence" to God. Still, these officials quickly salvaged nuns' reputations by blaming the "evil men" responsible for leading them "from virtue to dishonor." Only through civic oversight would Florentine nuns be preserved "in security and honor, and the convents flourish in liberty."[85] Other Italian urban regimes showed similar ambivalence in their regu-latory rhetoric. Forming a comparable magistracy in 1456, Genoese lawmakers decried the "petulance, audacity, and impudence" shown by local nuns but avoided explicit reference to sexual misbehavior. Innuendo was sufficient to raise the specter of promiscuity and justify civic intervention.[86] States also appealed to concern about nuns' sexuality as a way of disguising civic ambitions to exercise control over increasingly valuable local resources at the expense of the church. Civic regimes did not hesitate to put the protean figure of the wayward nun to political uses when it suited their purpose of extending jurisdiction into forbid-den ecclesiastical territory.

These same tensions conditioned the ways in which magistrates exercised convent surveillance. The night officers were assigned dual functions as protec-tors and prosecutors — functions that pitted nuns' intercessory role against their supposed carnality. Both magisterial functions, however, constructed a paternalistic identity for civic officers working on behalf of the common good. In their protective role, the night officers were charged with shielding convents from harassment, theft, assaults, and unlawful entry by laymen lured by the thrill of the forbidden. The need for such protection was real, especially at more vulnerable sites outside the walls, since fifteenth-century convents lacked the fortresslike quality of later structures. Although the story of young Lorenzo de' Medici scaling the walls of Le Murate in order to judge the nuns' piety firsthand may be apocryphal, it demonstrates nonetheless both the relative ease of entry and its varied motivations. Nor were such incidents unique to Florence. Break-ins at Venetian convents were known throughout the fifteenth century, as were night assaults on Roman convents by rowdy young barons.[87]

Reflecting this dual orientation, the Office of the Night adopted a two-pronged approach to convent supervision throughout its seventy-year history. The first prong enforced passive enclosure through a licensing procedure that it administered. Licensing was one of the most common forms of political and judicial regulation in Renaissance Italy, ranging from sumptuary provisions to medical permits. Laymen who desired legitimate convent entry needed a valid permit issued by the night officers, generally good for one year; civic authorization was required even for "necessary and honest" reasons such as providing medical care, offering legal advice, or making structural repairs.[88] Judging by subsequent denunciations, Florentines commonly construed the legislation as requiring permits even to enter convent parlors, although in fact it referred only to cloistered spaces. No formal licensing protocol remains, but the screening process did not seem especially rigorous. Nor did the laws mandate specific punishments; instead, unauthorized individuals could be punished in whatever way the night officers saw fit. According to Andrea Zorzi, this kind of extraordinary judicial latitude was intended to facilitate conflict resolution and apparently did not occasion widespread abuse.[89] The magistrates did not specify visitors' internal itinerary but depended instead on nuns' discretion. As noted earlier, only a few communities articulated how nuns should chaperone lay visitors entering the cloister. Laywomen normally did not require civic authorization from the night officers.[90]

Not surprisingly, the night officers yielded to the social force of kinship when issuing permits. Although civic officials initially decried the "excessive" conversation between nuns and kinsmen, the magistrates acknowledged that, far from being dead to the world, religious women remained vital participants in family affairs. A systematic survey of licenses issued between the 1450s and 1502 shows how easily blood ties trumped reclusion. Rather than wasting valuable administrative time on issuing individual entry permits to nuns' fathers and brothers, the night officers simply extended general visitation rights to them. These men could visit daughters or sisters whenever they wished, with no particular constraints. Male cousins and nephews generally enjoyed similar liberties throughout the late Quattrocento. Thus instead of confronting head-on the problem of what constituted an appropriate level of interaction between nuns and male kin, the night officers left it to later generations to work out.

Blood relations were joined by a steady stream of other visitors. From 1460 to 1502, the night officers issued an average of thirty to thirty-five access permits annually. Some were extended to specific convents undertaking construction projects, others to individuals such as physicians servicing several houses. In any given year, the number and range of tradesmen, professionals, and workmen granted unlimited entry privileges was staggering. Factors and procurators; confessors, chaplains, organists; barber surgeons, apothecaries, and physicians; greengrocers, bakers, butchers; lawyers, notaries, and stationers; carpenters, stonecutters, roofers, tilers, keymakers, flagmakers, painters, and barrel makers; goldbeaters, wool carders, tailors; leaseholders, farm laborers, and convent pensioners all gained blanket entry during the year their permit was valid.[91] The sheer range of access permits maps the extent to which convents were immersed in the life of the city as well as citizens' compliance with an increasingly familiar procedure. Especially prominent in the later Quattrocento were permits issued to silk merchants and other suppliers active in commercial textile production. As discussed in chapter 4, by 1500 virtually every convent in the dominion made gold thread, with production concentrated in the largest, poorest communities. Grasping the profound significance of this manufacturing activity to Florentine commercial life, the night officers took the pragmatic approach of issuing generic licenses to silk suppliers and brokers. Civic permits thus followed a similar trajectory to apostolic licenses for convent entry. Both civic and ecclesiastical officials were ever more permissive in granting access, yet nuns still shouldered the blame for maintaining permeable cloisters.

In their prosecutorial role, the night officers also investigated infractions, using the same procedures for policing sodomy. Charges against nuns or their male clerics could be made anonymously by dropping a note into one of the boxes set up in major civic churches for this purpose. Identification was required only if the accuser wished to collect a share of the fine offered as an incentive. This method of gathering information opened the investigatory process to the informal discipline of neighborhood gossip as well as to the potentially toxic effects of slander. Some accusations, which at times were copied verbatim in official records, were composed with real narrative flair, revealing the influence of popular vernacular writers like Boccaccio; most were brief and far more prosaic, providing little narrative detail. In addition, the night officers employed a number of spies who gathered information, sent reports from outlying cities, and made denunciations on their own. Nonetheless, the magistrates did not proceed arbitrarily but followed legal guidelines, often with the advice of lawyers. A majority vote was needed to convict offenders.

Denunciations made to the night officers reveal both an extraordinary picture of Florentine street life and an overriding concern with male sexuality. As Rocke has shown, the night officers were thoroughly preoccupied with sodomy; convent infractions paled by comparison. The relative number of accusations registered for each kind of transgression amply clarifies civic moral priorities. Only 111 of the 13,000 accusations recorded by the magistrates between 1460 and 1502 — a mere three-quarters of 1 percent — concerned offenses perpetrated by or against nuns.[92] Nuns figured as protagonists in an even smaller number of actual incidents, since the 111 denunciations included multiple accusations for the same misdeed as well as charges against male clergy employed by convents. Because unfounded allegations could be made repeatedly and legitimate scandals covered up, we should not imagine that civic records constitute an accurate census of transgressive behaviors one way or another. Still, the minuscule number of convent offenses in relation to sodomy accusations and to other forms of criminality paints a very different picture of convent morality from what literary tales suggest.

In most years, there were only a few accusations made against nunneries; the largest number were concentrated in the 1460s and 1470s when sodomy convictions also reached their peak. In some years, no convent incidents were reported. Tellingly, the number of denunciations against nuns, clerical personnel, and lay offenders did not reveal any correlation with the Savonarolan movement, despite the preacher's influence being felt in an uptick of sodomy cases. Savonarola's impact on convent life lay in the realm of moral suasion and the reform of individual houses; it did not spark a flurry of denunciations or increase official civic scrutiny of nuns.[93] Nor did the political turmoil and uncertainty caused by repeated regime changes between 1494 and 1530 generate noticeably different patterns of either accusation or conviction. Considering that the convent population more than doubled during the fifteenth century, this extraordinary equilibrium underscores both the limitations of civic policing efforts and the extent to which writers and scholars have overblown the prevalence of convent offenses.

Like sodomy denunciations, the vast majority of accusations against convents and their personnel were never pursued owing to insufficient evidence; the number of convictions was even smaller. Only 15 percent of the hundred-plus denunciations against convents resulted in conviction, mainly for unlawful entry by laymen and suspicious conduct on the part of nuns, clergy, and laity alike. Only two additional convictions were issued by the Otto di guardia between its assumption of policing functions in 1502 and the end of the republic three decades later.[94] Proving illicit sex was difficult, and most convictions for fornication of any sort stemmed from participants' confessions, not from official fact finding. When these sexual allegations are read in context, it becomes clear that they were primarily a way to register neighborhood dissatisfaction and to exert moral pressure on particular convents. Depending on the severity of the offense, punishments ranged from hefty, graded fines upward of 10 florins to ritual humiliation and exile. The night officers punished only laity; nuns and clergy remained beyond the pale of civic justice, being subject instead to ecclesiastical penalties.[95]

Denunciations also mapped geographical hot spots within and outside the city. Paradoxically, few convents within the densely packed urban core were the target of accusations, probably because nuns and neighbors monitored each other carefully and were highly interdependent both socially and economically. Conversely, the most egregious infractions concerned convents that were strewn along the western walls or located just outside the city. These thinly populated sites not only invited indiscretions but also nurtured local residents' anxieties regarding nuns' honor and its reflection on their district. When two laymen made an unlicensed visit to Montedomini outside Porta S. Gallo in 1468, an anonymous witness warned that "you magistrates know they did so in order to commit shameful acts."[96] Moreover, because houses on the urban periphery generally had small endowments, their vigorous participation in silk manufacture brought regular, troubling visits by suppliers and brokers. The two convents most frequently censured as carnally corrupt — S. Baldassare in Coverciano and S. Maria sul Prato near Ognissanti — were among the most active sites of commodity production, pointing to neighborhood disapproval of heavy lay traffic there.

The wider Florentine dominion also showed a distinct topography of suspicion. Almost 35 percent of accusations issued from subject cities, primarily the nearby towns of Prato and Pistoia vital to Florentine patronage systems and monastic placement. One of the most censured convents was the small Augustinian house of S. Margherita in Prato, best known as the staging ground for the tempestuous love affair between Fra Filippo Lippi and Suor Lucrezia Buti in the late 1450s.[97] After numerous charges hit S. Margherita of Prato in 1469–70, the magistrates empowered their notary to make an unprecedented civic inquiry there as part of "an honest endeavor." The night officers' zealous attention to the territorial periphery, where they stationed informants, strengthens scholarly claims that controlling public mores in outlying areas was an innovative spur to late medieval Italian state formation.[98] The magistrates had ample, if grudging, cooperation from the local citizenry. After accusing a layman of spending several nights in S. Margherita, the anonymous writer taunted the night officers: "If you don't believe this, send one of your spies to watch the convent about five hours after sunset and you'll see that I'm not lying."[99]

The 111 denunciations registered between 1460 and 1502 can be grouped into five categories situated on an escalating scale of severity: harassment, unlawful entry, suspicious conduct, fornication, and rape or abduction. Of these, only rape, abduction, and certain types of fornication counted as crimes prior to the magistracy's formation. Even construing sex crimes broadly, well over half of the denunciations submitted to the night officers concerned newly created misdeeds that bore little relation to sexuality. As Samuel Cohn has argued, the attraction of colorful tales found in criminal records has distorted our understanding of more "ordinary" criminality.[100] Although zesty stories undoubtedly enliven our understanding of urban mores and monastic conditions, they must be gauged in relation to their prevalence. At the same time, evaluating the narrative elements in denunciations, which blended fear of and reverence for religious women, illuminates the culture of suspicion in which Florentine nuns lived out their lives.

At the bottom end of the scale were four cases of harassment toward nuns, all occurring outside city walls or in subject cities. These were mainly verbal affronts to honor demanding magisterial redress. In 1460 several peasants from Castel Fiorentino complained to the night officers that they had placed their daughters in a convent "with the understanding that they would live decorously and comport themselves with honor." However, their intentions were thwarted by a certain layman named Piero di Ser Niccolò, who badgered the nuns day and night "and behaved very dishonorably in words and deeds." The following year, the lay factor of S. Gaggio lost his job for "speaking villainous and injurious words" to the abbess of Monticelli, while a baker was accused of harassing seven convents near and outside the city walls.[101]

At the opposite end of the scale were eight denunciations for violence against nuns' person in the form of abduction or rape. In Renaissance Italy, the crime of rape carried different meanings than it does today; raping a nun was considered not only an egregious offense against God but also a form of incest and the height of blasphemy.[102] Considering denunciations as a whole, it seems that nuns' personal security found stronger safeguards in considerations of honor than in physical enclosures. Niccolò Cellini of Prato reportedly entered S. Margherita with a companion "by force" and "forcibly violated one of the nuns, who he kept like a wife"—the contemporary euphemism for sexual relations. Another report suggests that charges of coerced sex were used to camouflage consensual relations; still others contain an unknown backstory. For instance, the abbess of S. Niccolò in Prato reported in 1460 that a certain Paolo Landi, his two sons, a miller, and another accomplice broke into the cloister via the door leading to the dormitory. A separate denunciation corroborated this break-in, citing robbery as a motive. The abbess explained that one of the nuns—Paolo's sister—presumed the miller was fetching grain and opened the door, at which point he and her brother snatched her and ran off into the piazza. Convent factors pursued them to no avail, since the other men were waiting nearby. Two months later, Paolo was caught, confessed, and fined, but it is not clear whether this abduction was part of a family dispute or a planned escape.[103]

Between these extremes lay the bulk of accusations, which can be split into three groups: unlawful entry (twenty-seven reports); suspicious conduct (thirty-seven reports); and fornication with nuns (thirty-five reports). Unlawful entry ranged from harmless offenses by tradesmen or physicians lacking the requisite license (these constituted the majority of cases) to frightening breaches of security. The magistrates put real teeth into convictions for these latter offenses, indicating their seriousness of purpose in protecting nuns' honor and safety. Since convents served as depositories for goods and money, property too was at stake. An unlikely trio made up of the Florentine canon Giorgio Dati, his clerk, and Benedetto Salutati—grandson of the famed humanist chancellor—was found guilty of clambering over the roof of S. Caterina one night around Easter 1471. Rather than expressing moral outrage over the men's behavior, the accuser instead advised the magistrates to "have the nuns enclosed so they can't be seen"; he also reminded them that "I want my share of the fine"—in this case, a staggering 400 florins apiece. Similarly, in 1474, the Poor Clares of Pistoia denounced a dissolute, young stove maker who scaled their walls intent on "violating them" and "forcing" some of them to do "odious and infamous" things.

Because the nuns wished to "preserve their faith and honor," they pleaded to have this menace removed. Comic literary tropes suffused the real-life story of "Bocco," a recidivist from Prato who habitually broke into local convents. In 1460, Bocco scaled the walls of S. Matteo in Prato under cover of darkness; finding the nuns' dormitory locked, he stole various "linen goods" and other things. A few days later he returned, this time collaborating with "a certain person" inside the convent. Having awakened the nuns with his clatter, Bocco hid in a closed chest from which he sprang knife in hand upon discovery, in true Boccaccian fashion. A stiff fine of 43 florins did little to deter him. Shortly after, he climbed another convent roof and then fled when a nun raised the alarm. Accompanying Bocco on some of these nocturnal adventures was a barber, "a known thief and sodomite." The offended nuns, together with the "good men" of Prato, entreated the night officers to punish them harshly in order to discourage "other thieves, sodomites, and other wicked types."[104] There were already sufficient grounds for prosecution, but the added slur of sodomy amplified the culprits' wickedness. As Helmut Puff has shown, accusations of sodomy formed the core of slanderous concoctions used to discredit or vilify political enemies, heretics, and "foreigners."[105]

The thirty-seven reports involving suspicious conduct ran the gamut from chatting with a nun in an exterior doorway to delivering letters or visiting a convent for an unseemly length of time. All of these activities aroused sexual suspicions, but these denunciations stopped short of making explicit charges. Many of these reports gave voice to the perennial anxiety about intimate relations between nuns and clergy; some targeted specific priests or laymen against whom accusers held a grudge. Still, these reports also attest to the high level of convent scrutiny by both neighbors and spies, who timed visits and eavesdropped on conversations. Two police spies on their way to morning mass at Le Murate spotted a silk broker and his companion going to SS. Jacopo e Lorenzo across the street "almost every morning around dawn." The priest-organist of S. Croce and a cleric of Orsanmichele were seen entering S. Jacopo di Ripoli after dark; "a half hour later they still hadn't left." Despite the suspicious nature of these visits to contemporaries, all parties were exonerated. Convent reputation played an important role in helping the magistrates to contextualize charges and set penalties. In one of the magistracy's rare convictions in 1469, the apothecary Antonio Vannozzi was accused of speaking with an eighteen-year-old nun in S. Margherita of Prato. When interrogated, he admitted conversing with an older nun, "aged 45 or more," who allegedly asked him to borrow some cloth for an upcom-

ing convent feast. Despite his attempt to establish honest grounds for the exchange, he was found guilty and fined a huge sum (400 florins).[106] Other tradesmen were fined for entering S. Margherita without a license or for speaking with
the nuns. Since this convent was a recurrent trouble spot, the night officers used
judicial example to quell the heat of street gossip as well as to discipline the house.

The final category — fornication — again spanned a wide range of actors and
circumstances. To a certain extent, sexual gossip creatively licensed "the explora-
tion of transgression and disorder," as Laura Gowing has argued for early modern London. Like sodomy slurs, heterosexual accusations served to amplify the
gravity of other charges; one group of Tuscan nuns entreated help from their
Medici patron by labeling their abbess both an "evil tyrant" and a "concubine."[107]
Many of the thirty-five denunciations were clearly intended to harm. These
reports encompassed venomous anticlerical attacks against convent confessors —
who had long been the objects of satire for failed celibacy — that painted their
sexual adventures in comically prolific, exclusively heterosexual terms. Even zealous pastoral care was occasionally censured. One 1474 report accused the city's
Dominican friars of making "excessive" visits to affiliated convents. If civic officials failed to address this problem, the writer vowed to seek remedy from the
pope himself "for the honor of our daughters. We want our convents to be
religious houses," the complaint continued, "not public places." Several denunciations blamed a layman for leading one or several nuns astray. Between 1469
and 1472, Jacopo Arrighi was denounced repeatedly for allegedly keeping three
nuns in S. Martino a Maiano as his mistresses as well as for having another
concubine in S. Maria sul Prato; each time he was exonerated.[108] Some charges of
fornication aimed to discredit an entire convent. One such report in 1470 ascribed a prodigious sexual energy to five nuns in S. Baldassare in Coverciano,
home to "many dishonest ways." This was the only accusation that directly
ascribed sexual agency to religious women. Not only did each nun allegedly have
at least three different lovers; a widow living in the convent supposedly served as
their procuress. After making "diligent" inquiries, the magistrates dismissed the
charges.[109]

Only a handful of denunciations used the most powerful linguistic lever available to censure religious women: the discourse of prostitution. The restraint with
which contemporaries equated convents with brothels contrasts sharply with the
casual use of this formula in literary tales and later historical assessments. Labeling a convent a whorehouse was not only intended to shock; it was also used to

raise the stakes immeasurably. Perhaps the single most fascinating use of this analogy came from an elderly nun in S. Caterina who, in denouncing two clerics, ended up accusing her own companions of debauchery. "I marvel that you officials have not yet lifted the veil from your eyes," this anonymous nun wrote in a 1481 letter to the night officers. "I believe you must be unaware how the hospital warden at Bonifazio and the priest, Francesco Lionelli, have turned this poor convent of Santa Caterina into a bordello. And I who write this letter am one of the nuns living here, one of its most ancient mothers."[110] Seeking civic intervention, this nun cast aspersions on her sisters in religion in order to drive home her point about the clerics' poor ministration. Despite this powerful rhetoric, the men were absolved of wrongdoing. Altogether, only three of the thirty-five denunciations resulted in conviction, all stemming from the confessions of the men charged.[111]

Although the figure of the wayward nun seems to be largely a product of contemporary anxieties, the prospect of nuns behaving like whores compelled magistrates to act. It is important, however, to locate their moralizing project in a broader framework of civic concerns that focused first and foremost on controlling male sexuality. Policing sodomy absorbed the lion's share of official energy; protecting nuns continually refocused accountability on men. Even the enduring fascination with eros in the convent frequently targeted laymen or clerics as the chief culprits. This contextualization reveals the magistracy's efforts to be less a misogynistic attempt to control religious women than a self-disciplining act undertaken by urban elites in the early process of state formation.[112] The city's ambitious moral agenda remained riddled with tensions leading to erratic implementation. Nor was its breadth of vision matched by a corresponding practical apparatus. Instead, magistrates relied in large part on informal neighborhood policing, which distributed power along capillary lines. Contrary to one scholar's claim that fifteenth-century Italian states displayed "full modernity," the Florentine state remained a complex, decentralized organism produced as much by the interactions of inquisitive neighbors and opportunistic nuns as by government fiat.[113] Moreover, the fact that some nuns found the state to be a useful means of influencing social dynamics that complemented the customary tools of family and church complicates our understanding of how early modern states exercised power. Some religious women actively seized on the protective functions of the night officers; others utilized the discursive power of sexual transgression to express personal animosities. Far from being simply the objects of state concern, nuns capitalized on directives aimed at their control. Their agency proved to be a two-sided coin, however: in utilizing this apparatus for short-term gains, Florentine nuns reinforced the extension of civic authority into their communities.

Ecclesiastical Reform Initiatives, 1500–1540

The cataclysms that rocked the Italian peninsula after 1494 gave new urgency to calls for tighter enclosure, which quickly became emblematic of a revivified religiosity. In Florence, both Savonarola and the movement he initiated considered nuns' enclosure to be an integral part of religious renewal. Bitter struggles between Savonarolan friars and his female followers to define his legacy in the first decades of the Cinquecento implicitly placed enclosure at the center of debate. Lorenzo Polizzotto has shown how this deeply divisive battle turned in part on competing visions of female holiness, pitting the desire of some religious women to preach and engage in public prophesy against more traditional views that stressed female passivity and interiority. When the friars of S. Marco advocated more stringent rules for convent ingress and egress, even for Dominican tertiaries, members of the Annalena, the Angiolini, and S. Lucia took a clear step back from their ministration. Several communities resisted the imposition of tighter enclosure in part by using visual images to remind viewers of their historic freedom of movement. Attempts to enforce enclosure in Belgian and German convents in these same years also met with resistance from nuns.[114] After 1500, enclosure shed its status as merely one significant feature of female monasticism across Europe to become the linchpin of an entire religious vision.

Reform efforts gained momentum from the perception that Italian military defeats reflected divine displeasure. The rich catalog of Italian sins invited harsh retribution; sacred virgins obviously had failed in their duties as intercessors. Tellingly, only after Italian city-states were humiliated by foreign invasions did the association between open reclusion and sexual dissipation become commonplace. In 1497 the celebrated Franciscan preacher Fra Timoteo of Lucca excoriated Venetians for their vices, among which was showing convents to visiting foreign lords. "These aren't convents," he claimed, "but whorehouses and public brothels." Nuns were among those blamed for the disastrous Venetian defeat in 1509, leading the patrician Girolamo Priuli to issue his notorious invective equating open convents with bordellos. New laws passed that year limited contact with nuns but soon became a dead letter because of patrician demand for sustained interaction with their female kin. Subsequent measures enacted by the

Council of Ten and the Venetian patriarch ordered iron grates installed in convent parlors and threatened noncompliant nuns with solitary confinement; in 1514, laywomen between the ages of ten and forty were prohibited from living in religious houses. The nuns of S. Zaccaria responded by throwing rocks at the men charged with installing the grates, although they later reached a compromise with officials. Only when civil and ecclesiastical authorities joined forces did Venice finally establish an office regulating convents. The hostility shown toward reforms initiated by Patriarch Antonio Contarini forced the Council of Ten to intervene, prompting the foundation of the Magistrato sopra i monasteri in 1521. Replying to nuns' numerous petitions protesting these developments, Leo X decisively supported the patriarch and nullified earlier enclosure privileges.[115]

As marauding armies crisscrossed north-central Italy, concerns about nuns' physical safety fed moral rationales for enclosure. Rape was a long-established military tactic used to humiliate and demoralize enemies; violating sacred virgins added blasphemous insult and a sense of impotence that suggested even God had abandoned the cause. Cesare Borgia's troops committed numerous "atrocities" against nuns in his campaign to subdue the Papal States in 1501; during the French sack of Ravenna in 1512, the Venetian diarist Sanuto reported that many nuns were savagely raped and murdered. When French and Spanish troops surrounded Florence to secure the Medici restoration, concern for both religious and laywomen mounted as "stories of more cruelties poured in daily."[116] That year, a benefactor of S. Jacopo rebuilt at his own expense the wall running from the garden to the parlor entrance "because he wanted the convent enclosure to be well preserved." The wall was judged "too low" and its gate "almost ruined," making it "very easy for someone outside to gain entrance." Still, the fact that monarchs and local ecclesiastical officials advocated tighter enclosure in parts of Europe untouched by invasion indicates that moral and ideological considerations weighed most heavily.[117]

After 1500, ecclesiastical authorities began to encase nuns in a multitude of restrictions in order to separate them from worldly influences. They set thresholds on interactions with kin, monitored letters going in and out of the convent, and devised new measures for visual reclusion. The most dramatic changes occurred in the built environment — higher garden walls, sealed-up windows, veiled grates in the parlor, fortified apertures — that limited nuns' visibility and accessibility to outsiders. These more obvious elements of enclosure were predicated on a series of smaller, incremental efforts to disentangle nuns from their urban networks, which transformed previous points of accommodation into explicit danger zones. The most hotly contested space was the convent parlor, where nuns conversed with friends and family through an open-worked grate. When making pastoral rounds in 1509, Archbishop Cosimo Pazzi repeatedly stressed the dangers of verbal and visual exchanges taking place there. Exhorting the nuns of S. Felicita to remain steadfast in their vows, Pazzi advised them "to take care in your conversations with laymen and others, because they are the means of alienating yourself from the true spiritual path." He cautioned the abbess to carefully supervise conversations at the parlor grate and turnstile, "since these are the beginnings of many evils." He made similar injunctions throughout his visitation, regardless of the degree of the nuns' discipline. Although the archbishop had nothing but praise for the Chiarito nuns, he nevertheless instructed them to elect an official "listener" to monitor conversations between nuns and laity. Conversely, he warned the nuns of S. Luca to "cut out and throw away" their usual habit of "running immediately to the grate and turnstile." At S. Maria al Monte — a major center for gold thread production — Pazzi fretted openly about exchanges with laity, although he approved of the nuns' poverty. "Above all watch yourselves in the parlor and in face-to-face dealings. Fashion this iron grate in such a way that your hands are not able to touch." Taking no chances, he commanded them under pain of excommunication "not to open or leave ajar the little communion windows to speak with anyone who wishes; keep them locked with a key."[118]

The appropriate level of interaction with kin, however, remained a thornier issue. Pazzi recognized that the ordinary pleasures of seeing family provided solace to nuns, most of whom lacked vocation. As a native Florentine, he also understood the financial hardships that complete separation would entail. Consequently, the archbishop tried to strike a tenuous balance between imperatives as he moved around the diocese. After issuing his usual caution that visitors were the beginning of "every evil," he instructed the Paradiso nuns to take a companion whenever they met with laity in the parlor. Because their rule permitted weekly conversations with kin "for the nuns' consolation," Pazzi had no choice except to comply. However, he stressed that the nuns needed the abbess's permission for visits beforehand and exhorted them to discuss only spiritual things that increased devotion. He also told them to replace their wooden grate with an iron one immediately.[119]

More innovative measures to achieve full reclusion surfaced in the early sixteenth century. The enlargement of female literacy by convent schools, the growing availability of vernacular printed materials, and the shift in Florentine political culture to more indirect forms of governance heightened the importance of epistolary exchanges between nuns and the outside world. Adriano Prosperi has shown how spiritual letters permitted Italian religious women to act as autonomous spiritual guides without need for male mediation.[120] Yet this most intimate of genres also hosted social conversations through which nuns exchanged news and gossip, requested gifts and favors, and revealed personal and emotional frustrations. Letters not only aroused suspicion in a changing religious climate but were a principal means by which nuns sustained their place in family circles. Consequently, disengaging nuns from secular affairs entailed regulating their correspondence closely. The constitutions for the Savonarolan tertiaries of S. Caterina da Siena promulgated in 1509 monitored both the recipients and content of nuns' letters. These religious women could write only to their fathers, mothers, and close kin about such everyday matters as "words of thanks, their health or illness, saying prayers and similar things." Grievous penalties were meted out to those who sent or received letters without showing them first to the prioress.[121]

Still, a certain flexibility and pragmatism distinguished these early Cinquecento reform efforts from later Tridentine measures. Although Pazzi, Savonarolan friars, and other local reformers breathed new life into old monastic prescriptions, they also showed a willingness to honor established practices considered to be "ancient" convent customs. These churchmen insisted on greater rigor, but they did not impose utter uniformity. For centuries, Florentine nuns had successfully defended exemptions based on historical precedent, and they used the same tactic right through Trent.[122] In this sense, nuns' stance was in fact deeply conservative: they defended what had long been the essence of Italian church practice, combating the logic of reform with the logic of tradition.

Both the rhetoric and efficacy of this defense can be seen in petitions emanating from S. Jacopo, which officially joined the Savonarolan fold in 1507. Deeply committed to the *Piagnone* cause, the nuns nevertheless importuned Julius II the following year to confirm their custom of "speaking with relatives and friends several times a year in the church, at the little window where the nuns take communion, in such a way that they can see those with whom they're speaking because the veil over the aperture is removed. Every elderly nun in the house affirmed that this practice had been observed since her childhood, and there is no recollection of any other custom." Worried that this practice contravened another bull issued fifty years earlier prohibiting visual contact when speaking with laity, the new convent supervisors sought papal approval so that "the nuns might retain peace of mind while following this same usage." After the papal deputy inspected the aperture and spoke with the eldest nuns, he decreed that "four or five times a year, all the nuns who live in this convent in future will be allowed to speak with kin, friends, and benefactors at the unveiled opening with only the approval of the prioress." He further empowered convent supervisors to increase the number of sessions "with the consent of the eldest nuns . . . especially on occasions when nuns professed." Despite the unconditional pronouncement that "this privilege shall endure in perpetuity," its exercise was obviously short lived.[123]

By the 1510s and 1520s, enclosure was already hardening as the ideological sign of renewal. In 1521, Leo X — hardly an ardent reformer — devised a new rule for Regular Franciscan Tertiaries that allowed strict enclosure for those who desired it. He also rewarded Observant nuns who were barred from pursuing spiritual graces by enclosure. Reflecting the politics of preferment, Leo ceded all indulgences attached to the churches of Rome and Florence to the Medici-favored nuns of S. Apollonia if they performed a fictive pilgrimage around their convent church; he issued a similar privilege to Le Murate in 1516.[124] Locally, the enclosure campaign found solid institutional backing in the 1517 Florentine synodal constitutions, which consolidated reform measures across the diocese. Ironically, these rulings were promulgated by the worldly Archbishop Giulio de' Medici before his ascent to the papal throne as Clement VII. Clerics not in service to a particular convent were prohibited from visiting without episcopal license; laymen needed permission from the archbishop or convent governor. Female visitors were welcome at the parlor grate as long as they were "of honest life and conversation." But nuns had to show any letters sent or received to their abbess on pain of imprisonment; "if they were love letters or less than decent," the rubrics imposed excommunication, a 50-florin fine, and six months in chains on the offending nun. Sexual misconduct elicited new punitive extremes. "All seducers of nuns," construed broadly to mean those who kissed or touched them, were declared infamous excommunicates, and the offending nun was condemned to life in prison.[125]

Physical and architectural changes figured prominently in these rulings as well. Convent parlors were mandated to have double grates set a palm width apart and constructed with tight latticework to prevent any hand from passing through "no matter how small." Grates had to be veiled when speaking with laymen, "except if the speaker is father, uncle, or other close relation" — the standard concession to kinship. Similarly, the turnstile was to be fitted with iron grates and configured so that no woman, however small, could enter or exit through it. Nuns' cells could not face a public street or neighbors' houses; windows had to have bars; all convents were required to have a prison for errant nuns. Tridentine enclosure rulings codified all of these features, albeit in more elaborate detail.

Finally, the 1517 synodal constitutions tackled the problem of passive enclosure. Laywomen over age twelve could not reside in a convent unless they intended to take vows. "The lute and the psalter do not go well together," contended the rubric. "Talk of marriage and children easily corrupts the purity of the virgin heart." These rulings not only uprooted established custom but flew in the face of fundamental urban needs for diverse residential options; in so doing, they also threatened to undercut prospective legacies to convents from female benefactors. Similarly, nuns were cut off from external festive life just as it became a fulcrum of Italian urban society. Women as well as men were barred from entering cloisters when novices assumed the habit or took final vows, nor could new brides visit nuns dressed in their wedding finery.[126] Whatever the level of compliance, these rulings highlight the contradictions in which Renaissance convents and society had become entangled.

The crisis besetting Florence from 1527 to 1530 gave new enclosure measures real purchase. In 1527, as plague and political turmoil raged, the confessor of the Poor Clares of Monticelli wrote a consolatory treatise for the nuns to strengthen their spiritual mettle. Amid massive disruption, this priest advised them "to avoid speaking with men if possible, even if they're your relatives; use as few words as necessary . . . and leave them well edified."[127] The destruction of extramural convents during the siege forced the permanent relocation of some inhabitants to urban monasteries or hospitals appropriated for this purpose. Even though hospitals and monastic institutions showed striking architectural similarities, nuns' new dwellings had to be refitted to meet higher standards of enclosure: grates installed, windows barred, walls heightened, portals fortified.[128]

As Florence returned to normalcy after the siege, enclosure took permanent root. In 1534, the convent governor of the former S. Niccolò dei Frieri (renamed S. Giovannino) commanded that nuns post guards at the door, station a permanent "listener" in the parlor, dispense with spiritual recreations such as plays, and abide by other restrictions. Only a century earlier, this convent had practiced open reclusion to better serve urban charitable and educational needs; now its fortresslike complex assumed an introverted quality that soon spawned its own contradictions and peculiar cultural forms.[129] Even the much-reviled Archbishop

Andrea Buondelmonti insisted on fuller enclosure to boost his legitimacy as a churchman. In March 1534, the nuns of S. Pier Maggiore protested vehemently after the archbishop demanded that they veil their parlor grates. Although nuns in this bastion of traditionalism did not hurl rocks like their Venetian counterparts, they did take legal action. Seeing this order as an assault on privilege, they refused to comply; in turn, the archbishop placed them under interdict. The nuns countersued to remove both interdict and directive, but their resistance came to naught. That month, they grudgingly hung the veils "by the archbishop's command."[130]

The long trajectory traced here demonstrates that, although Trent achieved greater consistency and uniformity than earlier measures, its tactics followed an established line of attack. Attempts to disengage religious women from the outside world not only were galvanized by the Observant movement but found new justification in the unsettled political climate of the early Cinquecento. The initiatives launched by Archbishop Pazzi marked the influence of reform sensibilities on the Florentine church well before the post-Tridentine episcopate of Alessandro de' Medici, usually taken to be the first local reformer since Antoninus. Accompanying these initiatives was the masculinization of the Florentine church apparent in the diminished ritual role played by the nuns of S. Pier Maggiore after 1500.[131] Not surprisingly, the escalation of enclosure also went hand in glove with an escalation in the number of forced professions. Importantly, however, the demise of open reclusion bore only tenuous relation to sexual activity. Evidence for nuns' immersion in the life of the city is abundant, whereas evidence for their widespread promiscuity remains sparse. The larger political culture and many forms of social experience permeated Renaissance Florentine convents, but they can hardly be considered clandestine brothels. Most Renaissance nuns lacked vocation and, without doubt, a few broke their vows. The vast majority of religious women, however, struggled to construct meaningful lives for themselves and to find the sacred in the everyday within tightening constraints. Soon Florentine nuns were squeezed still further between the double pincers of Duke Cosimo's new state magistracy governing convents and the imposition of compulsory *clausura* by Tridentine reformers, both of which had roots in the preceding century.[132]

Conclusion

Between the Black Death and the beginning of the Medici principate, convents were transformed from small, semiautonomous communities into large civic institutions serving family, church, and state. I have argued that fifteenth-century developments were pivotal to the ways this transformation played out. The first two chapters of my account emphasize the political uses to which convents were put by members of a composite mercantile elite. Gaining dominance over religious institutions enabled members of the Florentine upper classes to solidify political ascendance, create new footholds within the Italian church, and extend networks of clientage beyond their immediate neighborhoods. In turn, these inroads made by the upper classes in controlling religious institutions enabled convents to weather demographic crises and a powerful pronatalist discourse in the early Quattrocento. After 1450, new monastic recruitment patterns helped reconstitute urban social geography as the city grew from an assemblage of local enclaves into one of the most dynamic commercial centers of Renaissance Europe. The unique partnership struck between the papacy and Florentine oligarchy, which had been evolving since the fourteenth century, proved decisive in remaking the local monastic landscape. This rapid turnaround in convent fortunes in the mid-Quattrocento distinguished certain chronological features of the Florentine story from patterns of development in neighboring cities.

As I show in chapter 3, new economic relations between convents and the Florentine state that took hold after 1450 consolidated these political gains. *Monte* reforms not only entangled convents in a vast civic bookkeeping operation but made nuns more reliant on the public fisc for support. Through the instruments of public finance and the extension of civic charity, the Florentine commune impressed nuns into the city's spiritual service, giving Florentine religious women a more prominent intercessory and salvific role than they had a century before. These processes speak to the constitutive role that nuns and nunneries played in forming the Florentine state and in realigning church-state relations.

Accompanying these political changes were fundamental shifts in the social functions assigned to female monasticism. Over the course of the fifteenth century, nuns' families began to treat convents less as holding corporations to protect property interests and more as spearheads to establish wide-ranging patronage networks. As convents gained numerical strength in the mid-Quattrocento, both the Medici and their allies seized on new opportunities to translate webs of clientage into expanded political influence. Later in the century, the growing complexities of the marriage market demanded that countless girls take up the monastic life. In addition, political instability following repeated foreign invasions probably convinced some fathers and brothers that the convent represented one of the safest residential options for their kinswomen. Although the Italian church had been caught up in previous cycles of renewal, the late Quattrocento marked a turning point in the frequency with which genuine vocations, especially those associated with the Savonarolan movement, were channeled into traditional monastic pathways.

The convent economy illuminates another distinctive feature of Renaissance female monasticism. In the early fifteenth century, most Florentine convents had not yet developed significant investments in the public debt—a fact that sets their economies apart from those of early modern convents, which were more reliant on liquid capital investments. This shift not only reflects the continued development of innovative financial instruments across Italy but also points to new family property strategies underpinning nuns' corporate and private wealth. Rather than using property to subsidize nuns' annuities, Florentine families used declining *monte* investments to support them. As a result, propertied nuns lost some of their managerial role and financial discretion; since *monte* credits devolved on the institution after death, this form of personal wealth translated over time into larger institutional holdings in the public fisc. By the sixteenth century, it was standard Florentine practice to supplement nuns' living expenses through interest-bearing credits — a practice that denied nuns ready access to both capital and property and prevented the dispersal of family patrimonies. In these often-hidden ways, Renaissance convent economies augmented the social strategies by which Florentine aristocratic families consolidated their fortunes under the Medici dukes.

Pernicious poverty stemming from inadequate endowments also forced most Renaissance nuns to work for a living. Without doubt, fifteenth-century religious women engaged in a fuller spectrum of economic activities than either their late medieval predecessors or early modern successors. Economic diversification rendered convents more nimble, gave the Florentine economy much-needed elasticity, and spun a thick web of relationships — ones of dependence, patronage, and exchange — around Florentine religious women and their institutions. Chief among nuns' market activities was textile work, ranging from the drudgery of reeling silk to the lucrative job of spinning gold thread to the artistry of embroidery and lace making. Regardless of the task, nuns' invisible hands helped advance the city's international economic stature. Seizing the moral high ground, the Florentine commune adopted a statist model to protect private business interests; yet magistrates highlighted contradictions in civic policies when permitting business associates easy access to cloisters. As Tridentine strictures closed off market work, Florentine nuns became more reliant on their families, further fueling the privatization of early modern convents.

The Quattrocento also witnessed more concerted attempts to disengage religious women from the outside world, which exposed fundamental paradoxes at the heart of Renaissance monasticism. Inspired by the midcentury Observant movement, popes and prelates insisted on fuller reclusion, but their successors responded more willingly to lay demands for interaction with nuns. Similarly, civic mandates placed the night officers in a perennial double bind as both investigatory vice squad and convent guardians. These conflicted agendas help explain why cyclical calls for monastic reform often had failed outcomes. Moreover, the records of this innovative magistracy bear only tenuous witness to illicit sexual activity, which was more imagined than performed. It is time to lay the specter of the wayward nun to rest, or at least to recognize it as a politicized figure.

Attacks on open reclusion found new justification in the unsettled political atmosphere of the early Cinquecento, marked by cataclysmic foreign invasions. Not surprisingly, heightened calls for enclosure went hand in hand with a rapid rise in forced professions. Local initiatives launched by Archbishop Cosimo Pazzi, which wrapped an iron fist in the velvet glove of pastoral care, marked the influence of reform sensibilities on the Florentine church well before the post-Tridentine episcopate of Alessandro de' Medici. Shortly after Pazzi's death, the 1517 synodal constitutions codified many disparate enclosure measures—the installation of physical barriers, the monitoring of nuns' letters—yet neglected festering problems of lay intrusion in convent affairs. Florentine nuns used the logic of tradition and established privilege to defend their way of life but met with diminishing success after 1500.

This study also set out to evaluate the scope of female agency in relation to monastic life. Religious women were both the unwitting subjects and active agents of some of the momentous changes I have described, confounding any easy assessment, especially as historical conditions changed over time. There is no question that religious communities offered Florentine women considerable agency throughout the Renaissance. Evanescent female religious associations continued to nourish a pluralistic monastic landscape into the sixteenth century. Convent chapters facilitated their own recovery after 1400 by lowering spiritual dowries and adopting flexible payment schedules, especially for principal patrons. They determined in large part what capital projects to undertake and the volume of market work needed to underwrite them. Nuns extended their social reach both as individuals and as groups through broad-gauged clientage relations they themselves created, whether through market work, property management, educational activities, or political alliances. A few religious women acted as patrons and brokers in their own right by forging intermediate links in longer patronage chains and by making instrumental use of kinship that cut both ways. Class conditioned nuns' agency in significant ways; wealth and family connections, for example, allowed some religious women to exercise greater influence in the world. Yet on an aggregate level, sheer strength of numbers made large convents like Le Murate and S. Chiara political forces to be reckoned with, irrespective of their social composition.

Still, there is no question that Renaissance nuns and nunneries lost considerable decision-making power and scope for self-determination, even as their numbers grew beyond previous recognition. Changes in Quattrocento property regimes supporting individual nuns and their communities gave them less discretion in managing revenues; new recruitment patterns lessened their neighborhood influence while making them more visible on an urban stage. Immiseration forced many fifteenth-century nuns to compete for lay patrons, engage heavily in market production, and rely on civic charity for the most basic necessities of life. Even tertiaries who sought greater accommodation with the world found themselves under closer civic and ecclesiastical scrutiny as the century drew to a close. After 1500 growing patrician dominance within convent chapters made it difficult to sustain social inclusivity and a sense of spiritual egalitarianism. The stunning rise in convent populations placed added strain on already cramped spaces, propelled the rise of factions, and undercut close face-to-face relationships in many religious houses. Perhaps the clearest sign of eroding institutional autonomy was nuns' inability to negotiate new enclosure provisions as the sixteenth-century Italian church gained potency. Long before Florentine nuns confronted the double straits of Medicean state supervision and Tridentine reform, their communities had already navigated much of the initial passage from the late medieval to the early modern Italian church.

Acknowledgments

One of the joys of finishing a long project is having the opportunity to thank the individuals and institutions whose contributions were vital. This project was launched at the National Humanities Center under the sponsorship of the American Council of Learned Societies and the Gladys Krieble Delmas Foundation. I would like to thank the directors and library staff of the center for their invaluable assistance and the two sponsoring agencies for generous financial support. My cofellows, especially Melissa Bullard and Peter Lynch, as well as local colleagues Stanley Chojnacki, Barbara Harris, and Al Rabil, made my fellowship year in North Carolina stimulating and enjoyable. I also am indebted to the American Academy in Rome for providing a congenial writing environment on several occasions. My thanks go to the Ecole Française, Rome, for allowing me to use its extensive library resources and to Villa I Tatti, Florence, for continued hospitality. It is my pleasure to acknowledge the generous assistance of the Lila Acheson Wallace–Reader's Digest Publications Fund at Villa I Tatti in bringing this book to publication. I am happy to acknowledge the research support provided by the Emory University Research Committee, the Institute for Comparative and International Studies, and Emory College.

The staffs of various libraries and archives also deserve heartfelt thanks. I owe a special debt of gratitude to the members of the staff of the Archivio di Stato, Florence, for their many kindnesses over the years. Don Gilberto Aranci, archivist at the Archivio Arcivescovile, Florence, helped me track down a crucial manuscript. The staffs of the Biblioteca Riccardiana, Biblioteca Nazionale Centrale, and Biblioteca Medicea Laurenziana in Florence facilitated research in these repositories. Brief forays at the Vatican Archives and the British Library were made more productive by helpful staff members. Marie Hansen and the interlibrary loan staff at Emory University merit particular thanks for obtaining rare publications and other materials over the years.

This book owes a debt to many scholars with whom I have shared intellectual pleasures as well as the joys of friendship. Richard Goldthwaite read one chapter in draft and provided invaluable advice on all things economic; his bracing questions improved this project in countless ways. Judith Brown, who helped pioneer the study of Italian Renaissance nuns, offered thoughtful suggestions for improving the manuscript in its final stages. My former mentor Gene Brucker generously shared archival transcriptions that enrich the story told here. A number of colleagues who have made the study of Italian religious women such an exciting new field — Elissa Weaver, Saundra Weddle, Kate Lowe, Silvia Evangelisti, Catherine Turrill, Anne Jacobsen Schutte — contributed expert knowledge. This book has benefited greatly from their insights; of course, any faults that remain are my own responsibility. Other colleagues and friends, especially Nicholas Baker, Cristelle Baskins, Julia Delancey, Nicholas Eckstein, John Henderson, John Paoletti, Linda Pellecchia, David Peterson, Brenda Preyer, Michael Rocke, and Nicholas Terpstra, helped shape this book through convivial conversation.

Numerous Emory colleagues offered sound advice and encouragement. Special thanks go to Jim Roark for lending a willing ear on countless occasions and for showing me the conceptual power that resides in everyday language. Karen Bosnos listened patiently as I tried out new ideas, especially about women's work. History Department colleagues William Beik, Kristin Mann, Jamie Melton, Judith Miller, Matt Payne, and Stephen White offered constructive feedback at various points. Kim Culbertson of the Emory College Information Technology Division kindly prepared the graphs.

Work on this project was slowed considerably by a long illness. Two friends in particular — Robyn Fivush and Diane Jones-Palm — helped me weather some difficult times. I can never fully repay their incomparable love and support. My mother, Stella Strocchia, and my sister Susan Hall cheered me on over the years. Midway through research, I met long-lost relatives living in Florence — Felice, Rachele, Domenico, Flora, and Francesco Strocchia — who generously opened their hearts and home to me. Knowing them has given me a fresh perspective on contemporary Italian life. Tiberio and Gabriella Roselli enriched my research trips to Florence through their warmth and hospitality. My sincere thanks to all.

Notes

For archival source abbreviations used in the notes, see the bibliography.

Preface

1. Strasser, *State of Virginity*; Sperling, *Convents and the Body Politic*; Lehfeldt, *Religious Women*.

2. Trexler, "Celibacy." Throughout this study, I use the term "convent" to refer to organized groups of religious women incorporated under a formal monastic rule. The term "female religious communities" signals a broader, pluralistic spectrum of women religious, including tertiaries and unaffiliated penitents. Male religious institutions are called "monasteries" or "friaries," depending on their affiliation.

3. Bizzocchi, *Chiesa e potere*; Dameron, *Episcopal Power*; Dameron, *Florence and Its Church*; Peterson, "State-building."

4. Brucker, "Monasteries"; Herlihy and Klapisch-Zuber, *Les toscans*, 158. Trexler, "Celibacy," 15, put the total number of nuns in 1552 at 3,419, or 11.5 percent, of the urban female population.

CHAPTER 1 : The Growth of Florentine Convents

1. Villani, *Croniche*, bk. 11, chap. 94. Noting the inconsistencies in Villani's estimates, Herlihy and Klapisch-Zuber, *Les toscans*, 173–75, place the pre-plague population at about 120,000 persons.

2. Brucker, "Monasteries"; Herlihy and Klapisch-Zuber, *Les toscans*, 158. Trexler, "Celibacy," 15, puts the total number of nuns in 1552 at 3,419, or 11.5% of the urban female population. However, Batarra, *Popolazione di Firenze*, 9, cites the figure of 2,826 nuns in 1552. I am unable to account for this discrepancy.

3. Trexler, "Celibacy," 24–25; Zarri, "Monasteri femminili e città," 369, remarks that after Trent nuns from Bologna similarly dominated the region of Emilia-Romagna. There were five new convents founded in Prato between 1450 and 1518—S. Giorgio (1450), S. Caterina (1480), S. Vincenzo (1503), S. Trinita (1508), S. Clemente (1518)—which absorbed the illegitimate daughters of Florentine patricians as well as legitimate, middle-class girls from Florence and Prato. Di Agresti, *Sviluppi della riforma*, 59–60, reports that by 1591, twelve hundred nuns lived in the ten convents of Prato; of this number, only four hundred came from the city of Prato itself.

4. Litchfield, "Demographic Characteristics"; Sperling, *Convents and the Body Politic*,

18. According to Brucker, "Monasteries," 44–45, there was no corresponding growth among Florentine monks and friars, whose numbers rose from 750 in 1427 to 800 in 1500.

5. Trexler, "Celibacy," 26, noted that barely 200 nuns lived in the diocese of London in 1500. Leonard, *Nails in the Wall*, 12, states that about 250 nuns lived in Strasbourg's eight Dominican convents between 1470 and 1525 out of an urban population of twenty thousand. Unfortunately, Leonard does not provide a complete census.

6. In 1500, Valladolid had only seven convents, whereas Florence had thirty-seven, plus another seventeen female religious houses dispersed within a four-mile radius of the city. By the mid-sixteenth century, Valladolid counted thirteen convents housing 595 nuns, who represented 1.5% of the urban population of forty thousand. In comparison, the 3,823 Florentine nuns living in forty-seven urban convents in 1563 represented 5.5 to 6.5% of an estimated urban population of sixty thousand to seventy thousand. Another 970 nuns lived in fourteen suburban convents (Lehfeldt, *Religious Women in Golden Age Spain*, 16, 39; Trkulja, ed., *I fiorentini nel 1562*, vi–vii; Repetti, *Dizionario geografico fisisco storico*, 2:279).

7. Sebastiani, "Monasteri femminili milanesi," 6, maintains that Milan did not sustain the same rise in female religious institutions and personnel as Florence, although she does not provide concrete data. For Bologna, see notes 12 and 65 below.

8. As Cohn notes in "Nuns and Dowry Funds," 192–93, Trexler considered his findings to be provisional, although they were later uncritically accepted by scholars.

9. Hufton, "The Nun's Story."

10. Sensi, *Storie di bizzoche*.

11. Dameron, *Florence and Its Church*, 45, 47–51. The new houses were S. Elisabetta delle Convertite (1330), S. Elisabetta di Capitolo (1333), S. Giovanni Battista detto Mona Scotta (1334, later S. Chiara), S. Francesco de' Macci (1335), S. Apollonia (1339), S. Maria della Neve (1339, also called S. Maria degli Scalzi), S. Maria del Fiore detto Lapo (1340), S. Maria della Disciplina del Portico (1340), S. Niccolò Maggiore (1340), S. Baldassare a Coverciano (1341), S. Maria Regina Coeli detto Chiarito (1343), S. Caterina a S. Gaggio (1344), S. Gherardo (c. 1345, later S. Clemente), and S. Marta a Montughi (c. 1348). Weddle, "Identity and Alliance," has shown that site selection within the city was guided by a preference for relatively isolated, undeveloped neighborhoods, where there would be fewer distractions as well as space for expansion.

12. Zarri, "Monasteri femminili a Bologna," 138, 140, 143–44. Zarri based her census on the number of convents rather than on the number of inhabitants; her survey does not globally estimate either number prior to 1480, when Bologna counted twenty convents.

13. Richa, *Notizie istoriche delle chiese fiorentine*, 4:303; Trexler, "Celibacy," 23; BRF, Mss. Moreni, 317.

14. Few scholars have attempted a systematic pre- and post-plague census of female religious communities. Banker, *Death in the Community*, 24–26, 35, estimates that about 150 women in the nearby town of San Sepolcro lived in different types of religious houses in the early fourteenth century, representing 3.75% of the urban population of five thousand. Of this number, 101 were nuns living in three Franciscan convents; by 1356–80, their ranks had fallen to roughly 75 women.

15. ASF, Capitoli, Appendice, vol. 27. The bishop distributed 3,350 florins left by the merchant Giovacchino Ubaldini. On patterns of charitable bequests, see Cohn, *Cult of Remembrance*.

16. I use the list of magnates published by Lansing, *Florentine Magnates*, 239–42.

17. Lansing, *Florentine Magnates*, 132, 237.

18. AAF, VP, 1.1. The published inventory dates the visitation 1383 because it occurred before March 25, when the Florentine calendar changed to a new year. Acciaiuoli visited twenty-five female communities, not twenty-two as listed in *L'archivio della cancelleria arcivescovile di Firenze*, 13. Omitted from the published inventory are S. Niccolò Maggiore (fols. 12v–13r), S. Onofrio (13v–14r), and S. Baldassare in Coverciano (33r).

19. AAF, VP, 1.1, fol. 21r.

20. ASF, CRSPL, S. Jacopo, vol. 2, nos. 163 bis, 171, 176; for Montedomini, see ASF, NA, 9866, fols. 95r–96v, dated 31 July 1407, listing ten nuns, and ASF, NA, 9867, fol. 209v, dated 11 February 1417, listing thirteen nuns. I am grateful to Gene Brucker for transcriptions of these latter two documents.

21. Herlihy and Klapisch-Zuber, *Les toscans*, 177, put the urban population at sixty thousand in 1374. Religious women represented about one-half of 1% of the urban population in Villani's day and closer to three-quarters of 1% in 1384.

22. AAF, VP, 1.1, fols. 12v, 27v–28r, 29r–30r.

23. AAF, VP, 1.1, fols. 1v–4r, 13r, 14v–15r, 19r, 24r–v. I discuss the problems at S. Ambrogio at greater length in chapter 5.

24. AAF, SPM, Feste Ufizi, fol. 1r; ASF, CRSPL, SPM, vol. 76, fol. 65v; Molho, *Marriage Alliance*, 209, 365–75. The convent's *numerus clausus* had been set at twelve nuns by episcopal decree in 1313 (ASF, CRSPL, SPM, vol. 1, no. 21).

25. ASF, CRSPL, SPM, vol. 50, fol. 4v; vol. 68, fols. 19v, 68r; vol. 69, fol. 67r; vol. 70, fol. 79v.

26. Flora Portinari entered July 1375 and died November 1384; Taddea Dini took vows 1381 and died September 1386; Spera Cambi joined April 1380 and died August 1380; Piera Barucci died in 1396, six years after taking vows; Maddalena Bencivenni entered April 1394 and succumbed to plague July 1400; Bartolomea Ricasoli joined 1385, took vows in 1390, and had died by 1402 (ASF, CRSPL, SPM, vol. 51, fols. 3r, 35v, 50r, 93v; vol. 52, fol. 21v; vol. 68, fol. 23v; vol. 69, fols. 26r, 51r; vol. 70, fols. 11v, 60v; vol. 200, fol. 32r; AAF, SPM, Feste Ufizi, fol. 31v).

27. Brucker, *Florentine Politics*; Peterson, "War of the Eight Saints."

28. Strocchia, "When the Bishop Married the Abbess," 354–55. ASF, Dipl., SPM, 29 December 1395, states that Suor Antonia had been a professed nun for forty years and had led a commendable life. She was elected "unanimiter et concorditer et una voce nemine discordate," despite being the fifth most senior nun of eleven. Her death is recorded in ASF, Dipl., SPM, 4 August 1400.

29. Cohn, "Nuns and Dowry Funds," 76–97.

30. These communities included S. Orsola (1376), S. Girolamo e S. Francesco sulla Costa (1377), S. Girolamo detto Gesuate (1382, also called Le Poverine), SS. Jacopo e Lorenzo (1390), S. Onofrio (1390), S. Niccolò dei Frieri (1392), S. Brigida detto del Paradiso (1392), S. Verdiana (1395).

31. In 1378, two monastic dowries yielded almost a third of annual income at Monteluce in Perugia, one of the richest convents in Italy (Gardner, "Nuns' Altarpieces").

32. In 1412, nine-year-old Lorenza Corsini entered S. Pier Maggiore with a dowry of 200 florins — the convent's single highest Quattrocento entry payment — which represented one-third of the sum needed for a good marriage match. Only 100 florins were paid because Lorenza died a month after entry. Although her father was legally obligated for the entire sum, the nuns excused the remainder in view of the circumstances (ASF,

CRSPL, SPM, vol. 72, fols. 7v, 9r). Herlihy and Klapisch-Zuber, *Les toscans*, 417, give her dowry as 230 florins. Examples of late Trecento dowries can be found in ASF, CRSPL, SPM, vol. 69, fol. 26r; vol. 70, fol. 11v, and AAF, SPM, Feste Ufizi, fols. 13r, 31r–v.

33. Six novices entered between 1401–5 (ASF, CRSGF, 83, vol. 112, fols. 26r–27v, 43r).

34. ASF, Catasto, vol. 602, fol. 90r–v.

35. ASF, CRSGF, 90, vol. 1, fol. 4r; ASF, NA, 7943, fol. 68r; ASF, Mon. S. Brigida, vol. 235, fol. 5v.

36. Molho, *Marriage Alliance*, 28.

37. *Statuta*, 3:402–8.

38. Quoted in Rusconi, "St. Bernardino of Siena," 187.

39. AAF, VP, 2.1. Only twenty-six of the twenty-nine houses reported their populations. I have omitted the three nonreporting institutions from calculations of average size.

40. AAF, VP, 2.1, fol. 71v. The group's founder Agata reported that six of the ten women had already taken vows of some sort. They owned no goods but had "sufficient means" on which to live. The recluses had adopted the Benedictine rule in November 1423, prior to their move to Via Ghibellina (BNCF, II, II, 509, fol. 6v). The foundation pact with their parish superiors at S. Ambrogio is conserved in ASF, Dipl., S. Ambrogio, 2 December 1424. The other early Quattrocento foundation was S. Monaca (1442), the protégé of the monks of S. Maria del Carmine.

41. S. Agata, S. Orsola, S. Luca, S. Lucia, and S. Gherardo each housed only four to six religious women, including abbesses and novices. "Since ancient times" S. Ambrogio had set its ideal number at fifteen; now it housed six nuns and three novices, having lost its abbess and eight nuns to the 1400 plague (AAF, VP, 2.1, fols. 42v, 59r–v, 61r–63v; BNCF, II, X, 41).

42. The ecclesiastical portion of this census, which formed part of the same civic initiative to put tax assessments on an equal footing, was not carried out until 1428–29. However, I refer to this source as the 1427 *catasto* because that date has become so well known in the historical literature.

43. Herlihy and Klapisch-Zuber, *Les toscans*, 157; Brucker, "Monasteries," 46. The disparity in population estimates between my figures and those of these scholars stems primarily from the inclusion or exclusion of ancillary personnel, who figured in different portions of the tax survey. Herlihy and Klapisch-Zuber tallied a total of 575 *bocche* in urban convents and 359 in suburban houses based on the tax digests (*campioni*). However, using the more detailed individual returns (*portate*), I have securely eliminated 55 "mouths" from urban houses and an additional 12 from suburban convents, reducing the known number of nuns, novices, and professed servants from 553 to 520 (urban) and 359 to 347 (suburban) for a known total of 867. I then applied the average multiplier to houses that did not itemize "mouths" to arrive at a total number of about 800 religious women living in organized communities. Neither Herlihy and Klapisch-Zuber nor I include individual female penitents in this figure.

44. Molho, *Marriage Alliance*, 61–62.

45. Trexler, "Celibacy," 17–18.

46. Of the 189 choir nuns listed on fifteen convent tax rosters, 125 had surnames (66%). Thirteen of the fifteen rosters came from urban convents. These listed 158 nuns, 107 of whom had surnames (67.7%). The two rosters from ex-urban convents noted 18 of 31 nuns with surnames (58%) (ASF, Catasto, vols. 184, 192, 194). I have excluded the

roster of S. Maria a Monte, which reported first names only (ASF, Catasto, vol. 184, fol. 74r).

47. Molho, *Marriage Alliance*, 202, 365–75.

48. The convents were the Portico (twenty-four ages reported; this number includes choir nuns and *converse*); S. Maria di Candeli (eighteen); S. Giusto (seven); S. Giuliano (six); Chiarito (six); and S. Giovanni Battista (five). These data supplement and correct minor errors in Trexler, "Celibacy," 22–24.

49. Molho, " 'Tamquam vere mortua,' " 15n, speculates that these girls were in guardianship, but they were in fact novices.

50. ASF, NA, 13507, fol. 151r, reporting the ages of sixteen Montedomini choir nuns. ASF, Catasto, 602, fol. 206r–v, gives the ages of five choir nuns at S. Maria in Verzaia. Their average age was almost fifty-five; the youngest nun was age thirty-six. The 1438 *catasto* does not provide much additional information on this point, since returns filed by S. Maria di Candeli, S. Giusto, S. Giovanni Battista, and S. Giuliano listed exactly the same ages reported in 1427. Candeli had added a fifteen-year-old nun and a twelve-year-old servant (ASF, Catasto, vol. 603, fols. 162r–165v, 169r, 170v, 212r).

51. Molho, "Deception and Marriage Strategy"; Lowe, "Secular Brides and Convent Brides." Trexler, "Celibacy," considered age at entry, while Molho, " 'Tamquam vere mortua,' " based his analysis on age at profession.

52. Lowe, *Nuns' Chronicles*, 161, maintains that seniority accrued from date of entrance.

53. Strocchia, "Naming a Nun." Stressing the postulant's surety of vocation, the Brigettine order set the minimum entry age at eighteen. Male clerics of this order had to be twenty-five years old to take vows. By contrast, Observant Dominican friaries set the minimum age for entry at eighteen; Conventual friars might enter at fourteen (ASF, Mon. S. Brigida, vol. 61, fol. 7v; Hood, *Fra Angelico*, 292; Gilbert, "The Conversion of Fra Angelico"). Tridentine decrees required female novices to be sixteen years old.

54. Brown, "Monache a Firenze."

55. Quoted in Gregory, "Daughters, Dowries, and the Family," 223–24.

56. ASF, CRSGF, 133, vol. 39, fol. 79v. Agnola's age was left blank in the record. She professed five months later, in 1446, in order to claim her dowry from the fund (ASF, CRSGF, 133, vol. 40, fol. 59r). A virtually identical ceremony marked the entrance of a young servant nun at the same house the previous year (ASF, CRSGF, 133, vol. 39, fol. 70v).

57. ASF, CRSGF, 82, vol. 10, fol. 49r. Suor Filippa went on to a distinguished monastic career, culminating in her election as abbess in 1488 at age sixty-one. On girls' schooling and concepts of childhood, see Strocchia, "Learning the Virtues," and Strocchia, "Taken into Custody."

58. Molho, " 'Tamquam vere mortua,' " 15–16, reviews some examples of precocious ages at entry. Paolin, "Monache e donne," 213, quotes a nun who remarked in 1594 that her chapter frequently accepted girls from the age of four. This practice often stemmed from the fact that specific political circumstances determined the viability of other custodial arrangements.

59. Lowe, *Nuns' Chronicles*, 160–61; ASF, CRSGF, 81, vol. 3, fol. 30r.

60. Molho, *Marriage Alliance*, 306–7.

61. Lowe, "Secular Brides and Convent Brides," 56–60, analyzes this image in greater detail.

62. ASF, NA, 13497, fols. 72v–73v. Camilla Bardi went on to a distinguished monastic career. In 1494 she was elected abbess at age seventy-four, serving until her death in 1515 at age ninety-five.

63. Molho, " 'Tamquam vere mortua,' " 3.

64. Molho, *Marriage Alliance*, 411–15, estimates the urban population at 40,896 in 1480, while Goldthwaite, *Building of Renaissance Florence*, 33, puts it at 41,590.

65. Cohn, "Nuns and Dowry Funds," 84. Between 1448 and 1505, the number of Venetian convents rose from twenty-eight to forty-one (Sperling, *Convents and the Body Politic*, 27). By contrast, the number of Bolognese convents decreased in the mid-fifteenth century—the "moment of maximum crisis"—reaching a low of twenty in 1481 (Zarri, "Monasteri femminili a Bologna," 143–44). Convents affiliated with the Benedictine order declined from nine to six houses between the late Trecento and 1500 owing to demographic and economic problems, but this contraction was not limited to Benedictines (Zarri, "Monasteri femminili benedettini," 338–39).

66. Weddle, "Identity and Alliance," 401.

67. Bizzocchi, *Chiesa e potere;* Seidel Menchi, "Characteristics of Italian Anticlericalism"; Novi Chavarria, *Monache e gentildonne.*

68. Peterson, "State-building."

69. ASF, Catasto, vol. 194, fols. 123r–131v, 132r–135v, 135v–139v; vol. 989, fols. 58r, 253v.

70. Lowe, *Nuns' Chronicles*, 157–58.

71. Suor Giustina also claimed that four Jewish girls entered the house in the fifteenth century (Lowe, *Nuns' Chronicles*, 156–57).

72. Brucker, "Monasteries," 48; Lowe, "Female Strategies for Success," 211–12.

73. Strocchia, "Naming a Nun," 229–34; BNCF, II, II, 509, fol. 44v.

74. Suor Battista di Marsilio Giovanni of Rome brought a dowry of 1,500 scudi; Suor Eugenia Albizzi of Viterbo contributed 480 scudi (1461); Tommasa Gianfigliazzi, age sixty, gave 700 florins realized from the sale of her portion of the family palace (1477) (BNCF, II, II, 509, fols. 27r, 50r).

75. BNCF, II, II, 509, fols. 29r–v, 61r. One mark of stratification at Le Murate was differentiated spiritual duties. When commemorating lay benefactors, literate nuns were asked to recite the psalter, while those who could not read recited basic prayers instead (ASF, CRSGF, 81, vol. 91, fol. 11r).

76. ASF, Catasto, vol. 184, fol. 68r; vol. 989, fols. 373r–377v; Zarri, "Monasteri femminili di Bologna," 143.

77. ASF, Catasto, vol. 184, fols. 5r–6r; vol. 194, fols. 556v–557v; vol. 989, fols. 583r–584r, 819r–820v. The construction project at S. Verdiana is recorded in ASF, CRSGF, 90, vol. 62, fols. 1r–25r.

78. Only two of the dozen or more houses suppressed were closed on the grounds of poor discipline. Eugenius punished S. Luca and the Chiarito because their abbesses indulged in vanities and "illicit conversations." In 1435, the pope deprived the nuns of their goods for twenty-five years and transferred them to the convent of S. Caterina. Frictions ensued, despite papal injunctions that the transplants obey their new abbess and the original occupants strive to receive their new sisters "in charity" (BRF, Mss. Moreni, 200, pt. 4, pp. 103–6).

79. Van Enghen, "The Church in the Fifteenth Century."

80. In 1435, Eugenius incorporated several fourteenth-century foundations—S. Ghe-

rardo, S. Maria della Neve, S. Silvestro, S. Clemente — into the nearby Observant convent of S. Agata (Richa, *Notizie istoriche delle chiese fiorentine*, 5:245). Trexler, "Celibacy," 25–26nn, notes that later that year, the *signoria* opposed the mergers because "such a large number of nuns could not live chastely in so little space." The pope and priors reached an accord reversing the suppressions, but by 1478 these and other convents had been folded into S. Agata's portfolio (ASF, Catasto, vol. 989, fol. 27r). Nicholas V suppressed S. Martino a Mugnone outside the walls, where two elderly nuns and an aged abbess lived in a decaying complex (1451). Four years later, he suppressed S. Maria in Verzaia, which formerly headed a parish (ASF, NA, 13511, no. 263; ASF, NA, 2557, busta 4, fols. 516v–517r). Other mergers are discussed in chapter 2.

81. Trexler, "Celibacy," 7.

82. Inspired by flagellant processions, Lena di Luca da Panzano refused to leave the convent where she was living in temporary guardianship (1445); Francesco di Tommaso Giovanni's daughter entered the Poor Clares of Monticelli "willingly" and "happily" in 1446 (ASF, CS, ser. 2, vol. 9, fol. 119r; vol. 16 bis, fol. 5r). Molho, "'Tamquam vere mortua,'" 19–21, reviews these and other examples.

83. Two years after Alessandra's entry in 1453, the convent admitted five-year-old Giardesca Piccardi, who was similarly called to monastic life. In 1459, Elena Bonvanni joined the community "because she was inspired by God to become a nun . . . with the consent of her father, Zanobi, the abbess, . . . and all the nuns" (ASF, CRSGF, 79, vol. 455, fols. 12r, 18v, 25v). Among other examples from these years is the seventeen-year-old daughter of a respected physician "inspired by God," who joined neighboring S. Pier Maggiore in 1458 (AAF, SPM, Feste Ufizi, fol. 143r).

84. ASF, CRSGI, pt. 1, vol. 388, unfol.; ASF, Mss., vol. 170, no. 3. Suor Giustina Niccolini claimed that Antoninus personally consecrated fifty-eight Murate nuns (BNCF, II, II, 509, fol. 44r).

85. ASF, CS, ser. 2., vol. 58, fol. 193v; ASF, CRSPL, S. Jacopo, vol. 23, fols. 1v, 179r.

86. Two daughters of Piero del Chiaro, "now confined to Padua," were made nuns in S. Niccolò dei Frieri by their uncle (1447) (ASF, CRSGF, 133, vol. 39, fol. 93r). In 1446, Suor Maria Fortini paid the spiritual dowry for her niece Margherita at S. Pier Maggiore because the girl's father and uncle had been exiled as anti-Mediceans in 1434 (ASF, CRSPL, SPM, vol. 204, fol. 197r).

87. ASF, Mon. S. Luca, vol. 71, fol. 4r; ASF, CRSGF, 82, vol. 10, undated back flyleaf, probably written by the convent procurator Ser Francesco in the 1470s or 1480s.

88. Frick, *Dressing Renaissance Florence*, 103–4; Burke, "Visualizing Neighborhood."

89. ASF, NA, 14198, fol. 133r (Chiarito [1462]); ASF, NA, 2557, fol. 438r–v (S. Monaca [1455]); ASF, NA, 14193, fol. 174r, and ASF, NA, 7305, fol. 89r–v (S. Onofrio [1439, 1470]).

90. ASF, NA, 10084, fol. 13v (1467); ASF, CRSGF, 82, vol. 10, undated back flyleaf; Frick, *Dressing Renaissance Florence*, 141–44; Goldthwaite, "Economic and Social World of Italian Renaissance Maiolica."

91. AAF, SPM, Feste Ufizi, fol. 13r; Leonard, *Nails in the Wall*, 17.

92. ASF, CRSGF, 108, vol. 107, fols. 10r, 26v–39r, 56v.

93. AAF, SPM, Feste Ufizi, fol. 8r (1356); ASF, CRSPL, SPM, vol. 69, fols. 26r, 51r (1380). Giovanni di Jacopo Strozzi articulated his concerns on this score when making a dowry pact with S. Ambrogio for his daughter Margherita ("Suor Eugenia"). He paid 25 florins when she entered in July 1449 and promised the remaining 75 florins by the end

of October 1450. "Because currently there is plague about, it is agreed that if this girl dies . . . before October 1450, the convent cannot demand anything other than what she brought into the convent" (ASF, CRSGF, 79, vol. 455, fol. 7r).

94. ASF, CRSGF, 234, vol. 79, fols. 4v–5r.

95. Molho, *Florentine Public Finances*. See, for example, ASF, CRSGF, 83, vol. 113, fol. 119v.

96. BRF, Mss. Moreni, 103, fol. 65r–v.

97. ASF, CRSGF, 79, vol. 455, fol. 25v; vol. 22, fol. 17r.

98. ASF, CS, ser. 3, vol. 204, c. 124 ("Credo vi dovete rammentare che già è sette anni compiuti ch'io entrai qua al servizio di Dio in compagnia di sante venerabili madri, e più contenta sono stata l'un dì che l'altro e son mi affaticata sempre di esercitarmi e imparare le virtù che a nostre pari si richiede. Ma vogliendomi in tutta conformare colla detta compagnia, è necessario che io sia consecrata allo sposo mio Iesu et abbi il velo nero in capo simile alle mie pari"). This undated letter was probably written in 1435, the year after the Strozzi were exiled; Suor Lisabetta had appeared on the convent's 1427 *catasto* membership list.

99. ASF, CRSGF, 234, vol. 77, fol. 3r; vol. 79, fols. 29v–30r.

100. Molho, " 'Tamquam vere mortua,' " 3, 6, totaling 313 professions; Molho, *Marriage Alliance*, 61–62.

101. ASF, MAP, X, 575, letter to Cosimo de' Medici from the prioress of S. Maria Annunziata della Cella, 20 April, no year given; ASF, MAP, XII, 404, letter to Cosimo de' Medici from the abbess and nuns of S. Francesco, 14 March, no year given. On these and other nuns' letters, see Heazlewood, " 'Letters Are the Leaves,' " 12, 30. Kent, *Cosimo de' Medici*, illuminates numerous facets of Cosimo's patronage.

102. Tomas, *The Medici Women*.

103. ASF, CRSPL, SPM, vol. 74, fol. 11r; ASF, CRSGF, 90, vol. 60, fols. 4r, 32r. Ginevra's aunt Gemma Alessandri Strozzi also patronized S. Pier Maggiore. Among her gifts was a 50-florin grant in 1440 "to be distributed and allocated according to the convent's needs and requirements" (ASF, CRSPL, SPM, vol. 36, fol. 51r).

104. ASF, CRSGF, 83, vol. 113, fols. 5v, 8v, 46v, 87v, 100v; ASF, CRSGF, 79, vol. 455, fols. 3r–v, 4r, 12r, 17r, 22v; ASF, CRSGF, 82, vol. 10, fols. 85r–v.

105. ASF, MAP, XXVII, 178, letter to Lorenzo de' Medici from the Madonna delle Murate, 17 March 1471/72; ASF, MAP, XXII, 452, letter to Lorenzo de' Medici from Suor Filippa Portinari of S. Apollonia, 4 June 1472; Heazlewood, " 'Letters Are the Leaves,' " 68–69.

106. Eckstein, "The Widows' Might."

107. ASF, CRSGF, 133, vol. 39, fol. 70v.

108. Peterson, "Out of the Margins."

109. Brucker, "Monasteries," 46; ASF, Balie, vol. 40, fols. 75r–77r.

110. ASF, Catasto, vol. 184, fol. 70v; ASF, CRSGF, 82, vol. 1, fol. 373v. The new Florentine foundations were S. Caterina da Siena (chartered 1500), S. Maria degli Angiolini (1509), the Crocetta (1511), and S. Giuseppe (1518). Those in Prato were S. Vincenzo (1503), S. Trinita (1508), and S. Clemente (1518).

111. Civic orphanages in Florence and Bologna were notable for their sheer size among other features. By the late sixteenth century, the main Bolognese foundation housed between a thousand and seventeen hundred poor children (Terpstra, *Abandoned Children*, 40).

112. Goldthwaite, *Building of Renaissance Florence*, 33.

113. Brucker, "Monasteries," 48–50. For instance, ASF, Catasto, vol. 1008, fols. 508r–509r, listed Sandra di Simone Buondelmonti, age eighteen, "to be a nun in S. Pier Maggiore with half dowry." Her sister Laudomina entered S. Ambrogio in 1482 with the standard dowry because her mother, Maddalena, ceded a farm from her own goods; neither her husband nor sons could afford the entry payment (ASF, CRSGF, 79, vol. 58, fol. 130r). Similarly, Margherita di Girolamo Fortini, age four in 1480, was listed as "without dowry"; she entered S. Pier Maggiore in the early 1490s (ASF, Catasto, vol. 1021, fol. 178r–v).

114. Molho, *Marriage Alliance*, 304–10.

115. Frick, *Dressing Renaissance Florence*, 139–44.

116. Molho, *Marriage Alliance*, 73; ASF, CRSPL, SPM, vol. 79, fols. 18v, 19r; vol. 80, fol. 2r.

117. ASF, CRSPL, SPM, vol. 83, fol. 23r.

118. See for example ASF, CRSPL, S. Jacopo, vol. 42; Evangelisti, *Nuns*, 13; Evangelisti, "Rooms to Share."

119. Molho, *Marriage Alliance*, 306–7.

120. Molho, *Marriage Alliance*, 302–3; Landucci, *A Florentine Diary*, 7–8; BNCF, Ms. Landau Finlay, 72, fol. 57r; ASF, CRSPL, S. Agata, vol. 50, fols. 162v–163r.

121. *Acta sanctorum*, 14:352–53. Only six of the twenty-five nuns living in S. Orsola in 1465 had surnames; none of the fifty-nine nuns of S. Giorgio attesting to a 1496 contract had surnames (ASF, NA, 7304, fol. 79r; ASF, NA, 10089, fol. 160r).

122. ASF, CRSGF, 100, vol. 89, nos. 2, 3, 4. I use the status designations given by Molho, *Marriage Alliance*.

123. ASF, CRSGF, 100, vol. 131, nos. 51, 64; Heazlewood, "'Letters Are the Leaves,'" 35.

124. Polizzotto, "When Saints Fall Out," 522.

125. Zarri, *Le sante vive*.

126. Trexler, "Celibacy," 20.

127. Polizzotto, "When Saints Fall Out." The bibliography on Savonarola is vast. Key works include Polizzotto, *Elect Nation*; Weinstein, *Savonarola and Florence*; di Agresti, *Sviluppi della riforma*.

128. Strocchia, "Savonarolan Witnesses"; ASF, Balie, vol. 40, fols. 75r–77r.

129. ASF, Balie, vol. 40, fol. 77v; ASF, CRSGF, 106, vol. 12, fols. 32v–36v. The remaining dowries ranged from 80 to 100 florins (ASF, CRSGF, 106, vol. 12, fols. 1r–4v, 11r–v).

130. BNCF, Ms. Landau Finlay, 72, fols. 95v–104v. The average age of these women at entrance was 19.07 years; another five nuns joined the community in this period, but their ages are not known.

131. For example, the painter Francesco Rosselli, brother of the better-known artist Cosimo, placed three daughters in the house in 1499 but contributed nothing to their entry payments. Their grandmother Nanna paid the eldest girl's dowry outright, then repaid the monies Cosimo fronted for the other two girls, who were renamed Fede and Speranza (ASF, CRSGF, 106, vol. 12, fols. 81r, 132v–133v, 176v–177r).

132. Strocchia, "Savonarolan Witnesses"; Macey, *Bonfire Songs*.

133. Polizzotto, "When Saints Fall Out," 508–9.

134. ASF, CRSPL, S. Jacopo, vol. 42, fols. 2v, 4r; Strocchia, "Savonarolan Witnesses."

135. Brucker, "Monasteries," 50; Strocchia, "Taken into Custody."

136. BNCF, II, II, 509, fol. 93v; Strocchia, "Taken into Custody."

137. Landucci, *A Florentine Diary*, 163, reported that after being harassed by Alexander VI in 1499, the Countess of Imola "collected her property and had it sent here to Florence, and she also sent her daughters here, to be placed in the Murate," where she enjoyed a long-standing patronage relationship. Similarly, in 1502, Suor Lena Ridolfi, *ministra* of S. Orsola, noted that the widowed daughter of Count Antonio of Mirandola "was sent here today by her uncle Messer Ercole Bentivoglio on account of the war with Duke Valentino [Cesare Borgia]." About a year later, the chapter agreed to assume guardianship of her daughter and niece "for as long as may be necessary." The next day, Suor Lena fetched the youngsters from Prato (ASF, CRSGF, 100, vol. 89, no. 2, unfol.).

138. AAF, VP, 3.1, fascs. 3, 4.

139. Brown, "Monache a Firenze," 131–32.

140. The abbesses at S. Felicita were Lorenza Mozzi (r. 1386–1405), Margherita Macci (1405–42), Brigida Guicciardini (1442–80), Piera de' Rossi (1480–94), and Benedetta Machiavelli (1494–1520). Heading S. Ambrogio were Taddea di Giovanni (r. 1400–1414), Niccolosa Buonaccorsi (1414–68), Antonia Barducci (1468–69), and Maria Barbadori (1469–1508). In the fifteenth century, S. Pier Maggiore was captained by Lucia Falconieri (r. 1400–1411), Maddalena del Portico of Lucca (1411–60), Antonia Acciaiuoli (1460–74), Benedetta Riccoldi (1474–89), and Gostanza Alessandri (1489–1507).

141. Raffaella Manelli (r. 1520–21), Gostanza Gualterotti (1521–28), Maria Gondi (1528–34), Margherita Alamanni (1534–43), Lena Canigiani (1543–64), and Maddalena Ricasoli (1564–71), the last abbess holding life tenure.

142. Quoted in Trexler, "Celibacy," 20, his translation.

143. AAF, VP, 3.1, fasc. 4.

144. Strocchia, "Naming a Nun." The classic statement of this practice in lay society remains Klapisch-Zuber, "The Name 'Remade,'" in her *Women, Family, and Ritual in Renaissance Italy*, 283–309.

145. Evangelisti, "Memoria di antiche madri"; Evangelisti, "Moral Virtues and Personal Goods"; Weaver, *Convent Theatre*; Weaver, "Le muse in convento"; Lowe, *Nuns' Chronicles*.

CHAPTER 2: Nuns, Neighbors, and Kinsmen

1. Trexler, "Celibacy," 9–10.

2. For the fictive "marriage" between the abbess of S. Pier Maggiore and the Florentine bishop that formed part of local episcopal installation rites, see Strocchia, "When the Bishop Married the Abbess," and Miller, "Florentine Bishop's Ritual Entry." Top civic officials made an annual procession to S. Anna to celebrate the ouster of the tyrant Walter of Brienne on the saint's feast in 1343. Pontormo immortalized this enactment at the bottom of his St. Anne altarpiece, commissioned by the city fathers for the nuns, probably in the crisis-filled years between 1527 and 1529 (Crum and Wilkins, "In Defense of Florentine Republicanism"). The annual Corpus Christi procession stopped at S. Ambrogio to pick up the miraculous relic of the Holy Sacrament housed there (Borsook, "Cults and Imagery," and Strocchia, "Sisters in Spirit").

3. Weddle, "Identity and Alliance"; Rosenthal, "Spaces of Plebian Ritual."

4. Kent and Kent, *Neighbours and Neighbourhood in Renaissance Florence*, 2. Among the most important works on Italian urban neighborhoods are Muir and Weissman, "Social and Symbolic Places"; Kent and Kent, *Neighbours and Neighbourhood in Renaissance Florence*;

Eckstein, *District of the Green Dragon;* Kent, "Ties of Neighbourhood and Patronage"; and Klapisch-Zuber, "'Kin, Friends and Neighbors,'" in her *Women, Family, and Ritual in Renaissance Italy*, 68–93.

   5. Tomas, "Did Women Have a Space?"; Ruggiero, "Mean Streets."

   6. Kent and Kent, *Neighbours and Neighbourhood in Renaissance Florence;* Cohn, *Laboring Classes*, 25–32. Litchfield, *Dalla repubblica al granducato*, 9–13, documents the residential topography of cloth workers, whose displacement toward the periphery led to the increasing social homogeneity of those districts. See also Rosenthal, "Big Piero."

   7. Eckstein, "Neighborhood as Microcosm," 220; Eckstein, "Addressing Wealth in Renaissance Florence."

   8. S. Gaggio's initial members included the charismatic widow and cofounder Nera di Lapo Manieri, her daughter, the two daughters and niece of the other cofounder Tommaso Corsini, and another pious woman. Corsini moved into a nearby dwelling, where he pursued a penitential life until his death in 1366. One of his son's former employees became the convent chaplain. The community added another layer of kinship and *vicinanza* when it annexed a small convent located nearby in 1350 (Fantozzi Micali, *Monastero di San Gaggio*, 17–23). A certain Ghisla founded S. Pier Maggiore in 1066 for herself and her four daughters, one of whom became the first abbess (ASF, Dipl., SPM, nos. 1037 and 1038, both dated 27 February 1066; see ASF, CRSPL, SPM, vol. 1, filza 1, nos. 1–7, for later copies of the founding documents). S. Niccolò Maggiore, founded circa 1325 by Niccolò Gianfigliazzi, counted among its first occupants his mother, sister, and daughter; his sister served as the first abbess (ASF, S. Niccolò, vol. 1, no. 1; BRF, Mss. Moreni, 317, fols. 1, 9v, 10).

   9. ASF, CRSGF, 83, vol. 239, 34–35.

   10. ASF, CRSGF, 83, vol. 102, doc. 10; Fiorelli Malesci, *Chiesa di Santa Felicita*, 50.

   11. ASF, CRSPL, SPM, vols. 50, 51, 68, 69, 70. The 1370 list of twelve nuns and two novices is found in vol. 76, fol. 65v. Fourteen nuns entered the house between 1370 and 1394. Of them, at least eleven came from Chiavi and the two adjacent wards; one came from the district of S. Maria Novella, one from Lucca, and one lacked a surname.

   12. This information is culled primarily from AAF, VP, 1.1.

   13. This information is culled from ASF, Catasto, vols. 184, 192, 194.

   14. The convent of S. Giovanni Battista near present-day Porta Romana was often referred to as S. Giovanni Battista "de' Biliotti," since that family donated the original site. The nuns of S. Maria a Montedomini were called "the nuns of Simone Baroncelli" in their 1427 tax report (AAF, VP, 1.1, fol. 24r; ASF, Catasto, vol. 184, fol. 74r).

   15. Fantozzi Micali, *Monastero di San Gaggio*, 132. Martines, *Strong Words*, 137–66, analyzes the high financial and psychological costs of exile.

   16. Peterson, "War of the Eight Saints."

   17. Baxandale, "Exile in Practice."

   18. Martines, *Strong Words*, 19. In 1372 the wealthy, prominent cloth manufacturers Bartolomeo di Niccolò Albizzi and his brother Alessandro severed ties with their family and adopted the surname of Alessandri to legally separate themselves from relatives of lesser status (Brucker, *Florentine Politics*, 33–34, 51, 383n).

   19. In his 1427 tax return, Alessandro di Niccolò Alessandri called present-day Borgo degli Albizi "Borgo S. Pier Maggiore" (ASF, Catasto, vol. 56, fol. 133r). He elected burial in S. Pier Maggiore "in sepulture sua et antecessorum" (ASF, NA, 180, dated 8 May 1396).

   20. A 1370 list registered four Albizzi nuns, although a fifth lived in the convent (ASF,

CRSPL, SPM, vol. 76, fol. 65v). The two daughters of Bartolomeo Alessandri (born Albizzi) entered the convent in 1380 and 1382 (ASF, CRSPL, SPM, vol. 69, fols. 26r, 60r).

21. For small loans she made in 1374, see ASF, CRSPL, SPM, vol. 68, fol. 25r. She served multiple stints as treasurer from 1388 to 1413 (ASF, CRSPL, SPM, vol. 51, fol. 67r; AAF, SPM, Feste Ufizi, fols. 60r–v, 80v).

22. ASF, CRSPL, SPM, vol. 36, fol. 34r; vol. 38, p. 50; vol. 70, fols. 11v–12r; vol. 72, fols. 108v, 123r; AAF, SPM, Feste Ufizi, fol. 26r.

23. ASF, CRSPL, SPM, vol. 72, fols. 115v, 129v; vol. 73, fols. 112r, 122v; vol. 202, fol. 49r; AAF, SPM, Feste Ufizi, fol. 65v.

24. The presence of so many Albizzi and Alessandri nuns intensified the convent's pro-oligarchic political cast after the artisan-based Ciompi regime assumed power in 1378. To penalize the Alessandri for their opposition, the Ciompi declared two family members to be magnates, which barred them from holding communal office. Suor Caterina Albizzi's father Piero was exiled and the households of two other Albizzi nuns sacked and burned (Brucker, *Florentine Politics*, 33–34, 383n).

25. Strocchia, "When the Bishop Married the Abbess," 353–54.

26. Cardinal Piero Corsini badgered the S. Gaggio nuns throughout the 1370s and 1380s for permission to construct a large chapel in the convent church. Despite Corsini's ties to the community, the nuns rebuffed his request for fear of introducing "private interests" into a still rigorous religious environment. Only when his cousin Isabetta Corsini was elected abbess in 1387 did the chapter succumb to combined family pressures. Another request quickly followed for "a burial site near the said chapel for the entire family of Messer Filippo and his descendants." Once the nuns acceded, Corsini arranged a generous endowment in his 1403 will (Fantozzi Micali, *Monastero di San Gaggio*, 44–45).

27. ASF, CRSPL, SPM, vol. 68, fols. 31v–33v; vol. 70. fols. 83r, 101r.

28. ASF, CRSPL, SPM, vol. 73, fols. 72r, 75v. Similarly, the nuns of the Portico used two unsalaried procurators — the respected statesman Paolo Vettori and the dyer Michele di Francesco — to conduct business for them. Both men had daughters in the community (ASF, Catasto, vol. 602, fols. 129r–134v).

29. Trexler, "Celibacy," 19–20.

30. AAF, VP, 1.1, fol. 24r.

31. Some of these instances reflected the force of circumstance, although it is still worth noting the ingrained social habit. In 1427 the guardians of thirteen-year-old Francesco di Vieri Riccialbani placed his two sisters, aged ten and twelve, in S. Maria di Candeli near the former family residence (ASF, Catasto, vol. 36, fol. 523r–v).

32. Trexler, "Celibacy," 19–20; ASF, Catasto, vol. 184, fol. 68r.

33. ASF, Catasto, vol. 602, fols. 109r, 131r, 167r. The sisters Lena and Giuliana del Caccia entered S. Ambrogio in 1438 and 1446; Bandecha and Lorenza Brancacci joined the community in 1456 and 1459; Lucrezia and Camilla, the daughters of Carlo Strozzi, entered together in 1468 (ASF, CRSGF, 79, vol. 449, fol. 135v; vol. 455, fols. 3v, 22r–v, 39v).

34. Lucrezia Albizzi, who took the religious name Brigida, entered 17 July 1507 with a dowry of 157 florins paid by her father (ASF, CRSPL, SPM, vol. 2, fol. 105r).

35. Only two of the eight girls admitted between 1401 and 1414 came from Chiavi, but traditional patterns were restored once the house reached its full numerical complement (ASF, CRSPL, SPM, vol. 52, fols. 11r, 17r, 23v, 24v, 27r, 35r; vol. 72, fols. 7v, 132r). In 1401 one nun transferred from the devastated rural house of S. Martino a Mensola to live with her sister in S. Pier Maggiore — a move facilitated by their brother, a cathedral canon. Not

incidentally, these sisters shared joint ownership of a family farm, which reverted to the convent upon their deaths (ASF, CRSPL, SPM, vol. 36, fol. 33r).

36. See BNCF, II, X, 41, under calendar months.

37. ASF, CRSGF, 79, vol. 448, fols. 22v, 28v, 49v; vol. 449, fol. 135v; ASF, Dipl., S. Ambrogio, dated 1 January 1425.

38. Strocchia, "Learning the Virtues," and Strocchia, "Taken into Custody."

39. Martines, *Lawyers and Statecraft*, 26–40.

40. Although her entry date is unknown, Maria di Ser Benedetto Fortini witnessed a contract dated 20 September 1432 (ASF, Dipl., SPM, under date). Her learned brother Bartolomeo was exiled in the Medicean purge of 1434. He, Benedetto Fortini, and their descendants were "restored" to the city in September 1466 as part of the amnesty following the failed anti-Medicean coup (Vespasiano, *Le vite*, 2:409–13). Less is known about the other notary's daughter, Lucia di Ser Arrigo da San Miniato, who paid an unusually high dowry of 150 florins in 1437 (ASF, CRSPL, SPM, vol. 73, fol. 22r). Her brother Rinaldo had political and economic ties to the Fortini and to Francesco della Luna, another prominent statesman.

41. ASF, NA, 13511, no. 198.

42. Some years before he filed his 1457 tax return, Sandro Biliotti, who lived on the corner of Via Maggio in the Oltrarno ward of Nicchio, had put his fourteen-year-old illegitimate daughter Lena "in a convent in Pistoia to become a nun if she so wished." If she decided to marry instead, Sandro promised to furnish her with a dowry and trousseau (ASF, Catasto, vol. 788, fols. 406r–408r). Tellingly, he did not send her to S. Felicita, only a minute's walk from the family palace. The Biliotti stronghold of S. Giovanni Battista had been turned over to the Franciscans in 1452.

43. Romano, "Gender and the Urban Geography." Martines, *Strong Words*, 209–20, offers an illuminating analysis of gendered space featured in Renaissance amatory tales.

44. Klapisch-Zuber, "The 'Cruel Mother,' " in her *Women, Family, and Ritual in Renaissance Italy*, 117–31.

45. In 1373, Dada, a widow and notary's daughter, bequeathed her house to S. Pier Maggiore in return for a commemorative office and payment of her niece's dowry at the appropriate time, charging "the abbess's conscience." The convent followed through, paying this dowry in 1385 through the bank of another neighbor, Sandro Barucci, whose own daughter became a nun in the house. When Dada died (1403), "she was buried in the convent parlor opposite the door that goes into the convent." The nuns claimed the property and faithfully executed her memorial program for over a century (ASF, CRSPL, SPM, vol. 36, fol. 43r).

46. When the baker's widow, Dina, found herself in financial trouble in 1396, she struck a bargain with the nuns of S. Pier Maggiore. Some years earlier, she and her husband had rented a convent-owned house located next door to the convent. Her husband died after falling behind on the rent, leaving Dina no means of support. "Because of her poverty and out of mercy," Abbess Antonia Bardi forgave most of the debt in return for Dina's promise "to bake all the bread and roasts" for the nuns' consumption (ASF, CRSPL, SPM, vol. 200, fol. 17r).

47. On commemorative choices, see Strocchia, "Remembering the Family," and Cohn, *Cult of Remembrance*.

48. Cohn, "Nuns and Dowry Funds," 90.

49. Milner, "Florentine Piazza della Signoria."

50. Kent and Kent, *Neighbours and Neighbourhood in Renaissance Florence*, 5.

51. ASF, CRSGI, pt. 1, vol. 390.

52. Lorenza di Maestro Eufrosino, the daughter of a physician who had his shop at Canto de' Ricci, was described as "inspired by God and St. Peter" to become a nun; she brought the customary monastic dowry in 1458 (AAF, SPM, Feste Ufizi, fol. 143r). Suor Maria Fortini sponsored both her own niece Alazia, from the Chiavi ward, and her brother's niece, Benedetta Riccoldi, from Vaio, who joined the house circa 1454 and later made a distinguished career as abbess (1474–89). Benedetta's sister Margherita, however, had been enrolled at the Paradiso since 1443, although her 80-florin dowry was not paid by her uncle Bartolomeo Fortini until 1452. She rose to the rank of prioress by 1491 (ASF, Mon. S. Brigida, vol. 148, fol. 8r; ASF, NA, 6228, fol. 83r). Benedetta's grandfather Ser Pagolo Riccoldi had been active in late Trecento communal affairs (Witt, *Hercules at the Crossroads*, 141–42).

53. On deliberations to extend the Savonarolan apostolate at S. Jacopo, see Strocchia, "Savonarolan Witnesses."

54. From this meager sum, the convent had to pay for her bedding, clothing, and consecration, with Lorenzo picking up the rest of her board (ASF, CRSGF, 82, vol. 79, fols. 185v–186r).

55. Trexler, "Celibacy," 20. However, it should be noted that his key example of S. Frediano, an Augustinian convent after 1514, had a specific class dimension as a haven for girls from the Oltrarno.

56. For S. Gaggio, see ASF, NA, 10084, fol. 181v. For S. Felicita, see ASF, NA, 6218, fol. 309r, dated 1480, and ASF, CRSGF, 83, vol. 115, unnumbered front folio, dated 1485.

57. ASF, CRSPL, SPM, vol. 75, fol. 19r; ASF, CRSGF, 79, vol. 126, fols. 185v–186r.

58. Although Abbess Antonia died in 1474, she probably arranged this entrance some years before. The 1480 *catasto* return of the girls' father, Simone Buondelmonti, lists Andrea, neé Sandra, age eighteen, "to become a nun at S. Pier Maggiore with half dowry." The dowry of her younger sister, who entered S. Ambrogio in 1482, consisted of a farm valued at 130 florins suggello, which her mother Maddalena ceded from her own goods because neither her husband nor sons could muster the entry fee (ASF, Catasto, vol. 1008, fol. 508r–509r; ASF, CRSGF, 79, vol. 58, fol. 130r).

59. ASF, CRSPL, SPM, vol. 161, fol. 180v; ASF, CRSGF, 79, vol. 57, fols. 103v–104r; ASF, CRSGF, 82, vol. 10, fol. 86v.

60. The following discussion is based on BLF, Acq. e Doni, vol. 229, pts. 2 and 3, and Molho, *Marriage Alliance*, 172–77. Frick, *Dressing Renaissance Florence*, 141–44, discusses the Minerbetti girls' monastic trousseaux.

61. Burke, "Visualizing Neighborhood," argues that the artistic patronage of local churches was key to the expression of local community among principal families living in the district of S. Spirito.

62. On the use of convents for protection during these crisis periods, see Strocchia, "Taken into Custody."

63. Zarri, "Monasteri femminili e città."

64. ASF, CRSGF, 79, vol. 455, fols. 18v–19v; vol. 57, fols. 128v–129r; vol. 24, fol. 30r.

65. ASF, CRSPL, SPM, vol. 78, fol. 32v; vol. 161, fol. 366v; vol. 31, fol. 51r.

66. ASF, CRSPL, SPM, vol. 161, fol. 195r. Since her father was dead, her 50-florin dowry was paid by her maternal uncle Alessandro di Jacopo Alessandri. The 1480 tax report of her father Meglio listed her as Camilla "without dowry"; another sister Giovanna

was likewise listed as without dowry. Neither girl's age was given (ASF, Catasto, vol. 1022, fols. 8r–9v).

67. Suor Clementia entered in 1514 (ASF, CRSGF, 79, vol. 57, fols. 63v–64r; vol. 61, fols. 36v–37r).

68. *Concilium florentinum provinciale anno 1517*, 35, col. 263; Trexler, "Celibacy," 20.

69. Molho, *Marriage Alliance*, 61–62, 125.

70. Stephens, *Fall of the Florentine Republic*, 26–27.

71. Piero's 1480 tax return listed Gostanza as age ten with a dowry account worth 500 florins (ASF, Catasto, vol. 993, fols. 214r–215r). She entered S. Felicita in February 1486 with a 40-florin dowry (ASF, CRSGF, 83, vol. 115, fol. 2v).

72. ASF, Catasto, vol. 993, fols. 21r–22r; ASF, CRSGF, 82, vol. 10, fol. 86r–v.

73. ASF, CRSPL, SPM, vol. 78, fol. 86r; ASF, CRSGF, 83, vol. 115, fol. 42v; ASF, CRSGF, 82, vol. 10, fol. 88r.

74. Bizzocchi, "Chiesa e aristocrazia."

75. Similar gift transactions were common among patrician nuns in fifteenth-century Venice (Primhak, "Benedictine Communities").

76. Strocchia, "Naming a Nun."

77. Romano, "Gender and the Urban Geography," 344, citing the 1581 guide to Venice by Francesco Sansovino.

78. Bizzocchi, *Chiesa e potere;* Peterson, "State-building."

79. ASF, Catasto, vol. 989, fols. 48r–58r, 250r–254r.

80. The property survey is culled from ASF, CRSPL, SPM, vol. 30. In early 1527, the convent marked at least thirty-six properties with stone tondi bearing their emblem (ASF, CRSPL, SPM, vol. 134, fols. 15v, 26v).

81. ASF, Catasto, vol. 602, fols. 90r–v, 107v; vol. 989, fols. 635r–636v.

82. Fantozzi Micali, *Monastero di San Gaggio*, 23.

83. ASF, Decima Rep., vol. 70, fols. 111r–112r; ASF, Catasto, vol. 989, fols. 583r–584r; Brucker, "Monasteries."

84. Gaeta, *San Lorenzo*, xx–xxi.

85. Novelli, "Due documenti inediti."

86. ASF, CRSGF, 79, vol. 169, no. 76, dated 14 June 1423, copy made in 1780.

87. Piera's full account is in ASF, CRSGF, 90, vol. 60, fol. 35r; a more cursory record is located in vol. 41, fol. 41r.

88. Eckstein, "Neighborhood as Microcosm."

89. The following discussion is drawn from ASF, CRSPL, SPM, vol. 30.

90. ASF, CRSPL, S. Jacopo, vol. 29, fols. 53r–v, 54r.

91. Vespasiano recounted Eugenius's reform efforts in *Le vite*, 1:11–14.

92. Bizzocchi, *Chiesa e potere*, 32; Rubinstein, "Lay Patronage."

93. The consequences of monastic suppressions in other Italian cities have not been studied extensively. Roman convents experienced volatile portfolios because of mergers stemming from papal favoritism. For instance, in 1488, S. Maria in Julia, the Santuccie mother house, had insufficient income to support its occupants, so Innocent VIII joined the more robust convent of S. Ambrogio in Massima to it. This union (1488–89) prompted immediate litigation over property administration and the annual income assigned to S. Maria in Julia. In 1495 the houses agreed to substitute an annual payment of 12 ducats in place of more variable rental income and allow S. Ambrogio to elect its own abbess, subject to confirmation by her superior. However, the subordinate nuns continued

to litigate over various provisions until 1640, when they paid the huge sum of 32,325 scudi to free themselves from subjection (Novelli, "Due documenti inediti," 229, 235).

94. Through Eugenius's favor, the Dominican nuns of S. Caterina a Cafaggio obtained "the monastery titled S. Agnese at Borgo San Lorenzo" (ASF, Catasto, vol. 602, fol. 89r–v). To the Paradiso, situated south of the city, he ceded the holdings of S. Maria della Neve on Via S. Gallo, which gave it a vested interest on the northern side of town (ASF, Mon. S. Brigida, vol. 235, fol. 43r). Eugenius's generosity to the Paradiso is mentioned by Vespasiano, *Le vite*, 1:14, who mistakenly claims that the pope gave S. Maria della Neve to a group of Augustinian canons.

95. S. Apollonia absorbed the hospital of S. Paolo a Pinti in 1438, Mantignano in 1441, and S. Giusto a Camporlese in 1446 (Spencer, *Andrea del Castagno and His Patrons*, 103). To demonstrate his admiration for these exemplary nuns, Antoninus granted them S. Giusto a Camporlese, whose church reportedly was in a "pessimo statu." By terms of the agreement, S. Apollonia was required to repair it within three years; the abbess was assigned patronage rights in perpetuity and the former patrons were required to give her an annual wax tribute (Richa, *Notizie istoriche delle chiese fiorentine*, 8:303).

96. ASF, CRSGF, 82, vol. 1, fol. 312r–v. By terms of the bull, S. Apollonia could not take full possession until the current hospital warden either resigned or died. A year later, he tendered his resignation, giving the convent clear ownership of the "hospital, its accounts and possessions" (ASF, CRSGF, 82, vol. 1, fol. 316r). The former holdings of S. Paolo are recorded on fols. 2v–101r. Because the hospital was located in the parish of S. Pier Maggiore, it was sometimes called the "spedale di S. Pier Maggiore" or, alternately, the "spedale di Donati" after its lay patrons.

97. Eugenius authorized the nuns to select the priest who officiated there (ASF, CRSGF, 82, vol. 1, fol. 331r, dated 1 November 1444). The original supplication is in ASV, Reg. Suppl., vol. 400, fol. 219v.

98. In a series of acts made in 1439, Eugenius conceded plenary indulgences *in articulo mortis* to nuns' confessors and *commessi*. Extended spiritual graces were given to nuns, novices, and convent servants who performed an internal spiritual itinerary in the choir and cloister. The pope also granted them the perpetual right to keep all the sacraments in the convent church (ASF, CRSGF, 82, vol. 1, fols. 315r, 317v, 318r).

99. ASF, CRSGF, 82, vol. 1, fols. 316r–317r. The agreement stipulated that a new warden would be elected within four months by Abbess Cecilia Donati or whatever Donati nun might reside in S. Apollonia. In the absence of a Donati nun in the future, these rights would devolve on Donati lay patrons. The agreement also specified that the Donati arms painted over the hospital door could not be altered or erased.

100. ASF, CRSGF, 82, vol. 1, fol. 329r–330v, dated 13 September 1443.

101. ASF, CRSGF, 82, vol. 111, unfol., under date 22 February 1454.

102. *Bull. fran.*, 2:638–39, dated 5 May 1464. This account is also given in ASF, CRSGF, 82, vol. 1, fols. 355v–356r.

103. ASF, Decima Rep., vol. 70, fols. 14r–15r.

104. Although Eugenius ordered the merger in July 1441, the six Mantignano nuns, minus the abbess, did not physically relocate until March 1442 (ASF, CRSGF, 82, vol. 1, fol. 326r–v). Richa, *Notizie istoriche delle chiese fiorentine*, 8:302–3, notes that the church of Mantignano dated from 1084; the convent also was under direct papal protection. Thomas, *Art and Piety*, 83, claims that Mantignano had been significant both as a religious community and as a hospital, although the latter dated only from 1441. Eugenius required

the S. Apollonia nuns to maintain a women's hospital at the former site so it would not lapse into a secular state (ASF, CRSGF, vol. 1, fol. 326r–v). In 1565, this hospital was suppressed "because the *casa* is half-ruined and located in a place where it would not be possible to exercise this hospitality toward women without scandal." Instead, S. Apollonia was required to dower four poor girls from the Mantignano area annually, using proceeds from the original annexation (ASF, CRSGF, vol. 1, fols. 375r–376r).

105. ASF, CRSGF, 82, vol. 1, fols. 319v–320r, 326r–v; ASF, Catasto, vol. 195, fols. 41v, 251v; vol. 602, fol. 109r. Mantignano housed seven nuns, while S. Apollonia listed twenty-nine choir nuns, five novices, and six servant nuns in 1438.

106. This inventory is now archived as ASF, CRSGF, 82, vol. 120. With the acquisition of Mantignano, S. Apollonia also gained two important relics: an arm of St. Thomas, archbishop of Canterbury, and the head of one of the martyred virgin companions of St. Ursula (Richa, *Notizie istoriche delle chiese fiorentine*, 8:315).

107. Mantignano acquired its first house in Borgo S. Frediano in 1310, added four more houses in 1315, and bought additional properties piecemeal (ASF, CRSGF, 82, vol. 1, fols. 126r–v, 141r, 171r, 204r–v). The nuns obtained license from Urban V to use this urban refuge in August 1370 (ASF, CRSGF, 82, vol. 1, fol. 246r).

108. The landholdings acquired by Mantignano and S. Paolo a Pinti between 1060 and 1300 and then transferred to S. Apollonia are itemized in ASF, CRSGF, 82, vol. 1, fols. 1v–101r.

109. ASF, CRSGF, 82, vol. 1, fol. 328r, dated 1 January 1443.

110. ASF, Decima Rep., vol. 70, fols. 14r–15r. S. Apollonia also kept Mantignano's rural patrimony intact over the years; see the inventories dated 1477 and 1506 noted in ASF, CRSGF, 82, vol. 5.

111. ASF, CRSGF, 82, vol. 99, lists renters from 1450 to 1536. Some of the leases lasted over fifty years. In addition to rent payments, S. Apollonia frequently required tokens of homage, such as annual tribute of a goose or candles.

112. Suor Piccarda Gianfigliazzi, granddaughter of the renowned statesman Rinaldo, was entrusted with a valuable farm holding near Mantignano in 1435, which obliged her to arrange an annual mass in perpetuity for the donor, Bartolo Gottoli da Prato, and to keep a lamp lit over his tomb in the convent church. After Piccarda's death, the property devolved to Mantignano, whose nuns were charged with tending his memory. This obligation then became the responsibility of S. Apollonia (ASF, CRSGF, 82, vol. 1, fols. 306v–307r). In 1452, S. Ambrogio reached an accord with S. Apollonia regarding a vineyard purchased twenty years earlier by two sisters, Abbess Niccolosa Buonaccorsi of S. Ambrogio and Suor Maddalena, a former nun at Mantignano. Because the women had purchased the vineyard with a joint legacy left them by a third sister, Caterina, also a nun at S. Ambrogio, S. Ambrogio expected to get the lion's share upon the abbess's death. However, Abbess Niccolosa persuaded her chapter to donate her share to Maddalena, giving S. Apollonia eventual title to the entire property (ASF, CRSGF, 82, vol. 111, under date 12 November 1452).

113. Thomas, *Art and Piety*, 83–87, 114–15, notes that the merger permitted S. Apollonia to extend the existing cloister, build another one, and make alterations to the dormitory. Only when construction was complete did the nuns begin decorating and furnishing their church, a job contracted to Neri di Bicci in 1464–73.

114. Bacarelli, "Per l'architettura fiorentina." In 1418 Abbess Cecilia Donati obtained permission from Martin V to acquire a house next door belonging to the hospital of S. Maria a S. Gallo in order to build a new infirmary. With this property in hand,

S. Apollonia purchased five other contiguous houses to expand the cloister. Although Bacarelli cites the documents undergirding expansion, she does not note the influx of funds from Mantignano.

115. Bacarelli, "Per l'architettura fiorentina," 138–41. The nuns petitioned Eugenius again in November 1444 to alienate additional convent goods for their building campaign (ASV, Reg. Suppl., vol. 400, fols. 219v–220r).

116. These tax exemptions were granted in stages. In 1435, Eugenius confirmed the privileges enjoyed by S. Apollonia since "time immemorial" exempting them from tithes on holdings in the dioceses of Florence and Fiesole and on goods given by oblates and on those supporting nuns' board, provided they continued to observe the rule. The first liberation from ecclesiastical taxes and episcopal jurisdiction came on 31 May 1440, in recognition of the nuns' "fervor, continence, good habits," and insufficient income. These privileges were confirmed three years later (ASF, CRSGF, 82, vol. 1, fols. 306r–v, 319r–v; ASF, Dipl., S. Apollonia, dated 14 June 1443). The convent then became one of the many Italian "abbazie nullius diocesis," exempt from diocesan control, directly under papal jurisdiction. These exemptions had been granted by the papacy since the seventh century (Filosa, "L'origine delle abbazie nullius").

117. ASF, CRSGF, 82, vol. 1, fols. 319r–v, 350r–351v. Pius II did not show the same favoritism toward the nuns. In November 1459 he partially overturned their privileges, "considering their income," which resulted in a levy of 20 ducats to support local clergy. The nuns petitioned Archbishop Orlando Bonarli in February 1460 to overturn this levy, but apostolic commissioners upheld the new taxes. His successor Paul II favored the nuns enough to entrust a rich cargo of liturgical vestments and furnishings to their keeping in 1465, along with gold coins worth 6,000 ducats belonging to the Cardinal of Aquileia (ASF, CRSGF, 82, vol. 1, fols. 352v–354r, 357r–v; ASF, CRSGF, 82, vol. 111, at date 12 February 1460).

118. ASF, NA, 5234, fols. 259v–260r, 286r–v. Bartolomea Biliotti had served as abbess of S. Niccolò Maggiore in 1405 before transferring to Mantignano by 1413, where she served as abbess for almost thirty years.

119. ASF, CRSGF, 82, vol. 1, fols. 321r–325r; Richa, *Notizie istoriche delle chiese fiorentine*, 8:306–8. The convent of Mantignano maintained strong ties to the Biliotti family. In September 1438 the nuns elected two members of the clan as their procurators "to proceed in litigation of whatever sort and in their businesses." After her resignation, Abbess Bartolomea selected Tommaso Biliotti "to act in her lawsuits and business affairs" (ASF, CRSGF, 82, vol. 1, fols. 313v, 325v).

120. Richa, *Notizie istoriche delle chiese fiorentine*, 8:310. ASF, CRSGF, 82, vol. 1, fol. 291r–v, lists the six nuns living in Mantignano in July 1425. This group must have closely resembled the group transferred in 1442 and included Piera di Maestro Piero Pulci, Isabetta di Piero di Ser Signa, Margherita di Antonio Covoni, Caterina di Andrea Rossi, Piccarda d'Antonio di Rinaldo Gianfigliazzi, and Maddalena di Stefano Buonaccorsi.

121. Since the Mantignano nuns retained their seniority by profession date, three of them — Piera Pulci, Caterina de' Rossi, and Maddalena Buonaccorsi — figured among the most senior chapter members (ASF, CRSGF, 82, vol. 111, at date 22 February 1454).

122. The fresco also included the arms of Nicholas V, who completed the commission (Bacarelli, "Per l'architettura fiorentina," 141; Thomas, *Art and Piety*, 83–87). Richa, *Notizie istoriche delle chiese fiorentine*, 8:309–10, notes that an undated panel painting hang-

ing in the refectory depicted Cecilia Donati at the feet of Eugenius; it was accompanied by a small scroll bearing an inscription citing her achievements in obtaining Mantignano.

123. To subsidize expansion in the 1450s, S. Apollonia increased its fees for boarders to roughly 20 florins annually, almost double the normal market rate (ASF, CRSGF, 82, vol. 11).

124. See ASF, Decima Granducale, vols. 3780, 3781, 3782, and 3783, organized by quarter.

125. Thomas, *Art and Piety*, 64–67; Simari, "Profilo storico-architettonico"; Richa, *Notizie istoriche delle chiese fiorentine*, 9:246–49.

126. Lehfeldt, "Convents as Litigants." The Benedictine nuns of S. Maria a Verzaia also headed a parish in 1422, but Eugenius suppressed the convent (AAF, VP, 2.1, fol. 66v). The old Oltrarno parish of S. Felice in Piazza was not associated with the Dominican nuns of S. Pier Martire until August 1557, when they were transferred there from their former location inside Porta Romana (Richa, *Notizie istoriche delle chiese fiorentine*, 10:202, 206).

127. AAF, VP, 3.1, fasc. 4.

128. ASF, CRSGF, 79, vol. 458, fol. 1r; ASF, CRSPL, SPM, vols. 36, 81, 130, 164, 165. Strocchia, *Death and Ritual*, 94–95, discusses parish burial rights.

129. ASF, CRSPL, SPM, vol. 1, no. 25.

130. ASF, Dipl., SPM, dated 4 September 1365; copy in vol. 4, tomo 1, unfol., and in vol. 61, no. 188.

131. AAF, SPM, Feste Ufizi, fol. 113r–v.

132. ASF, CRSPL, SPM, vol. 1, no. 27; vol. 61, no. 261; BRF, Mss. Moreni, vol. 212, p. 591.

133. The following discussion is based on Novelli, "Due documenti inediti." The Santuccie house in Florence was located at the corner of present-day Via dell'Agnolo and Via della Rosa.

134. *Bull. rom.*, 5:270–73; ASF, CRSPL, SPM, vol. 61, no. 326.

135. Sire, *Knights of Malta*, 158–74, discusses the development of the Jerusalemite order in Italy.

136. ASF, CRSPL, SPM, vol. 61, no. 328, dated 15 February 1481. In recognition of their contribution to the Turkish campaign, the papal commissioner ceded a plenary indulgence to the nuns and lay annuitants of S. Pier Maggiore along with the right to choose their own confessor.

137. This history is recounted in ASF, CRSPL, SPM, vol. 61, no. 327. The bull of suppression is published in *Bull. rom.*, 5:270–73.

138. ASF, CRSPL, SPM, vol. 1, no. 31, dated 8 December 1481.

139. ASF, CRSPL, SPM, vol. 53, fols. 74v, 75r.

140. ASF, CRSPL, SPM, vol. 1, no. 29, 31; vol. 61, no. 342.

141. ASF, CRSPL, SPM, vol. 78, fol. 62r; Weissman, *Ritual Brotherhood*, 206–20; Strocchia, "Sisters in Spirit."

142. ASF, CRSGF, 79, vol. 169, no. 36, dated 6 August 1368.

143. ASF, CRSGF, 79, vol. 169, no. 77.

144. BNCF, II, II, 509, fols. 9v–10r.

145. ASF, CRSGF, 79, vol. 169, no. 88; Nunes, *Dom Frey Gomez*, 1:311. My thanks to Ed Friedman for help with the translation.

146. Weddle, "Identity and Alliance," 408, also notes Benci's possible political motiva-

tions as a Medicean trying to make inroads in a traditionally hostile quarter. I discuss Benci's patronage at greater length in chapter 3.

CHAPTER 3 : The Renaissance Convent Economy

1. Gennaro, "Clare, Agnes, and Their Earliest Followers."

2. Relations between foreign policy and communal finance in the late Trecento and early Quattrocento have been studied by various scholars, although there is not a strong consensus about the overall state of the fifteenth-century Florentine economy. Foundational works include Molho, *Florentine Public Finances*; Brucker, *Florentine Politics and Society*; Brucker, *Civic World*; and Becker, *Studies in the Rise of the Territorial State*.

3. Peterson, "War of the Eight Saints." The chaplain of S. Pier Maggiore complained bitterly that the 1375 impost was higher than any previous exaction, forcing the convent "to borrow much money" from friends and benefactors. The convent also alienated four houses and a farm "for the officials of the Florentine commune"; a decade later, only the farm had been restored (AAF, SPM, Feste Ufizi, fols. 14r–15r, 24r; AAF, VP, 1.1, fol. 28r). Like monasteries, convents often repurchased alienated property and absorbed the loss. In 1383, S. Pier Maggiore negotiated with a barrel maker to buy back the confiscated house he had purchased during the war. Although willing to sell, he bargained to maintain lifetime usufruct, after which the property reverted to the convent. Unfortunately the account does not give any monetary values for these transactions.

4. Molho, *Marriage Alliance*.

5. McNamara, *Sisters in Arms*, 274.

6. The tally of forty-eight women's religious houses (twenty-seven urban, twenty-one suburban) given by Herlihy and Klapisch-Zuber, *Les toscans*, 156–58, is open to slight adjustment, since one foundation (the Paradiso) was occupied by both male and female religious, while a few convents had hospitals attached to them and might be counted toward different categories.

7. My figure for mean assets differs from the average value of 3,760 florins given by Brucker, "Monasteries," 53; this difference stems from our respective method of calculation. I used the data provided in individual returns (*portate*) in 1427, whereas Brucker used the summary made by tax officials (*campioni*) and combined returns from 1427, 1430, and 1438 in various ways. I also have corrected a few minor errors in Brucker's tables that misidentified houses with similar names. In addition, I counted the Paradiso as a female rather than male community, since the majority of inhabitants were nuns and the convent was governed by an abbess. I excluded Le Murate from my calculations because it claimed no property assets in 1427.

8. Strocchia, "Taken into Custody."

9. ASF, Catasto, vol. 989, fol. 18r–v.

10. ASF, Catasto, vol. 184, fol. 51r; vol. 194, fols. 121r–123r. For boarding fees, see Strocchia, "Taken into Custody."

11. Hay, *Church in Italy*, 61–62.

12. ASF, Catasto, vol. 194, fols. 123r–131v.

13. AAF, VP, 1.1, fol. 29v.

14. ASF, Catasto, vol. 194, fols. 132r–135v, claiming twenty-four nuns and ten priests as *bocche*.

15. Convents holding corporate *monte* credits included S. Felicita, S. Gaggio, S. Jacopo di Ripoli, and the Paradiso. In addition, S. Domenico nel Maglio reported *monte* income held privately by one of the nuns (ASF, Catasto, vols. 184, 185, 192, 194).

16. Peterson, "State-building," 130–31. Shortly before the *catasto* was enacted, for example, S. Jacopo had been compensated with credits worth 1,500 florins for properties forcibly sold to the politically active citizens Giovanni Guicciardini and Lorenzo Ridolfi (ASF, CRSPL, S. Jacopo, vol. 26, fol. 102r, dated 1425).

17. ASF, Catasto, vol. 602.

18. Brucker, "Monasteries," 51.

19. This sum was calculated using the figures supplied by Brucker for twenty-two male houses reporting assets. I have eliminated the Paradiso from this list.

20. Peterson, "State-building," 126.

21. Sperling, *Convents and the Body Politic*, 257. For purposes of this comparison, the florin and ducat can be considered roughly equivalent.

22. Primhak, "Women in Religious Communities," 102, 157. In 1521, S. Zaccaria was divided into two communities inhabiting the same complex.

23. Twenty-eight percent of nuns entering the Observant house of S. Servolo between 1434 and 1543 were *converse*. The proportion at conventual houses was certainly higher (Primhak, "Women in Religious Communities," 115–17).

24. Primhak, "Benedictine Communities," 93–95; Radke, "Nuns and Their Art." Primhak, "Women in Religious Communities," 153–55, notes expenses and protocols for nuns' consecrations.

25. On Venetian women's disposition of property, see Chojnacki, *Women and Men*, 115–68. Sperling, *Convents and Body Politic*, 72–114, addresses nuns' role in propagating the "myth of Venice."

26. One of the best introductions to Italian public finance is Mueller, *Venetian Money Market*.

27. Conti, *L'imposta diretta*, 36.

28. Molho, *Marriage Alliance*, 40.

29. In the 1420s the cash-strapped commune paid only 3.75% on *monte* shares originally scheduled to yield 5% interest; shares scheduled at 8% got only 6% interest. Similarly, the market value of *monte* shares declined precipitously in the 1420s and 1430s. *Monte* credits were assessed at 50% of their face value in the 1427 *catasto* (Molho, *Florentine Public Finances*, 102, 161).

30. ASF, Catasto, vol. 602, fols. 106r–115v.

31. By 1438, the convent had been gifted with one major credit (2,595 florins) earning 8% interest. One donor had given a credit of 400 florins earmarked for the infirmary. *Monte* investments grew when Lapaccio de' Bardi, a traditional Franciscan patron, donated credits with a face value of 1,944 florins in 1442 (ASF, NA, 5234, fol. 286r–v, dated 28 May 1442).

32. ASF, Catasto, vol. 602, fol. 110v.

33. ASF, Catasto, vol. 184, fols. 35r, 74r.

34. AAF, VP, 2.1.

35. While virtually all of the thirty-seven Neapolitan convents surveyed by Archbishop Filamarino in 1642 owned some property, revenues from landed wealth formed only a secondary source of income. Other revenue streams came from teaching fees, which

reached as high as 18% of total income at some convents, and from the sale of wine, linen, and handiwork (Russo, *Monasteri femminili*, 21–27). For revenues at Venetian convents, see Sperling, *Convents and the Body Politic*, 178–84, 201–2.

36. Lehfeldt, *Religious Women in Golden Age Spain*, 48–54. Investments in state-funded credit schemes carried reasonably good returns, typically yielding about 7% interest.

37. ASF, Catasto, vol. 421, fol. 23r ("E più ho d'incarico ogni spesa la quale m'ocorresse per infirmità o per altro bisogno per la mia persona, da pane e vino e carne tre volte la settimana in fuori che mi dà il mio convento; ogni altra cosa ho trarre di dette substanzie").

38. ASF, S. Niccolò Maggiore, vol. 4, fol. 1v, dated 14 January 1433/4, written partly in the hand of the artist Bicci di Lorenzo.

39. Evangelisti, "Moral Virtues and Personal Goods," 48.

40. Zarri, "Third Status."

41. Facchiano, "Monachesimo femminile nel Mezzogiorno," illuminates property relationships in southern Italian convents.

42. AAF, VP, 2.1, fols. 42r, 47r.

43. Moorman, *History of the Franciscan Order*, 409.

44. AAF, VP, 2.1, fol. 60r.

45. AAF, VP, 3.1, fascs. 2, 4. At the Chiarito, fully professed nuns were obliged to pay 10 soldi per month from their earnings, newer nuns 7 soldi, and servants 5 soldi "when they are healthy" (ASF, CRSPL, Chiarito, vol. 3, fol. 2r).

46. ASF, Auditore, vol. 4894, fol. 357r–v.

47. ASF, CRSPL, SPM, vol. 70, fols. 94r, 127v; vol. 36, fol. 34r.

48. ASF, CRSPL, SPM, vol. 72, fols. 9v, 115v, 129v; vol. 52, fol. 62r.

49. ASF, CRSGF, 79, vol. 116, fol. 5v; vol. 169, no. 76, dated 14 June 1423.

50. In 1451, the commune levied a 25% charge on taxable property transferred from laity to tax-exempt corporations like convents, prompting strong pushback from Archbishop Antoninus, who forced its repeal (Peterson, "State-building"). Tax officials also tracked *monte* accounts and real estate transferred from laity to religious institutions and personnel to detect fraud; see ASF, Catasto, vols. 420 and 638. In 1427, a quarter or more of land in the surrounding countryside was under ecclesiastical ownership (Conti, *Formazione della struttura agraria*).

51. These figures are derived from ASF, Catasto, vols. 184 and 185. I estimated the population of S. Maria a Monticelli, which did not report the number of *bocche*, at the mean population of sixteen.

52. ASF, Catasto, vol. 602, fols. 149r, 108r.

53. ASF, Catasto, vol. 185, fols. 473r, 430r; vol. 184, fols. 17r–18v; vol. 194, fols. 655r–v, 658v, 666r–v. Brucker, "Monasteries," 47, lists S. Domenico's assets for 1427–38 at 5,143 florins. However, this figure does not jibe with reported holdings for 1427 cited above, for 1430 (4,765 florins) or 1438 (4,004 florins) found in ASF, Catasto, vol. 195, fol. 118r. Nevertheless, its rank as the fourth wealthiest urban convent is not affected by this discrepancy.

54. For instance, she and another nun, Ghita Adimari, bought three pieces of land from a shoemaker in 1437 for 96.5 florins. The two nuns split the annual rents during their lifetimes; with the proceeds, they established mass programs and other religious feasts to take effect after death. Suor Ghita Capponi also directed 1 florin per year from this legacy to her "disciple," Suor Ginevra Buondelmonti, for her lifetime (ASF, CRSGF, 108, vol. 119, fol. 34r, dated 16 January 1436/7).

55. For Augsburg, see Cuneo, "Basilica"; "Le sopradette monache anno più oblighi delle sopradette entrate, cioè a vestirsi e farsi le spese nell'infermità e governarne disciepole e farne più rinovali l'anno per l'anima di chi gli a loro lasciati, e de sopradetti danari avanzano poco"; ASF, Catasto, vol. 184, fol. 18v.

56. ASF, CRSGF, 108, vol. 12, fol. 26v; vol. 14, fol. 55r–v.

57. ASF, Catasto, vol. 184, fols. 30r–31v, 46r.

58. ASF, CRSGF, 234, vol. 1, fols. 2v–3r; vol. 79, fol. 6v.

59. Klapisch-Zuber, "The 'Cruel Mother,'" in her *Women, Family, and Ritual in Renaissance Italy*, 117–31.

60. For instance, payments to S. Felicita between 1385 and 1404 could be delinquent by two or three years, although most payments were made annually (ASF, CRSGF, 83, vol. 112, fol. 26r–v).

61. Evangelisti, "Monastic Poverty."

62. ASF, CRSPL, S. Jacopo, vol. 26, fols. 67r, 104v. Suor Tommasa's shares were to be distributed with the condition that "le dette due monache sieno comite et obbligata fare ogn'anno la piatanza e festa di San Lorenzo e fare dire al convento l'uficio de' morti per l'anima della madre della detta Suor Tommasa e sua." A note in a different hand reads, "Nota che la detta Suora Tommasa dichiarò nell'ultimo della sua vita che l'una parte lassava a Suora Costanza Barucci e l'altra a Suora Niccolosa Barucci."

63. ASF, CRSPL, S. Jacopo, vol. 26, fol. 196r–v.

64. The following discussion is based on ASF, Catasto, vol. 602. fols. 148v–149v.

65. Russo, *Monasteri femminili*, 33–36.

66. Primhak, "Women in Religious Communities," 229.

67. Bestor, "Marriage Transactions in Renaissance Italy."

68. ASF, CRSGF, 90, vol. 60, fol. 25 r–v; ASF, CRSPL, SPM, vol. 79, fol. 76v; vol. 87, fol. 132r.

69. ASF, Acq. e Doni, vol. 293, unfol., dated 18 July 1499; ASF, CRSGF, 81, vol. 100, letters 190, 196, 198, 252, among others. See also Lowe, "Female Strategies," 219–20, and Lowe, "Rainha D. Leonor of Portugal's Patronage."

70. Bynum, *Holy Feast and Holy Fast*.

71. On admonitions that Dominican nuns restrict fasting, see Roberts, "Plautilla Nelli's *Last Supper*," and Leonard, *Nails in the Wall*, 28.

72. AAF, VP, 1.1, fols. 1v–4r.

73. Conversely, monasteries and friaries bore other expenses when extending hospitality to traveling friars and "outsiders." S. Maria Novella claimed that it accommodated twenty-four itinerant friars and fed about ten visitors daily (ASF, Catasto, vol. 184, fols. 125r–132r).

74. AAF, VP, 3.1, fascs. 2, 4.

75. ASF, Catasto, vol. 602, fol. 255r. For ecclesiastical censures of prebends from the twelfth century on, see McNamara, *Sisters in Arms*, 274–80.

76. Frick, *Dressing Renaissance Florence*, 141–44.

77. Several studies have examined the material culture of early modern Italian convents, although to date there has been no comparative study over time. Evangelisti takes up the transmission of nuns' cells and other personal goods in "'Farne quello che pare e piace'" and in "Moral Virtues and Personal Goods."

78. ASF, Catasto, vol. 421. fols. 10r, 88r.

79. ASF, Catasto, vol. 602, fol. 255v.

80. Primhak, "Women in Religious Communities," 210, 216–18, quoting from the 1472 tax report of S. Lorenzo.

81. ASF, Catasto, vol. 184, fols. 51r, 61v; vol. 602, fols. 91r–93r.

82. ASF, Catasto, vol. 602, fol. 255v. S. Pier Maggiore had to alienate several properties, sell miscellaneous goods, and take in two recruits simply to pay for necessary building repairs in the 1430s (ASF, CRSPL, SPM, vol. 73).

83. ASF, Catasto, vol. 602, fol. 252r–255v.

84. Sperling, *Convents and the Body Politic*, 180.

85. ASF, CRSGF, 83, vol. 112, fols. 103r–v, 104v–105v.

86. Molho, *Florentine Public Finances*, 58.

87. ASF, Dipl., SPM, 7 September 1420; ASF, CRSPL, SPM, vol. 73, fol. 119r.

88. ASF, CRSPL, SPM, vol. 73, fol. 72v.

89. The convent's *monte* portfolio, which had no credits in 1427, grew to a nominal value of 1,155 florins by 1438 and 1,795 florins by 1446 (ASF, Catasto, vol. 602, fols. 254v–255r; ASF, CRSPL, SPM, vol. 205, fol. 48r).

90. Alessandro Machiavelli and Giovanni Barducci, both men of standing in the city and parish, consigned *monte* accounts worth 200 and 400 florins respectively to endow chapels where masses could be performed for the family dead. One of the convent chaplains established another chapel using his credits, directing two years of interest payments as compensation to the painter and craftsman who made the glass windows. In 1438 the convent's newest recruit, Suor Maddalena Guidetti, brought a dowry consisting of interest on her mother's *monte* account paid for five consecutive years (ASF, CRSGF, 83, vol. 113, fols. 6v, 7v–8r, 13r–v, 57v; ASF, Catasto, vol. 602, fol. 146v). These and other smaller donations raised convent *monte* holdings from 2,404 to 3,434 florins.

91. Molho, *Marriage Alliance*, 42. In the seventeenth and eighteenth centuries, the nuns of S. Domenico, among others, held investments in the public savings banks of the Monte delle Graticole and Monte di Pietà (ASF, CRSGF, 108, vol. 147, fascs. 2, 3). On the development and role of the Monte di Pietà, see Menning, *Charity and State*.

92. ASF, Catasto, vol. 602, fols. 90r, 91r–83r, 118v.

93. Face value of convent credits grew from 1,530 to 2,400 florins between 1431 and 1437 (ASF, CRSPL, S. Jacopo, vol. 8, no. 7; vol. 26, fols. 102r–v, 104v, 112r). Molho, *Marriage Alliance*, 42.

94. ASF, CRSGF, 82, vol. 111, under dates 14 January 1433/4, 4 November 1435, 17 April 1439, 15 December 1441, and 30 July 1443.

95. For instance, in 1438, S. Gaggio asked that the bulk of its 62-florin interest payment be applied to its communal impost; four years later, it used the cash to purchase a large amount of grain from the commune (ASF, CRSGF, 234, vol. 1, fol. 20v; vol. 2, fol. 22v; vol. 78, fols. 106r–107r).

96. Molho, *Marriage Alliance*, 35–38; Rocke, *Forbidden Friendships*, 62. The Convertite nuns kept copies of the relevant legislation in the convent (ASF, CRSGF, 126, vol. 70).

97. Conti, *L'imposta diretta*, 35.

98. This summary is based on Molho, *Marriage Alliance*, 48–60, and Conti, *L'imposta diretta*, 50–66.

99. ASF, PR, vol. 142, fol. 402r.

100. Conti, *L'imposta diretta*, 8, 18–19. These arrangements highlighted and to some extent compromised nuns' intercessory role in the cult of remembrance. In 1469, *monte*

officials gave S. Ambrogio about two-thirds of its annual salt consumption as payment on the endowment of the Barducci chapel. Although the chapel was undergoing renovation, the convent was still obliged to perform the usual masses and pay other expenses. After consulting their patron Stagio Barducci, the nuns decided to accept the offered payment in salt, which was stored in-house for later consumption, and the deficit was marked against the communal treasury (ASF, CRSGF, 79, vol. 21, fol. 51v).

101. ASF, CRSGF, 79, vol. 20, fols. 87r, 89v.

102. ASF, CRSGF, 108, vol. 147, fasc. 1, nos. 1, 2.

103. Tomas, *Medici Women*, 85–90. Medici clients in Pisa included Ognissanti, S. Viti, S. Francesco, S. Maria, S. Silvestro, S. Domenico, S. Caterina, S. Paolo, and S. Maria. For subsidies extended to them, see ASF, PR, vols. 171, 172, 173, 175, 178.

104. *Statuta*, 3:402–8; Peterson, "State-building," 133.

105. ASF, PR, vol. 199, fol. 22r.

106. Kent, "Lorenzo de' Medici."

107. Lowe, "Patronage and Territoriality"; Lowe, "A Matter of Piety."

108. ASF, PR, vol. 133, fols. 137v–138r; vol. 141, fol. 162r–v.

109. ASF, PR, vol. 150, fols. 78v–79r; vol. 156, fols. 53v–54r; vol. 165, fols. 103v–104r; vol. 169, fol. 129r–v; vol. 171, fol. 8r–v; vol. 173, fols. 190v–191r. My thanks to Gene Brucker for several of these references.

110. Molho, *Florentine Public Finances*, 51; for the Murate claim, see ASF, PR, vol. 169, fol. 129r–v.

111. Ilardi, "Crosses and Carets," 1128.

112. ASF, MAP, XII, 404, letter to Cosimo de' Medici from the abbess of S. Francesco, 14 March, no year given ("Ci rimettiamo per l'amore di Dio et di San Francesco a ricorrere alla vostra misericordia, non per vivere nè per le nostre persone, che stiamo contente sola a quello che ci è di necessità, ma per rifare la casa di Sancto Francesco ch' è molto piccola e male in punto, e non veggiamo modo di pote[r] vivere a stremità non che acconciarla. È sì piccolo il luogho dove noi dormiamo che non vi possiamo fare le letta che sieno abastanza").

113. ASF, MAP, XXII, 38, letter to Lorenzo de' Medici from the Madonna delle Murate, 13 December 1465; Heazlewood, " 'Letters Are the Leaves,' " 68.

114. BNF, II, II, 509, fol. 42v.

115. ASF, MAP, XXVII, 348, 21 May 1479, letter to Lorenzo de' Medici from Suor Domitilla Strozzi, abbess of S. Chiara Novella ("sempre obligatissima fare e far fare spetiale prege per la conservatione del vostro felice stato come cotidianamente ogni giorno").

116. Tomas, *Medici Women*. ASF, MAP, LXXXV, 176, letter to Lucrezia from the prioress of S. Domenico dated 1476, no month given ("Siamo obligatissime a pregare a Dio . . . et così facciamo, e simile per lo stato vostro e de' vostro magnifici figliuoli acciò che l'abbiate sempre felice con salute").

117. For an overview of Florentine economic structures, see Dini, "L'economia fiorentina." Brucker summarizes the major areas of scholarly dispute in "Economic Foundations of Laurentian Florence."

118. Molho, *Marriage Alliance*, 363–64; Cohn, "Women and Work," 120n. Goldthwaite, *Building of Renaissance Florence*, 301, notes that the lira-florin ratio "rose more or less steadily from 3 ½:1 to 7:1" between 1350 and 1500.

119. ASF, Catasto, vol. 989, fols. 373r–377v. S. Jacopo claimed ten houses and a shop as

the sum total of its urban property, along with nine farms, twenty-three pieces of land of varying sizes and yields, and a vineyard. The nuns owed debts of 150 florins to their local spicer, butcher, chicken vendor, physician, and wood supplier among others. Quote at fol. 377v: "Preghiamo le vostre carità, signori ufficiali, che noi vi siamo raccomandate perchè noi siamo qua giù abandonate da ogni persona per rispetto della guerra e della moria. Noi guadagniamo più niente perchè le botteghe non ce ne vogliono dare per rispetto di questa moria che abbiamo all'uscio cioè la schala. Non ci parebbe fatica pagare se noi guadagnasimo. Sarà ci forza d'andare accattare e limosinare. Fateci meno male che voi potete."

120. ASF, Catasto, vol. 989, fols. 321r–322r. The value of their *monte* credits is noted in ASF, PR, vol. 199, fol. 43r–v. On the growth of a school at this convent, Strocchia, "Learning the Virtues."

121. ASF, PR, vols. 171, 172, 173, 175, 177, 178.

122. ASF, CRSGF, 82, vol. 1, fols. 368r–v, 373v, 374r.

123. ASF, PR, vol. 199, fols. 9v–10r, 41v, provisions granted for the year April 1508 to March 1509. Le Murate won the largest concession that year, since its 180 nuns were known to be "extremely poor and to live on alms which for the most part come from outside the city."

124. Carnesecchi, "Monache in Firenze," 1:29, lists the convents and their populations, totaling 1,467 nuns.

125. ASF, MAP, CXLV, 294, letter to Goro Gheri, bishop of Fano from Suor Elisabetta, abbess, Monastero del Paradiso, 5 July 1519 ("Noi abbiamo dal comune di Firenze 16 staia di sale l'anno per vigore di fiorini 2233 di monte. E perché siamo cresciute circa bocche 30 più che il sol[i]to, siamo sute constrette soprapigliare detto sale e abbiamo debito qualche staio. E per avere sopra preso, il proveditore non ne vuole dare un carico che sono otto staie innanzi tempo, e noi ne abbiamo di bisogno"); Heazlewood, " 'Letters Are the Leaves,' " 112–13.

126. Tomas, *Medici Women*, 139.

127. ASF, Catasto, vol. 989. fol. 711v ("In detto munistero si fa oratione pel buono stato di questa città, che sono più utile tale oratione di simile religiose persone che non sono dumila cavagli"). For Dei's quote, see Trexler, "Celibacy," 6.

128. Richards, "Community and Poverty."

129. ASF, Acq. e Doni, vol. 293, unfol. Communal officials also sent "copiose elemosine" to the Buonomini di San Martino "pro remedio civitatibis et populi florentini et ut ira Dei placetur."

130. Polizzotto, *Elect Nation*, 188–91; di Agresti, *Sviluppi della riforma*, 19–24.

131. Tomas, *Medici Women*, 170.

132. ASF, PR, vol. 199, fol. 33r. On S. Jacopo's Savonarolan allegiances, see Strocchia, "Savonarolan Witnesses."

133. ASF, CRSPL, S. Jacopo, vol. 2, no. 202, packet dated 17 June 1485.

134. ASF, CRSPL, S. Jacopo, vol. 21, fol. 20r ("Debbono adunque le monache continuamente pregare il Signore nelle commune e private oratione per la excelsa republica fiorentina, e per i cittadini che quella anno a regiere, ricevendo tanti e sì grandi beneficii dal loro").

135. ASF, CRSPL, S. Jacopo, vol. 2, no. 202, packets dated 18 June 1550 and 17 June 1485.

136. Sperling, *Convents and the Body Politic*, 171.

CHAPTER 4: Invisible Hands

1. Venarde, *Women's Monasticism*, 103–32.

2. Greci, "Donne e corporazioni."

3. Klapisch-Zuber, "Women Servants in Florence"; Klapisch-Zuber, "Female Celibacy and Service," in her *Women, Family, and Ritual in Renaissance Italy*, 165–77; Trexler, "Florentine Prostitution."

4. Cohn, "Women and Work"; Chabot, "La reconnaissance du travail." For an earlier consideration of female occupations in fifteenth-century Italy, see Herlihy, *Opera Muliebria*, 154–68.

5. Lehfeldt, *Religious Women in Golden Age Spain*; Oliva, *The Convent and the Community*; Sánchez, *The Empress, the Queen, and the Nun*.

6. Gilchrist, *Gender and Material Culture*, 85–90, concludes that because commercial enterprise in fifteenth-century English nunneries was limited, religious women functioned primarily as consumers. Yet she does not explore in any depth the shift from small-scale production to a cash economy based on "temporalities and spiritualities" taking place at the same time.

7. ASF, Catasto, vol. 184, fol. 63r.

8. ASF, Mon. S. Luca, vol. 79, fol. 91r.

9. On child labor, see Franceschi, "Les enfants au travail."

10. Davidsohn, *Le origini*, 137–39, documents the existence of a convent-based weaving workshop run by *converse* in the ninth century.

11. The bibliography on women and work in early modern Europe is vast. Several of the classic studies relevant to this discussion are Hufton, "Women and the Family Economy," and Davis, "Women in the Crafts." More recent studies include Chojnacka, *Working Women*, and the articles collected in *Il lavoro delle donne*.

12. Lowe, "Women's Work," 142. Goldthwaite, *Building of Renaissance Florence*, 289–300, notes that most unsalaried workers probably considered themselves fortunate to work as many as 200 days per year or at most 270 days annually.

13. Chabot, "La reconnaissance du travail."

14. ASF, Catasto, vol. 602, fol. 243v.

15. ASF, CRSGF, 125, vol. 8. This volume is conserved in the fondo of S. Clemente. I am grateful to Elissa Weaver for bringing this document to my attention. For the establishment of the convent, known as S. Maria della Misericordia, see Pulci, *Florentine Drama*, 10–21.

16. ASF, CRSPL, Chiarito, vol. 1, fol. 46v; vol. 2, fol. 18v.

17. The following discussion is drawn from Strocchia, "Learning the Virtues."

18. ASF, Catasto, vol. 602, fol. 651r–v; vol. 989, fols. 76r–78v, quote at 78v.

19. Radke, "Nuns and Their Art," 433, notes the impressive quality of needlework and objects manufactured in gold and silver in some Venetian convents. The Poor Clares of Perugia were famous for embroidered altarcloths, church draperies, and clerical vestments (Wood, *Women, Art and Spirituality*, 104).

20. For their sister's marriage in 1473, the heirs of Niccolò Buoninsegni parceled out small trousseaux commissions to different convents. A nun in S. Niccolò Maggiore earned 1 florin for sewing nine undershirts; another nun in S. Domenico nel Maglio made six similar garments of finer quality; a Murate nun made 370 *braccia* of silk ribbon (ASF, Acq. e

Doni, vol. 293, unfol.). The nuns of S. Agata earned 30 florins in 1524 for making the wedding finery of wellborn Silvia Ricasoli, who shortly before had been in their care (ASF, CRSPL, S. Agata, vol. 50, fol. 42v).

21. Franceschi, *Oltre il "Tumulto,"* 130–32. Earlier studies indicated that foreign male weavers displaced female weavers in the late Trecento; see for example Brown, "A Woman's Place Was the Home."

22. Benvenuti Papi, "Mendicant Friars," 99–100, discusses the class associations of spinning linen. Income from spinning linen at S. Maria de' Candeli from 1385 to 1450 is recorded in ASF, CRSGF, 128, vol. 80.

23. See de Roover's classic study, "Andrea Banchi."

24. Goldthwaite, "Entrepreneurial Silk Weaver," 117.

25. Goldthwaite, "Entrepreneurial Silk Weaver," 69.

26. Franceschi, "Un'industria 'nuova' e prestigiosa." Dini, "L'industria serica," provides a good overview.

27. Franceschi, "Un'industria 'nuova' e prestigiosa," 168.

28. Bonds, "Genoese Noblewomen."

29. For instance, the nuns reeled batches of "seta da Brugia, seta catanzana, seta spagnola," among other types (ASF, CRSGF, 108, vol. 54, fol. 16r).

30. ASF, CRSGF, 108, vol. 54, fols. 16r, 21v, 31r, 33v, 35v, 46r. Their other dealers were Domenico Borghini, Marabottino and company, Francesco d'Andrea Bartoli, and Giannozzo Biliotti.

31. ASF, CRSGF, 108, vol. 54, fol. 27r.

32. ASF, CRSGF, 108, vol. 54, fols. 16r, 17r.

33. ASF, CRSGF, 108, vol. 54, fols. 16r, 21r–23r.

34. ASF, CRSGF, 108, vol. 54, fols. 67r, 92v–93v.

35. De Roover, *L'arte della seta*, 88; Dini, "Una manifattura di battiloro."

36. Reyerson, "Women in Business," 120.

37. De Roover, *L'arte della seta*, 88, notes that the process of manufacturing metallic thread changed between the fourteenth and fifteenth centuries. In the Trecento, the core thread was first wrapped with a thin, supple layer of animal gut before being wound with the gold strips. In the fifteenth and sixteenth centuries, this middle layer was eliminated and the strips were instead wrapped directly around the thread.

38. ASF, Mss., vol. 90, fols. 61r, 62r, 69r, 70v.

39. De Roover, *L'arte della seta*, 91. On Scholastica's cultivation of patronal relationships, see Kent, "Lorenzo de' Medici."

40. Dini, "Una manifattura di battiloro," 108; ASF, CS, ser. 5, vol. 1744, fol. 156v.

41. The Convertite claimed assets of 515 florins in 1427–38, giving it the smallest endowment of twenty-five urban communities reporting assets. Le Murate reported no property holdings (Brucker, "Monasteries," 47). The Convertite population figure of one hundred to two hundred women given by Cohen, *Evolution of Women's Asylums*, 37, is too high for the fifteenth century.

42. Dini, "Una manifattura di battiloro," 108.

43. De Roover, *L'arte della seta*, 89. For Gondi's dealings with S. Gaggio, see ASF, CRSGF, 234, vol. 81.

44. Molà, *Silk Industry*, 35.

45. The role of the night officers is discussed further in chapter 5. For the prosecution of sodomy, Rocke, *Forbidden Friendships*.

46. ASF, UN, vol. 12, fol. 70r; vol. 13, fol. 54v; vol. 14, fol. 78r; vol. 15, fol. 91r; vol. 16, fol. 92v.

47. ASF, UN, vol. 27, fol. 113v.

48. See for example ASF, UN, vol. 27, fol. 116v; vol. 28, fols. 90v–92r.

49. Goldthwaite, "Entrepreneurial Silk Weaver," 94–96; Franceschi, "Les enfants au travail," 76–77.

50. Goldthwaite, "Entrepreneurial Silk Weaver," 99.

51. Cohn, *Laboring Classes*, 9.

52. Terpstra, "Making a Living."

53. AAF, VP, 3.1, fasc. 2.

54. ASF, CRSGF, 126, vol. 62, fol. 71v.

55. ASF, Mon. S. Brigida, vol. 147, fol. 2v.

56. Goldthwaite, "Entrepreneurial Silk Weaver," 72.

57. AAF, VP, 3.1, fasc. 2.

58. ASF, CRSGF, 100, vol. 89, no. 3; Thomas, *Art and Piety*, 97.

59. ASF, Catasto, vol. 184, fol. 47r–v. Fantozzi Micali, *Monastero di S. Gaggio*, 24, 45, notes that the nuns made repairs and placed stalls in the choir but does not correlate these projects with manufacturing activities.

60. ASF, CRSGF, 234, vol. 1; vol. 80, fol. 131v ("disse per mandare a Livorno a uno cittadino, il quale lo ricercava per la sua donna di tal prezzo e valore").

61. ASF, CRSGF, 234, vol. 2, fol. 47r–v; ASF, Catasto, vol. 602, fol. 243v; ASF, NA, 10084, fols. 181r–v, 291v–292r.

62. ASF, CRSGF, 234, vol. 81, fol. 1r.

63. The following analysis is based on accounts covering the period February 1469 through March 1480 in ASF, CRSGF, 234, vol. 81. Gold leaf was figured at 12 *oncie* per *libbra*, giving the total of 564.75 *libbre*, or an annual average of 616 ounces. The nuns' total earnings for this production amounted to 5,088 lire, which I averaged at the mean for these years (113 soldi per florin), giving the sum of 900.53 florins.

64. De Roover, *L'arte della seta*, 92.

65. ASF, CRSGF, 234, vol. 81, fols. 21v, 146r, 163v, 199v, 200v, 202v.

66. ASF, CRSGF, 234, vol. 81, fols. 45r–49r.

67. ASF, CRSGF, 234, vol. 81, fols. 94v, 128r. The crucifix was completed two years later, in 1478.

68. Lowe, "Women's Work," 140; Lowe, "Nuns and Choice"; Winkelmes, "Taking Part." Radke, "Nuns and Their Art," documents how wellborn Venetian nuns made "informed aesthetic and programmatic choices" about their visual and spatial environment.

69. ASF, CRSGF, 234, vol. 81, fols. 28v, 50r, 62v–63r, 106v, 163v.

70. ASF, CRSGF, 234, vol. 81, fol. 37v; vol. 83, fols. 7v–8r, 21v–22r, 78r.

71. ASF, CRSGF, 234, vol. 82, fol. 1r ("commettendo al lui liberamente . . . che ritragga da chi ha a dare i paghi, chi a avere. Di poi le monache trarranno da questo libro e metteranno a libri loro che terranno dentro. Questo vogliono si faccia per potere con più riposo e pace di mente servire a Dio, e non si avere [sic] a travagliare con tanta gente di fuora. E quando avranno tratto di questo libro e messo alloro, li stratanno la partita di questo e acciochè per tale segno s'intenda essere acconcio al libro loro"). These secondary ledgers have not survived.

72. ASF, CRSGF, 234, vol. 83, fols. 8r, 102v–145v.

73. Goldthwaite, "Entrepreneurial Silk Weaver," 113–15.

74. Fantozzi Micali, *Monastero di San Gaggio*, 25–26.

75. ASF, CRSGF, 234, vol. 84; vol. 85, fol. 64v. Annual deficits from 1532 to 1543 are documented in vol. 44.

76. After 1530, dowries increased to 150–200 florins, with each nun bringing additional goods and furnishings worth 90–110 florins (ASF, CRSGF, 234, vol. 84, fols. 94v, 96v, 97v; vol. 85, fol. 125v). In 1533, the nuns received 150 florins from the cathedral *operai* to help rebuild the dormitory as well as smaller sums from individual patrons (ASF, CRSGF, 234, vol. 85, fol. 44v; Fantozzi Micali, *Monastero di San Gaggio*, 26).

77. ASF, Catasto, vol. 603, fol. 58v.

78. Gregori, Roche, and Bacarelli, eds., *Il 'Paradiso' in Pian di Ripoli*, documents many of the architectural and decorative initiatives undertaken in the 1450s and 1460s but does not link these projects with market production. ASF, Mon. S. Brigida, vol. 147, fol. 136v, notes the payment of 1 florin "per fare le finestre ove stanno le suore a richamare."

79. ASF, Mon. S. Brigida, vol. 148, fol. 37r.

80. This account book of S. Brigida, running from 1439 to 1455, is conserved among the records of S. Luca and recently has been recataloged under ASF, Mon. S. Luca, vol. 79. For purchase of raw materials and for spinning thread, see fols. 90v, 91r, 97v–98r, 151r.

81. In the 1480s, the nuns dealt mainly with Bartolomeo del Tovaglia, one of the dealers for the S. Gaggio workshop. In addition, the nuns had a running account with the firm of Lorenzo de' Medici. By the mid-1490s, their principal suppliers were Francesco and Giovanni Pandolfini.

82. ASF, NA, 13511, no. 198, dated 20 November 1443; ASF, Catasto, vol. 989, fol. 159r; AAF, VP, 3.1, fasc. 3.

83. Ilardi, "Renaissance Florence"; Ilardi, *Occhiali alla corte*, 26; Guidotti, "Appunti per una storia della produzione vetraria di Firenze."

84. For the use of eyeglasses by the Lapo nuns, see Strocchia, "Learning the Virtues," 8. The nuns of S. Pier Maggiore bought five pair of eyeglasses from the Paradiso workshop in 1463 (ASF, Mon. S. Brigida, vol. 149, fol. 33r–v). Prices ranged from 9 or 11 soldi to double that amount or more.

85. Comprehensive figures for eyeglass production are derived from Guidotti, "Produzione di occhiali."

86. ASF, Catasto, vol. 989, fol. 159r; AAF, VP, 3.1, fasc. 3.

87. In 1483–84, the convent purchased nine chairs "per le ricamatrici" (ASF, Mon. S. Brigida, vol. 152, fols. 208v, 221v, 225r).

88. This technique, developed in fifteenth-century Florence, involved laying down gold thread horizontally. These threads were then tacked down using irregularly spaced couching stitches in colored silk, which helped embroiderers prevent the piece from appearing visually distorted when viewed from different angles (Parker, *Subversive Stitch*, 11, 79, 108).

89. Garzelli, *Il ricamo*.

90. Santoro, *Tessuti figurati*; Degl'Innocenti, *I tessuti della fede*.

91. Improta and Padoa Rizzo, "Paolo Schiavo." The commission is documented in ASF, Mon. S. Brigida, vol. 149, fols. 22v, 58r–v.

92. Boskovits, "Ancora su Paolo Schiavo"; Gregori, Roche, and Bacarelli, eds., *Il 'Paradiso' in Pian di Ripoli*, 48, 100.

93. Sframeli, " 'Ricamato da mano angelica,' " attributes its facture to Suor Margherita del Caccia. The piece is now conserved in the Cleveland Museum of Art.

94. ASF, Mon. S. Brigida, vol. 148, fol. 2v. The generic term *fregio*, which translates as "a hanging" or "frieze," is used in several commissions rather than more specific nomenclature, such as *paliotto*. When the meaning of *fregio* seems clear from the context, I have substituted a more precise English term.

95. ASF, Mon. S. Luca, vol. 79, fols. 142r, 143r, 161v–162r.

96. ASF, Mon. S. Brigida, vol. 149, fols. 15v, 22v, 58v, 145r, 209r. On Sienese embroidery workshops, see Ciatti, "Appunti per una storia dei tessuti a Siena"; for Sassetti's patronal rights, see Improta and Padoa Rizzo, "Paolo Schiavo," 36.

97. ASF, Mon. S. Brigida, vol. 154, fol. 33r.

98. ASF, Mon. S. Brigida, vol. 147, fol. 27r.

99. ASF, Mon. S. Brigida, vol. 147, fols.138r, 138v, 140v.

100. ASF, Mon. S. Brigida, vol. 147, fols. 27r, 30r, 36v, 37r, 38v, 39r.

101. ASF, Mon. S. Brigida, vol. 147, fols. 138r, 142v, 154r.

102. ASF, Mon. S. Brigida, vol. 147, fols. 12v, 21r; vol. 149, fol. 33r; vol. 152, fols. 26v, 28r; vol. 154, fol. 6v.

103. Di Agresti, *Sviluppi della riforma*, 19.

104. ASF, CRSPL, S. Jacopo, vol. 42, fol. 1v. The nuns were allowed to keep about half of the 186 florins earned in 1514–15. It is not stated where the surplus was deposited or to what uses it was put. Since S. Jacopo had been making gold thread since the 1440s, the nuns had a highly developed organization. Among their officers were an "uficiale del lavoro" and several "maestre del lavoro," who organized work, managed accounts, and instructed newcomers in craft skills. For the convent's Savonarolan affiliations, see Strocchia, "Savonarolan Witnesses."

105. The following discussion is based on ASF, Mon. S. Brigida, vol. 154.

106. ASF, CRSGF, 98, vol. 25, fol. 41r. ASF, Mon. S. Brigida, vol. 147, fol. 31r, notes the 1471 sale to Vespasiano. Other clients included a nun's sister, the daughter of a female annuitant living in the house, and the wife of a tenant.

107. ASF, Mon. S. Brigida, vol. 159, covering the period 1519–50; AAF, VP, 3.1, fasc. 3.

108. ASF, Catasto, vol. 989, fols. 153r–160v.

109. Kent, *Lorenzo de' Medici*, 15–16, notes that Lorenzo's appointment as *operaio* in 1463 kicked off his civic career.

110. ASF, Mon. S. Brigida, vol. 267. Among the institutions acquired between 1478 and 1538 were the abbey of Mamma and the church of S. Fabbiano and abbey of S. Casciano, both in the diocese of Volterra.

111. ASF, CRSGF, 98, vol. 26, fols. 1r, 29r; vol. 27, fols. 5v, 11v. Other buyers between 1490 and 1510 included the nuns of S. Francesco and the silk firm of Lionardo Antinori.

112. ASF, Mon. S. Luca, vol. 40, 1r. This commercial account book, kept by Infanghati from 1514 to 1516, includes his accounts with eighteen laywomen who worked for him as "maestre della seta."

113. These figures are based on ASF, CRSGF, 98, vol. 27.

114. ASF, CS, ser. 2, vol. 59, fol. 67r–v, gives an incomplete list of abbesses, which I have supplemented from internal convent records.

115. In the early sixteenth century, S. Orsola kept a separate section of accounts for "guadagno della sala e della telaia e delle altre suore" (ASF, CRSGF, 100, vol. 89, nos. 3, 4, and 5). For S. Monaca, see ASF, MAP, LXXXIV, 165.

116. The first mention of this commodity is in a document dated 13 April 1507 (ASF, CRSGF, 98, vol. 27, fol. 3r). The accounts use the terms *trine* and *reticelle* interchangeably.

117. This work is known as *Il burato*, issued in four parts.

118. Molà, *Silk Industry*, 299; Goldthwaite, "Entrepreneurial Silk Weaver," 118.

119. ASF, CRSPL, S. Piero, vol. 58, unfol. For S. Orsola, see ASF, Guardaroba Medicea, vol. 23, fols. 78r, 87r. My thanks to Bruce Edelstein for this latter reference.

120. ASF, CRSGF, 98, vols. 27, 28, 29, and 30. My calculations end in 1590 because volume 31, covering the period 1590 to 1600, does not report annual income or expenses, nor does it aggregate earnings in the usual way.

121. For a moving description of the nuns' ordeal, see ASF, CS, ser. 2, vol. 58, fols. 195v–199r; for their continued textile activities, see ASF, CRSGF, 98, vol. 27, fol. 56r.

122. ASF, CRSGF, 98, vol. 27, fols. 62v, 66v, 79r–v. Dowries ranged from 170 to 210 florins; prior to the siege, they stood at 80 to 100 florins.

123. ASF, CRSGF, 98, vol. 28, fols. 85r, 118r.

124. Evangelisti, "Art and the Advent of Clausura"; Evangelisti, " 'We Do Not Have It.' "

125. Riccoboni, *Life and Death in a Venetian Convent*; Strocchia, "Savonarolan Witnesses."

126. ASF, CRSGF, 98, vol. 25, fols. 10r, 12v, 14v, documents the production of texts in the 1460s for friars identified by place of origin rather than surname.

127. Driver, "Nuns as Patrons, Artists, Readers," 238; Hutchinson, "Devotional Reading"; Rhodes, "Syon Abbey."

128. AAF, VP, 3.1, fasc. 3; ASF, Mon. S. Brigida, vol. 145, fol. 5r.

129. Piattoli, "Monastero del Paradiso"; Piattoli, "Un capitolo di storia dell'arte libraria."

130. Gill, "Women and the Production of Religious Literature"; ASF, Mon. S. Luca, vol. 76, fol. 82r; ASF, Mon. S. Brigida, vol. 148, fols. 2v, 19v.

131. The nuns of S. Maria Maddalena in Siena copied books for male houses from the 1440s to the 1470s. In Florence, the nuns of S. Francesco worked for the wealthy hospital of S. Maria Nuova in the late 1480s, while Le Murate produced a diurnal for S. Ambrogio in 1511 (Lowe, Women's Work," 137, 141).

132. ASF, CRSGF, 98, vol. 25, fols. 10r, 60v; Lowe, "Women's Work," 141.

133. Weaver, "Le muse in convento"; Miglio, "Lettere dal monastero"; Bryce, " 'Les livres des Florentines.' "

134. Basic bibliography on this enterprise includes Nesi, *Diario della stamperia di Ripoli*; Bologna, "La stamperia fiorentina del monastero di S. Jacopo di Ripoli"; Fineschi, *Notizie storiche sopra la stamperia di Ripoli*; and most recently Conway, *Diario of the Printing Press of San Jacopo di Ripoli*.

135. Conway, *Diario of the Printing Press of San Jacopo di Ripoli*, 345–53.

136. ASF, CRSGF, 234, vol. 1, fol. 3r; vol. 77, fol. 66v. The Paradiso scriptorium produced a number of books for internal use. For example, in 1479 an unnamed nun with a beautiful book hand copied the vernacular sermons of S. Bernardo, along with sayings taken from Seneca, Socrates, Augustine, and St. Gregory, organized in a familiar compendium format (BNCF, Conv. Sopp., D. 1. 1326).

137. ASF, CRSPL, SPM, vol. 75, fol. 3r. This book had belonged to Lisabetta Fioravanti, a deceased nun in the convent.

138. Piera de' Medici's missal is conserved in BLF, Conv. Sopp, Vallombrosa, codex 235. For the S. Jacopo volume, see Pierattini, "Suor Fiammetta Frescobaldi," 109. Suor Lucrezia Panciatichi's obituary is recorded in ASF, CRSPL, S. Jacopo. vol. 23, fol. 122v.

139. Levi d'Ancona, *Miniatura e miniatori*, 11, 400; the volume is now conserved as BLF, Conv. Sopp., vol. 90. On other activities of these two nuns, see Strocchia, "Sisters in Spirit."

140. Lowe, "Women's Work."

141. The following discussion is based on Strocchia, "Learning the Virtues," and Strocchia, "Taken into Custody."

142. For an introduction to the establishment of custodial institutions for women and girls in grand ducal Florence, see Cohen, *Evolution of Women's Asylum*, and Terpstra, "Mothers, Sisters, and Daughters."

143. AAF, VP, 3.1, fasc. 3 ("Nel nostro monastero non entra donne per alcuna cagione nè altre persone senza necessità, ne sappiamo avere conversazione di persone sospette").

144. ASF, CRSGF, 108, vol. 107, fol. 40r, dated 1496.

145. Esch, "Roman Customs Registers," notes the thousands of devotional items, including barrels of enameled and glass rosary beads, imported into Rome for sale to pilgrims. Domestic inventories make reference to similar items, although their materials and cost must have varied enormously. The inventory made after Lorenzo de' Medici's death in 1492 included large numbers of devotional items such as Agnus Dei, rosaries, and sculpted and painted religious images (*Libro d'inventario dei beni di Lorenzo il Magnifico*, indexed by name of object).

146. Turrill, "*Compagnie* and *Discepole*." Nelli was not the first Florentine nun to show such well-developed artistic skills, although her oeuvre is certainly the largest and best known. According to Parronchi, "Due note para-uccellesche," 174–79, Paolo Uccello's daughter Suor Antonia, a nun in S. Donato in Polverosa, was listed in the painters' guild as a "pittoressa" at the time of her death in 1490.

147. Brucker, "Ecclesiastical Courts," 251.

CHAPTER 5 : Contesting the Boundaries of Enclosure

1. Seidel Menchi, "Characteristics of Italian Anticlericalism." Martines, *Strong Words*, 199–229, probes amatory tales featuring such stock characters as the goatish cleric and the lustful nun. Daichman, "Misconduct in the Medieval Nunnery," treats this topic unconvincingly.

2. Superficial treatments that trade on the sensationalism of convent sex include Canosa, *Il velo e il cappuccio*, and Mandoli, *Vita licenziosa*. A sample of one hundred petitions submitted to the Holy Penitentiary by male and female religious includes numerous cases of fornication; Tamburini, *Santi e peccatori*. Yet these examples obscure the fact that the vast majority of supplications came from laity seeking dispensation to marry within prohibited degrees of kinship. A more balanced view of this important archive is offered by Brucker, "Religious Sensibilities."

3. Ruggiero, *Boundaries of Eros*; Brown, *Immodest Acts*. No criticism of these authors is intended.

4. Lehfeldt, "Convents as Litigants"; Lehfeldt, *Religious Women in Golden Age Spain*; Gill, "*Scandala*," 178. The subject of women's active apostolate can be approached through Scott, "Urban Spaces."

5. Atkinson, "Precious Balsam"; Makowski, *Canon Law*, 74, 126–27. McNamara, *Sisters in Arms*, 3, discusses the restoration of a "secondary" virginity.

6. Gowing, *Domestic Dangers*.

7. Giuliani, "Genesi e primo secolo di vita del magistrato sopra monasteri."

8. Gill, "Open Monasteries"; Gill, "Penitents, *Pinzochere,* and *Mantellate.*"

9. Lehfeldt, "Spatial Discipline and Its Limits."

10. Pius V strengthened earlier enclosure provisions in *Circa pastoralis* (1566). Most studies to date have focused on post-Tridentine enclosure. Some of the most insightful discussions include Medioli, "An Unequal Law"; Medioli, "Dimensions of the Cloister"; Strasser, "Cloistering Women's Past"; Evangelisti, " 'We Do Not Have It.' "

11. The following discussion is based on Makowski, *Canon Law.* I disagree with Gill's contention, "*Scandala,*" 177, that *Periculoso* did not represent "a dramatic turning point" in the history of women's religious institutions. Although the directive was not enforced consistently, it furnished a crucial legal instrument for zealous bishops and reformers.

12. Weaver, "The Convent Wall in Tuscan Convent Drama"; ASF, CRSPL, S. Jacopo, vol. 25, fol. 33v.

13. Gill, "*Scandala,*" 185–91.

14. Novelli, "Due documenti inediti."

15. Johnson, *Equal in Monastic Profession,* 153–55, argues that mobility was essential to the prosperity of thirteenth-century French nuns.

16. ASF, Dipl., SPM, dated 24 September 1304; the 1632 Italian version is in ASF, CRSPL, SPM, vol. 1, filza 1, no. 18. Lotterio granted them "il potere uscire del monastero e parlare a parlatorio et altrove a chi fussi di bisogno per gl'affari dei detto monastero."

17. ASF, CRSPL, SPM, vol. 83, fols. 130r, 135r, 142r; AAF, VP, 2.1, fol. 42r.

18. For one excursion from S. Ambrogio in 1506, see ASF, CRSGF, 79, vol. 27, fol. 204v. Primhak, "Benedictine Communities"; Cuneo, "Basilica Cycle."

19. Relevant bibliography can be found in Miller, "Why the Bishop Had to Get Married," and Strocchia, "When the Bishop Married the Abbess."

20. Miller, "Why the Bishop Had to Get Married," 1084.

21. Zarri, *Recinti,* 346–62.

22. Holmes, *Fra Filippo Lippi,* 106.

23. Strocchia, "Sisters in Spirit."

24. Exposed repeatedly to warfare, the nuns of S. Piero a Monticelli decided in 1398 to purchase a house in Florence "where we might flee in times of trouble. It is a necessity for us to have one" (ASF, CRSPL, S. Piero, vol. 24, fol. 39r). The convent of Mantignano, located a few miles south of the city, also owned a safe house in Florence.

25. ASF, Acq. e Doni, vol. 293, unfol. The founders were Piera Viviani, Margherita Cambi, Francesca da Panzano, Giovanna di Ser Filippo, and Francesca Ricci, "che stavano molte unite e visitavano gli spedali e facevano opera buone."

26. ASF, CRSGF, 133, vol. 62, fols. 1v, 2r. Thomas, *Art and Piety,* 294–96, notes that in 1442 three nuns from this house supplicated Eugenius in person.

27. ASF, CRSGF, 133, vol. 39, fols. 12v, 39v, and unfoliated insert.

28. Sensi, "Anchoresses and Penitents."

29. Thomas, *Art and Piety,* 222–23, 360n. For their attendance at Savonarola's sermons, see di Agresti, *Sviluppi della riforma,* 19.

30. ASF, Mss., vol. 170, no. 3, fols. 53v–54r, 57v.

31. The other hermitage of S. Girolamo was occupied by a certain Suor Angela; no other information was recorded (AAF, VP, 2.1, fols. 71r, 72v; BNCF, II, II, 509, fol. 4r–v).

32. Gill, "Penitents, *Pinzochere,* and *Mantellate,*" 32–34; McLaughlin, "Creating and

Recreating Communities of Women"; Pennings, "Semi-Religious Women"; Sebastiani, "Da bizzocche a monache."

33. Terpstra, "Mothers, Sisters, and Daughters"; Baernstein, *A Convent Tale.*

34. Benvenuti Papi, "Mendicant Friars," reviews the late medieval evidence for these communities. ASF, Acq. e Doni, vol. 293, unfol., lists these local founders as Caterina Colombini da Siena, Niccolosa da Firenze, and Agnolina da Prato.

35. AAF, VP, 2.1, fol. 74r–v. The report listed six of the eight inhabitants, all called *domina*, the respectful term for laywomen. Only two had surnames, and at least one came from the *contado.*

36. In his bull dated 11 September 1443, Eugenius declared that he "tolerated" the Gesuate but did not "approve" of them (*Bull. rom.,* 1:345). For the Roman Oblates, see Esposito, "St. Francesca."

37. The group was called "donne devote della Vergine Maria in sulla Piazza del Carmine." They reported no assets in 1427, 483 florins in assets in 1430, and 371 florins in 1438 (ASF, Catasto, vol. 195, fol. 274r). In 1445 these *devote* purchased some farmland from a local key maker and shoemaker at reduced prices (ASF, Catasto, vol. 638, fol. 83r). Eckstein, "The Widows' Might," examines the relationship between female devotional life in this area and the imagery of the Brancacci chapel.

38. About eighty pious laywomen, "among the most devout women of Florence and from the best, most respected families," formed this group. Dedicated to the famous icon of S. Maria del Popolo housed in the Carmine, they were assigned a side chapel for common prayer. Despite rejecting formal vows, the company nonetheless assumed a recognizable organizational structure when it elected the widow Lisa Serragli as "prioress" (ASF, Acq. e Doni, vol. 293, unfol.; Eckstein, "The Widows' Might").

39. McNamara, *Sisters in Arms,* 392. Herlihy and Klapisch-Zuber, *Les toscans,* 153–56.

40. ASF, Catasto, vol. 821, fol. 440r–v; ASF, Decima Rep., vol. 70, fol. 427v; Pulci, *Florentine Drama,* 15–20.

41. ASF, NA, 13497, fols. 166r–167v.

42. ASF, CRSPL, S. Jacopo, vol. 25, fol. 33v.

43. Martines, *Strong Words,* 208; Makowski, *Canon Law,* 71, 74.

44. ASF, CRSPL, S. Jacopo, vol. 25, fols. 34r–35v.

45. ASF, CRSPL, S. Jacopo, vol. 25, fols. 27r–28r.

46. Peterson, "The Cathedral, the Florentine Church, and Ecclesiastical Government in the Early Quattrocento," provides an excellent overview of the problems vexing the Florentine church.

47. AAF, VP, 1.1, fols. 1r–34v, report for S. Maria a Verzaia at 20r. In addition, S. Giusto alle Mura was admonished for allowing "certain dishonest windows" in unnamed locations (AAF, VP, 1.1, fol. 16r–v).

48. AAF, VP, 1.1, fols. 1v–4r.

49. ASF, CRSPL, SPM, vol. 70, fols. 125v, 130v; vol. 52, fol. 44v.

50. ASF, CRSPL, SPM, vol. 52, fol. 71v. For alliances with the Gambacorta family, see Brucker, *Civic World,* 202–8.

51. ASF, CRSPL, SPM, vol. 72, fols. 120v, 129v.

52. The moral ambiguity surrounding dancing is discussed by Bryce, "Performing for Strangers," and Ciappelli, *Carnevale e Quaresima,* 147.

53. Peterson, "Florence's *Universitas Cleri.*"

54. AAF, VP, 2.1, fols. 41v–42r. An autograph copy of Pseudo-Augustine's *Soliloquies* and other short works copied by Antonia Acciaiuoli in 1423 is conserved as Lyell Manuscript 73, Bodleian Library, Oxford University.

55. AAF, VP, 2.1, fols. 41v–80r, 133r–v.

56. Uffman, "Inside and Outside the Convent Walls"; Medioli, "An Unequal Law," 138–39.

57. *Bull. rom.*, 5:6–10, 21–26, dated 30 June 1436.

58. *Bull. fran.*, 1:77.

59. Nunes, *Dom Frey Gomez*, 1:311.

60. Holmes, "Giovanni Benci's Patronage"; Weddle, " 'Women in Wolves' Mouths.' "

61. ASF, CRSPL, SPM, vol. 7, doc. 609. For instance, in 1480 the nuns of S. Felicita consigned a tomb located "inside the convent near the chapter room" to the sons of a local barber (ASF, CRSGF, 83, vol. 114, fol. 26r).

62. ASF, CRSGF, 82, vol. 10, fol. 92r. This phrase is taken from Strasser, "Brides of Christ."

63. Thomas, *Art and Piety*, 217; Weaver, *Convent Theatre.*

64. Bryce, "Performing for Strangers," 1089.

65. Licenses were not necessary in some cases. When the Perugian convent of Monteluce was transferred to the Observant Franciscans in 1448, the city's principal citizens and numerous noblewomen gathered in the cloister to welcome the new occupants. After the keys and seal were consigned to the new abbess, the crowd departed except for the laywomen, who remained for several days. This was understood to be an intrinsic part of the transfer ceremony (Fantozzi, "La riforma osservante," 373). Printed Franciscan bulls currently end with the tenure of Innocent VIII.

66. *Bull. fran.*, 2:90, 328, 807–8.

67. *Bull. fran.*, 3:198–99, 529–31, 573.

68. Of the forty-nine permits issued from September 1489 to September 1490, twenty-six concerned Italian convents. Spain garnered fourteen, France seven, and other regions two (*Bull. fran.*, 4:597–734).

69. *Bull. fran.*, 4:564, 625–26, 630–31.

70. Early sixteenth-century popes issued a huge array of apostolic privileges as new revenue sources. For instance, Julius granted assorted privileges to Pierfrancesco Machiavelli, his wife, Francesca Agli; to Bernardo Manetti and his wife, Loretta Ricasoli; and to Caterina Ricasoli in exchange for various "favors." Among the entitlements was the women's right to enter Florentine convents without impediment (ASF, CRSGF, 79, vol. 169, no. 174).

71. Strocchia, "Taken into Custody."

72. In her 1463 testament, Betta, widow of Simone Guasconi, left lifetime income from a vineyard to her devoted servant Antonia. The property devolved to S. Apollonia on condition that Betta's daughter, Abbess Piera Guasconi, allow Antonia to live in the convent; if she refused, the legacy was void. The convent accepted these terms after Betta's death in 1474 (ASF, CRSGF, 82, vol. 110, under date 2 May 1463; vol. 79, fol. 264r). For the Annalena guardianship, see ASF, Mss., vol. 170, no. 3, fol. 57v.

73. Quoted in Weddle, " 'Women in Wolves' Mouths,' " 121.

74. Chojnacki, *Women and Men*, 37–38.

75. ASF, PR, vol. 111, fol. 45r–v. Composed of nine guildsmen serving annual terms of

office, convent guardians had to be at least fifty years old, married, and deemed wise. Magistrates could not refuse service if selected, nor did their tenure invoke normal civic prohibitions against holding multiple offices.

76. Established on 17 April 1432, the Office of the Night absorbed the functions of the convent guardians on 5 August 1433 (ASF, PR, vol. 123, 31v–36v; vol. 124, fol. 148r). The combined magistracy, now composed of six men, was known as Ufficiali di notte e conservatori dell'onestà dei monasteri. Rocke, *Forbidden Friendships*, 26–36, discusses the concerns giving rise to the sodomy commission. Few records survive from 1421 to 1433, and early records are incomplete, only becoming more systematic after 1465. The 1454 enabling legislation is found in ASF, PR, vol. 145, fols. 2v–3v.

77. Rocke, *Forbidden Friendships*, 19.

78. ASF, UN, vol. 36, fols. 1r, 8r, 19r. Strasser, *State of Virginity*.

79. Romano, "Gender and the Urban Geography."

80. The provisions dated 15 February 1446 and 10 April 1454 are excerpted in ASF, Acq. e Doni, vol. 293, unfol. The 1456 measure regarding the Annalena is printed in Zippel, "Le monache d'Annalena."

81. Brucker, *Society of Renaissance Florence*, 179–212, gives a sampling of documents concerned with public mores. For Eugenius's jurisdictional battles with the priors, see Brucker, *Renaissance Florence*, 192, and Hay, *Church in Italy*, 63.

82. Brucker, "Ecclesiastical Courts."

83. Lay magistracies supervising convents were established in Bologna, Brescia, Carpi, Mantua, Milan, Mirandola, Modena, Parma, Perugia, Piacenza, Ravenna, and Venice (Chojnacki, *Women and Men*, 40). Arcangeli, "Ragioni politiche della disciplina monastica," offers a nuanced case study. Zorzi, "Judicial System," 55, discusses Florentine judicial pragmatism.

84. ASF, PR, vol. 111, fol. 45r–v ("Per la fragilità del sesso e le spesse molestie, le quali da ciaschuna generatione d'uomini tutto 'l dì sono date alle sacre monache, e ancora per la troppa conversatione degli uomini con esse ancora sotto specie di parentado, come la sperienza notoriamente dimostra, quasi tutti i monasteri delle monache così della città di Firenze come quegli presso a quattro miglia, a mancamento di fama male reggimento, e presso che alla loro distructione si conoscono essere ridotti").

85. Brucker, *Society of Renaissance Florence*, 206–7.

86. Rosi, "Le monache nella vita genovese," 19.

87. Lowe, *Nuns' Chronicles*, 106, 169, contends that the concentration of young, unattached women in Venetian convents made their victimization easier, while reports of consensual sex may have piqued male interest in taking nuns as lovers. Stinger, *The Renaissance in Rome*, 14, notes a night assault on a Roman convent by unruly young barons in 1460. The episode featuring Lorenzo de' Medici is recorded in BNCF, II, II, 509, fols. 42v–43r.

88. ASF, UN, vol. 12, fol. 64r.

89. Zorzi, "Judicial System in Florence," 55–56.

90. Two women were accused of violating enclosure under suspicious circumstances. In 1494 Margherita di Nicholino, "who lives near the field of Ognissanti near the gate," entered S. Maria sul Prato to "bring chickens to those nuns." Although the accuser considered this "a great shame," Margherita was absolved of wrongdoing. Gentile, wife of Domenico Nenni, was denounced for entering S. Martino outside Porta al Prato without a

license; she confessed to bringing the nuns unspecified things. In consideration of "the nuns' honor," she was forbidden to enter any convent or convent church (ASF, UN, vol. 29, fol. 47v; vol. 27, fols. 85v, 141v).

91. ASF, UN, vol. 11, fols. 103v–111r.

92. To take a single year, only three of the 305 accusations recorded between November 1480 and November 1481 concerned nuns (ASF, UN, vol. 20). I calculate the raw number of accusations, even if made several times about the same incident. When compound charges were made, such as suspicious dealings coupled with fornication, I count the more serious offense only. Figures for sodomy accusations are taken from Rocke, *Forbidden Friendships*, 60.

93. Di Agresti, *Sviluppi della riforma*.

94. ASF, OGBR, vol. 230, fols. 35v, 163v.

95. In 1457, the prior of S. Fabbiano in Prato was found guilty of having consensual affairs with three nuns. He was excommunicated, absolved by the Holy Penitentiary, and resumed his duties by 1463. What happened to the nuns is unknown (ASF, Acq. e Doni, vol. 293, unfol.; ASF, CRSGF, 260, vol. 217, fols. 46v–48r).

96. ASF, UN, vol. 12, fol. 28r.

97. Holmes, *Fra Filippo Lippi*, 10–11, 106, 108, critically appraises both the nature of this relationship and the documentation for it.

98. ASF, UN, vol. 14, fols. 13v–14v. Lansing, "Gender and Civic Authority"; Mazzi, "Croniche di periferia." Cohn challenges Mazzi's findings and methodology in "Sex and Violence."

99. ASF, UN, vol. 12, fol. 25v.

100. Cohn, "Sex and Violence."

101. ASF, UN, vol. 4, fols. 26v–27r; vol. 6, unfol., under date 19 August 1461; vol. 8, unfol., under date 7 October 1461.

102. Ruggiero, *Boundaries of Eros*, 70–108. Cohn, "Sex and Violence," 203n, notes that late medieval penalties for raping nuns in the central Italian town of Foligno were significantly harsher than for raping virgins, wives, and widows.

103. ASF, UN, vol. 5, fols. 54v, 71v, 82r, 87v; vol. 13, fol. 20r.

104. ASF, UN, vol. 15, fol. 67r; vol. 17, fol. 53r–v; vol. 5, fol. 37r–v.

105. Puff, *Sodomy*, 107–66.

106. ASF, UN, vol. 18, pt. 2, fol. 32r; vol. 20, fol. 41v; vol. 14, fol. 3r; vol. 15, fol. 67v.

107. Gowing, *Common Bodies*, 106; ASF, MAP, XIX, 356, letter to Piero de' Medici from the nuns of S. Chiara at Castel Fiorentino, dated 19 May 1493.

108. ASF, UN, vol. 17, fol. 35v; vol. 13, fols. 18v, 19r, 76v; vol. 16, fol. 29r. Arrighi probably had a thwarted love relationship with one of the Maiano nuns, whom he reportedly visited after she was transferred to S. Maria sul Prato.

109. ASF, UN, vol. 15, fol. 27r.

110. ASF, UN, vol. 20, fol. 50v.

111. A civic functionary confessed to an ongoing liaison with a nun in S. Maria sul Prato; he was fined 25 florins and forced to do public penance in 1473. A curate was found guilty of leading a "contumacious life" that included having sex with a nun (also in S. Maria sul Prato); he was banished from the city in 1473. In 1476, a certain Giovanni di Piero confessed to entering S. Baldassare in Coverciano "many times day and night," although he did not admit to carnal knowledge; he was fined only 10 florins, suggesting the magistrates had a weak case (ASF, UN, vol. 16, fols. 87r, 103r; vol. 18, pt. 2, fol. 56r).

112. Ruggiero, *Boundaries of Eros.*

113. Fubini, *Italia quattrocentesca*, 36.

114. Polizzotto, "When Saints Fall Out"; Thomas, *Art and Piety*, 229; Evangelisti, *Nuns*, 159.

115. Pedani, "L'osservanza imposta"; Giuliani, "Genesi e primo secolo di vita del magistrato sopra monasteri," 46–48, 56–66.

116. Baldini, *Il velo segreto*, 75; Landucci, *A Florentine Diary*, 251.

117. ASF, CRSPL, S. Jacopo, vol. 21, fol. 28r–v. On comparable architectural changes in Spain, see Lehfeldt, "Spatial Discipline."

118. AAF, VP, 3.1, fascs. 2, 4.

119. AAF, VP, 3.1, fasc. 3.

120. Prosperi, "Spiritual Letters."

121. Brit. Lib., Add. Mss., 22777, fols. 39v–41r.

122. Evangelisti, " 'We Do Not Have It.' "

123. ASF, CRSPL, S. Jacopo, vol. 21, fol. 11r–v. On the nuns' Savonarolan allegiances, see Strocchia, "Savonarolan Witnesses."

124. *Bull. rom.*, 5:764–67; ASF, CRSGF, 82, vol. 1, fols. 368r, 373r, 374v; BNCF, II, II, 509, fol. 76v.

125. *Sacrorum conciliorum*, 35:257–58.

126. *Sacrorum conciliorum*, 35:258–61.

127. BRF, Mss. Moreni., 316, fol. 28r.

128. The Poor Clares of Monticelli moved into a former plague hospital near S. Croce after it was adapted for claustration, while the nuns of S. Niccolò dei Frieri were transferred to new quarters on Via S. Gallo following similar changes to a former monastery (ASF, CS, 2, vol. 58, fol. 197v; ASF, CRSGF, 133, vol. 60, p. 39).

129. ASF, CRSGF, 133, vol. 60, pp. 45–46; Evangelisti, "Monastic Poverty."

130. ASF, CRSPL, SPM, vol. 87, fols. 107r, 108v.

131. Strocchia, "When the Bishop Married the Abbess."

132. Evangelisti, "Art and the Advent of Clausura," provides a lucid overview of both state and church reforms.

Bibliography

ARCHIVAL SOURCES

AAF   Archivio Arcivescovile, Florence
     SPM, Feste Ufizi   San Pier Maggiore, Feste, Ufizi, e Mortori, 1351–1466
     VP   Visite Pastorali
ASF   Archivio di Stato, Florence
     Acq. e Doni   Acquisti e Doni
     Auditore   Auditore dei Benefici Ecclesiastici poi Segreteria del Regio Diritto
     Balie   Balie
     Capitoli   Capitoli
     Catasto   Catasto
     Ceppo   Ceppo
     CS   Carte Strozziane
     Decima Granducale   Decima Granducale
     Decima Rep.   Decima Repubblicana
     Dipl.   Diplomatico
         S. Ambrogio   Sant'Ambrogio
         S. Apollonia   Sant'Apollonia
         SPM   San Pier Maggiore
     CRSGF   Corporazioni Religiose Soppresse dal Governo Francese
     CRSGI   Corporazioni Religiose Soppresse dal Governo Italiano
     CRSPL   Corporazioni Religiose Soppresse da Pietro Leopoldo
         Chiarito   S. Maria Regina Coeli detta del Chiarito
         S. Agata   Sant'Agata
         S. Jacopo   San Jacopo di Ripoli
         S. Piero   San Piero a Monticelli
         SPM   San Pier Maggiore
     Guardaroba Medicea   Guardaroba Medicea
     MAP   Mediceo Avanti il Principato
     Mss.   Manoscritti
     Mon. S. Brigida   Monastero S. Brigida detto del Paradiso

Mon. S. Luca	Monastero San Luca
NA	Notarile Antecosimiano
OGBR	Otto di Guardia e Balia della Repubblica
PR	Provvisioni, Registri
S. Niccolò	San Niccolò Maggiore
UN	Ufficiali di Notte e Conservatori dell'Onestà dei Monasteri

ASV	Archivio Segreto Vaticano, Vatican City
Reg. Suppl.	Registra Supplicationum
RV	Registra Vaticana
BLF	Biblioteca Medicea Laurenziana, Florence
Acq. e Doni	Acquisti e Doni
Conv. Sopp.	Conventi Soppressi
BNCF	Biblioteca Nazionale Centrale, Florence
Conv. Sopp.	Conventi Soppressi
Fondo Principale	Fondo Principale
Ms. Landau Finlay	Ms. Landau Finlay
BRF	Biblioteca Riccardiana, Florence
Mss. Moreni	Manoscritti Moreni
Mss. Ricc.	Manoscritti Riccardiana
Brit. Lib.	British Library, London
Add. Mss.	Additional Manuscripts

"Constitutioni delle suore della penitentia a Santo Domenico del terzo ordine del monastero di San Vincentio di Firenze vocato Annalena." University of Pennsylvania Library. Ms. Codex 104.

PRINTED PRIMARY SOURCES

Acta sanctorum. Ed. Jean Baptiste Carnandet. New ed. 67 vols. Paris, 1863.

L'archivio della cancelleria arcivescovile di Firenze: Inventario delle visite pastorali. Ed. Gilberto Aranci. Florence, 1998.

Bull. fran.   *Bullarium franciscanum: Continens bullas brevia supplicationes tempore romani pontificis Innocenti VIII pro tribus ordinibus S.P.N. Francisci obtenta.* N.s., vol. 4, pts. 1 (1484–89) and 2 (1489–92). Ed. Caesar Cenci. Grottoferrata, 1989–90.

   Bullarium franciscanum: Continens constitutions, epistolas, diplomata romanorum pontificum Calixti III, Pii II, et Pauli II. N.s., vol. 2 (1455–71). Ed. Joseph M. Pou y Marti. Quaracchi, 1939.

   Bullarium franciscanum: Continens constitutions, epistolas, diplomata romanorum pontificum, Eugenius IV et Nicolai V ad tres ordines S.P.N. Francisci spectantia. N.s., vol. 1 (1431–55). Ed. Ulricus Hüntermann. Quaracchi, 1929.

   Bullarium franciscanum: Continens constitutions, epistolas, diplomata romanorum pontificum, Sixti IV. N.s., vol. 3 (1471–84). Ed. Joseph M. Pou y Marti. Quaracchi, 1949.

Bull. rom.   *Bullarum, diplomatum et privilegiorum sanctorum romanorum pontificum taurinensus editio.* Vol. 5 (Eugenius IV [1431]–Leo X [1521]). Ed. Francisco Gaude. Augustae Taurinorum, 1860.

Il burato: Libro de recami. Venice, 1527.

Cereta, Laura. *Collected Letters of a Renaissance Feminist.* Ed. and trans. Diana Robin. Chicago, 1997.

Concilium florentinum provinciale anno 1517. In *Sacrorum conciliorum, nova et amplissima collectio.* Ed. J. D. Mansi. Paris, 1902. 35:215–318.

Constitutiones synodales cleri florentini Cosmi de Pacciis, archiepiscopi florentini anno dom. incarnationis 1508. Florence, 1509.

Landucci, Luca. *A Florentine Diary from 1450 to 1516, Continued by an Anonymous Writer till 1542.* Trans. Alice de Rosen Jarvis. Annot. Iodoco del Badia. London, 1927.

Libro d'inventario dei beni di Lorenzo il Magnifico. Ed. Marco Spallanzani and Giovanna Gaeta Bertelà. Florence, 1992.

Masi, Bartolomeo. *Ricordanze di Bartolomeo Masi, calderaio fiorentino dal 1478 al 1526.* Ed. Giuseppe Corazzini. Florence, 1906.

Neri di Bicci. *Le ricordanze (10 marzo 1453–24 aprile 1475).* Ed. Bruno Santi. Pisa, 1976.

Pulci, Antonia. *Florentine Drama for Convent and Festival: Seven Sacred Plays.* Ed. James Wyatt Cook and Barbara Collier Cook. Chicago, 1996.

Riccoboni, Bartolomea. *Life and Death in a Venetian Convent: The Chronicle and Necrology of Corpus Domini, 1395–1436.* Trans. Daniel Bornstein. Chicago, 2000.

Statuta populi et communis florentiae: Publica auctoritate, collecta, castigata et praeposita anno salutis 1415. 3 vols. Friburg, 1778–83.

Vespasiano da Bisticci. *Le vite.* 2 vols. Ed. Aulo Greco. Florence, 1970–76.

Villani, Giovanni, Matteo, and Filippo. *Croniche.* Trieste, 1857.

SECONDARY WORKS

Arcangeli, Letizia. "Ragioni politiche della disciplina monastica: Il caso di Parma tra Quattro e Cinquecento." In *Donna, disciplina, creanza cristiana dal XV al XVII secolo: Studi e testi a stampa.* Ed. Gabriella Zarri. Rome, 1996. 165–87.

Arenal, Electa, and Stacey Schlau. *Untold Sisters: Hispanic Nuns in Their Own Works.* Albuquerque, NM, 1989.

Artusi, Luciano, and Antonio Patruno. *Ora et labora: L'antico complesso religioso e l'opera pia di Sant'Ambrogio in Firenze.* Florence, 1996.

Atkinson, Clarissa. "Precious Balsam in a Fragile Glass: The Ideology of Virginity in the Later Middle Ages." *Journal of Family History* 8 (1983): 131–43.

Bacarelli, Giuseppina. "Per l'architettura fiorentina del Quattrocento: Il chiostro di Sant'Apollonia." *Rivista d'arte* 37 (1984): 133–63.

Baernstein, P. Renée. *A Convent Tale: A Century of Sisterhood in Spanish Milan.* New York, 2002.

———. "In Widow's Habit: Women between Convent and Family in Sixteenth-Century Milan." *Sixteenth Century Journal* 25 (1994): 787–807.

Baldini, Claudia. *Il velo segreto: Monache di clausura nella storia di Ravenna (X–XIX secolo).* Ravenna, 1998.

Banker, James. *Death in the Community: Memorialization and Confraternities in an Italian Commune in the Late Middle Ages.* Athens, GA, 1988.

Battara, Pietro. *La popolazione di Firenze alla metà del '500.* Florence, 1935.

Battistini, Francesco. *Gelsi, bozzoli e caldaie: L'industria della seta in Toscana tra città, borghi e campagne (sec. XVI–XVIII).* Florence, 1998.

Baxandale, Susannah Foster. "Exile in Practice: The Alberti Family in and out of Florence." *Renaissance Quarterly* 44 (1991): 720–56.

Becker, Marvin B. *Studies in the Rise of the Territorial State.* Vol. 2 of *Florence in Transition.* Baltimore, MD, 1968.

Benvenuti Papi, Anna. "Mendicant Friars and Female Pinzochere in Tuscany." In Bornstein and Rusconi, 84–103.

Bestor, Jane Fair. "Marriage Transactions in Renaissance Italy and Mauss's *Essay on the Gift.*" *Past and Present* 164 (1999): 6–46.

Bizzocchi, Roberto. "Chiesa e aristocrazia nella Firenze del Quattrocento." *Archivio storico italiano* 142 (1984): 191–282.

———. *Chiesa e potere nella Toscana del Quattrocento.* Bologna, 1987.

Bologna, Pietro. "La stamperia fiorentina del monastero di S. Jacopo di Ripoli e le sue edizioni." *Giornale storico della letteratura italiana* 20 (1892): 349–78; 21 (1893): 49–69.

Bonds, William N. "Genoese Noblewomen and Gold Thread Manufacturing." *Medievalia et Humanistica* 17 (1966): 79–81.

Bornstein, Daniel E. "Women and Religion in Late Medieval Italy: History and Historiography." In Bornstein and Rusconi, 1–27.

Bornstein, Daniel E., and Roberto Rusconi, eds. *Women and Religion in Medieval and Renaissance Italy.* Chicago, 1996.

Borsook, Eve. "Cults and Imagery at Sant'Ambrogio in Florence." *Mitteilungen des Kunsthistorischen Institutes in Florenz* 25 (1981): 147–202.

Boskovits, Miklós. "Ancora su Paolo Schiavo: Una scheda biografica e una proposta di catalogo." *Arte cristiana* 83 (1995): 332–40.

Brown, Judith C. "Everyday Life, Longevity, and Nuns in Early Modern Florence." In *Renaissance Culture and the Everyday.* Ed. Patricia Fumerton and Simon Hunt. Philadelphia, 1999. 115–38.

———. *Immodest Acts: The Life of a Lesbian Nun in Renaissance Italy.* New York, 1986.

———. "Monache a Firenze all'inizio dell'età moderna: Un'analisi demografica." *Quaderni storici* 85 (1994): 117–52.

———. "A Woman's Place Was in the Home: Women's Work in Renaissance Tuscany." In *Rewriting the Renaissance: The Discourses of Sexual Difference in Early Modern Europe.* Ed. Margaret W. Ferguson, Maureen Quilligan, and Nancy J. Vickers. Chicago, 1986. 206–24.

Brown, Judith C., and Robert C. Davis, eds. *Gender and Society in Renaissance Italy.* London, 1998.

Brucker, Gene A. *The Civic World of Early Renaissance Florence.* Princeton, NJ, 1977.

———. "Ecclesiastical Courts in Fifteenth-Century Florence and Fiesole." *Medieval Studies* 53 (1991): 229–57.

———. "The Economic Foundations of Laurentian Florence." In *Lorenzo il Magnifico e il suo mondo.* Ed. Gian Carlo Garfagnini. Florence, 1994. 3–15.

———. *Florentine Politics and Society, 1343–1378.* Princeton, NJ, 1962.

———. "Monasteries, Friaries, and Nunneries in Quattrocento Florence." In Verdon and Henderson, 41–62.

———. "Religious Sensibilities in Early Modern Europe: Examples from the Records of the Holy Pentitentiary." In *Culture, Society, and Religion in Early Modern Europe: Essays by the Students and Colleagues of William J. Bouwsma.* Ed. Ellery Schalk. Waterloo, ON, 1988. 13–25.

———. *Renaissance Florence.* Berkeley, CA, 1969.

———. *The Society of Renaissance Florence: A Documentary Study.* New York, 1971.

Bryce, Judith. " 'Les livres des Florentines': Reconsidering Women's Literacy in Quattro-cento Florence." In *At the Margins: Minority Groups in Pre-Modern Italy.* Ed. Stephen J. Milner. Minneapolis, MN, 2005. 131–61.

———. "Performing for Strangers: Women, Dance and Music in Quattrocento Florence." *Renaissance Quarterly* 54 (2001): 1074–1107.

Burke, Jill. "Visualizing Neighborhood in Renaissance Florence: Santo Spirito and Santa Maria del Carmine." *Journal of Urban History* 32 (2006): 693–710.

Bynum, Carolyn Walker. *Holy Feast and Holy Fast: The Religious Significance of Food to Medieval Women.* Berkeley, CA, 1987.

Canosa, Romano. *Il velo e il cappuccio: Monacazioni forzate e sessualità nei conventi femminili in Italia tra Quattrocento e Settecento.* Rome, 1991.

Carnesecchi, Carlo. "Monache in Firenze nel 1515." In *Miscellanea fiorentina di erudizione e storia.* 2 vols. Ed. Iodoco del Badia. 1902. Rpt., Rome, 1978. 1:29.

Chabot, Isabelle. "La reconnaissance du travail des femmes dans la Florence du bas Moyen Age: contexte idéologique et réalité." In *La donna nell'economia, sec. XIII–XVIII.* Ed. Simonetta Cavaciocchi. Prato, 1990. 563–76.

Chojnacka, Monica. *Working Women of Early Modern Venice.* Baltimore, MD, 2001.

Chojnacki, Stanley. *Women and Men in Renaissance Venice: Twelve Essays on Patrician Society.* Baltimore, MD, 2000.

Ciappelli, Giovanni. *Carnevale e Quaresima: Comportamenti sociali e cultura a Firenze nel Rinascimento.* Rome, 1997.

Ciatti, Marco. "Appunti per una storia dei tessuti a Siena e il patrimonio delle contrade." In *Paramenti e arredi sacri nelle contrade di Siena.* Ed. Caterina Pallavicino. Florence, 1986. 23–74.

Cohen, Sherrill. *The Evolution of Women's Asylums since 1500: From Refuges for Ex-Prostitutes to Shelters for Battered Women.* New York, 1992.

Cohn, Samuel K., Jr. *The Cult of Remembrance and the Black Death: Six Renaissance Cities in Central Italy.* Baltimore, MD, 1992.

———. *The Laboring Classes in Renaissance Florence.* New York, 1980.

———. "Nuns and Dowry Funds: Women's Choices in the Renaissance." In Cohn, *Women in the Streets,* 76–97.

———. "Sex and Violence on the Periphery: The Territorial State in Early Renaissance Florence." In Cohn, *Women in the Streets,* 98–136.

———. *Women in the Streets: Essays on Sex and Power in Renaissance Italy.* Baltimore, 1996.

———. "Women and Work in Renaissance Italy." In Brown and Davis, 107–26.

Connell, William J., ed. *Society and Individual in Renaissance Florence.* Berkeley, CA, 2002.

Conti, Elio. *La formazione della struttura agraria moderna nel contado fiorentino.* Rome, 1965.

———. *L'imposta diretta a Firenze nel Quattrocento (1427–1494).* Rome, 1984.

Conway, Melissa. *The Diario of the Printing Press of San Jacopo di Ripoli (1476–1484).* Florence, 1999.

Crum, Roger J., and David G. Wilkins, "In Defense of Florentine Republicanism: Saint Anne and Florentine Art, 1343–1575." In *Interpreting Cultural Symbols: Saint Anne in Late Medieval Society.* Ed. Kathleen Ashley and Pamela Sheingorn. Athens, GA, 1990. 131–68.

Crum, Roger J., and John T. Paoletti, eds. *Renaissance Florence: A Social History*. Cambridge, UK, 2006.

Cuneo, Pia F. "The Basilica Cycle of Saint Katherine's Convent: Art and Female Community in Early-Renaissance Augsburg." *Woman's Art Journal* 19 (1998): 21–25.

Daichman, Graciela. "Misconduct in the Medieval Nunnery: Fact, Not Fiction." In *That Gentle Strength: Historical Perspectives on Women in Christianity*. Ed. Lynda L. Coon, Katherina J. Haldane, and Elizabeth W. Sommer. Charlottesville, VA, 1990. 97–117.

Dameron, George W. *Episcopal Power and Florentine Society, 1000–1320*. Cambridge, MA, 1991.

———. *Florence and Its Church in the Age of Dante*. Philadelphia, 2005.

Davidsohn, Robert. *Le origini*. Vol. 1 of *Storia di Firenze*. Florence, 1972.

Davis, Natalie Zemon. "Women in the Crafts in Sixteenth-Century Lyon." In Hanawalt, 167–97.

Degl'Innocenti, Daniela. *I tessuti della fede: Bordi figurati del XV e XVI secolo dalle collezioni del Museo del Tessuto*. Prato, 2000.

de Roover, Florence Edler. "Andrea Banchi, Florentine Silk Manufacturer and Merchant in the Fifteenth Century." *Studies in Medieval and Renaissance History* 3 (1966): 223–85.

———. *L'arte della seta a Firenze nei secoli XIV e XV.* Ed. Sergio Tognetti. Florence, 1999.

di Agresti, Domenico. *Sviluppi della riforma monastica savonaroliana*. Florence, 1980.

Dini, Bruni. "L'economia fiorentina dal 1450 al 1530." In *La Toscana al tempo di Lorenzo il Magnifico: Politica, economia, cultura, arte*. 3 vols. Florence, 1996. 3:799–823.

———. "L'industria serica in Italia, secc. XIII–XV." In Dini, *Saggi su una economia-mondo*, 51–85.

———. "Una manifattura di battiloro nel Quattrocento." In Dini, *Saggi su una economia-mondo*, 87–115.

———. *Saggi su una economia-mondo: Firenze e l'Italia fra Mediterraneo ed Europa (secc. XIII–XVI)*. Pisa, 1995.

Driver, Martha W. "Nuns as Patrons, Artists, Readers: Bridgettine Woodcuts in Printed Books Produced for the English Market." In *Art into Life*. Ed. Carol Garrett Fisher and Kathleen L. Scott. East Lansing, MI, 1995. 237–67.

Eckstein, Nicholas A. "Addressing Wealth in Renaissance Florence: Some New Soundings from the *Catasto* of 1427." *Journal of Urban History* 32 (2006): 711–28.

———. *The District of the Green Dragon: Neighbourhood Life and Social Change in Renaissance Florence*. Florence, 1995.

———. "Neighborhood as Microcosm." In Crum and Paoletti, 219–39.

———. "The Widows' Might: Women's Identity and Devotion in the Brancacci Chapel." *Oxford Art Journal* 28 (2005): 99–118.

Esch, Arnold. "Roman Customs Registers, 1470–80: Items of Interest to Historians of Art and Material Culture." *Journal of the Warburg and Courtauld Institutes* 58 (1995): 72–87.

Esposito, Anna. "St. Francesca and the Female Religious Communities of Fifteenth-Century Rome." In Bornstein and Rusconi, 197–218.

Evangelisti, Silvia. "Art and the Advent of Clausura: The Convent of Saint Catherine of Siena in Tridentine Florence." In Nelson, 67–82.

———. "'Farne quello che pare e piace . . .': L'uso e la trasmissione delle celle nel monastero di Santa Giulia di Brescia (1597–1688)." *Quaderni Storici* 88 (1995): 85–110.

———. "Memoria di antiche madri: I generi della storiografia monastica femminile in

Italia (secc. XV–XVIII)." In *Fuentes directas para la historia de las mujeres (siglos VIII–XVIII)*. Vol. 1 of *La voz del silencio*. Ed. Cristina Segura Graiño. Madrid, 1992. 221–49.

———. "Monastic Poverty and Material Culture in Early Modern Italian Convents." *The Historical Journal* 47 (2004): 1–20.

———. "Moral Virtues and Personal Goods: The Double Representation of Female Monastic Identity (Florence, Sixteenth and Seventeenth Centuries)." *Yearbook of the Department of History and Civilization, Florence, European University Institute* 5 (1996): 27–54.

———. *Nuns: A History of Convent Life, 1450–1700*. Oxford, UK, 2007.

———. "Rooms to Share: Convent Cells and Social Relations in Early Modern Italy." *Past and Present* (2006), S1:55–71.

———. " 'We Do Not Have It, and We Do Not Want It': Women, Power, and Convent Reform in Florence." *Sixteenth Century Journal* 34 (2003): 677–700.

Facchiano, Annamaria. "Monachesimo femminile nel Mezzogiorno, medievale e moderno." In Zarri, 169–91.

Fantozzi, Antonio. "La riforma osservante dei monasteri delle clarisse nell'Italia centrale." *Archivum Franciscanum Historicum* 23 (1930): 361–82.

Fantozzi Micali, Osanna, Franco Lombardi, and Piero Roselli. *Il monastero di San Gaggio a Firenze: La storia, il piano di recupero*. Florence, 1996.

Faselli, Rosalia Bonito. "Il motivo della melagrana dei tessuti italiani al tempo di Piero della Francesca." In *Tessuti italiani al tempo di Piero della Francesca*. Ed. Giuseppina Puletti. San Sepolcro, 1992. 36–43.

Filosa, Maria. "L'origine delle abbazie nullius." In *Le abbazie nullius: Giurisdizione spirituale e feudale nelle comunità femminili fino a Pio IX*. Ed. Francesca Marangelli. Conversano, 1984. 133–42.

Fineschi, Vincenzio. *Notizie storiche sopra la stamperia di Ripoli*. Florence, 1781.

Fiorelli Malesci, Francesca. *La chiesa di Santa Felicita a Firenze*. Florence, 1986.

Franceschi, Franco. "Les enfants au travail dans l'industrie textile Florentine des XIVe et XVe siècles." *Médiévales* 30 (1996): 69–82.

———. "Un'industria 'nuova' e prestigiosa: La seta." In vol. 2 of *La grande storia dell'Artigianato*. Ed. Franco Franceschi and Gloria Fossi. Florence, 1999. 167–89.

———. *Oltre il "Tumulto": I fiorentini dell'Arte della Lana fra Tre e Quattrocento*. Florence, 1993.

Frick, Carole Collier. *Dressing Renaissance Florence: Families, Fortunes, and Fine Clothing*. Baltimore, MD, 2002.

Fubini, Riccardo. *Italia quattrocentesca: Politica e diplomazia nell'età di Lorenzo il Magnifico*. Milan, 1994.

Gaeta, Franco. *San Lorenzo*. Venice, 1959.

Gardner, Julian. "Nuns' Altarpieces: Agendas for Research." *Römisches Jahrbuch der Biblioteca Herziana* 30 (1995): 25–57.

Garzelli, Annarosa. *Il ricamo nella attività artistica di Pollaiolo, Botticelli, Bartolomeo di Giovanni*. Florence, 1973.

Gennaro, Clara. "Clare, Agnes, and Their Earliest Followers: From the Poor Ladies of San Damiano to the Poor Clares." In Bornstein and Rusconi, 39–56.

Gilbert, Creighton. "The Conversion of Fra Angelico." In *Scritti di storia dell'arte in onore di Roberto Salvini*. Florence, 1984. 281–87.

Gilchrist, Roberta. *Gender and Material Culture: The Archaeology of Religious Women.* London, 1994.

Gill, Katherine. "Open Monasteries for Women in Late Medieval and Early Modern Italy: Two Roman Examples." In Monson, 15–47.

———. "Penitents, *Pinzochere,* and *Mantellate:* Varieties of Women's Religious Communities in Central Italy, c. 1300–1520." PhD diss. Princeton University, 1994.

———. "*Scandala:* Controversies concerning *Clausura* and Women's Religious Communities in Late Medieval Italy." In *Christendom and Its Discontents: Exclusion, Persecution, and Rebellion, 1000–1500.* Ed. Scott L. Waugh and Peter D. Diehl. Cambridge, UK, 1996. 177–203.

———. "Women and the Production of Religious Literature in the Vernacular, 1300–1500." In Matter and Coakley, 64–104.

Giuliani, Innocenzo. "Genesi e primo secolo di vita del magistrato sopra monasteri: Venezia, 1519–1620." *Le veneziane francescane* 28 (1961): 42–68, 106–69.

Goldthwaite, Richard A. *The Building of Renaissance Florence: An Economic and Social History.* Baltimore, MD, 1980.

———. "The Economic and Social World of Italian Renaissance Maiolica." *Renaissance Quarterly* 42 (1989): 1–32.

———. "An Entrepreneurial Silk Weaver in Renaissance Florence." *I Tatti Studies* 10 (2005): 69–126.

———. *Wealth and the Demand for Art in Italy, 1300–1600.* Baltimore, MD, 1993.

Gowing, Laura. *Common Bodies: Women, Touch and Power in Seventeenth-Century England.* New Haven, CT, 2003.

———. *Domestic Dangers: Women, Words, and Sex in Early Modern London.* Oxford, UK, 1996.

Greci, Roberto. "Donne e corporazioni: La fluidità di un rapporto." In *Il lavoro delle donne.* Ed. Angela Groppi. Rome, 1996. 71–91.

Gregori, Mina, Giuseppe Roche, and Giuseppina Bacarelli, eds. *Il 'Paradiso' in Pian di Ripoli: Studi e ricerche su un antico monastero.* Florence, 1985.

Gregory, Heather. "Daughters, Dowries, and the Family in Fifteenth-Century Florence." *Rinascimento,* ser. 2, 27 (1987): 215–37.

Groppi, Angela, ed. *Il lavoro delle donne.* Rome, 1996.

Guidotti, Alessandro. "Appunti per una storia della produzione vetraria di Firenze e del suo territorio pre-Cinquecentesca." In *Archeologia e storia della produzione del vetro preindustriale.* Ed. Marja Mendera. Florence, 1991. 161–75.

———. "Produzione di occhiali (lenti, montature, custodie) nella Firenze del '400: I documenti del monastero di S. Brigida al Paradiso." *Atti della Fondazione Giorgio Ronchi* 58 (2003): 689–700.

Hanawalt, Barbara A., ed. *Women and Work in Preindustrial Europe.* Bloomington, IN, 1986.

Hay, Denys. *The Church in Italy in the Fifteenth Century.* Cambridge, UK, 1977.

Heazlewood, Justine. " 'Letters Are the Leaves, Prayers Are the Fruit': Florentine Nuns in the City." MA thesis, Monash University, 1999.

Herlihy, David. *Opera Muliebria: Women and Work in Medieval Europe.* Philadelphia, 1990.

Herlihy, David, and Christiane Klapisch-Zuber. *Les toscans et leurs familles.* Paris, 1978.

Hills, Helen, ed. *Architecture and the Politics of Gender in Early Modern Europe.* Aldershot, UK, 2003.

Holmes, Megan. *Fra Filippo Lippi: The Carmelite Painter.* New Haven, CT, 1999.

———. "Giovanni Benci's Patronage of the Nunnery, Le Murate." In *Art, Memory, and Family in Renaissance Florence.* Ed. Giovanni Ciappelli and Patricia Lee Rubin. Cambridge, UK, 2000. 114–34.

Hood, William. *Fra Angelico at San Marco.* New Haven, CT, 1993.

Howell, Martha. "Fixing Movables: Gifts by Testament in Late Medieval Douai." *Past and Present* 150 (1996): 3–45.

Hufton, Olwen. "The Nuns' Story." In Nelson, 19–29.

———. "Women and the Family Economy in Eighteenth-Century France." *French Historical Studies* 9 (1975): 1–22.

Hutchinson, Ann M. "Devotional Reading in the Monastery and in the Late Medieval Household." In *De Cella in Seculum: Religious and Secular Life and Devotion in Late Medieval England.* Ed. Michael G. Sargent. Southampton, UK, 1989. 215–27.

Ilardi, Vincent. "Crosses and Carets: Renaissance Patronage and Coded Letters of Recommendation." *American Historical Review* 92 (1987): 1127–49.

———. *Occhiali alla corte di Francesco e Galeazzo Maria Sforza.* Milan, 1976.

———. "Renaissance Florence: The Optical Capital of the World." *Journal of European Economic History* 22 (1993): 507–41.

Improta, Maria Cristina, and Anna Padoa Rizzo. "Paolo Schiavo fornitore di disegni per ricami." *Rivista d'arte* 41 (1989): 25–56.

Johnson, Penelope D. *Equal in Monastic Profession: Religious Women in Medieval France.* Chicago, 1991.

Kent, Dale V. *Cosimo de' Medici and the Florentine Renaissance: The Patron's Oeuvre.* New Haven, CT, 2000.

Kent, Dale V., and Francis W. Kent. *Neighbours and Neighbourhood in Renaissance Florence: The District of the Red Lion in the Fifteenth Century.* Locust Valley, NY, 1982.

Kent, Francis W. *Lorenzo de' Medici and the Art of Magnificence.* Baltimore, MD, 2004.

———. "Lorenzo de' Medici, Madonna Scholastica Rondinelli e la politica di mecenatismo architettonico nel convento delle Murate a Firenze (1471–72)." In *Arte, committenza ed economia a Roma e nelle corti del Rinascimento (1420–1530).* Ed. Arnold Esch and Christoph L. Frummel. Torino, 1995. 351–82.

———. "Ties of Neighbourhood and Patronage in Quattrocento Florence." In *Patronage, Art, and Society in Renaissance Italy.* Ed. Francis W. Kent and Patricia Simons. Oxford, UK, 1987. 79–98.

Klapisch-Zuber, Christiane. *Women, Family, and Ritual in Renaissance Italy.* Trans. Lydia G. Cochrane. Chicago, 1985.

———. "Women Servants in Florence during the Fourteenth and Fifteenth Centuries." In Hanawalt, 56–80.

Lansing, Carol. *The Florentine Magnates: Lineage and Faction in a Medieval Commune.* Princeton, NJ, 1991.

———. "Gender and Civic Authority: Sexual Control in a Medieval Italian Town." *Journal of Social History* 31 (1997): 33–59.

Lehfeldt, Elizabeth A. "Convents as Litigants: Dowry and Inheritance Disputes in Early-Modern Spain." *Journal of Social History* 33 (2000): 645–64.

———. *Religious Women in Golden Age Spain: The Permeable Cloister.* Aldershot, UK, 2005.

———. "Spatial Discipline and Its Limits: Nuns and the Built Environment in Early Modern Spain." In Hills, 131–49.

Leonard, Amy. *Nails in the Wall: Catholic Nuns in Reformation Germany.* Chicago, 2005.

Levi D'Ancona, Mirella. *Miniatura e miniatori a Firenze dal XIV al XVI secolo: Documenti per la storia della miniatura.* Florence, 1962.

Litchfield, R. Burr. *Dalla repubblica al granducato: Il nuovo assetto socio-spaziale di Firenze, 1551–1632.* Trans. Gigliola Fragnito and Franek Sznura. Florence, 1991.

———. "Demographic Characteristics of Florentine Patrician Families, Sixteenth to Nineteenth Centuries." *Journal of Economic History* 29 (1969): 191–205.

Lowe, K. J. P. "Female Strategies for Success in a Male-Ordered World: The Benedictine Convent of Le Murate in Florence in the Fifteenth and Early Sixteenth Centuries." *Studies in Church History* 27 (1990): 209–21.

———. "A Matter of Piety or of Family Tradition and Custom? The Religious Patronage of Piero de' Medici and Lucrezia Tornabuoni." In *Piero de' Medici "il Gottoso" (1416–1469).* Ed. Andreas Beyer and Bruce Boucher. Berlin, 1993. 55–69.

———. "Nuns and Choice: Artistic Decision Making in Medicean Florence." In *With and Without the Medici: Studies in Tuscan Art and Patronage, 1434–1530.* Ed. Eckart Marchand and Alison Wright. Aldershot, UK, 1998. 129–53.

———. *Nuns' Chronicles and Convent Culture in Renaissance and Counter-Reformation Italy.* Cambridge, UK, 2003.

———. "Patronage and Territoriality in Early Sixteenth-Century Florence." *Renaissance Studies* 7 (1993): 258–71.

———. "Rainha D. Leonor of Portugal's Patronage in Renaissance Florence and Cultural Exchange." In *Cultural Links between Portugal and Italy in the Renaissance.* Ed. K. J. P. Lowe. Oxford, UK, 2000. 225–48.

———. "Secular Brides and Convent Brides: Wedding Ceremonies in Italy during the Renaissance and Counter-Reformation." In *Marriage in Italy, 1300–1600.* Ed. Trevor Dean and K. J. P. Lowe. Cambridge, UK, 1998. 41–65.

———. "Women's Work at the Benedictine Convent of Le Murate in Florence: Suor Battista Carducci's Roman Missal of 1509." In *Women and the Book: Assessing the Visual Evidence.* Ed. Lesley Smith and Jane H. M. Taylor. London, 1997. 133–46.

Macey, Patrick. *Bonfire Songs: Savonarola's Musical Legacy.* Oxford, UK, 1998.

Makowski, Elizabeth. *Canon Law and Cloistered Women: Periculoso and Its Commentators, 1298–1545.* Washington, DC, 1997.

Mandoli, Coriolano. *Vita licenziosa delle monache dei monasteri di Sant'Andrea di Fucecchio e di Santa Cristiana di Santa Croce sull'Arno (XVI secolo).* Fucecchio, 1999.

Martines, Lauro. *Lawyers and Statecraft in Renaissance Florence.* Princeton, NJ, 1968.

———. *Strong Words: Writing and Social Strain in the Italian Renaissance.* Baltimore, MD, 2001.

Matter, E. Ann, and John Coakley, eds. *Creative Women in Medieval and Early Modern Italy: A Religious and Artistic Renaissance.* Philadelphia, 1994.

Mazzi, Maria Serena. "Croniche di periferia dello stato fiorentino: Reati contro la morale nel primo Quattrocento." *Studi storici* 27 (1987): 609–35.

McLaughlin, Mary Martin. "Creating and Recreating Communities of Women: The Case of Corpus Domini, Ferrara, 1406–1452." In *Sisters and Workers in the Middle Ages.* Ed. Judith M. Bennett. Chicago, 1989. 261–88.

McNamara, Jo Ann. *Sisters in Arms: Catholic Nuns through Two Millennia.* Cambridge, MA, 1996.

Medioli, Francesca. "The Dimensions of the Cloister: Enclosure, Constraint, and Protection in Seventeenth-Century Italy." In Schutte, Kuehn, and Seidel Menchi, 165–80.

———. "An Unequal Law: The Enforcement of Clausura before and after the Council of Trent." In *Women in Renaissance and Early Modern Europe*. Ed. Christine Meek. Dublin, 2000. 136–52.

Menning, Carol Bresnahan. *Charity and State in Late Renaissance Italy: The Monte di Pietà of Florence*. Ithaca, NY, 1993.

Miglio, Luisa. "Lettere dal monastero: Scrittura e cultura scritta nei conventi femminili toscani del '400." In *Libro, scrittura, documento della civiltà monastica e conventuale nel basso medioevo (secoli XIII–XV)*. Ed. Giuseppe Avarucci, Rosa Marisa Borraccini, and Gianmario Borri. Spoleto, 1999. 133–63.

Miller, Maureen C. "The Florentine Bishop's Ritual Entry and the Origins of the Medieval Episcopal Adventus." *Revue d'histoire ecclésiastique* 98 (2003): 5–28.

———. "Why the Bishop of Florence Had to Get Married." *Speculum* 81 (2006): 1055–91.

Milner, Stephen J. "The Florentine Piazza della Signoria as Practiced Place." In Crum and Paoletti, 83–103.

Molà, Luca. *The Silk Industry of Renaissance Venice*. Baltimore, MD, 2000.

Molho, Anthony. "Deception and Marriage Strategy in Renaissance Florence: The Case of Women's Ages." *Renaissance Quarterly* 41 (1988): 193–217.

———. *Florentine Public Finances in the Early Renaissance, 1400–1433*. Cambridge, MA, 1971.

———. *Marriage Alliance in Late Medieval Florence*. Cambridge, MA, 1994.

———. " 'Tamquam vere mortua': Le professioni religiose femminili nella Firenze del tardo medioevo." *Società e storia* 43 (1989): 1–44.

Monson, Craig A., ed. *The Crannied Wall: Women, Religion, and the Arts in Early Modern Europe*. Ann Arbor, MI, 1992.

Moorman, J. H. R. *A History of the Franciscan Order from Its Origins to the Year 1517*. Oxford, UK, 1968.

Mueller, Reinhold C. *The Venetian Money Market: Banks, Panics, and the Public Debt, 1200–1500*. Baltimore, MD, 1997.

Muir, Edward, and Ronald F. E. Weissman, "Social and Symbolic Places in Renaissance Venice and Florence." In *The Power of Place: Bringing Together Geographical and Sociological Imaginations*. Ed. John A. Agnew and James S. Duncan. London, 1989. 81–103.

Nelson, Jonathan, ed. *Suor Plautilla Nelli (1523–1588): The First Woman Painter of Florence*. Florence, 2000.

Nesi, Emilia. *Il diario della stamperia di Ripoli*. Florence, 1903.

Novelli, Leandro. "Due documenti inediti relative alle monache benedettine dette 'santuccie.' " *Benedictina* 22 (1975): 189–253.

Novi Chavarria, Elisa. *Monache e gentildonne, un labile confine: Poteri politici e identità religiose nei monasteri napoletani: secoli XVI–XVII*. Milan, 2001.

Nunes, Eduardo. *Dom Frey Gomez, abade de Florença, 1420–1440*. Vol 1. Braga, PT, 1963.

Oliva, Marilyn. *The Convent and the Community in Late Medieval England: Female Monasteries in the Diocese of Norwich, 1350–1540*. Rochester, NY, 1998.

Paolin, Giovanna. "Monache e donne nel Friuli del Cinquecento." In *Società e cultura del Cinquecento nel Friuli occidentale: Studi*. Ed. Andrea del Col. Pordenone, 1984. 201–28.

Parker, Rozsika. *The Subversive Stitch: Embroidery and the Making of the Feminine.* London, 1984.

Parronchi, Alessandro. "Due note para-uccellesche." *Arte antica e moderna* 30 (1965): 169–80.

Pedani, Maria Pia. "L'osservanza imposta: I monasteri conventuali femminili a Venezia nei primi anni del cinquecento." *Archivio veneto* 144 (1995): 113–25.

Pennings, Joyce. "Semi-Religious Women in Fifteenth-Century Rome." *Mededelingen van het Nederlands Instituut te Rome*, n.s., 12 (1987): 115–45.

Peterson, David S. "The Cathedral, the Florentine Church, and Ecclesiastical Government in the Early Quattrocento." In *La cattedrale e la città: Saggi sul Duomo di Firenze.* Vol. 1 of *Atti del VII centenario del Duomo di Firenze.* 2 vols. Ed. Timothy Verdon and Annalisa Innocenti. Florence, 2001. 1:55–78.

———. "Florence's *Universitas Cleri* in the Early Fifteenth Century." *Renaissance Studies* 2 (1988): 85–96.

———. "Out of the Margins: Religion and the Church in Renaissance Italy." *Renaissance Quarterly* 53 (2000): 835–79.

———. "State-building, Church Reform, and the Politics of Legitimacy in Florence, 1375–1460." In *Florentine Tuscany: Structures and Practices of Power.* Ed. William J. Connell and Andrea Zorzi. Cambridge, UK, 2000. 122–43.

———. "The War of the Eight Saints in Florentine Memory and Oblivion." In Connell, 173–214.

Piattoli, Renato. "Un capitolo di storia dell'arte libraria ai primi del Quattrocento: Rapporto tra il monastero fiorentino del Paradiso e l'ordine francescano." *Studi Francescani* 29 (1932): 1–21.

———. "Il monastero del Paradiso presso Firenze nella storia dell'arte del primo Quattrocento." *Rivista d'arte* 18 (1936): 287–96.

Pierattini, Giovanna. "Suor Fiammetta Frescobaldi, cronista del monastero domenicano di Sant'Iacopo a Ripoli in Firenze (1523–1586)." *Memorie Domenicane* 56 (1939): 101–16; 233–39.

Polizzotto, Lorenzo. *The Elect Nation: The Savonarolan Movement in Florence, 1494–1545.* Oxford, UK, 1994.

———. "When Saints Fall Out: Women and the Savonarolan Reform in Early Sixteenth-Century Florence." *Renaissance Quarterly* 46 (1993): 486–525.

Primhak, Victoria. "Benedictine Communities in Venetian Society: The Convent of S. Zaccaria." In *Women in Italian Renaissance Culture and Society.* Ed. Letitia Panizza. Oxford, UK, 2000. 92–104.

———. "Women in Religious Communities: The Benedictine Convents in Venice, 1400–1550." PhD diss., University of London, 1991.

Prosperi, Adriano. "Spiritual Letters." In *Women and Faith: Catholic Religious Life in Italy from Late Antiquity to the Present.* Ed. Lucetta Scaraffia and Gabriella Zarri. Cambridge, MA, 1999. 113–28.

Puff, Helmut. *Sodomy in Reformation Germany and Switzerland, 1400–1600.* Chicago, 2003.

Radke, Gary. "Nuns and Their Art: The Case of San Zaccaria in Renaissance Venice." *Renaissance Quarterly* 54 (2001): 430–59.

Repetti, Emilio. *Dizionario geografico fisico storico della Toscana.* 5 vols. Florence, 1833–43.

Reyerson, Kathryn L. "Women in Business in Medieval Montpellier." In Hanawalt, 117–44.

Richa, Giuseppe. *Notizie istoriche delle chiese fiorentine.* 10 vols. Florence, 1754–62.

Richards, Marie. "Community and Poverty in the Reformed Order of St. Clare in the Fifteenth Century." *Journal of Religious History* 19 (1995): 10–25.

Rhodes, J. T. "Syon Abbey and Its Religious Publications in the Sixteenth Century." *Journal of Ecclesiastical History* 44 (1993): 11–25.

Roberts, Ann. "Plautilla Nelli's *Last Supper* and the Tradition of Dominican Refectory Decorations." In Nelson, 45–55.

Rocke, Michael. *Forbidden Friendships: Homosexuality and Male Culture in Renaissance Florence*. New York, 1996.

Romano, Dennis. "Gender and the Urban Geography of Renaissance Venice." *Journal of Social History* 23 (1989): 339–53.

Rosenthal, David. "Big Piero, the Empire of the Meadow, and the Parish of Santa Lucia: Claiming Neighborhood in the Early Modern City." *Journal of Urban History* 32 (2006): 677–92.

———. "The Spaces of Plebian Ritual and the Boundaries of Transgression." In Crum and Paoletti, 161–81.

Rosi, Michele. "Le monache nella vita genovese dal secolo XV al XVII." *Atti della società ligure di storia patria* 27 (1895): 7–205.

Rubinstein, Nicolai. "Lay Patronage and Observant Reform in Fifteenth-Century Florence." In Verdon and Henderson, 63–82.

Ruggiero, Guido. *The Boundaries of Eros: Sex Crime and Sexuality in Renaissance Venice*. New York, 1985.

———. "Mean Streets, Familiar Streets; or, The Fat Woodcarver and the Masculine Spaces of Renaissance Florence." In Crum and Paoletti, 295–310.

Rusconi, Roberto. "St. Bernardino of Siena, the Wife, and Possessions." In Bornstein and Rusconi, 182–96.

Russo, Carla. *I monasteri femminili di clausura a Napoli nel secolo XVII*. Naples, 1970.

Sánchez, Magdalena S. *The Empress, the Queen, and the Nun: Women and Power at the Court of Philip III of Spain*. Baltimore, MD, 1998.

Santoro, José Luiz. *Tessuti figurati a Firenze nel Quattrocento*. Florence, 1981.

Schutte, Anne Jacobson, Thomas Kuehn, and Silvana Seidel Menchi, eds. *Time, Space, and Women's Lives in Early Modern Europe*. Kirksville, MO, 2001.

Scott, Karen. "Urban Spaces, Women's Networks, and the Lay Apostolate in the Siena of Catherine Benincasa." In Matter and Coakley, 105–19.

Sebastiani, Lucia. "Da bizzocche a monache." In Zarri, 193–218.

———. "Monasteri femminili milanesi tra medioevo e età moderna." In *Florence and Milan: Comparisons and Relations*. 2 vols. Ed. Craig Hugh Smyth and Gian Carlo Garfagnini. Florence, 1989. 2:3–15.

Seidel Menchi, Silvana. "Characteristics of Italian Anticlericalism." In *Anticlericalism in Late Medieval and Early Modern Europe*. Ed. Peter A. Dykema and Heiko A. Oberman. Leiden, NL, 1993. 271–81.

Sensi, Mario. "Anchoresses and Penitents in Thirteenth- and Fourteenth-Century Umbria." In Bornstein and Rusconi, 56–83.

———. *Storie di bizzoche tra Umbria e Marche*. Rome, 1995.

Sframeli, Maria. " 'Ricamato da mano angelica': Un'attribuzione settecentesca per l'*Incoronazione della Vergine* di Paolo Schiavo." *Arte cristiana* 83 (1995): 323–31.

Simari, Maria Matilde. "Profilo storico-architettonico di un monastero fiorentino del Quattrocento: Santa Monaca." *Rivista d'arte* 39 (1987): 147–214.

Sire, H. J. A. *The Knights of Malta*. New Haven, CT, 1994.

Spencer, John R. *Andrea del Castagno and His Patrons*. Durham, NC, 1991.

Sperling, Jutta Gisela. *Convents and the Body Politic in Late Renaissance Venice*. Chicago, 1999.

Stephens, John. *The Fall of the Florentine Republic, 1512–1530*. Oxford, UK, 1983.

Stinger, Charles L. *The Renaissance in Rome*. Bloomington, IN, 1985.

Strasser, Ulrike. "Brides of Christ, Daughters of Men: Nuremberg Poor Clares in Defense of Their Identity." *Magistra* 1 (1995): 193–248.

———. "Cloistering Women's Past: Conflicting Accounts of Enclosure in a Seventeenth-Century Munich Nunnery." In *Gender in Early Modern German History*. Ed. Ulinka Rublack. Cambridge, UK, 2002. 221–46.

———. *State of Virginity: Gender, Religion, and Politics in an Early Modern Catholic State*. Ann Arbor, MI, 2004.

Strocchia, Sharon T. *Death and Ritual in Renaissance Florence*. Baltimore, MD, 1992.

———. "Gender and the Rites of Honour in Italian Renaissance Cities." In Brown and Davis, 39–60.

———. "Learning the Virtues: Convent Schools and Female Culture in Renaissance Florence." In *Women's Education in Early Modern Europe: A History, 1500–1800*. Ed. Barbara J. Whitehead. New York, 1999. 3–46.

———. "Naming a Nun: Spiritual Exemplars and Corporate Identity in Florentine Convents, 1450–1530." In Connell, 215–40.

———. "Remembering the Family: Women, Kin, and Commemorative Masses in Renaissance Florence." *Renaissance Quarterly* 42 (1989): 635–54.

———. "Savonarolan Witnesses: The Nuns of San Jacopo and the Piagnone Movement in Sixteenth-Century Florence." *Sixteenth Century Journal* 38 (2007): 393–418.

———. "Sisters in Spirit: The Nuns of Sant'Ambrogio and Their Consorority in Early Sixteenth Century Florence." *Sixteenth Century Journal* 33 (2002): 745–77.

———. "Taken into Custody: Girls and Convent Guardianship in Renaissance Florence." *Renaissance Studies* 17 (2003): 177–200.

———. "When the Bishop Married the Abbess: Masculinity and Power in Florentine Episcopal Entry Rites, 1300–1600." *Gender & History* 19 (2007): 346–68.

Tamburini, Filippo. *Santi e peccatori: Confessioni e suppliche dai Registri della Penitenzieria dell'Archivio Segreto Vaticano (1451–1586)*. Milan, 1995.

Terpstra, Nicholas. *Abandoned Children of the Italian Renaissance*. Baltimore, MD, 2005.

———. "Making a Living, Making a Life: Work in the Orphanages of Florence and Bologna." *Sixteenth Century Journal* 31 (2000): 1063–79.

———. "Mothers, Sisters, and Daughters: Girls and Conservatory Guardianship in Late Renaissance Florence." *Renaissance Studies* 17 (2003): 201–27.

Thomas, Anabel. *Art and Piety in the Female Religious Communities of Renaissance Italy: Iconography, Space, and the Religious Woman's Perspective*. Cambridge, UK, 2003.

Tomas, Natalie R. "Did Women Have a Space?" In Crum and Paoletti, 311–28.

———. *The Medici Women: Gender and Power in Renaissance Florence*. Aldershot, UK, 2003.

Trexler, Richard C. "Celibacy in the Renaissance." In Trexler, *The Women of Renaissance Florence*, 6–30.

———. "Florentine Prostitution in the Fifteenth Century." In Trexler, *The Women of Renaissance Florence*, 31–65.

———. *The Women of Renaissance Florence.* Vol. 2 of *Power and Dependence in Renaissance Florence.* Binghamton, NY, 1993.

Trkulja, Silvia Meloni, ed. *I fiorentini nel 1562: Descritione delle bocche della città et stato di Fiorenza fatta l'anno 1562.* Florence, 1991.

Turrill, Catherine. "*Compagnie* and *Discepole:* The Presence of Other Women Artists at Santa Caterina da Siena." In Nelson, 83–110.

Uffmann, Heike. "Inside and Outside the Convent Walls: The Norm and Practice of Enclosure in the Reformed Nunneries of Late Medieval Germany." *Medieval History Journal* 4 (2001): 83–108.

Van Enghen, John. "The Church in the Fifteenth Century." In *The Handbook of European History, 1400–1600: Late Middle Ages, Renaissance, and Reformation.* Ed. Thomas A. Brady Jr., Heiko A. Oberman, and James D. Tracy. Leiden, NL, 1994. 301–26.

Venarde, Bruce L. *Women's Monasticism and Medieval Society: Nunneries in France and England, 890–1215.* Ithaca, NY, 1997.

Verdon, Timothy, and John Henderson, eds. *Christianity and the Renaissance: Image and Religious Imagination in the Quattrocento.* Syracuse, NY, 1990.

Weaver, Elissa. *Convent Theatre in Early Modern Italy: Spiritual Fun and Learning for Women.* Cambridge, UK, 2002.

———. "The Convent Wall in Tuscan Convent Drama." In Monson, 73–86.

———. "Le muse in convento: La scrittura profana delle monache italiane (1450–1650)." In *Donna e fede: Santità e vita religiosa in Italia.* Ed. Luisa Scaraffia and Gabriella Zarri. Rome, 1994. 253–76.

Weddle, Saundra L. "Identity and Alliance: Urban Presence, Spatial Privilege, and Florentine Renaissance Convents." In Crum and Paoletti, 394–412.

———. " 'Women in Wolves' Mouths': Nuns' Reputations and Architecture at the Convent of Le Murate in Florence." In Hills, 115–29.

Weinstein, Donald. *Savonarola and Florence: Prophecy and Patriotism in the Renaissance.* Princeton, NJ, 1970.

Weissman, Ronald F. E. *Ritual Brotherhood in Renaissance Florence.* New York, 1982.

Winkelmes, Mary-anne. "Taking Part: Benedictine Nuns as Patrons of Art and Architecture." In *Picturing Women in Renaissance and Baroque Italy.* Ed. Geraldine A. Johnson and Sara F. Matthews Grieco. Cambridge, UK, 1997. 91–110.

Witt, Ronald G. *Hercules at the Crossroads: The Life, Works, and Thought of Coluccio Salutati.* Durham, NC, 1983.

Wood, Jeryldene M. *Women, Art, and Spirituality: The Poor Clares of Early Modern Italy.* Cambridge, UK, 1996.

Zarri, Gabriella. "I monasteri femminili benedettini nella diocesi di Bologna (secoli XIII–XVII)." *Ravennatensia* 9 (1981): 333–71.

———. "I monasteri femminili a Bologna tra il XIII e il XVII secolo." In *Atti e memorie: Deputazione di storia patria per le provincie di Romagna,* n.s., 24 (1973): 133–224.

———. "Monasteri femminili e città (secoli XV–XVIII)." In *La chiesa e il potere politico dal medioevo all'età contemporanea.* Ed. Georgio Chittolini and Giovanni Miccoli. Turin, 1986, 359–429.

———. *Recinti: Donne, clausura e matrimonio nella prima età moderna.* Bologna, 2000.

———. *Le sante vive: Profezie di corte e devozione femminile tra '400 e '500.* Turin, 1990.

———. "The Third Status." In Schutte, Kuehn, and Seidel Menchi, 181–99.

————, ed. *Il monachesimo femminile in Italia dall'alto medioevo al secolo XVII a confronto con l'oggi.* Verona, 1997.

Zippel, Giuseppe. "Le monache d'Annalena e il Savonarola." *Rivista d'Italia* 4 (1901): 231–49.

Zorzi, Andrea. "The Judicial System in Florence in the Fourteenth and Fifteenth Centuries." In *Crime, Society, and the Law in Renaissance Italy.* Ed. Trevor Dean and Kate Lowe. Cambridge, UK, 1994. 40–58.

Zucchi, Alberto. "Il monastero di Annalena in Firenze." *Memorie domenicane* 68 (1951): 231–49.

Index